MONEY AND CAPITAL

This book renews the Marxian theory of the general equivalent by highlighting the contradiction between the social functions of money (unit of account, means of circulation) and its private functions (store of value, accumulation).

It draws a clear distinction between the monetary base and the commodity base of money and thus avoids the confusion between money and credit on the one hand, and money and capital on the other, which are found in other heterodox monetary theories. It accounts for the new forms of monetary constraints weighing on the banking systems under and inconvertible fiat money standard, the class relationships underlying the interventions of monetary authorities and governments, and presents a definition of the state which emphasises its mode of intervention on the collective and social conditions of capitalisms which are money and labour power. The emphasis on the contradiction between these two types of monetary functions gives a more fundamental account of the conflict between the international role and the national origin of the dollar than the Triffin dilemma, which has been constantly overcome or deferred by the US since 1960. The author explains this evolution by demonstrating how, from the 1950s onwards, the dollar began a process of acquiring relative autonomy from the US economy. By focusing on the role and international functions of the dollar, he offers a fresh look at the 2008 crisis and its consequences for the international monetary system, but also for a possible post-capitalist financial system – which post-revolutionary Russia experimented with in the form of the NEP, and whose contemporary implementation is foreshadowed by the rise of digital central bank currencies.

The book thereby provides a necessary update to the tools and concepts inherited from Marx for analysing and understanding money, capital and the state.

Laurent Baronian is an Assistant Professor in Economics at the University Sorbonne Paris Nord, France. His research interests include the history of economic thought, monetary theory and history, labour in the age of information and communication technologies, and the theory and practice of the commons.

Routledge Frontiers of Political Economy

Globalization and the Decline of American Power
The Political Economy of the American Fall
Cyrus Bina

Marx and Le Capital
Evaluation, History, Reception
Edited by Marcello Musto

Permanent Economic Disorder
Shahzavar Karimzadi

Temporary Economic Crises
Shahzavar Karimzadi

Money and Capital
A Critique of Monetary Thought, the Dollar and Post-Capitalism
Laurent Baronian

Modern Money and the Rise and Fall of Capitalist Finance
Trusts, Personae, and Indebtedness
Jongchul Kim

Innovation, Complexity and Economic Evolution
From Theory to Policy
Pier Paolo Saviotti

For more information about this series, please visit: www.routledge.com/Routledge-Frontiers-of-Political-Economy/book-series/SE0345

MONEY AND CAPITAL

A Critique of Monetary Thought, the Dollar and Post-Capitalism

Laurent Baronian

Routledge
Taylor & Francis Group
LONDON AND NEW YORK

First published 2023
by Routledge
4 Park Square, Milton Park, Abingdon, Oxon OX14 4RN

and by Routledge
605 Third Avenue, New York, NY 10158

Routledge is an imprint of the Taylor & Francis Group, an informa business

British Library Cataloguing-in-Publication Data
A catalogue record for this book is available from the British Library

Library of Congress Cataloging-in-Publication Data
Names: Baronian, Laurent, author.
Title: Money and capital : a critique of monetary thought, the dollar and post-capitalism / Laurent Baronian.
Description: 1 Edition. | New York, NY : Routledge, 2023.
Identifiers: LCCN 2022036726 (print) | LCCN 2022036727 (ebook)
Subjects: LCSH: Money—Social aspects. | Dollar, American. | Capital. | Capitalism. | Monetary policy.
Classification: LCC HG221 .B326 2023 (print) | LCC HG221 (ebook) | DDC 332.4—dc23/eng/20220926
LC record available at https://lccn.loc.gov/2022036726
LC ebook record available at https://lccn.loc.gov/2022036727

ISBN: 978-0-367-20405-1 (hbk)
ISBN: 978-1-032-42425-5 (pbk)
ISBN: 978-0-429-26129-9 (ebk)

DOI: 10.4324/9780429261299

For Product Safety Concerns and Information please contact our EU representative:
GPSR@taylorandfrancis.com
Taylor & Francis Verlag GmbH,
Kaufingerstraße 24,
80331 München, Germany.

In memory of François Chesnais

CONTENTS

INTRODUCTION

I.1 The money of the Greeks: the other before the gods

In his first lecture at the Collège de France, Foucault sought to link money to state power by invoking the case of 5th-century Corinth, whose tyrant Cypselos is said to have introduced money from scratch into the city's exchange circuits in order to restore a social equilibrium disturbed by the weight of peasant debts and the excessive wealth of the great landowners (Foucault, 2013: 133–34). By taxing a tenth of the wealth of the rich and partially redistributing this tribute to the poor, Cypselos would provide a distant historical example of the necessary link between money and the state, as well as its identity with debt: "The appearance of money is linked to the constitution of [...] power whose raison d'être is to intervene in the regime of property, in the interplay of debts and settlements" (Foucault, 2013: 139). Yet, Foucault admits that the complex system set up by Cypselos would hardly have been imaginable without "the circulation of a constant substitute in the distributions and returns" for which Lydian money served very likely as a model at this time (Foucault, 2013: 136). Not only did debt not wait for money to bind individuals and groups by obligations, but power has always been secondary to the deterritorialising power of money. For if state power is inseparable from war, it is because it is first constituted in relation to the Other, before exercising its hold within its own borders:[1] "Exchanges are peacefully resolved wars, and wars are the result of unsuccessful transactions" (Lévi-Strauss, 1969: 67). And money does not differ from debt because it determines a relationship of exchange where debt defines a relationship of obligations, but rather because it mediates a relationship to the Other, where debt determines a personal relationship. It is from its character as both anonymous and objective – hence, as we shall see, the role of the State itself in coinage – that its power of exchangeability with the Stranger comes. There is no monetary universality; there is only a universalisation through money.

DOI: 10.4324/9780429261299-1

This was the great novelty of the Greeks compared to the peoples of the Near East, who had long been familiar with the technologies of coinage as well as with the various monetary functions: to replace the seal mark, which embodies the power or authority of the Sovereign, with the authentication sign of the monetary substance (Seaford, 2004: 119). Henceforth, the coin would no longer embody a personal or divine power, but rather it would embody the mark itself that transforms it into an authentic coin. Severed from the link that attached it to the power of its issuer, the coinage worth its own weight is destined to pass from hand to hand to pose as a pure form of exchangeability. Foucault observes that Cypselos and later Solon established their power through the institution of money in opposite ways: the former by keeping the debts of the peasants, the latter by cancelling them (Foucault, 2013: 141). But in both cases, as Foucault himself notes, the operation consisted in shifting the holding of power from an agricultural aristocracy to the rich merchants and manufacturers by favouring crafts and wage labour (p. 133). In fact, Corinth and the whole of Greece were constantly intensifying their trade with the Near East, which supplied them with wheat in particular. Even before the Greeks, Croesus had shifted the Lydian trade from electrum to silver money, not only because of the abundant silver veins at Siphnos, but because of the strong demand for silver by the Orientals.[2] Money is not a creation ex nihilo, dependent on a new form of political power. On the contrary, it was on money as a condition of openness to Otherness that the conditions for the continued power of the rich in Corinth and elsewhere in Greece depend.

It is true, however, that the Greeks included money in sacrificial rituals, stimulating theories about the religious origins of ancient money. But it was precisely because these rituals already existed that the introduction into the temples of money, as an object that was more durable and easily appropriated than other sacrificial objects, reinforced the individual appropriation resulting from sacrificial redistributions. Above all, the replacement of perishable treasures by durable monetary wealth coincided with the increase in trade, including with the Barbarians, as well as stimulating the partial monetarisation of social relations (Seaford, 2004: 112): the money enclosed within the temple walls was a projection of the polis outside. Still the Eastern line! Before the exchange with the gods (Bensa and Wiegratz, 1992: 74), it is the exchange with the Other that first gives rise to the constitution of monetary treasures and determines money as a general form of value.

It is the two inseparable dimensions of the form of exchangeability and the form of value that animate Aristotle's reflections on money, its functions and its effects in society. It is well known that Aristotle describes chrematistics as a deviation from the natural use of money defined as a convention (*nomisma*) to facilitate exchange and solve the problem of the double coincidence of wants. Aristotle clearly shows how the desire for enrichment finds its source in money considered as the unique representative of social wealth. But he doesn't just denounce the inversion of the means – getting money to acquire goods or practise one's art – into an end, and hence the deviation of the use of money from its natural destination; he also observes the transformation of natural ends into mere means of enrichment:

> The quality of courage, for example, is not intended to make wealth, but to inspire trust; neither is this the aim of the general's or of the physician's art; but the one aims at victory and the other at health. Nevertheless, some men turn every quality or art into a means of getting wealth; this they conceive to be the end, and to the promotion of the end they think all things must contribute.
>
> *(Aristotle, 1996: 14)*

If this reversal of ends into means is contrary to nature, it is because money was created for exchange. By drawing the ultimate consequences of the possible functions of money at a time when exchange value was far from having penetrated society's production relations, Aristotle discovers the possibility of a social production entirely turned towards exchange value and dependent on the speculation of entrepreneurs.[3]

Foucault believes that he finds proof of the religious character of the monetary object in the fact that the maker of counterfeit money was treated as sacrilegious (Foucault, 2013: 141), but 2,000 years later, "At the very time when, in England, they stopped burning witches, they began to hang counterfeiters of money" (Marx, 1867b: 783).

I.2 The two modes of being of money in economic thought

That money fulfils both exchange and hoarding functions probably explains why a contemporary theorist of money still asks:

> Is money a *process* or a *thing*? Is it a *commodity* or a *social relation*? What explains the *value* of money? What are money's key *functions*? Why are there so many competing (and contradictory) *definitions* of money? What were the *origins* of money, and how important are they for understanding how it works now?.
>
> *(Dodd, 2014: 6)*

In fact, since the debate between monetary orthodoxy and heterodoxy began with the Bank Charter Act of 1844,[4] monetary thought has continued to fuel this perplexity. For orthodoxy, money is conceived as an instrument pure and simple for the exchange of commodities and the distribution of resources, whereas the heterodox conception of money is seen from the outset as a credit currency, as money-capital intended to finance investment and the capitalist trade in commodities. Hence, in terms of monetary policy, the constant concern of the orthodox to ensure the conditions of money's neutrality with respect to trade (Tutin, 2009), whereas the heterodox insist upon the importance of easy access conditions to money as a source of growth and employment for companies.

But this opposition over the nature and role of money has always developed against a background of a common recognition of the social dimension of money: for the orthodox, money basically fulfils a function as an instrument for the circulation of goods and services whose exchange and distribution guarantee social well-being; for the heterodox, money is defined as a common unit of account guaranteeing the homogenisation of reciprocal debts and their settlement by an ultimate means of payment representing that unit of account. Heterodoxy claims that money is a public good in order to condemn the artificially created monetary scarcity of the orthodox and to advocate an active monetary policy in favour of growth and financial stability. But the orthodox also have their own conception of the public good: that of a currency whose neutrality ensures the formation of an equilibrium according to the agents' preferences and resources.

Behind the attacks of the heterodox, it is the private function of money as a store of value that is targeted, insofar as keeping money out of circulation limits and contradicts its function as a means of exchange and settlement in the service of social production. The euthanasia of the rentiers sought by Keynes is nothing other than the abolition of the private function of appropriation of social wealth objectified in money. However, monetary orthodoxy in its canonical form, namely the quantity theory, hardly recognises the store of value function, except as a means of regulating the quantity of money in circulation and thus the value of money. This is why the more the development of capitalism increases the monetary wealth of the rentiers, the more the defence of the quantity theory in the field of monetary thought takes the place of a defence of the interests of savers against the productive classes, entrepreneurs and employees. Thus, for example, Keynes criticised Ricardo's theory of interest, which assumed that the monetary rate of interest merely reflected the real rate of profit in industry (Keynes, 1936: 190–92). For Keynes, this was to make the false assumption that the rate of interest corresponded to the rate at which the full employment of factors was assured. But through this identity, Ricardo assumed more deeply that loan capital was entirely at the service of industry, for money has no other function than to ensure the circulation of goods. It is in the hands of Milton Friedman, as we shall see, that the return of quantity theory comes, without stating it, to defend money as a store of value, as appropriate social wealth in the objective form of a financial asset.

Schumpeter reflected this bipolarisation of the field of monetary thought by contrasting the "credit theory of money" with the "monetary theory of credit". But while he places himself among the former, it is to adopt as his starting point "capitalist finance" defined as "a clearing system that cancels claims and debts and carries forward the differences – so that 'money' payments come in only as a special case without any particularly fundamental importance" (Schumpeter, 1954: 686). Since the financing of capitalist production is entirely based on the credit system and transactions are essentially carried out on credit, credit-based monetary theories define money as a unit of account in which the reciprocal debts of agents are valued (Keynes, 1930). According to this conception, money also exists as a means of payment, but this means of payment itself represents a kind of debt that derives its superiority over other debt instruments from its legally decreed quality as a means of tax settlement (Knapp, 1924): "money as means of payment is just a debt. The payment of a debt is an exchange of debts" (Hicks, 1989: 104). Thus, in credit-based theories of money, the ultimate means-of-payment character of money is purely conventional and does not derive from the general medium-of-exchange function of money, which, in monetary theories of credit, distinguishes it from credit. Therefore, in these theories, the store of value function is a function derived from the liquidity that the quality of ultimate means of settlement confers on money. "Liquidity cannot be defined except in terms of exchangeability for money" (Hicks, 1989: 42). And we will see how Keynes, who was the only theorist of this approach for whom the liquidity preference is not limited to a demand for money for transaction and precautionary reasons, transformed money into a financial asset. Among the monetary theories of credit, the quantity theory of money probably owes its strength and flexibility to the fact that it defines money and its functions independently of its capitalist uses.[5] By giving rise to it from market circulation, it defines money as a means of exchange which is distinguished from all other instruments of circulation by the fact that, as a general means of exchange, money is fixed exogenously, either because it is itself a particular commodity (in the case of precious metals) or because it is issued by a monetary authority outside the exchange process (in the case of fiat money). But quantity theory does not justify the store of value function of money any more than credit-based theories of money do, except by the fact that, insofar as it is derived from the world of commodities, it itself possesses a value. Hence the possibility of money being replaced by all sorts of goods or assets whose value is deemed to be as stable as money. Both the credit-based and the quantity theories of money conceive of money essentially in terms of its social function as a unit of account for society's debts or as a general medium of exchange for market circulation. Although they recognise in the function of the store of value a function of private appropriation or holding of social wealth, this function derives sometimes from its function as the ultimate means of payment, and sometimes from its existence as a value independent of its monetary form. In a mode of production where social labour is exchanged through the circulation of individuals' private labour, where social wealth is embodied in a private object – even if this object belongs to a system of payments considered as public property – it is through the private function of store of value that money is integrated into the economic structure of market exchanges. The whole point of monetary theory is to derive the social and private functions from the nature of money itself.

Compared to monetary orthodoxy, institutionalist theory has had the great merit of recognising the dual dimension of the general equivalent through what it calls the ambivalence of money (Aglietta and Orléan, 1998). In it, money is defined both as the "social medium par excellence of market societies" that makes the payments system itself a public good, and as the "absolute liquidity" that arouses a desire for unrestricted private appropriation (Aglietta, 2016: 67). But in institutionalism, this desire for appropriation results precisely from the liquid character of money, i.e. its absolute exchangeability. And this exchangeability, in turn, emerges from a process of mimetic rivalry between exchangers seeking to impose their own wealth as an object desirable by all (Aglietta and Orléan, 2002: 75).[6] But once money is imposed at the end of this struggle of "wealth-pretenders" (Lordon and Orléan, 2006: 19), the desire for private appropriation is exacerbated the moment that trust in the payments system where agents' mutual debts are settled is eroded. Thus, the ambivalence of money does not belong to money itself but to the antagonistic social relationship presupposed in market society. Institutionalists start from this already constituted commodity society to found a desire that would, in turn, condition the existence and the motor of such an economic system. This is the flaw in all institutionalisms that start from the existing reality, as it immediately appears, and then explain it by anthropological or psychological foundations that are themselves historically determined and conditioned by the social organisation that they are trying to explain. This anthropological-institutional doublet carries the theory into a circle where the human and the institution reflect each other's image ad infinitum, as when one passes along a corridor with mirrored walls.

Therefore, to prevent the unleashing of the forces of private appropriation, it is necessary to establish rules that create ethical trust in money and the payments system. But since money emerges from the frantic and anguished quest for absolute wealth and not from the process of objectification of the exchange value of commodities, i.e. of the social labour contained in them, the unleashing of these forces which is expressed in crises is interpreted basically as the effect of the exchangers' loss of trust in the payments system, and not of the immanent character of the economic form in which social labour is presented as an object distinct not only from the activities of the producers, but from the product of their social activity. This is why, according to this view, currency crises invariably manifest themselves as crises of trust, leading to a search for "an anchor outside the financial system" (Aglietta and Cartelier, 1998: 143) (precious metal, foreign currency, substitute commodity). But this view does not explain why financial crises may instead lead to a search for the very money of the payments system in crisis. Contrary to this view, the common feature of crises is that they provoke distrust of all means of payment except money as a general equivalent or, insofar as they are global crises, as a universal equivalent (gold, dollar). Crises of trust reveal precisely that money has a specific nature in capitalist market societies which distinguishes it entirely from all forms of settlement and which lies in its existence as an objectified form of social labour.[7]

I.3 Anal eroticism and phylogeny of capitalism

Psychoanalysis has also established for itself this double dimension of flow and object in the exchange relation. Indeed, it very quickly discovered in the equation "excrement = money" the double function of retention and expulsion in the child's instinctual life. However, the status of anal retention in the child's relationship to its mother is undoubtedly the most complex and uncertain aspect of the pregenital pulsional life (Gibeault, 1989: 65–66). This is because the anal pleasure of retention (possession) cannot be separated from the oral pleasure of incorporation (acquisition). Now, if introjection supposes the indifferentiation between the child and its environment, anal retention implies a relationship to the faeces defined as an external or exteriorisable object, so that a common possession by two children, for example, is possible. Psychoanalysis generally associates the desire to make money with the oral aggressive impulses that accompany the desire to introject (Borneman, 1978: 35). But one can just as easily earn money by sacrificing one's labour, coupled with abstinence: a form of openness to the Other that refers precisely to the external dimension of the expelled object, hence to the anal dimension of the desire to possess. It is true that there is no such thing as anal masochism as such, but Freud had nevertheless noted the relationship between the passivity proper to anal eroticism and that which characterises erogenous masochism, in particular in the game of retention/expulsion where the retention drive favours the delay in satisfaction (Gibeault, 1989: 65). However, if retention implies the exteriority of the retained object, it is the sadistic dimension that opens the way to the object itself, precisely through the desire to destroy and dominate it. In the narcissistic challenge of retaining one's faeces, sadism accounts for the pleasure linked to the mastery and domination of the object because the retention is not always done under the sign of love but also in a movement of hatred and attack. It can therefore be as much the expression of the pleasure procured by the satisfaction of the mother who has been obeyed as the expression of a desire to dominate the mother by refusing to respond to her request for expulsion. In both cases, there is objectification of the faeces. This double possibility accounts for the ambivalence of the desire for possession itself, where one side of the alternative (pleasing the mother) envelops and prolongs the pleasure of the gift of faeces to the mother. On the other side, the retention is sterile and purely narcissistic (avarice).[8]

The relationship between the ontogeny of the infant and the phylogeny of societies is to be situated not in the mnemonic traces of a supposed archaic heritage (Marcuse, 1955) but at the level of individual and social practices, it being understood that social practice is only the desiring-production itself in conditions determined by the state of the existing productive forces and relations of production (Deleuze and Guattari, 1983: 38). However, the drive to enrichment is not sufficient to elaborate a phylogeny of capitalism because here money has to be invested, not hoarded. But since the desire to possess implies the objective character of what one desires to possess, it already contains the conditions for such an outward movement. The great discovery that Freud makes in 1917[9] is indeed that of the presence in the desire to possess of a more fundamental pleasure than the auto-erotic satisfaction of retention that he had assumed until then: the pleasure in production, of stools in this case, and of the sacrifice of its production in exchange for maternal love: the first conscious creation, the first creative action of the newborn towards the mother. But, as we have seen, they are immediately a means for the child to exercise his power over his parents: if he defecates when the mother wishes, he is appreciated as smart, clean, etc. If he defecates elsewhere than in his mother's house, he is appreciated as a child. If he defecates elsewhere than where he is expected to, but also if he does not defecate when the parent puts him on the potty, for example, he is challenged or called unclean, etc. By playing with their faeces, children discover their power over these great beings that are their parents. There are three possibilities for the child in possession of his excrement, which can be found in the character types of the adult: obedience to injunctions (rational behaviour of homo eoconomicus), capricious expulsion (prodigality) and retention (avarice). The first two cases refer to the social function of money, i.e. money as a general medium of exchange. Only the third refers to the private function of money as a store of value. We have seen that the pleasure of retaining one's faeces in order to increase excitement during expulsion redoubles the pleasure derived from the feeling of power over one's parents induced by that retention. This is how retention mixes the pleasure of enrichment (incorporation and retention are closely associated, see below) with the pleasure of power over others, that is, social power. Now the pleasure of enrichment is the pleasure of retaining something whose final destiny is to be given up (faeces retained for too long produce intestinal complications, etc.) whereas, conversely, the social power made possible by the retention of faeces implies the retention of this object, this social production, in one's own hands. This is why faeces possess by nature this double social and private dimension which characterises money: at the same time object of exchange with the outside world and object of private wealth: form of exchangeability and form of value. In the order of the economy of desire, the historical strength of capitalism lies in the compromise that this mode of social production makes between these two tendencies.

Marx often borrows the vocabulary of psychology when it comes to explaining the motives of capital accumulation.[10] First of all, the capitalist shares with the hoarder "the passion for wealth as wealth [Bereicherunstrieb]" (Marx, 1867a: 588). But Marx immediately points out that the capitalist's individual mania becomes an effect of the social mechanism, in which he is only a cog (Marx, 1867a: 588). Here, then, capital rests not only on the ingredients of the market economy – money and commodities – but on characters, drives and manias which are born of the development of money in social relations and which find in it not only the conditions for their unlimited development, but their social justification. This justification comes precisely from the fact that the drive to enrichment is satisfied only on the condition of permanently increasing social production and thus the productive forces of society. It is only in this sense that the drive to enrichment forms the spring of capitalism's historical mission and links the ontogeny of the infant to the phylogeny of capitalism. However, the drive to enrichment does not only find its social justification in capital; it is a condition of the capitalist's survival by virtue of the laws of competition to which each capital in activity is subjected and which force him "to keep constantly extending his capital, in order to preserve it" (Marx, 1867a: 588). But as much as this thirst for enrichment necessarily joins avarice in the historical beginnings of capitalism (avarice which Weber describes as asceticism), with the progress of capitalism and the abundance of wealth it creates, it coexists with the desire for enjoyment. Moreover, the display of wealth and a certain level of waste are as indispensable as the renunciation of enjoyment was for the first capitalists. And this coexistence of the drives for enrichment and enjoyment is all the more valid in that at the monopoly stage of capitalist production, which we entered at the turn of the 20th century, the drive for enrichment is constrained by the very limits of capital accumulation. Thus, the figure of the capitalist bears at its deepest core the contradiction immanent to money itself and whose ontogeny we have traversed in the child, between its function of accumulation and its function of circulation, but by reversing the contradiction proper to money. For by satisfying his desire for private enjoyment, the capitalist activates the social function of money as a means of circulation, whereas by realising his impulse to enrichment, he fulfils the historical mission of capital by converting this appropriate social wealth into new means of social production. In the first case, it enriches other capitalists; in the second case, it enriches its own capital. In all cases, the capitalists taken together earn what they spend, while the wage-earners spend what they earn (Kalecki). Yet, when he replaces his original avarice with his desire for enjoyment, the capitalist, Marx observes, "ceases to be the mere incarnation of capital" (Marx, 1867a: 589). Is this not one of the proofs that the development of capitalism itself engenders, in the very person of its functionary, the development of impulses which not only no longer respond to the historical mission of capital, but blur the private dimension of money by stimulating its existence as a pure and simple means of general exchange?[11]

★★★

No one better than Klossowski has grasped the importance of the role of money in the organisation of the Sadian phantasm; no one has better related the ambivalence of anal sadism to the contradictory nature and functions of money. In *Living Currency* (2017), money is not only a general equivalent; it is also a sign of the unvaluable character of the phantasm: a universally intelligible equivalent (as abstract wealth) of the perverse phantasm that is unintelligible and unchangeable. It is that fundamental supplement which transforms the human principle of the gift of love or exchange into the inhuman game of corruptions, of the monetary appropriation of bodies, of prostitution as the essential structure of intersubjectivities. Money is then this phantasmatic diversion of the human principles of love, which authorises the commercial slavery of bodies and beings (Marty, 2011). It is a diversion of wealth – for which it is exchanged in its mediating function as a means of circulation – in favour of the perverse phantasm. In this sense, money is, in the domain of objects, the non-exchangeable par excellence. For under this equivalent function of the invaluable, in fact, money means the destruction of the riches of which it is the equivalent in the market order. "Money, even as it represents and guarantees what exists, now becomes a sign of *what does not exist*, namely, the phantasm" (Klossowski, 2017: 69). Money carries with it this transgression of existing norms since it offers the freedom to choose or refuse this or that good among all those that exist before it. Through this freedom, it questions the value of what exists in favour of what does not exist. What does not exist according to the market order exists in "*money not spent* and thus *not given to what exists*" (Klossowski, 2017: 69). It is in this sense that the store of value function is the perverse function par excellence of money.

If Sade is the secret and obscure inspiration of the French Revolution, it is because his own perversion is nothing other than the staging of the perverse effects of money without the mediation of money itself. We have examined how anality presupposes the oral urge for which there is hardly any separation between the self and the environment. Now, in Sade and Klossowski, the oral background subsists in all commerce between men, which is always an exchange of bodies through the secret language of body signs (Klossowski, 2017: 69). And it is the very nature of the phantasm to abolish all ownership of the body. Thus, money only mediates the exchange of bodies when property rights are established. It is the perverse form of this exchange, substituting a de facto prostitution, both material and moral. Money replaces the immediate communication of beings through the exchange of their bodies with prostitution through the exchange of goods. Under these conditions, as soon as the phantasm, which is in itself invaluable, ungraspable, useless and arbitrary – that is to say, which is opposed by nature to the instinct of conservation and reproduction – is converted into money, it becomes a rare object and gives rise to purely sumptuary expenditure.[12] But insofar as money is both the equivalent of the invaluable of the perverse phantasm and the general equivalent of ordinary wealth, it is trade itself which, through the circulation of money, makes the "closed world of anomalies" communicable with the world of institutional norms. Nevertheless, there remains a distorted communication between the clandestinity of private phantasms and the transparency of the commercial exchanges of a society that favours, at the same time as it covers with the modest veil of money, the crimes of the pervert.

***

In the same year that Freud discovered the relationship between anal retention and avarice in *The Rat Man* (1909, the consultation took place two years before the text was published), the US experienced the greatest money shortage crisis in its history, which would determine its future and that of the international monetary system. The banking crisis of 1907 was actually triggered by the widespread distrust that the bursting of a speculative bubble had caused in finance companies and by contagion in the banks that did business with them. The 1907 crisis had the characteristic of being a "pure" liquidity crisis (Mendez and Tutin, 2010: 44). That is, it occurred at a time when banks were chronically short of cash, as they are every autumn when Midwestern farmers borrow to start their crops and ship them to the various markets. In the absence of a central bank, the New York banks from which the reserves ultimately came had to borrow gold on the London market in exchange for finance bills issued on their behalf by financial companies. In addition, the earthquake in San Francisco a year earlier forced insurers to transfer gold from London to the US to compensate their policyholders. Faced with these gold outflows, the Bank of England decided to raise its discount rate and, in the process, advised not to renew the finance bills of New York banks, precipitating the liquidity crisis in the US, which, according to Friedman and Schwartz, caused the worst contraction of the money supply in the country's history (1963: 158).

The crisis of 1907 was the direct cause of the plan to create a central bank whose main function would be to inject liquidity when tensions arose in the banking and financial system. Even though resistance from all sides delayed the project for a long time, the crisis had indeed revealed two major flaws in the US monetary system. First, the clearing houses, which performed some of the functions of a central bank, did not lend directly and could not create money. They did issue loan certificates but these did not function as means of payment. Second, the extreme fragmentation of the US banking system implied a complete decentralisation of reserves which limited the system's ability to react to liquidity shocks. The duck hunters' meeting at which the top bankers and federal officials posed at Jekyll Island was intended to create a system of federal banks to provide liquidity to banks in times of stress or panic (Markham, 2002: 43). Finally, the Federal Reserve Act of 1913 allowed banks to issue "elastic money" through the issuance of Federal Reserve notes. More importantly, it allowed Federal Reserve Banks, in addition to setting the discount rate, to buy and sell US Treasury bonds, securities issued by state and county governments, and bills of exchange.

Thus, by 1916, with the help of the war, a Fed report revealed that it had become the creditor of foreign countries in every corner of the world (Markham, 2002: 73). 1,500 banks in the US were involved in issuing and selling securities as well as foreign borrowing. And the pace of US financing increased as the war progressed. Moreover, as soon as the US declared war on Germany, Wilson declared an embargo on the gold reserves that had been growing since the beginning of the war. But above all, the declaration of war gave rise to Liberty loans by means of bond issues that did more than attract national savings to finance the government's war effort: it installed all the ingredients of the US model of liberal democracy in the age of mass consumption, just as the Russian proletariat had broken free from the Tsarist yoke and was taking control of its own destiny. In the same year that Freud posited the primacy of pleasure in the production of faeces in children, the US experimented with Liberty Bonds, the monetary flexibility that the Fed was now offering the government, including the mechanisms that banks use today to finance their speculative activities: repurchase agreements (repos), whose role and mechanisms we will examine later. Thus,

> To provide immediate funds [while waiting for the Liberty Bonds counterpart funds to arrive], certificates of indebtedness were issued by the government in anticipation of the Liberty Loan proceeds. The secretary issued some $4 billion of those certificates in 1917 to meet government expenses. The certificates were used to provide liquidity through repurchase transactions – that is, the certificates were purchased by the Federal Reserve Bank of New York for short intervals and then resold to the original sellers. This 'repo' process was also used for repurchases of banker's acceptances.
>
> *(Markham, 2002: 76)*

And indeed, the Secretary of the Treasury remarked that the first Liberty Loan was "the largest single piece of financing ever undertaken by the government of the United States" (ibid.). All means of mass culture were used. Posters and advertisements were used to encourage the purchase of Liberty Bonds. Movie stars like Charles Chaplin and Douglas Fairbanks were used to promote them. More than a million newspaper articles praised them, not to mention editorials, cartoons and newspaper advertisements. Citizens were urged to go into debt to buy them through certificates of participation, while savings stamps and war savings stamps were issued to attract small savers and thus lay the groundwork for the indebted man. What is more, their issue was a new opportunity for speculation, as they were oversubscribed, so that more than half of all adults had bought Liberty Bonds in one way or another. This issue alone created a huge capital borrowing market for the industry. Finally, 1917 marked the end of British hegemony, well before the crisis of 1931 and the Great Depression.[13]

I.4 Outline of the book

Marx's theory of the general equivalent does not differ from other approaches to money either by the link it establishes between money and labour-value, or by the genesis of money from the commodity, or even by the unity of functions it determines. The difference lies, rather, in that it posits, through its commodity genesis, money as both a form of general exchangeability and a general form of value. These two modes of being of money determine in Marx the different categories of the credit system and explain the very possibility of crises in the capitalist mode of production (Chapter 1). The role of the central bank and the instruments of monetary policy were undoubtedly the immediate stakes in the polemic between the Currency School and the Banking School, but the scope of the debate in the history of monetary thought cannot be explained in any other way than by the modes of being of money that these two schools claim through the monetary functions that they promote in their interventions, and which condition their respective fetishisms of capital (Chapter 2). Since monetary orthodoxy defines money as a pure means of exchange with no other use than to facilitate transactions, the whole history of modern monetary thought up to Friedman is a long series of attempts to justify a demand for money for its own sake, i.e. to determine it as a general form of value while conceiving it exclusively as a form of general exchangeability (Chapter 4). The examination of Keynes's attempt from the *Tract on Monetary Reform* to the *General Theory* will show how, torn between a conception of money defined as a unit of account in which banks grant credit to firms and his theory of liquidity preference, Keynes transforms money demanded for its own sake into a liquid financial asset (Chapter 3) and thus paves the way for the internal polemics of post-Keynesianism between the structuralists (liquidity preference approach) and the horizontalists (circuit approach) (Chapter 5). But it is in the Modern Monetary Theory that Keynes's chartalism coupled with a credit theory of money finds its radical utopian form and inspires a monetary universalism reducing money in history to a kind of debt (Chapter 6).

While the international monetary system had been entirely organised around the dollar since the Bretton Woods Agreement, in 1960 Robert Triffin set out, in the form of a dilemma, the fundamental contradiction of a monetary system in which global liquidity is provided by the currency of a particular state. We shall see that this dilemma arose for the dollar in the aftermath of the First World War, at a time when the Keynesian state was replacing the liberal state, which was entirely focused on its external financial equilibrium: thus, well before the neoliberal turn of the 1970s, the free circulation of money worldwide was the condition, the object, the springboard and the field of action of the early neoliberal project: neoliberalism is first and foremost an ordomonetarism (Chapter 7). But above all, Triffin's dilemma expresses a deeper contradiction between the different functions that the dollar fulfils as a universal currency and as a national currency, a contradiction itself redoubled by the contradictory functions that the dollar fulfils within its two spheres of circulation. However, the bewitched destiny of the dollar will show, through the formation of the Eurodollar market in particular, that this dilemma will have been constantly pushed back by a process that must be described as the relative autonomisation of the dollar, which gradually transformed the Fed into a genuine universal Bank, no less than the US Treasury bill into a pillar of the international financial system (Chapter 8). In this process of autonomisation, the currency crises that hit the peripheral regions of world capitalism from the 1980s onwards present themselves as phases of the birth of the dollar as a universal currency whose degree of penetration of international financial circuits relativises the claims of competing currencies to assume the current role of the dollar (Chapter 9). However, the dollar did not become autonomous from the US markets without relaxing the monetary constraint on global production and trade and thus without effecting a relative decommodification of universal social activity. Both through this loosening and through the role of the Fed and the US Treasury, developments in the international monetary system are engendering the very conditions by which, on the basis of a strengthening of market production, Lenin's NEP transformed the banking and financial system of Soviet Russia into a global system of accounting, planning and resource allocation (Chapter 10). It is to this end only that central bank digital currency projects promise to revolutionise the payments systems of today's world (Conclusion).

Notes

1 Even Hobbes, arguably the most inclined of the contract theorists to attribute the origin of the State to the state of internecine warfare, cannot help but cite the defence "from the invasion of foreigners" as the primary reason for the formation of Leviathan, before "the injuries of one another" (Hobbes, 1651: 114).

2 Excavations have revealed that Lydian electrum coins remained within a narrow perimeter of circulation, due in part to the uncertainty of their value, the proportion of gold and silver being difficult to establish, whereas the silver coins of Corinth and Aegina went as far as Egypt (Seaford, 2004: 135). Picard, who argues that owl treasures were not used for trade, nevertheless acknowledges that the Near East has an exception in Alexandria (p. 125). Finally, Schaps (1997) has noted the simultaneity of coinage, agora and retail trade in Athens. For even though the Lydians created the first minted coins, the Greeks were the first to make pervasive daily use of them (Seaford, 2004: 113).

3 "[T]he fundamental speculation of a capitalist society has two facets: the acquisition of capital assets and the putting out of commitments to pay cash embodied in the liabilities used to finance such capital acquisitions" (Minsky, 1975: 86).

4 One could probably go back to the Bullionist controversy of 1810, on the occasion of the return of the convertibility of the pound into gold at the end of the Napoleonic Wars, but this debate did not have the same magnitude regarding either the practical issues or the theoretical arguments of the parties involved as the 1844 debate (see Fetter, 1965).

5 It is true that Wicksell develops a quantity theory based on a system of pure credit money centred on the debt relationship between the bank and the firm. But in this system, only the banks issue this credit money, which is therefore the only means of payment for firms and households. Wicksell's aim is to show the cumulative effects on the quantity of money and prices of the difference between the bank interest rate and the natural interest rate, i.e. the real rate of profit (Wicksell, 1978: 190 ff.).

6 The presentation of this mimetic rivalry claims to be based on the anthropology of René Girard, but it owes much more to Menger (1892) for the self-validation mechanism she describes. Just as their conception of the ambivalence of money is taken directly from Simmel (1900): "In so far as money becomes the absolutely commensurate expression and equivalent of all values, it rises to abstract heights way above the whole broad diversity of objects" (Simmel, 1900: 254). But for him the drive for wealth, which arises from this extension, forms a social pathology expressing itself in the relativisation and depreciation of all things subjected to a process of quantification and comparison.

7 To illustrate the role of trust in crises, Aglietta systematically uses examples of mistrust in subordinate currencies in the international monetary system:

> What matters is the immediacy of the feverish search for protection of existing wealth. The result of this search ends up polarising on a new common belief whose support is often external to the previous monetary space, often a foreign currency that becomes the new accepted unit of measurement. This is why mimicry is the general process of extreme currency crises in the critical moment when the official currency itself is rejected.
>
> *(Aglietta, 2016: 208)*

But what we need to understand is why this research focuses on a new objective medium that is considered the sole representative of the social wealth of a country whose currency it is not.

8 Classical liberalism thus would proceed from an anal fixation on the desire to possess that the clinic attributes to a negative ambivalence towards the mother.

> Because the person who takes pleasure in possessing thinks that everyone wants to dispossess him of his money in the same way that his mother used to dispossess him of his faeces, he regards the people around him with extreme distrust. He is the type of person who constantly proclaims everywhere that man is evil 'by nature', that the desire to possess is 'human nature' and that the idea of the community of goods is 'unnatural'.
>
> *(Borneman, 1978: 45)*

From this point of view, capitalism would have given to a character formation, which is rare in other social systems, a field of deployment unknown elsewhere. This social regression would undoubtedly result from the decline of the feudal lord figure, which would have found in the development of money the objective conditions for this fixation.

9 "On transformations of instinct as exemplified in anal erotism" (1917).

10 "Hence there is immanent in capital an inclination [*Trieb*] and constant tendency, to heighten the productiveness of labour, in order to cheapen commodities, and by such cheapening to cheapen the labourer himself" (Marx, 1867: 324–25).

11 With regard to the desire to possess money, Arvane (2015) distinguishes between avarice, which refers to money as a value, and greed, which understands money as the equivalent of all possible riches, as potential enjoyment. These two urges are matched by two feelings towards those who possess money: jealousy and envy. The jealous person wants to keep and prevent money from circulating; the envious person wants to benefit from other people's money as a means of circulation, as it has a liberating power. Thus, greed relates to money as a general form of value and greed to money as a form of general exchangeability, to the general equivalent as money.

12 It is in this sense that the potlach falls out of the economic market circuit and that the primitive monies which are its support are a simulacrum of the commodity monies and behave like their playful diversion by retrospection.

13 "Great Britain found itself nearly bankrupt in 1917, a sharp contrast to its dominant position in international finance in the prewar years. It owed $400 million on a maturing loan that had been underwritten by J.P. Morgan & Co., but the United States advanced almost $700 million to Great Britain, allowing it to continue the war effort. Even with the massive requirements of the Liberty Loans, Wall Street continued to finance foreign governments. On August 22, 1917, J.P. Morgan & Co., acting for the British government, placed $15 million of ninety-day British Treasury bills in the United States. This was intended to become a weekly affair. 'U.S. Consols' and U.S. registered '4s' were also being sold in the United States during the war by Great Britain" (Markham, 2002: 78).

PART 1

The modes of being of money

1

MONEY, ITS MODES OF BEING AND ITS FUNCTIONS

1.1 Marx against monetary utopias

For the contemporary reader, the genesis of the general equivalent in *Capital* belongs to the rank of theoretical curiosities, not only because it borrows its form of exposition and its vocabulary from Hegel's logic, but because the money which emerges from the development of exchange relations finds its ultimate incarnation in a commodity, in gold or silver. And since the whole movement of money is based on the development of the value-form, the whole theory of labour-value seems to be called into question by inspiring a conception of money that would not survive the abandonment of the gold standard system.

For Marx, the difficulty to be faced in the exposition of the formation of the general equivalent consists less in demonstrating that money is a commodity than in grasping the process which leads a commodity to become money (Marx, 1867: 102). But for Proudhon's monetary disciples, against whom Marx first expounded his theory of money (*Grundrisse*), the commodity nature of money was not at all self-evident and conferred on its producer an exorbitant privilege vis-à-vis ordinary exchangers (Marx, 1857–58: 64). Thus, Alfred Darimon, for example, called for the abolition of metallic money and, in its place, for the issue of banknotes which, while denominated in francs, would directly represent hours of labour (Darimon, 1856: 9), thus drawing inspiration from the monetary reforms of John Gray (1848). In this way, the exchange of goods would take place and expand without the disruption and limitations caused by the variation of production costs and the scarcity of precious metals. Producers would exchange the product of their labour for the equivalent in hourly vouchers in order to obtain in return the goods produced by others for the amount of the same number of working hours. Thus, the hour of labour would be the authentic unit of measurement of the exchange value of commodities and no trader would

DOI: 10.4324/9780429261299-3

be able to take advantage of the possession of metallic money to derive from the exchange a higher value than that embodied in gold (Marx, 1859: 321). Against these monetary utopias, it was all the more decisive to demonstrate the necessity of the commodity form of money as Gray and Proudhon themselves based their reforms on the theory of labour-value and recognised in metallic money, unlike Say, for example, a commodity whose value is determined by the labour time necessary for its production. The *Grundrisse* are like the reverse side of *Capital*: before explaining how the exchange value of the commodity is expressed in a commodity-money, it was necessary to discover why money is materialised in a commodity.

The general question raised by the meaning of the reform envisaged by the proponents of the time-coupon is:

> is it possible to revolutioniste the existing relations of production and the corresponding relations of distribution by means of changes in the instrument of circulation – changes in the organization of circulation? A further question: can such a transformation of circulation be accomplished without touching the existing relations of production and the social relations based on them?
>
> *(Marx, 1857–58)*

The utopianism of the reform lies precisely in the illusion that a change in the form of money would abolish the capitalist relation of exploitation in commodity production and guarantee the equality of the producer-traders by remunerating them according to the time actually worked.

Marx first of all objects to the issue of time-money on the grounds that the value of commodities as socially necessary labour time is never equal to the labour time actually contained in them. This is because the socially necessary value defines an ideal quantity born of the exchange relation itself, although value is theoretically and practically prior to prices and conditions the exchange relations. On the one hand, the value of a commodity cannot be determined other than by the average of its market prices; on the other hand, these variable prices oscillate perpetually around the average value of the commodity (Marx, 1857–58: 76–77). The ambiguity of the status of value, which has given rise to so many interpretations and criticisms of Marxian labour-value theory (Elson, 2015), merely expresses the specific character of social labour in market society, where the living labour time that society decides to spend on the production of a good is fixed indirectly, through the mediation of the exchange of the products of labour performed by private individuals (Baronian, 2013). Thus, value and price are unequal because the social conditions of production impose themselves on individual value only through prices. Value is indeed a substance, but a social substance which does not exist outside the exchange relation between commodities, just as social labour time expressed in value is itself an ideal quantity which results from the average of market prices or from the average of the incessant variations of the exchange relation between the commodity and its monetary equivalent.

Now, an issue of paper labour money would imply conditions of production and exchange which would precisely make money superfluous:

> if the conditions under which the price of a commodity=its exchange value are assumed as fulfilled, i.e. balance of demand and supply; of production and consumption; in the final analysis, proportionate production [...], then the question of money becomes quite secondary, and especially the question of whether blue or green tickets, metal or paper ones, are issued, or in what form social book-keeping will be done. It is then the height of absurdity to keep up the pretence that investigations of the actual money relationships should be instituted.
>
> *(Marx, 1857–58: 90)*

This is why, as we shall see, the status of the money equation in general equilibrium models is purely formal. Walras's auctioneer, like Darimon's central banker, should ensure not only the coordination of social exchanges, but also, by this very function, the organisation of social production. Either the Bank "would be either the despotic governing production and managing distribution, or indeed nothing more than a board to carry on the book-keeping and accounting for society working in common" (Marx, 1857–58: 93). Because of the difference, inherent in commodity production, between value and price, money can never directly represent the labour time incorporated in the commodity. For "the labour-time ticket, which represents the *average labour time*, would never correspond to the *actual labour time* and never be convertible into it" (Marx, 1857–58: 76–77). The specific character of the commodity mode of production has taught us two things: the commodity must express its exchange value in a distinct object representing its social existence, and this object cannot directly express the labour time contained in the commodity. Therefore, the difference between money and commodity does not derive from the arbitrary privilege of precious metals over other commodities, but from the deeper difference between socially necessary value and individual value which explains why values are measured by a different standard than labour time. The nominal difference between price and value is conditioned by their real difference (Marx, 1857–58: 78). So far, however, money does not necessarily have to be fixed in a commodity. All we know for the moment is that money represents the social form of the labour contained in the commodity, and that this labour, by virtue of the very nature of the commodity mode of production, must necessarily be objectified in a currency distinct from the commodity in which it is contained. If labour time, because of its ideal character, cannot form a concrete unit of measurement, this ideality does not require that the exchange value of the commodity is necessarily expressed in the material of another commodity. No doubt, a decentralised economy excludes by its very nature a currency measured in working hours, but nothing so far requires that socially necessary labour be expressed in the product of a certain labour.

1.2 The market society and its object

Moreover, exchange value could just as well be expressed in a simple sign or symbol of its value (Marx, 1857–58: 76). The difference between value and price basically reveals only the difference, proper to the commodity, between the natural and the social existence of the commodity, and this difference is manifested precisely in its relation to another commodity. Thus, even when in the relation of two commodities, the second expresses in its concrete existence the value of the first (20 yards of linen = 1 coat), this relation puts them as equal to a third term which "exists initially in the head, in the imagination, just as general ratios" (Marx, 1857–58: 81). The account of the genesis of the general equivalent shows precisely how this third ideal term acquires a concrete form of existence in money. But, for now, the object of the standard does not matter, provided that the price standard itself is fixed once and for all. For what matters above all in the choice of a concrete value unit of measurement is that it possesses all the properties of value which the commodity lacks in its natural existence: as a value, the commodity must be divisible, which as a product it is not. As a value, it is universal, as opposed to the particular existence of use value; as a value, it is always exchangeable, whereas the exchange of a particular commodity depends on the need of the buyer. As a value, it itself determines the measure of its exchangeability, whereas social need determines the exchangeability of the product.

Before being determinations of money, divisibility, universality, exchangeability and its measurement are first of all determinations of the commodity as a value. Therefore, in order to compare commodities, it is sufficient to transform them mentally into numerical magnitudes:

> Not a single atom of real gold is used to estimate the value of a thousand bales of cotton in terms of a certain number of ounces of gold and then to express this number of ounces in £. s. d., the names of account of the ounce.
> *(Marx, 1859: 312)*

This ideality is illustrated by numerous historical examples that show us that the unit of account of money may exist only ideally in relation to circulating currencies, which may be monetised according to quite other standards (currencies circulating under Charlemagne's empire). Nevertheless, in actual exchange, these magnitudes must be realised in a sign of value distinct from the goods. For as long as money, as an object distinct from commodities, represents the exchange value of all commodities, it can only express social labour time through its own material magnitude. If money were to express social labour time directly, its nature as money would be negated, which presupposes that the commodity never directly represents social labour time, but instead is exchanged for an object which symbolises this labour time as a quantum of itself, as a quantum of its own objectivity. The quantum of labour time that the commodity represents in money "is both measured and given its general, exchangeable form corresponding to the concept" (Marx, 1857–58: 104). Insofar as this sign expresses the value of all commodities, it would suffice for it to be "the symbol of the commodity as a commodity" (Marx, 1857–58: 82), not a particular commodity. The need to express exchange value in an object other than the commodity does not imply at this stage that it must be expressed in a particular commodity. At this point, all that Marx can oppose to the Proudhonians is that they can never abolish money as long as value remains the social form of the labour products.

However, when we say that value manifests itself in the exchange relation, we have seen that this means that the living labour of producers acquires its social character through the mediation of the exchange of the products of this labour. It is therefore necessary that the product of labour as a commodity be exchanged for a product of labour that represents the social character of labour. At an undeveloped stage of exchange, money can take the most exotic forms and be embodied in objects that owe nothing to human labour. These various monetary forms have led institutionalists to say that money is a universal fact that can be observed in all societies whose history has left us traces (Théret, 2008: 814). But in a productive system entirely turned towards exchange, where the labour of individuals is realised as social labour in the exchange of the products of work as commodities, the universal representative of value must also materialise in the product of a given labour. If the social basis from which we start is composed of independent producers who exchange their products as commodities, how could money arise elsewhere than in the process of exchange and thus present itself first of all as a particular commodity? We shall see that this is the case in societies in which, according to the common opinion of economists, there were abstract monetary units devoid of a commodity basis (Mesopotamia, ancient Egypt). Marx only settles the account of the Proudhonians once he has established the fundamental character of the commodity relation of production in general. From the moment when individuals do not organise the distribution of social labour in advance, but a posteriori through the exchange of the products of their private labour (where they do not exchange labour time as such, but on the contrary labour time materialised, objectified in the product of labour), money, in turn, takes the form of determined labour.

> Labour time itself cannot be money directly (to demand this would be the same as demanding that every commodity should be directly its own money), precisely because in fact it always exists (as an object) only in the form of particular products. As a general object it can only exist symbolically, again in a particular commodity which is posited as money.
>
> *(Marx, 1857–58: 104–05)*

If labour itself were to present itself as the universal money, it would have to represent universal labour even before the exchange. It would then be the collective character of production which would determine the worker's participation in the consumption of products. "Instead of a division of labour which necessarily arises from the exchange of exchange values, labour would be organised in such a way that the individual's share in common consumption would directly follow" (Marx, 1867–58:108). Exchange would take place not after, but before production, as a prior distribution of labour according to the collective needs of society. Consequently, this exchange would include from the outset the participation of the individual in the world of society's products and his labour would also present itself from the outset as social labour. The existence of a universally exchangeable commodity means, first of all, that economic agents refer to it as the only adequate social mode of existence for their labour. It completes the process by which social activity is mediated by the circulation of the products of labour as commodities, by which therefore individuals "exist for each other only as things" (Marx, 1858: 468). From this moment onwards, money will no longer seem to owe its existence to the fact that commodities have chosen it as the general form of value. On the contrary, it will appear that they relate to this equivalent because it is money. This opens up the possibility of replacing commodity-money with a monetary form that is more in line with the stage of development of exchange and communication and that corrects the defects of the previous form of money (Marx, 1857–58: 61). But whatever the monetary form, none will be able to abolish the necessity for commodities to be exchanged for the objective form in which their value is represented.

1.3 The two modes of being and the contradictory functions of money

We can now better grasp the notion of general or universal equivalent, and we will soon see why it has given rise to the most varied interpretations among Marxists. Insofar as money arises not from a convention but from the relation of commodity to commodity, i.e. from the development of exchange value, and thus mediates exchange, it presents itself at first sight as a form of the immediate exchangeability of commodities.[1] We shall call this mode of being of the general equivalent-money *the form of general exchangeability*. However, this mode by which money is exchanged in law for all other commodities belongs to it because and insofar as not all commodities are in this universally exchangeable form. Thus, money presents itself simultaneously and contradictorily as a form that is both distinct from and common to commodities, i.e. as a form of objectivity of their value.[2]

This form of objectivity determines money in a mode of being that we should call the general form of value. Through the unity of these two modes of being of money, is expressed the nature of the commodity mode of production in which money is both the social form of the labour contained in commodities and the object of private appropriation for the exchangers. This is why "general equivalent" designates money as the objectified social form of the private labour of social individuals.[3] The paradox of this dual mode is that it is as a private object that money fulfils its social function as a medium of exchange, while conversely it is as social wealth that money fulfils its private function as a store of value.

When they try to define it, theorists of money usually first state the three generic functions of money – unit of account, medium of exchange or circulation, and store of value (Wicksell, Fisher, etc.) – before classifying them in order of historical appearance or practical importance, depending on the conception of the nature of money that they are trying to explain. But it never occurred to any economist, with a few exceptions (Aglietta and Orléan, 2002), that these functions contradict each other and manifest opposing dimensions of money. Thus, as a means of circulation, which orthodoxy makes the main function of money, money manifests itself as a form of general exchangeability, whereas the function of store of value refers to money as a general form of value. As a means of circulation, money fulfils a social function of distributing the products of society's labour (Marx, 1857–58: 131; 1859: 332). However, the trust in the social character of the production whose circulation is ensured by money makes it appear as "evanescent and ideal, something merely imaginative" (Marx, 1895: 568). Therefore, this function allows money to be replaced by any symbol of itself that society chooses by convention to best meet the requirements of this function (Campbell, 2004: 84). However, while custom or convention is the source of the forms of money in circulation, it is never the source of the general equivalent character that money necessarily takes on in the market. Now, as a general equivalent, as the ultimate means of payment, as the general form of value, both its quantity and its materiality become essential (Marx, 1857–58: 161–62).[4] Thus, where the means of circulation fulfils a social function, money as a store of value presents itself instead as a private mode of existence of social wealth. Marx undoubtedly insisted a lot on the social virtues of this reserve function, which allows circulating money to find its channels of adduction and derivation, as required by variations in the value and quantities of circulating goods (Marx, 1859: 369–70). But precisely these virtues derive from the very form of the means of circulation, which consists of a thing distinct and common to the values in circulation and with which these must necessarily be exchanged. Thus, they are inseparable from the mode of existence of money as appropriable wealth.

1.4 The ambivalence of the value-measurement function and the ideality of the unit of account

It is the ambivalence of the mode of existence of the general equivalent which gives the value-measurement function its distinctive character in relation to the unit of account or price standard, and with which it is confused in many Marxist theorists of money. The function of value measurement arises as soon as a commodity relates to another commodity and immediately finds in it the measure of its exchange value. Thus, barter does not represent the historically primitive form of exchange, as monetary institutionalism believes it must denounce (Servet, 1993), but determines the *logically primitive form of the equivalent* in which the exchange value of the commodity is separated and embodied in the product of the others' labour, that is, in another commodity. Monetary exchange does not obscure real exchange; on the contrary, it reveals its essential nature, namely that social labour takes the form of the exchange of the products of private labour. If barter constitutes the canonical figure of exchange in neoclassical theory, it is precisely because utility as a value relation and as a motive for exchange is masked by monetary exchange. This is why money does not fulfil the function of measuring values (these values are given in the preferences of individuals and the quantities of goods present in the market), but of a price standard whose value is entirely dependent on the purchasing power of money as determined by its quantity and the commodities in circulation. If we want to express the difference of these functions from the point of view of monetary gold, we would say that it measures the values of commodities as materialised labour time, while it forms the price standard as a fixed weight of metal measuring other quanta of metal (Marx, 1859: 309).[5] Thus, the function of value measurement defines money as the embodiment of social labour where the unit of account refers to a certain quantum of gold expressed in units measuring other quantities of the same metal.[6] Since money as a measure of value is not itself expressed as a ratio but as a quantity of a certain material such as gold or silver, for example, insofar as it is itself value, it relates to itself as a quantity of its own material.[7]

No doubt at the time of the gold standard, there was a contradiction between the function of value measurement and the function as means of circulation. For the first function, the money material was essential, although its concrete presence was not necessary; for the second function, only the quantity was important, although its concrete presence is necessary under this function (Marx, 1859: 355). But as soon as the monetary system becomes based entirely on fiat money, not only does this contradiction disappear, but so do all forms of tangible existence of money. From now on, the means of circulation become mere symbolic representatives of an abstract unit of account, just as the unit of account becomes the only common denominator of all monetary forms in circulation. This evolution of money provides the basis for all monetary theories according to which money and the hierarchy of means of payment represent purely conventional institutions (see Mehrling, 2012). Certainly, in its function as a representative of social wealth, i.e. as a general form of value, money must be present in its concrete existence as an objectification of the exchange value of goods. But precisely as a store of value, money ceases to fulfil its specifically monetary functions as they emerge in the course of the circulation of goods. It can therefore be replaced by any other store of value (see Hicks, 1989). Thus, except when it operates as a means of payment, money is sometimes ideal, sometimes replaced by a symbol of itself, and sometimes replaced by other forms of embodiment of value.[8] It is in fact the nature of the general equivalent of money that makes the store of value function a specifically monetary function (Hicks, 1989: 42). And Keynes himself, despite his chartalist definition of money, actually relies on the general equivalent character of money to account for agents' preference for liquidity and thus to explain why money does not enter circulation entirely (Testart, 2001: 32).[9]

Harvey underlined the contradiction, never resolved but always carried over to higher levels of the monetary hierarchy, between the function of value measurement and the function of money as a means of circulation. We shall see how this contradiction is expressed in Triffin's dilemma, which has affected the dollar since the inter-war period. But it should already be noted that it is in the function of value measurement that the contradiction lies. For under this function, money fulfils both a social function as a unit in which all commodities are mutually valued, and a private function by determining the wealth of the holders of all assets denominated in it, its own value being expressed by its purchasing power over all other commodities. As a unit of account, however, money represents a purely ideal magnitude that is separate from its various particular money carriers and coincides with them only insofar as they have been decreed ultimate means of payment, i.e. general equivalents. As a unit of account, money, as a purely abstract quantity, is reduced to its social role as a unit measuring the value of goods. It therefore only fulfils a private function when it refers to itself as a unit of account of a separate monetary medium (banknotes, deposits, bank reserves). Thus, Wicksell, who confuses the measurement of value with the unit of account, can state:

> as a measure of value any commodity whatever might serve. Indeed, compared with the two others, this is not really a function at all, for it has no relation to the thing itself or to any of its external physical properties.
>
> *(Wicksell, 1978: 7)*

Now it is not indifferent to the function of value measurement whether the thing in question is gold or silver, since under this function money relates to other goods as exchange value. However, once the unit of account has been fixed, whether it is a specific weight of gold or of silver, its existence becomes purely ideal and independent of both the money carriers denominated in it and the goods that express their price in it. More generally, it is because of the reduction of money to its unit of account function that current monetary thought on the different forms of money establishes the hierarchy of their relations on a purely conventional basis, without realising that this hierarchy is required by the nature of money as a general equivalent, whatever the variety of means of payment that the monetary authorities declare to be the ultimate means of payment. Underlying this institutional conception of means of payment is the idea that it is up to these authorities, through their function as a lender of last resort, to broaden the range of convertible means of payment at par with the ultimate means of settlement in order to, if not eliminate, at least mitigate the crises of the money-based mode of production (Mehrling, 2012, 2013; Poszar, 2014).[10]

Suzanne de Brunhoff's great contribution to the Marxist theory of money is to have stated the market constraint of the general equivalent within the fiat money payment system and to have analysed the new conditions of this constraint (1971, 1976 and 1978). For her, the notion of general equivalent means two things that do not have the same theoretical meaning, nor the same practical scope. General equivalence means, of course, that money represents the value of all commodities and that, conversely, all commodities relate to each other through their relationship to money. But general equivalence also and above all means that all goods must be exchanged for money to validate their existence as goods, or even their existence as social use values (Marx, 1867: 116). Money as a general equivalent therefore designates both the general representative of all values, and the monetary constraint which weighs on the exchange of values. This constraint is specific to any market economy, irreducible to the capitalist mode of production, and continues to impose itself as such in the most abstract and ethereal forms of monetary circulation. Thus, the dual aspect of the monetary constraint – both specific to the capitalist economy as a commodity economy and distinct from the capitalist economy as capitalist – explains the special status of the first section of *Capital*: both separate from the later sections and at the same time absolutely indispensable to the intelligibility of the rest of the book (1967). Not only does Suzanne de Brunhoff explain this special status, she justifies it, and she makes it cast its shadow over all the later parts of *Capital*.[11] Even if she minimises the question of the particular mode of production to which the genesis of the general equivalent refers (Orléan, 2018: 66), she nevertheless draws from the analysis of this genesis a decisive lesson about the social structure corresponding to this genesis. Whatever the mode of production in which money intervenes as a general equivalent, the economic sanction of the market reflects the fact that the commodity and money are never socially neutral. The social relation that founds the existence and determines the role of money is "the index of an essential division of society, on which the economic power of money rests" (Brunhoff, 1976: 47). It is, as we have seen, this essential division that determines money both as a general form of exchangeability and as a general form of value, and it is through this latter mode of being that money imposes its commodity constraint.

1.5 The social and private functions of interest-bearing capital

If money carries within it its transformation into capital, i.e. into a value which is valorised, it is because it thus overcomes the contradiction between its function as a general means of exchange (form of general exchangeability) and its function as a store of value (general form of value). Money as capital circulates but only with a view to accumulating, to returning to its starting point in increased quantity. In the same way, money is accumulated, but only to return immediately to the sphere of circulation. It is thus the resolved tension between its two functions. Through the cyclical return of money to its starting point, its function as a means of circulation is put at the service of its function of private accumulation of social wealth in its general form. Conversely, this accumulation serves primarily as a means of increasing capitalist production and expanding commodity circulation and thus subordinates itself to the social function of money as a means of circulation. This is what distinguishes the capitalist from the hoarder. "The never-ending augmentation of exchange value, which the miser strives after, by seeking to save his money from circulation, is attained by the more acute capitalist, by constantly throwing it afresh into circulation" (Marx, 1867: 164). But this movement by which value valorises itself by alternately taking the forms of money and commodity is a movement of self-valorisation which "requires some independent form, by means of which its identity may at any time be established. And this form it possesses only in the shape of money" (Marx, 1867 165). Thus, as a value in process, money has to enter into circulation in order to initiate the movement of its growth, while as a medium of exchange, it continues its cyclical movement back to its owner. It thus realises its existence as a value which returns in increased quantity in the form of a store of value. Thus, "instead of simply representing the relations of commodities, it enters now, so to say, into private relations with itself" (Marx, 1867: 165). Insofar as self-valorisation is measured by money itself in its function as a unit of account, it fulfils both a social function as a measurement unit of all circulating forms of value (commodities, money) and a private function as a measure of its own begetting, "as the father differentiates himself from himself *qua* the son" (Marx, 1867 166).

But at the same time, surplus value (profit), as the result of the specific movement of money-capital, of money as capital, brings the contradiction of money to a higher level, because money-capital includes in its concept the tendency to make money out of money without passing through all the phases of circulation that its process of growth requires, i.e. exchange against commodities and its conversion into the only commodity whose use value consists in creating value, namely labour power. This is why money as capital finds its final and definitive form in interest-bearing capital, in loan capital, where the general formula of capital, M-C-M′, is reduced to the purified formula M-M′ for the owner of money (Chesnais, 2016: 67–71). The fetishism of money-capital that it expresses finds its source directly in the fact that money seems to resolve in its own movement the tension immanent to money itself between its two essential attributes. That money as capital and interest as the price of money result from the development of the very nature of money is illustrated by the fact that usury and, more generally, interest-bearing loans are observed in all societies where money circulation takes place (Pierre Manigat, 2022a). It is when social production is subject to the metabolism of money and when the latter finds in labour power the source of its growth that the laws on usury disappear. Under capitalism, interest lending overcomes the contradictions of money but by subjecting it to the laws of the valorisation of industrial capital. Or rather, it is by submitting to the demands of capitalist production that loan capital finds the conditions for its generalisation and thus that money overcomes the contradictions between the different functions it fulfils in simple commodity circulation.

Now it is precisely through this formula that the contradiction of money between its private dimension as a general form of value and its social dimension as a form of general exchangeability is reconducted and radicalised. For in interest-bearing capital, the contradictory functions of money fall to different classes of capitalist society. For the lender, the process of self-valorisation of money is in fact reduced to a pure and simple increase independent of all the hazards and diverse forms it takes and through which it fulfils its social function of means of circulation. For the borrower, however, money, insofar as it is invested in productive capital, only fulfils the social functions of a medium of exchange – with ordinary commodities and above all with the labour power through whose activity it is valorised. Whether the borrower is the manager of a joint-stock company or an owner-borrower, the purpose of money valorisation is the accumulation of capital for its own sake and the honouring of its commitments as a borrower or as agent of the Principal, i.e. the shareholder.[12] It is with this separation between legal and economic properties that the interest on capital seems to be entirely separated from the production process and that the idea of capital-fetish (Marx, 1861–63: 458) comes to an end. Hence the contradiction between the demands of the possessor of money, for whom it only fulfils a private function of continual increase of the reserve of value, and the constraints of circulation that the borrower faces in the social uses he makes of loan capital. Thus, the movement of its own continuous increase, which interest-bearing capital pursues in its tendency to overshoot the necessary moments of circulation, carries with it, in turn, the propensity to burst into crisis. At the societal level, it is the whole credit system and speculation that rests "upon the necessity to extend the range of, and to overcome the barrier to, circulation and exchange. This appears more colossal, more classical, in the relationship between peoples than in the relationship between individuals" (Marx, 1857–58: 343).

1.6 The necessities of money and the possibility of crises

However, this necessity constantly clashes with money itself, which is required for the exchange of the products of society's labour and which, as a distinct object, contains the possibility that this social process will break down and thus enter into crisis. For money separates exchange into two separate acts "locally evolved primitive, traditionally pious and sentimentally absurd obstacles standing in the way of social metabolism" (Marx, 1859: 332). Moreover, "money functions as a means of circulation only because in it the values of commodities have independent reality" (Marx, 1867: 126). But, however, this same separation makes possible the dislocation of the moments of this process of exchange, so that the possibility of crisis lies solely in the separation of sale from purchase (Marx, 1861–63: 132). Now, when the moments of sale and purchase are separated in time, when goods circulate on the basis of credit, the latter replaces money in its function as a means of circulation, which will now be presented as a means of payment. The means of payment presupposes the function of store of value or rather hoarding, since it comes into play after the instruments of credit have circulated the goods in order to convert them into their form of social existence. Insofar as money as a means of payment is the objective general form of this social existence, it can be kept, in turn, as a reserve and, as such, as a private form of social wealth. Just as the function of store of value was the unity of the first two functions, the function of the means of payment, by which the private form of social wealth finds its way back into the process of social exchange, thus unites in itself both the function of value measurement – "In so far as the payments balance one another, money functions only ideally as money of account, as a measure of value" (Marx, 1867: 148), this time within the circulation, not outside it as is the case with hoarding.

Under these conditions, crises occur because accounts have to be settled on a certain date and their specifically monetary character is shown by the fact that money "abandons the merely ideal figure of money of account and is transformed into money of value". But "The money famine continues, whether payments have to be made in gold or in credit money such as banknotes" (Marx, 1867: 149).[13] But money as a means of payment does not simply make commercial crises possible, but, since it presupposes at the same time and makes possible "numerous *pro forma* transactions, before the final exchange of commodities between producer and consumer takes place" (Marx, 1859: 334), it provides the basis for modern crises of the credit system, in a word, for financial crises. But this separation expresses nothing other than the objective form of existence of money, which, as an appropriable object, fulfils a private function as the sole material representative of social wealth. "As long as the *social* character of labour ap- pears as the *money existence* of commodities, and thus as a *thing* external to actual production, money crises — independent of or as an in- tensification of actual crises—are inevitable" (Marx, 1895: 514). The crisis thus means nothing other than the abolition of the social functions of circulating money in favour of its sole private function as a store of value.

Interest-bearing capital is born precisely from the withdrawal of money from the sphere of circulation and its constitution as a store of value (Dobb, 1946). Money in its autonomous existence comes from circulation and appears there as its result: "it closes its own circle by means of circulation. In this aspect, its role as *capital* is already latent" (Marx, 1857–58: 151). The money that is taken out of circulation and amassed presupposes the development of the first two determinations (measure unit and instrument of circulation); otherwise, only gold and silver are amassed, but not money. So if it were devoid of any relation to circulation, money would not be currency: money has only a relative autonomy and maintains a negative relation to circulation. It is in fact the realised price of the commodity and satisfies any need insofar as it can be exchanged for the object of any need, where it is perfectly indifferent to the particularity, whatever it may be. Thus, money is not only the form of universal wealth, but the content of this wealth. In it, "the concept of wealth is so to speak realised in a particular object, *individualised*" (Marx, 1857–58: 153). In its determinacy of form, money is the pure abstraction of all particular wealth and exists as universal wealth only in my imagination. But as the material representative of universal wealth, it is realised only insofar as it is rejected in circulation, where it disappears in exchange for the particular and singular modalities of wealth. It represents the form par excellence of private wealth only insofar as it is destined to fulfil its social functions of circulation. Or, as a social form, money only has content by being rejected in circulation. It follows from the contradiction between the social and private functions of money that, as a singularised tangible object,

> I can carry it around with me in my pocket as the universal social power and the universal social nexus, the social substance. Money puts social power as a thing into the hands of the private person, who as such uses this power.
>
> *(Marx, 1858: 431; 1857–58: 154)*

The miser and the profligate are opposed from this point of view by the fact that the former transforms money into a sterile object of abstract enjoyment, whereas the latter makes society enjoy its ephemeral and constantly renewed enjoyments. In order to keep money in its pure form, the miser sacrifices all particular wealth, whereas the profligate gives content to this form by sacrificing her wealth for the benefit of others. But stinginess is also distinguished from the lust for wealth by the fact that the capitalist also maintains "it in constant tension with circulation" (Marx, 1859: 366). In both lust for wealth and greed, the aim is to maintain money in its function as private wealth at all costs, but in the first case the accumulation implies a permanent flow of social labour in return for the flow of accumulated money; in the other case, it is a matter of blocking all social flows to the point of the withering away of oneself as well as of things. But, however, its nature as money-capital contradicts its social function as a condition of production: it has to return in such a way that it earns interest for its lender as a form of private income, separate and independent from the social production of which it is an extracted part. When it is lent as capital, money is opposed to social production as a private condition of this production, i.e. as private wealth which can be diverted from its social destination in order to either be kept in its liquid form (liquidity preference) or to be converted into financial securities whose profitability is based on an already existing production of value. The more capitalist production develops as a social mode of production, the more the financial sphere – in which the means of payment unused in the productive sphere circulate – expands and offers alternative possibilities of valorisation to productive capital.

If, therefore, interest-bearing capital implies the tendency to free itself from the contingencies of social circulation, conversely, as a movement that opposes its mere existence as an immobile store of value, it can give rise to purely speculative operations by exchanging itself for fictitious forms of value and provoke a crisis that immediately presents itself as a financial crisis. Here, the crisis arises from the fact that these forms (shares, bonds, certificates of deposit, repos, etc.) lose the trust that agents have in them:

> in a period of crisis, the circulation of bills collapses completely; nobody can make use of a promise to pay since everyone will accept only cash payment; only the banknote retains, at least thus far in England, its ability to circulate, because the nation with its total wealth backs up the Bank of England.
>
> *(Marx, 1895: 537)*[14]

The banking system as an instituted payment system, in turn, overcomes this contradiction by its function of issuing money both independent of pre-existing reserves and subject to the needs and demand for credit by agents participating in social production. The development of this institutional basis has led heterodox monetary thought to describe money as a public good, while assuming that money issuance mostly responds to the needs of social production (Aglietta, 2016). The banking system, through the pre-validation it provides to the products of capital, operates as if capitalist production were a directly social production (Campbell, 2002: 222). But in doing so, it displaces the contradiction between its issuance of circulation means and the necessity of their convertibility into ultimate means of payment, i.e. into general equivalents. For whatever the form of money circulating in society, the values produced, even if pre-validated by bank money (de Brunhoff), will never prevent money from imposing itself as something both distinct from other instruments of credit and from commodities themselves, and into which they must be converted in order to validate the social character of the labour or income they represent.

1.7 Note on Hilferding's monetary theory

Like the institutionalists, Hilferding posits the existence of a commodity society, i.e. a social relationship in which the commodity enters directly as a fragment of the social product, where it therefore confronts the totality of social production in the form of other commodities. As a result, money appears as a simple necessity arising from the generalisation of exchange.

> The concerted action of commodities in exchange transforms private, individual and concrete labour time into the general, socially necessary and abstract labour time which is the essence of value. As the value of commodities comes to be measured in multifarious exchanges, so it comes to be measured increasingly in terms of a single commodity, and this needs only to become established as the standard of value in order to become money.
>
> *(Hilferding, 1910: 33)*

Money is therefore a commodity like any other and "the necessity for it to have value arises directly out of the nature of the commodity producing society" (*Ibidem*). It is curious to note that Hilferding provides a stronger proof of the necessity of commodity-money than of the necessity of money, whose existence derives only from the extension of exchange and not from the structure of the commodity order, from the simple and immediate relationship between two commodities. For what interests Hilferding in a commodity society where production decisions are private and decentralised is the law of distribution of social labour. This law is the law of prices, which must be expressed in an instrument for measuring and circulating goods produced independently from each other. Hilferding avoids drawing the consequences of the fact that in these conditions the value of commodities must be expressed in a distinct and separate object in order to concentrate on the commodity character of money. But he immediately minimises the importance of this character by virtue of the conditions of money circulation. Since money only fulfils the social functions of measurement and circulation of goods, its purely circulatory and ephemeral mode of existence allows it to be replaced by simple signs of value:

> Money can be dispensed with as an expression of equivalence. But it is indispensable as a symbol of value because it is a necessary means of giving society's sanction to the value of a commodity. Thanks to money, it is possible for value to be reconverted from its monetary form into any other commodity. However, since the monetary expression of value is ephemeral, and unimportant in itself (except when the process C -M -C is interrupted and the money itself has to be stored for a longer or shorter time in order to make possible the completion of the M -C sequence at a later date), what is important for our purpose is the social aspect of money - its quality of being the value equivalent of a commodity. This social aspect of money finds its palpable expression in the substance used as money for example, gold. But it can also be expressed directly through conscious social regulation or, since the state is the conscious organ of commodity producing society, by state regulation. Hence the state can designate any token - for example, a piece of paper appropriately labelled - as a representative of money, a money token.
>
> *(Hilferdsing, 1910: 38)*

Thus, the part of social exchange corresponding to what Hilferding calls the "minimum of circulation" escapes the anarchy of commodity production "A certain minimum of commodities with a given value must be bought and sold whatever the circumstances. The exclusion of the effects of anarchic production manifests itself in the possibility of replacing gold by mere value tokens" (Hilferding, 1910: 39). This replacement is made possible precisely because money here fulfils a purely social function of circulation and is not intended to be kept as a store of value (p. 78). Thus, the function of value measurement is transformed into a mere unit of account and the value of these units represented in the money in circulation is entirely determined by the value of the mass of goods against which it is exchanged. At equal speeds of circulation, the value of money is determined by the "socially necessary value in circulation" (Hilferding, 1910: 47).

Since these signs of value have become legal means of payment, the state now has the power to expand these means of payment in times of crisis and thus to forcibly convert commodities and assets into the general equivalent through the lender-of-last-resort function of the central bank (Hilferding, 1910: 66). In this way, Hilferding abolishes the law of the market, according to which goods must necessarily be converted into money in order to realise the value contained in them. Thus, he abolishes the general form dimension of the value of money, according to which the social labour of the commodity is represented in an objectified form.

Notes

1 "To the elementary relative value form of a commodity, there corresponds the single equivalent form of one other commodity. Thus, in the relative expression of value of the linen, the coat assumes the form of equivalent, or of being directly exchangeable, only in relation to a single commodity, the linen" (Marx, 1867: 72).

2 "In order to express the value of the linen as a congelation of human labour, that value must be expressed as having objective existence, as being a something materially different from the linen itself, and yet a something com- mon to the linen and all other commodities" (Marx, 1867: 61).

3 Rubin, who insists on the value-form of the commodity, defines the general equivalent only according to the general exchangeability of money: the money-form is thus defined as a form of general exchangeability. What is lacking in this definition is precisely the objective character of the equivalent that associates the function of appropriable wealth with the social functions of money. Michael Williams (2000) tries to demonstrate that as a social form fulfilling the various monetary functions, money does not need to be embodied in a commodity. But by pushing the commodity out of the money-form, he at the same time evacuates the form of objectivity that this social form necessarily takes on the basis of commodity exchange (Williams, 2000: 445).

4 Paulani (2014) relies on the social character of value and thus on the abstract mode of existence of the commodity to justify money and the more developed forms of value as abstract forms and thus free from their commodity gangue. But in calling an illusion the determination of money as "true wealth" (2014: 787), she stumbles on the fact that as a social form, money presents itself as something that is in a general way the unique representative of social wealth but for which in times of crisis all particular wealth is sacrificed.

5 Germer (2005) justifies commodity-money in Marx by the fact that as a measure of values, money must itself possess value and therefore contain social labour time (2005: 33).

6 For John Weeks (2012), the theory of commodity-money is justified by the need to establish a nominal anchor for prices, which is not offered by the neoclassical theory in which money is primarily imposed as a means of circulation. Conversely, Peter Hans Matthews (1996) gets rid of the need for commodity-money by confusing the functions of value measurement and price standard. Why go through the commodity form of money at all, since as a price standard, money has a purely conventional existence. Thus, he adopts the circuitist conception according to which the value of money is determined by the quantity of labour it commands, regardless of the purchasing power of money over the goods consumed by workers (p. 207). Similarly, Marcello Messori (1997) argues that it is possible to dispense with commodity-money while maintaining the relationship of money to abstract labour based on the relationship between money and labour power, i.e. based on specifically capitalist forms of the monetary relationship (1997: 77).

7 Eckhard Hein (2006) understands money in Marx as an ideal and socially accepted representative of the value of commodities because social labour time is qualitatively and quantitatively different from the concrete labour time embodied in the commodity. Thus, the labour time actually embodied in gold cannot determine the value of gold. In reality, it is not the concrete labour producing gold which directly represents social labour, but the socially necessary labour, except that, as it forms the substance of the general form of exchangeability, it is not expressed in any commodity but itself. It is therefore not so much concrete labour as the concrete material of gold that

expresses the social existence of ordinary commodities. In general, Hein feels obliged to get rid of the commodity basis of money in order to get rid of Marx's metallism, but without taking into account the fact that the regime of inconvertible money preserves the commodity constraint of money.

8 The transition to a regime of pure fiat money since the end of the Bretton Woods system has made it all the easier to adopt the Marxian theory of money because the substance of value that money represents is social, and therefore ideal. Geert Reuten (2005) wants a theory of money without labour-value and proposes to demonstrate that for Marx only money constitutes the value of goods. All his conceptual contortions aim at ridding money of its relation to labour and thus making it an expression of value in general, whatever the substance of this value. His interpretation is based on the fact that abstract labour, insofar as it expresses an ideal quantity which is not really contained in the individual commodity, determines value as an ideal quantity which only money brings into concrete existence. He fails to see that money determines above all the form of objectivity that value necessarily takes as a social relation. In the same way, Arthur, who considers value exclusively as a social form, independently of the content contained in this form, does not consider it necessary to make human labour the fundamental social relation through which society is produced and reproduced. From this point of view, money is presented as a simple unit of the various values (2005: 116). This therefore amounts to emptying money of its commodity content but also of its functions (2005: 117), and making it a purely empty form that can accommodate all value contents as well as adopt all bodily envelopes.

9 Costas Lapavitsas (2017), who seeks to base the current system of credit money on commodity-money (2017: 94), sees the commodity constraint it imposes on bank currencies as only a factor limiting the quantity of money issued by banks, which could otherwise issue means of payment in excess of circulation needs (2017: 120). Not only does the principle of his approach curiously follow the quantitative approach, but he ignores the fact that money differs from other financial assets not because it is a commodity (2017: 261) but because it is a general equivalent, even when stripped of its commodity basis.

10 We shall see later that it is also for having reduced money to its function as a unit of account that Keynes makes the roles of money coexist within his theory of preference for liquidity, which are not only contradictory to each other but occupy separate spheres of circulation.

11 Nelson distinguishes between theories of credit money and theories of commodity-money according to the nature of the material constituting the money (65–66). But the essential difference lies not in the nature of the material but in the nature of the relation conditioning the circulation of this material: commodity relation on the one hand, credit relation on the other. She detects in Marx hints of a theory of credit money based on the wrong presupposition that any non-commodity form of money would amount to making money a mere form of credit. But what distinguishes money from credit lies precisely in its character as a general equivalent, and this character can be embodied in a currency in both credit money and commodity-money. The issue is not to substitute a theory of credit money for a theory of commodity-money (76), but to substitute a theory of money as a general equivalent without a commodity basis for a theory of commodity-money. The problem with theories of credit money is precisely that they eliminate the monetary character of money and thus the monetary constraint that continues to prevail even on the basis of credit money.

12 We are not concerned here with the alliances, agreements and mixing of functions that can be observed within the capitalist bourgeoisie in general. For an analysis of its internal relations, see Duménil and Lévy (2018).

13 Davis (2010: 412) also underlines the fact that, whatever the nature and character of a society's monetary institutions, the fundamental contradictions of commodity production must necessarily be perpetuated from the moment money represents social wealth as something separate and appropriable.

14 Here, Marx leaves open the possibility that public debt securities should provide the universal equivalent in times of crisis.

> As explored in Capital, the Bank of England was a 'semi-government institution' which was able to issue notes in excess of the bullion on reserve in its vaults, thus creating 'fictitious capital.' Not only was all government tax revenue deposited with the Bank, but its notes were also backed by the total wealth of the nation.
>
> *(Davis, 2010: 411)*

Leaving aside the fact that she calls "fictitious capital" what is merely a representative of gold, namely the Bank of England note, Davis makes it clear that the creation of the Bank of England contains the seeds of the credit system as it developed without precious metals. Insofar as the Bank holds the accounts of the state and thus the totality of the taxes collected by the state, the mass of notes issued by the Bank will be able to draw on the wealth of the nation as a substitute for precious metals, while at the same time, devoid of any commodity basis, this issue of credit money gives the Bank and the banking system in general enormous power over this social wealth.

2

THE PARADOXES OF THE CURRENCY SCHOOL-BANKING SCHOOL DEBATE

2.1 Return to the function of money as a means of payment

We must clarify the status of the function of means of payment, which we have said synthesises the social and private functions of money. In reality, under this function, money does not intervene either as a measure of value or as a means of circulation, but as a means of final settlement of a debt contract between the buyer and seller of a commodity (commercial draft, bill of exchange, etc.). This function therefore implies that the social functions of money are entrusted to debt instruments which, denominated in official units of account, ensure the circulation of commodities. The more credit develops, the more the means of payment function expands and the more its function as a means of circulation is pushed back into the retail trade. And precisely because money does not enter circulation until the moment of final payment, the means of payment function implies its existence as a store of value. Thus, when it enters circulation, money presents itself as "as a mere transient agent in the interchange of products, but as the individual incarnation of social labour, as the independent form of existence of exchange value, as the universal commodity" (Marx, 1867: 148). It is in its function as a means of payment that money imposes itself as a general equivalent.

The first two functions of the equivalent, i.e. measure of value and means of circulation, in a way represented the preconditions of commodity circulation: the measure of value function appeared as soon as one commodity was related to another, and the means of circulation resulted from the extension of this commodity relationship. The latter simply reflected a higher degree of commodity circulation than the former. Circulation does not in itself produce these two functions of the equivalent, but rather they appear as conditions without which no circulation would be possible. The transition to the functions of money as a universal commodity, however, derives exclusively from circulation, "without

DOI: 10.4324/9780429261299-4

the society's aid or desire". Though it is a product of circulation, money has become detached from it "contrary to initial agreement" (Marx, 1859: 487) which subjected the equivalent form to the circulation of particular commodities. At the beginning, it is only a form of exchange value, which arises from the process of circulation, but soon it is promoted to autonomy, thanks to its function as a general means of payment and becomes the determining goal of circulation.

It is with capitalist production that commodity production becomes entirely submitted to the need to make money or, as Keynes would say, that commodity production is transformed into the monetary economy of production. With it, money becomes both the goal and the means of commodity production. The production and circulation of commodities appear as a process of valorisation of value. If the formula of simple commodity production was C-M-C, commodity-money-commodity, the formula of capitalist production is M-C… P…C′-M′ . Money appears as the starting and ending points of the whole process. Because money, as we know, is the absolute form of value, the process of capital appears as a process of the self-increase of money. Yet, capital is not money, nor even the commodity (C) or the productive elements taken in themselves (P). Capital is neither M, nor C, nor P, but the process by which value, advanced in money, passes through all its forms, to return in greater quantity in its form advanced at the beginning, in the form of money. M only serves to buy the productive elements (means of production and workers), P to create value and surplus value, C′ to be exchanged again for money, but with a higher value than the value originally advanced. Only the process of creating surplus value by labour power within the sphere of production defines capital in its real movement (Marx, 1894: 342). The fact that capital has money as its point of departure and arrival, and that moreover money regularly flows back into the hands of the capitalist in increasing quantity, makes the money trade, i.e. the interest-bearing loan, a special branch of capitalist production, subordinated to the needs of the valorisation of productive capital. Interest now represents a part of the surplus value created and realised in the spheres of production and circulation, the profit of enterprise representing the difference between gross profit and interest. Thus, the formula of capital, insofar as it is based on the credit system, becomes M-M-C… (P) …C′-M′-M′. The money-capitalist advances through the banking and financial institutions the money to the industrial capitalist, i.e. the manager, who takes charge of valorising it by carrying out the different phases of the whole process of productive or commercial capital, in order to return to its owner, at the due date, the money lent increased by a part of the profit realised, i.e. the interest. From now on, the banking and financial system ensures two distinct functions whose interweaving makes it difficult to understand the monetary functions in a capitalist regime. On the one hand, it must ensure the reproduction of existing capital, by means of circulating credit instruments (discounting bills of exchange, notes, demand deposits, etc.). On the other hand, it is responsible for ensuring the funding for the expansion of capitalist production, by means of interest-bearing money-capital credit (Fine, 1985).

2.2 The two sides of the fetishism of finance capital

The erroneous and contradictory conceptions of money theorists as well as of agents of finance capital in general stem from the diversity of functions that money assumes in the circulation of capital. In the first place, insofar as capital defines a mode of production based on exchange value, money, in addition to its function as a measure of value, plays the dual role of a general means of circulation of commodities-capital and of a universal commodity, of a means of purchase and a means of payment. But in neither of these capacities does money appear as capital in the different phases of commodity circulation. It merely converts the value represented in the particular commodity into its general value form or, on the contrary, converts itself into a commodity. For it to appear as the money form of capital, it is necessary to consider the whole process of production and circulation in which it intervenes as a transitory form of capital-value. Apart from the consideration of this overall relationship, money only fulfils the generic functions of a measure of value, a means of circulation and a general means of payment.

But second, insofar as capitalist production does not simply consist in the production of commodities but in the valorisation of value, the monetary circuit appears as the form par excellence of the circulation of capital and the cyclical figure of money-capital, i.e. as the characteristic form of rotation of capital. Money appears as the alpha and omega of the whole process of capital. Thus, once this mode of production has become generalised, it seems natural to the agents of production that money should regularly fructify and flow back to its owner in increased quantity. "In the capitalist system of production, every sum of money is able to function as capital, that is, to produce a profit" (Hilferding, 1910: 99). Therefore, for the one who advances money to a third party, it does not matter whether the money is used to set up a business, pay debts or is spent on consumer goods. It is not as a universal commodity, the absolute representative of exchange value, that he has given it to the borrower, but as capital. As such, money acquires a new use value, that of being able to produce profit. So, "In this capacity of potential capital, of a means of producing profit, it becomes a commodity, but a commodity *sui generis*" (Marx, 1895: 337). Money thus appears as capital in two ways: in its relation to the whole process of production and circulation of capital, and in the relation between the lender and the borrower:

> Commodities and money are here capital not because commodities change into money, or money into commodities, not in their actual relations to sellers or buyers, but only in their ideal relations to the capitalist himself (subjectively speaking), or as phases in the process of reproduction (objectively speaking).
>
> *(Marx, 1895: 341)*

It is therefore as capital in itself that the owner lends her money to the industrial or commercial capitalist, because in a society ordered to the conditions of existence of the capitalist mode of production, where wage-labour therefore exists, money and commodities can at any time act as capital and thus valorise themselves. Interest-bearing capital assumes that the use value of the money lent consists in making money. Being the absolute form of exchange value and the starting and ending points of the capital cycle, it contains within itself the faculty "being able to serve as capital and, as such, to produce the average profit under average conditions" (Marx, 1895: 350). The interest rate, by expressing itself irrationally as the price of money, proves that the increase of money has become the goal of exchange: as a measure of value and a means of circulation, money fulfils these functions only insofar as its process of circulation brings it back in increased quantity. It is exchanged for commodities, means of production and labour power, but only as a means of its preservation and increase. For the lender, however, things are not so complicated. Because the interest rate remains the same regardless of the profit made by the industrial capitalist, because the interest rate is conceptually and actually distinguished from the corporate profit, and because the interest rate is determined above all in relation to the world market rather than to the national profit rate, the lender regards her money as capital in itself, capital par excellence, so that interest appears to derive from money as money. Profit of enterprise then seems to represent an overprofit beyond the interest rate, generated because of an exceptional market position, interest alone appearing as natural profit on the production and sale of goods. But however one justifies the existence of the interest rate, it is in the interest-bearing capital itself, i.e. financial capital, that the social relation of production is reduced to the relation of an object, i.e. money, to itself, that the conception of capital as a fetish reaches its height in interest-bearing capital, "being a conception which attributes to the accumulated product of labour, and at that in the fixed form of money, the inherent secret power, as an automaton, of creating surplus value in geometrical progression" (Marx, 1895: 396). Consequently, the fetishism of interest-bearing capital cannot be equated with the fetishism of money. The latter, as we have seen, occurs when the social relationship between the different agents of production crystallises in a distinct and external object to which all the products of labour are related. It is because money expresses social labour in an alienated form that it functions as a fetish, as an abstract object of need whose social nature seems to derive from its objective form. But with money lent at interest, it no longer represents only in objective form the social relation of commodity production, but the relation of capital to labour under the aspect of the self-increase of money. Money no longer presents itself simply as a fetish, but as an automaton fetish. From now on, capital represented in money confronts all the agents of production, whether they are entrepreneurs or workers, and seems to impose the capitalist form of production on them from outside.

However, as capitalist production develops, in both extension and concentration, on the one hand, and the accumulation and concentration of money-capital in the reservoirs of circulation, on the other, the functional and social separation between capital per se and productive capital tends to become more general and to form two separate spheres. Increasingly dependent on the conditions for granting credit, not only to start a business but to maintain its continuity and expansion, productive capital becomes more and more conditioned by financial capital, although the latter owes its existence and prosperity to productive capital alone

> So long as credit was granted only for a short time, Hilferding points out, and only as circulating capital, it was relatively easy to terminate the relationship. The enterprise could repay the loan at the end of the turnover period, and then look for another source of credit. This ceases to be the case when a part of the fixed capital is also obtained through a loan. The obligation can now only be liquidated over a long period of time, and in consequence the enterprise becomes tied to the bank. In this relationship the bank is the more powerful party. The bank always disposes over capital in its liquid, readily available, form: money capital. The enterprise, on the other hand, has to depend upon reconverting commodities into money. Should the circulation process come to a halt, or prices fall, the enterprise will require additional capital which can only be obtained in the form of credit. Under a developed credit system, an enterprise maintains its own capital at a minimum; any sudden need for additional liquid funds involves obtaining credit, and failure to do so may lead to bankruptcy.
>
> *(Hilferding, 1910: 95)*

What is improperly called the "dictatorship of creditors" illustrates the fact that on the one hand industrial capitalists are dependent on the demands of finance, but on the other hand, through it, they are placed in a state of now global competition, with finance capital acting directly on the whole of the globe and beyond.

With the development of the banking system and the generalisation of credit for the financing of enterprises, interest-bearing capital confers on money an ambiguous nature: on the one hand, as we have seen, the existence of the interest rate as the price of money makes it the absolute embodiment of capital, independently of the actual reproduction of this capital, of which it is the condition. But on the other hand, insofar as it conditions the production of commodities in general, money derives its quality of universal commodity from its function as a general means of exchange for the particular commodities, so that the interest on this universal commodity derives less from its quality of money-*capital* than from the rate of profit which the circulation of *commodities*-capital brings to the borrower. In its first aspect, therefore, the price of money expresses only the allegedly innate quality of money to behave as capital. In its second aspect, it expresses its quality as a universal representative of social wealth. In the first case, money is lent as capital par excellence; in the second case, it is offered and demanded as a specific commodity.

2.3 The confusions of the banker's political economy

2.3.1 The money fetishism of the Currency school

It is for having conceived of money as capital par excellence that the Banking school (BS) opposed the Currency school (CS) in relation to the Bank Charter Act of 1844, which provided for the separation of the issue department from the banking department of the Bank of England and for a monetary issuing policy strictly based on the Bank's gold reserves (Arnon, 2011: 194). The debate therefore focused on the organisation of the Bank of England necessary to regulate the issue of banknotes and, more generally, national credit. For the CS, strict control of money issue was aimed at preventing over-issuance, which, by causing prices to rise, led to gold outflows due to the depreciation of the note and the loss of competitiveness of British products. For the BS, however, there can be no over-issuance of banknotes when convertibility into gold is guaranteed, since money is issued in return for the demand for credit, and the latter depends on prices and income. The causality therefore runs from credit to money as a means of payment and not the other way round. Thus, their opposition implies a deeper difference in the very nature of money and its relation to capital. For the CS, which reduced money to its social function as a simple intermediary of exchange and thus conceived of productive elements as the only real forms of capital, only productive capital created profits. According to this conception, borrowers never ask for money for its own sake, but only because their demand for real capital requires that they come into possession of means of circulation. This justifies not only the size, but also the very idea of the interest rate as the price of money: since the supply and demand for money are identical with the supply and demand for real capital, the interest rate is merely the monetary expression of the rate of profit, insofar as the demand for real capital, and hence for the money to acquire it, increases as the anticipated rate of profit increases.[1]

Following this "real" conception of the rate of interest, some, like Norman, clearly distinguish the demand for money-capital from the demand for money as such, so as to justify the high interest rates charged by the Bank of England as the price of capital in general and not as the price of money, i.e. as the price of the money form of capital, distinct from other forms of capital (Marx, 1894: 416). Others, like Overstone, the main inspiration for the Bank Act, equate the demand for money with the demand for capital and thus the interest rate with the rate of profit of real capital. To this conception of the interest rate, Marx objected with the representatives of the BS that there is no link between the interest rate and the demand for real capital (Tooke, 1844: 33). Overstone, for example, before the parliamentary committee which followed the crisis of 1857 (Report of Select Committee on Bank Acts, communicated from the Commons to the Lords), with manifest bad faith confused the increase in the value of capital resulting from a high rate of profit with the increase resulting from an increased demand for money-capital.[2] But whatever the cause of an increased demand for money-capital, it "and consequently the 'value of capital', [that] may rise even though the profit may decrease; as soon as the relative supply of money capital shrinks, its 'value' increases" (Marx, 1895: 418). And if the high rate of interest coincides with a high rate of profit, this may well indicate a falling corporate profit, with the rate of interest rising accordingly. Although this demand may increase for reasons independent of the rate of profit, Overstone makes this confusion in order not to have to explain a high interest rate in times of monetary tension by a shortage of means of circulation or, what amounts to the same thing, by an increase in the demand for money, i.e. the money form of capital. This would force him to admit that the high interest rate artificially causes a scarcity in the supply of money in order to comply with the binding issuing rules of the Bank Act of 1844, which he himself had inspired.

Overstone so strongly rejects the idea that the rate of interest can represent the price of money-capital and that the demand for money can represent anything other than a mere demand for means of circulation, that he equates the demand for discounting with a demand for money to buy capital, the rate of interest being justified here by the assumed rate of profit (in other words, he confuses borrowing with discounting):

> This smug logician assumes that bills of exchange are discounted only for the purpose of expanding business, and that business is expanded because it is profitable. The first assumption is wrong. The ordinary businessman discounts, in order to anticipate the money form of his capital and thereby to keep his process of reproduction in flow; not in order to expand his business or secure additional capital, but in order to balance the credit he gives by the credit he receives.
>
> *(Marx, 1895: 423)*

Now it is because, like Norman, he conceives of money as a mere means of circulation that he can justify the demand for money as a demand for real capital and equate the rate of interest with the real rate of profit. If money were conceived as money-capital, i.e. as a specific form of capital, the interest rate would immediately appear as a form of arbitrary appropriation on social production. This conception of money directly inspired the Bank Act itself, since it was intended to transform the whole mass of gold into a means of circulation by equating the outflow of gold with a contraction of the means of circulation and the inflow with an expansion. But although all monetary experience has shown the contrary, since either the authorised mass never circulated in full or, as in the crisis of 1857, it was insufficient, this conception reproduced the Humean mechanism according to which prices were directly affected by the inflow and outflow of gold. In reality, these inflows and outflows only modified the interest rate and it is indeed the fluctuations in the supply and demand of money that determined the variations in the interest rate. The paradox of the banking legislation of 1844, insofar as it led to the sacrifice of the whole process of social reproduction in order to preserve the gold reserves of the Bank of England, consists in conceiving of money as a simple means of exchanging commodities, but by using this conception for the promotion of money in its function as a store of value, i.e. as an absolute commodity.

But above all, by ignoring the function of money as a means of payment, the CS proponents do not explain the causes of a high demand for money in times of crisis and hence recommend monetary policies that would aggravate the crisis. As long as the reproduction process is smooth, the extension of trade credit continues in parallel with capital accumulation.[3] During this period, there is an identity between money and credit instruments. Both are means of circulation as well as, to a large extent, means of payment. During the prosperity phase, confidence reigns among productive and financial agents. But it is not, as institutionalists believe, on money that their confidence rests, but on the capitalist system itself, as a social mode of production: "It is faith in the social character of production which allows the money form of products to assume the aspect of something that is only evanescent and ideal, something merely imaginative" (Marx, 1894: 598). Yet as soon as a halt occurs for one reason or another, "a superabundance of industrial capital becomes available, but in a form in which it cannot perform its functions" (Marx, 1894: 481). Consequently, there are huge quantities of commodity-capital, but unsaleable. It is then that credit tightens. When the crisis breaks out, the demand for money, reaching its highest point, does not represent a demand for real capital; on the contrary, capital is in excess and commodities are unsaleable. What is demanded at the time of the crisis is money, not as a means of circulation, but as the ultimate means of payment, since credit instruments no longer enjoy the confidence of agents after this credit has been overstretched.[4] It is therefore at the moment when money is most needed, the crisis having evacuated all means of circulation based on commercial credit, that bankers inspired by the false and partial ideas of CS increase the interest rate and block their reserves. Hence the paradox that, although apparently based on a purely functional conception of money, the proponents of CS fall into the most absurd money fetishism by sacrificing an enormous mass of value in the form of commodities for the sake of preserving the value of what they otherwise regarded as a mere means of circulation. It is in this sense that CS and, later, its heir monetarism, form a kind of rentier political economy.

2.3.2 The interest-bearing capital fetishism of the Banking school

Where the CS confuses money and capital, the BS on the contrary artificially distinguishes money as a means of circulation from money-capital, currency from capital, for the reason that money circulates in cash between consumers and traders and that it is replaced by credit in transactions between capitalists. The BS actually mistakes the difference between the monetary form of income and the monetary form of capital for a difference between the means of circulation function of money and the function of capital-money. But the two differences do not overlap at all. For example, some money circulates as a medium between traders (between capitalists) and between traders and consumers. In both cases, money functions as a means of circulation. But the BS makes a conceptual difference between these different forms of circulation by relying on phases of the economic cycle where money in circulation is low, while the capital at the disposal of banks, or rather the assets representing this capital are abundant, and vice versa. This confusion arises from the fact that in the business world, which functions essentially on the basis of credit, money in circulation serves essentially as a means of payment (and not as a means of purchase, as is the case with consumer cash payments, whether with a credit card or with notes and coins) (Marx, 1894: 456).

The BS further justifies this opposition between currency and capital by the fact that in times of crisis the demand for additional capital, gold and banknotes, does not affect the quantity of domestic means of circulation. Moreover, the increase in commercial credit in the form of bills of exchange, determined by the needs of trade, has no influence on the volume of notes in circulation.[5] On the one hand, Marx pointed out that the means of internal circulation necessarily circulate capital, even if this circulation includes a circulation of income, as illustrated by the payment of wages by the capitalist and the purchase of goods by the wage earner from the merchant. On the other hand, it is not because the demand for money as a simple means of payment does not mingle with the circulation of currency, that it does not constitute a means of circulation as such, even if it is a circulation of capital. The export of gold, the immediate reflux of advanced banknotes or the simple transfer of money from one account to another certainly does not cause an increase in the mass of current circulation. But it is wrong to deduce that the monetary facilities offered by the banks are identical to the borrowing of additional loan capital and, therefore, that the circulation of money as a means of payment does not increase, while the means of circulation remain stable (Marx, 1894: 456). The function of means of payment has nothing to do with capital as such, even though, as we have seen, the credit system develops this function of money as never before. It is true that in a period of credit shortage coinciding with a slowdown of production following a crisis of overproduction, the mass of circulation necessary for the consumption of income decreases and the mass necessary for the circulation of capital increases. But one cannot deduce from this difference in the functions of the circulating money, a conceptual difference between currency and capital (Marx, 1894: 447). Finally, this increase in the demand for means of payment in times of crisis can in no way be explained by a shortage of capital, except in the exceptional case of a raw materials shortage crisis: an increased demand for monetary facilities does not imply a shortage of capital; it is not "a lack *of commodity* capital which causes the stringency" (Marx, 1894: 458); it is capital in its money form that is demanded.

Conversely, the BS relies on periods of prosperity, when credit between capitalists is in full operation and the demand for the means of circulation is particularly strong, to distinguish the demand for currency from the demand for capital. Here again, the artificial distinction between currency and capital is based on particular moments of the circulation process which the BS interprets by confusing the determinations of money with the different forms of circulation of this money. Fullarton, for example, derives the principle of a conceptual difference between the two from the fact that in times of crisis the demand for capital is very high, while the demand for circulation is lower. Marx observes that in this particular case it is not the demand for capital that is particularly sensitive, but rather the difficulty of meeting this high demand. In other words, in times of crisis, banks, including the Central Bank, have to mobilise their capital to advance money, i.e. to lend capital, as the assets for which it used to exchange its notes are depreciated or even worthless. This is what we saw with the unconventional policies that followed the 2008 crisis, when the Fed bought junk bonds or even injected liquidity directly through the issuance of treasury bills, thus at the expense of the US taxpayer. However, this liquidity never served as circulating money but only served to clear the accounts of banks and credit institutions in difficulty or on the verge of bankruptcy. It is true that in this case, the aim was to ensure the liquidity of the banking and financial system, but through a huge expansion of the Fed's balance sheet. If the BS therefore tends to distinguish theoretically between currency and capital, it is because, like the CS, it adopts the point of view of the bank, but this time in its dual function of guarantor of currency and lender of money. The bank issues its own banknotes in exchange for bills of exchange, etc., and thus ensures the circulation of goods. Here, money functions as a means of circulation and this money costs the bank nothing, except for the paper and the printing. These notes are debts of the bank established in its name, which certainly earn money through discounting, seigniorage, etc., but are no less different from its capital. But when its credit is exhausted, as in times of tightness or crisis, it has to advance its own capital to meet the demand for loans. Hence the idea that in times of crisis the demand for capital increases, whereas in reality it is a demand for the monetary form of capital, for money as a means of payment. For there are two possibilities. Either the crisis manifests itself in the form of gold outflows, and it is money as a means of payment that is demanded; yet, as universal money, this money is money-capital: "It is not a contradiction here between a demand for money as a means of payment and a demand for capital. The contradiction is rather between capital in its money form and capital in its commodity form" (Marx, 1894: 457). Or it is a demand dedicated to the domestic circulation, but in this case it is not a demand for capital as such that is being addressed, since the markets are overflowing with commodity-capital, it is a demand for money, for the money form of capital.

But it is above all in its understanding of the significance of gold outflows that the money-capital fetishism of the BS is revealed. Although it distinguishes the functions of currency and means of payment, we have seen that it defines the former as a form of circulation of income, the latter as a form of circulation of capital. Thus, the greater or lesser export or import of precious metals is a "question of capital", whereas it is in reality a question of money, even if the function is specific to it (Marx, 1894: 450). Its distinction "amounts to saying that the demand for *international* media of circulation and payment differs from the demand for *internal* media of circulation and payment" (Marx, 1894: 451). Therefore, just as strangely as with the CS – and even though it develops against the latter a most flexible and institutional theory of internal circulation; even though it recognises the identity of money and credit, which both ensure the circulation of goods in times of confidence (Tooke, 1844: 121–22); and even though it mocks the fetishism of money and the sacrifices which their opponents impose on industrialists and merchants on the altar of money – when the Bank is driven to the point of bloodletting, the BS joins in their sacrificial rite. Because gold and banknotes constitute the real capital of the Bank, as well as the securities and other assets which it can exchange for them at any time, the BS makes money-capital, the transitory but necessary form of capital, the capital par excellence[6] by attributing to it the natural property of producing interest. While the CS is ready to sacrifice real wealth for the benefit of commodity-money, insofar as money represents the universal commodity, the BS agrees to sacrifice it to save money-capital, i.e. money insofar as it embodies capital.

No doubt, money does not fulfil the same function and the bank does not play the same role in the mechanism of social reproduction in the CS and the BS. But if the BS is won over by the same money fetishism as soon as it comes to the Bank's capital, it is because it does not question the gold standard system any more than the advocates of the CS (Sumner, 1992). Their controversy is really about how the gold standard works and the role of monetary policy in its operation. In a sense, this controversy was triggered by a misunderstanding of Ricardo's quantity theory of money, on which the CS is based (Skaggs, 2016). Ricardo had developed the principle that the quantity of money in circulation determines the general price level by relying on a period when the Bank of England had suspended the convertibility of its notes. In fact, the dichotomous approach of the real and the monetary in quantity theory derives from the observation of the mechanism of inconvertible money. Even the BS, in spite of its theory of prices, will align itself with the positions of the SC with regard to the inconvertible state note (Fullarton, 1845: 22 and 29). Hence the reduction of money to its function as a means of circulation in quantity theory. Since real economic relations are independent of monetary relations and determine them, the only real economic utility that one is prepared to attribute to money is to facilitate the exchange of the products of productive capital. The CS continued to defend this principle even though the whole gold standard system revolved around the convertible banknote. Under these conditions, the Bank of England note, which is only a debt of the Bank redeemable in gold, could not influence prices any more than any other credit instrument. Tooke objected that it is the level of prices and commercial transactions that determines the quantity of credit money needed to circulate goods (Arnon, 2011: 217–18).

2.3.4 The law of reflux and the quantitativism of the Banking school

We know indeed that Tooke and Fullarton rely on the law of reflux to challenge the quantity approach (Fullarton, 1845: 68; Le Maux, 2012). But they did so by relying on the difference between the convertible banknote and the inconvertible banknote, which acts on prices in the same way as an increase in metallic money would. The convertible banknote, however, is a credit instrument; it is issued as an advance only. In other words, it necessarily flows back to the bank that issued it when the advance is repaid (Fullarton, 1845: 86). It

> can therefore affect prices only *provisionally,* for in order to repay the advances a sum exactly equal to those advances has to be taken from the final income. An advance from the bank enables the borrower to spend to-day an income which he will in fact receive only later, but he will not spend that income since it will be used to repay the advance.
>
> *(Rist, 1940: 198)*

But this is only true if the banks actually practice the law of reflux and limit themselves to making short-term loans and not advances which tie up their funds for long periods. This is why the law of reflux is actually part of a general portfolio choice theory for convertible notes (Skaggs, 1991) and not part of the real bills doctrine. Where the latter prescribes that banks should make advances against short-term real securities to avoid inflationary excesses, the law of reflux only describes the mechanism by which the automatic return of convertible notes to the issuing banks prevents any excess issuance from having a lasting influence on the price level.

One of the paradoxes of the CS/BS debate is that while the BS promotes a more flexible monetary policy towards credit, Bank of England reserves, etc., it actually has a much more restrictive conception of money compared to the CS (Diatkine, 1995: 37). The reason why it considers it absurd to control the circulation of banknotes to the exclusion of all other credit instruments issued by banks and merchants is that, in its view, banknotes are no more money than these instruments (Cassidy, 1998: 517). For Tooke, for example, the error of Overstone, Torrens and Norman was to regard the convertible banknote as identical with gold, though it is itself "merely commercial bills payable on sight, and not bearing interest, drawn on and accepted by a banker". And the deposit "is similarly a banker's undertaking to pay on sight" (Rist, 1940: 203–04). When the customer of a bank has a bill of exchange discounted, the bank substitutes its promise to pay for that of the acceptor; whether this promise is evidenced by a note or scriptural money transferable by means of cheques, circulating from hand to hand, or by an entry in its books transferable by means of cheques, the economic effects are identically the same (Fullarton, 1845: 51).

Because Tooke and Fullarton did not distinguish between convertible banknotes and other credit instruments, Wray imagines that money includes all liquid assets in circulation, including gold coins (1990: 107). However, for the BS, only gold and inconvertible money can be defined as money, all other means of circulation, insofar as they are convertible into gold, being instruments of credit. But Wray makes this error of interpretation because according to him money is in essence credit. This leads him to claim that the CS defends a restrictive conception of money, including only gold and notes issued by the Bank of England and local banks, whereas in reality it has a broader conception of money than the BS, for which notes are to be classified as credit instruments. But as gold does not circulate in the domestic sphere except in the form of gold coins, which are themselves largely replaced by small denomination notes, all means of circulation seem to behave as money in the BS, unlike the CS, for which only notes are considered as money, the amount of which must be regulated according to the reserves of the Bank of England's issue department (Arnon, 2011: 188). The misunderstanding stems from the fact that, while the BS clearly distinguishes between money and credit, it is the CS that, like Wray and the Modern Monetary Theory club, confuses the two. And it is because it confuses the two that the CS seeks to impose a rule of issue on the central bank, just as it is because the BS never confuses them that, as will be seen below, it can rely on the law of reflux to regulate the amount of means of circulation without needing any rule for the Bank (Tooke, 1848: 185).

This is why quantity theory made a comeback at the very moment when the regime of inconvertible credit money, i.e. a monetary regime without a commodity basis, became widespread (Wray, 1990: 107). The CS provided the conceptual basis for this regime by defining the bank note issued by the central bank as money in its own right. Moreover, in his Plan for Monetary Reform (1824), Ricardo himself considered that an ideal monetary regime would be one in which only inconvertible banknotes, the issue of which would be strictly controlled by the central bank, entered into circulation. For Tooke and Fullarton, only precious metals are money in the true sense of the word, but they are only used for foreign exchange or small divisional money, as credit has replaced money in almost all spheres of domestic circulation (Fullarton, 1845: 36). This is why a gold outflow resulting from a bad harvest or an exceptional price rise should not, up to a certain point, lead to restrictions in the issuance of banknotes. For the BS, "money" issued in the form of deposits in exchange for loans granted by banks is of the same nature as "money" issued by the banks of issue, because for the latter, too, any advance that is granted results in the issue of a banknote, and banknotes are money. What is known as money is therefore only a credit instrument.

But if, however, the CS considers the Bank of England note on the same footing as gold, it is because a hierarchy of credit instruments had been established, marked by the Bank of England notes being given the status of legal tender, and the development of the interbank market where reciprocal payments by banks are made in the form of banknotes or transfers to the Bank, so that the banks are only concerned with their capacity to repay in banknotes the deposits entrusted to them, leaving the central bank to transform these banknotes into gold. Tooke agreed with the CS that the note of the central bank as well as its monopoly should be regulated. Moreover, he considered it necessary for the Bank of England to hold a much larger precautionary reserve than it did before the Bank Act (1840: 185; Smith, 2003: 41). Hence the rule imposed by the CS on the central bank to regulate the quantity of money in the market by increasing or decreasing the amount of its notes or current accounts by purchases or sales of securities, and without waiting for private banks to approach it with offers of bills of exchange to be rediscounted (Rist, 1940: 208). By entrusting the issue of banknotes to a single bank, the central bank was given the means of action and control to unify the country's monetary circulation (Rist, 1940: 226).

So Tooke also follows the CS's quantity rule for small denomination notes which are in fact only substitutes for divisional gold. And he goes so far as to minimise the difference between bills of exchange and banknotes, though the former must be converted into the latter when discounted (Arnon, 2011: 231). For they are in fact two substitutes for each other that both differ from metallic money. However, even though Tooke differentiates between capital and circulation (between credit and money), he sees an identity between the quantity of credit granted and the quantity of money income spent on the market of consumer goods (Tooke, 1844: 35–36). Here, he follows Smith and his theory of labour-commanded (as will the Schmittian theory) according to which the price level is ultimately determined by the income distributed (1844: 71–72).[7]

Therefore, according to Tooke, since the credit instruments are equivalent, it would be absurd to control only the issue of banknotes. Credit abuses cannot be combated by limiting their issuance alone but by controlling credit in general, through the discount rate in particular. Crises are in fact the result of an excess of credit in all its forms without exception: commercial paper, credit purchases of goods, excess of deposit creation. This is what Tooke calls overbanking (1840: 262) and which is itself the result of a state of demand determined by prices. Thus, speculation arises from a determined state of the market and not from the multiplication of banknotes or deposits (Fullarton, 1845: 100), which is rather a result of it.[8] Moreover, credit is only created by banks at the request of the public. Banks do not create banknotes and deposits at will. This is what differentiates the bank note from the state note: "The State creates paper money at will but cannot withdraw it from circulation; the banks do not create credit instruments at will, but can withdraw them by ceasing to renew credits" (see also Fullarton, 1845: 63–64; Tooke, 1848: 177; Rist, 1940: 213). The normal price level from which the speculative level deviates is ultimately determined by consumer incomes (wages, managerial profits, interest and rents) and the crisis occurs precisely when these incomes are not sufficient to absorb the goods at speculative prices. For Tooke, therefore, Bank of England notes should be used to provide additional, momentary money to prevent bankruptcies and the drying up of liquidity.

The criticism of the CS by the BS is therefore only valid in a convertible currency regime. If we were to switch back to inconvertible money, Tooke and Fullarton would agree that prices would be affected by the level of issue (Tooke, 1844: 70–71). And they recognise that money spent by the government on public works, etc., does not flow back to the banks and cause the price level and wage level to rise (Smith, 2003: 46). This paper money "will constitute a fresh source of demand, and must be forced into and permeate all the channels of circulation" (Tooke, 1844: 69). Under such conditions, "every fresh issue" will be followed by the "rise of commodities and wages and a fall of the exchanges", for the state has thereby increased the nation's income. This is also related to the modern quantity theory of money and its rules of central bank independence and balanced budgets, in a context where, here too, the economic role of the state has increased enormously compared to the British state of the mid-19th century.

Like Norman, the CS sometimes artificially distinguishes between the demand for money and the demand for capital, so as to define the interest rate as the effect of the supply of and demand for money as a specific commodity distinct from the supply of and demand for commodities-capital; or, like Overstone, it identifies the demand for capital and the demand for money-capital in order to prove falsely that the rise in the interest rate in times of crisis is not due to a scarcity of the means of circulation. On the one hand, Overstone asserts that the price of goods is determined by the quantity of currency in circulation, while on the other hand he identifies the interest rate and its fluctuations with the fluctuations of the real rate of profit. In reality, like Norman, he conceives of money essentially as a means of circulation as well as an absolute commodity whose price is precisely given by the interest rate.

The BS confuses money and capital but artificially distinguishes currency and capital, i.e. it considers money under its determinations of money-capital without considering the formal determinations of money as money. Thus, Tooke conceives currency as a mere means of circulation and capital as loan capital, as interest-bearing capital (1844: 34). But he does not envisage that money in its function as a means of circulation can replace capital or, on the contrary, that the function of means of payment can regulate consumer credit. The basis for this artificial separation lies in the view of the bank adopted by Tooke, according to which the notes issued for circulation do not affect the bank's credit and do not represent its capital. He thus confuses the money form of income and the money form of capital with circulation and capital. In the same way, Fullarton transforms the different functions of money into differences of determination: means of circulation = currency and means of payment = capital.

The CS and the BS reflect each other as in a darkened mirror: money-capital and productive capital are in an inverted relationship. While the CS defends the interests of the savers and claims on production by its conception of money and the interest rate, it claims that productive capital constitutes the only really existing capital in relation to which money itself serves as a simple means to circulate the goods and services representing this capital. The BS, however, supports the interests of industrialists and merchants with its law of reflux and its conception of credit, but conceives money-capital, or rather the capital held by the bank in the form of reserves of precious metals, convertible notes or debt securities of all kinds, as capital par excellence. The CS grants everything to the means of circulation but this is to better defend money in its private function as a store of value; the BS grants nothing to the means of circulation but this is to guarantee the social circulation of money-capital. The CS fetishism of money as well as the BS fetishism of interest-bearing capital operates through displacement and condensation. And it is in this displacement and condensation of concepts that the ideological background of any kind of fetishism lies.

Notes

1 The rate of interest

> is not regulated by the rate at which the Bank will lend, whether it be 5, 4, or 3 per cent, but by the rate of profits which can be made by the employment of capital, and which is totally independent of the quantity, or of the value of money.
>
> *(Ricardo, 1821: 363)*

2 It is on the basis of this qualitative distinction between the interest rate and profit of enterprise that neoclassical theory can make the hypothesis of a zero rate of profit under perfect competition on the one hand, and justify the interest rate as a remuneration for abstinence or renouncing of liquidity on the other.

3 "Inasmuch as [the bills of exchange] ultimately neutralise one another through the balancing of claims and debts, they act absolutely as money, although there is no eventual transformation into actual money. Just as these mutual advances of producers and merchants make up the real foundation of credit, so does the instrument of their circulation, the bill of exchange, form the basis of credit money proper, of banknotes, etc. These do not rest upon the circulation of money, be it metallic or government-issued paper money, but rather upon the circulation of bills of exchange" (Marx, 1894: 397–98).

4 "As long as the state of business is such that returns of loans made come in regularly and credit thus remains unshaken, the expansion and contraction of circulation depend simply upon the requirements of industrialists and merchants. [...] Once the crisis has broken out, it becomes from then on only a question of means of payment" (Marx, 1894: 524–25).

5 "The volume of circulating bills of exchange has no influence on note circulation and is influenced by the latter only in times of money tightness, when the quantity of bills increases and their quality deteriorates. Finally, in a period of crisis, the circulation of bills collapses completely; nobody can make use of a promise to pay since everyone will accept only cash payment; only the banknote retains, at least thus far in England, its ability to circulate, because the nation with its total wealth backs up the Bank of England" (Marx, 1894: 537).

6 "That the greatest sacrifices of real wealth are necessary to maintain the metallic basis in a critical moment has been admitted by both Tooke and Loyd-Overstone" (Marx, 1894: 567).

7 This makes Arnon say that Tooke's theory of prices is an Income Theory of Prices (2011: 232). This aspect of Tooke's theory should be seen in the context of the reactivation of the quantity theory of money in the 20th century. For this reactivation occurred at a time when not only was the share of wages in borrowers' expenditure incomparably greater than in Tooke's time, but the means of circulation used by wage earners were no longer distinct from those used by the original borrowers, i.e. companies: deposits, cheques, credit cards, etc. The banking practice of the 20th century therefore no longer establishes the practical difference between the means of circulation of capital and the means of circulation of labour, and thus the difference between credit and money established by Tooke on the basis of this practical difference (1844: 21).

8 But as soon as the marketisation of the banks' balance sheet develops, the banks enter the dance and the difference between bank-financed speculation and bank speculation as such disappears.

PART 2

Critique of monetary thought

3

KEYNES'S TWO MONIES

3.1 The contingency of orthodox monies

Money, in its two modes of being as a form of general exchangeability and as a general form of value, is thus born of the immediate commodity-to-commodity relationship. Thus, it is integrated into the structure of market relations by virtue of the very nature of this social relation of production, where the social existence of individuals is mediated by the private exchange of the objective products of their labour. Money is not only the means of circulating these products, but also the form of objective value against which they must necessarily be exchanged in order to impose themselves as products of social labour. In the neoclassical theory of exchange, even though the social relation between individuals takes the form of a quantitative relation between things (see Walras), it is the utilitarian relation of individuals to things that determines the relation of value between these things (Jevons, 1871: 2; Menger, 1871: 228). Thus, insofar as it is a subjective theory, the theory of value-utility does not imply the existence of money as a form of objectivity of value. Under these conditions, only the function of means of circulation, i.e. money as a form of general exchangeability, explains the presence of money in exchange. The only way for neoclassical theory to integrate money as an economic form necessary for exchange is therefore to found a demand for money on the motives of the traders themselves. But since money has only an indirect utility, given by its power to get directly useful goods, its value depends directly on its quantity relative to the quantity of useful goods to be exchanged, where the value of the latter is determined exclusively according to the preferences and resources of the agents. Thus, the value-utility theory necessarily implies the exogenous character of money, and finds in quantity theory the monetary conception corresponding to its presuppositions. For without a quantitative rule derived from the values of the commodities themselves, it is as if

DOI: 10.4324/9780429261299-6

some unknown cause, like a helicopter hovering over the markets, "had diffused a certain amount of [money] through the country; and, consistently with such an opinion, ascribed its value solely to its quantity" (Senior, 1840: 10).

Yet, it is true that the quantity approach to money did not have to wait for neoclassical theory to come to form monetary orthodoxy. Indeed, it found its first systematic expression in the labour-value theorist par excellence, Ricardo. For him, the value of money is, as for any commodity, determined by its cost of production, i.e. the quantity of labour necessary for its production (Ricardo, 1821: 18). From this point of view, the quantity of money is entirely determined by prices, and these by the proportions of labour time. In reality, the influence of the quantity of money on prices begins either with the transition to inconvertible money or with a trade balance in surplus or deficit. This is in any case Ricardo's opinion. Because of its function as a universal means of circulation, a shortage or surplus of money in circulation inevitably lowers or raises prices and thus raises or lowers the value of money. The return to convertibility and the resumption of the mechanism of gold entry and exit points would bring the value of money back to its production cost (Kojima, 1951: 81).

However, it is clear that for Ricardo the value of money is determined by labour time only because it is a commodity, and that precious metals have historically played the role of a general equivalent. The determination of the quantity of money by prices within a system of free metallic circulation is thus for him a completely contingent relationship which does not result from the immanent development of exchange value. The quantity conception of money, which Ricardo limits to exceptional situations and short-term phenomena, must necessarily prevail as a General Theory as soon as metallic circulation is abolished, a fortiori when we move to a regime of fiat money. However, there is a deeper reason why Ricardo defends the quantity theory, which concerns the theory of value itself. For Ricardo, money is not introduced as a necessary form of exchange value, because social labour is presented from the outset as abstract labour incorporated in the commodity. It is therefore not necessary for the labour embodied in the commodity to be represented in a separate commodity which represents its exchange value in order to realise itself as abstract labour or social labour. Money is not the necessary objective form of exchange value, but only the measure and instrument of exchange. This is what the classical and neoclassical approaches to quantity theory have in common: neither theory implies that the exchange value of the commodity has to separate itself and adopt a separate form of existence. The quantity theory is the natural monetary theory of all approaches in which the exchange value of commodities is realised before exchange.

Laidler and Rowe (1980) point out that from the 1870s onwards, the monetary theory analysed the demand for money by treating money not as value for its own sake, i.e. as a general form of value, but as real cash, as purchasing power over goods and services available on the market.[1] In neoclassical theory, which endorsed Ricardo's dichotomy between the real and the monetary, the demand for money arises directly from the requirements of money circulation, where purchases and sales are separated in time and where receipts and expenditures occur at different times in the processes of production and exchange (Patinkin, 1989: 13–15). The problem of a demand for money distinct from the demand for consumption goods is undoubtedly due to the development of the rentier class, whose existence is justified in neoclassical theory not in the manner of Malthus – as a source of demand – but as the holder of a resource as necessary as the resources of the productive classes (Bukharin, 1919).

But the importance in economic theory of the demand function of money as desired cash stems above all from the need to justify the existence of money where the object and purpose of exchange is the consumption of goods and services, and where money is therefore entirely absorbed in its function as a means of circulation. This is because even in its function as a unit of account, neoclassical models don't need money, and so arbitrarily chose a numeraire among the goods used to give the relative prices of other goods and services on the market (Allingham, 2008). However, once these models succeed in demonstrating the existence of equilibrium prices, i.e. prices such that supply and demand are fully satisfied, the very function of the means of circulation becomes superfluous, insofar as equilibrium prices have eliminated the problem of the double coincidence of needs and transaction costs (Bridel, 2002: 268).

This explains why the problem of the demand for money coincided with the triumph of the quantity theory, where the functions of unit of account and means of circulation are the sole justifications for the presence of money on the market. And what unites classical and neoclassical theories is precisely that they share the basic presuppositions of quantity theory: the ex ante equality of savings and investments, the former necessarily being converted into the latter since money is not demanded for its own sake; and the dichotomy principle, relative prices being fixed independently of monetary prices, whatever the theory of value underlying price determination in general:

> the quantity theory does not separate the classical sheep from the nonclassical goats, because the quantity theory, properly formulated, is accepted by virtually all economists, however their views might otherwise differ. In particular, the quantity theory, as a long-term proposition, was endorsed by Keynes. The controversies were all about the short-term adjustments.
>
> *(Niehans, 1987: 413)*

Not only does money not represent the value of goods in these two functions, but any increase or decrease in the quantity of money in circulation modifies the level of monetary prices without changing its real price, whether this price expresses quantities of labour or degrees of utility.

The entire history of the formation of Keynes's *General Theory* from his *Tract* onwards is animated by the search for an account of the demand for money for its own sake that owes nothing to the contingencies of market circulation. But, as we shall see, since Keynes derives his observations of the conditions of this demand exclusively from the financial sphere, whose circuits are separate from industrial circulation (*Treatise*), he defines the money demanded for itself as a liquid financial asset and the price of money as the price of liquidity. And as in Keynes's case the interest rate both expresses and determines the liquidity preference, it will suffice for monetarism, as we shall see with Friedman, to neutralise the role of the interest rate in the demand for money in order to reformulate the quantity theory on the very basis of the Keynesian definition of money as an asset.

3.2 The financial liberation of the interest rate

Keynes objects to the classical theory of the interest rate, i.e. to the theory of Ricardo and the neoclassicals, as being fundamentally non-monetary, even when it introduces a specific money market (Keynes, 1936: 175). For what determines supply and demand on the money market is not money itself, but non-consumed goods, real funds available for capital accumulation (Tily, 2007: 153). Money is only the representative of these real goods and owes its existence only to its function as an instrument of measurement and circulation of this real wealth awaiting consumption. It cannot even be said that as a stock it fulfils a store of value function, since the classics do not acknowledge hoarding: savings are by definition destined to be invested; they are ex ante equal to investment (Bertocco, 2013: 314). For money is never demanded for its own sake, but only for the convenience of exchange or the transfer of goods whose value it represents and which it circulates (Keynes, 1936: 182). This is also why, in the classical money market, it is always supply that precedes demand, it is always the supply of savings that determines the demand for investment and sets its limit (Chick, 1983: 178). Therefore, any supply of money that would exceed the current value of this given amount of real savings would have no effect on the creation of new wealth: money represents wealth, but does not create it, and does not even give rise to it. The monetary interest rate therefore does not determine the supply of and demand for money, i.e. the supply of and demand for money as a general form of value, but the supply of and demand for future means of consumption, or rather the price of foregoing present wealth for future consumption. Similarly, on the demand side, the interest rate is the price of having future income today. And even when a money rate coexists with a real rate, as in Wicksell, the inequality of these rates only affects the structure of relative prices and income distribution, not the absolute quantity of goods produced (Wicksell, 1898: 143–44).

In the *General Theory*, the rejection of the loanable funds theory is expressed above all by the principle of the identity between savings and investment. Savings are in fact a balance that adjusts itself, that "always and necessarily accommodates itself to [investment]" (Keynes, 1973a: 276). It is not "the dog", as "common sense" would have it, but "the tail of the dog". With this image, Keynes means that investment always drags savings "along with it, at an equal pace" (*Ibidem*).

The rate of interest cannot therefore represent the price equalising these two variables:

> The novelty in my treatment of saving and investment consists, not in my maintaining their necessary aggregate equality, but in the proposition that it is, not the rate of interest, but the level of incomes which [...] ensures this equality.
>
> *(Keynes, 1973b: 211)*

Yet, Keynes belatedly recognised this identity, on the advice of Robertson who found it strange that profits in the *Treatise*, i.e. the savings of entrepreneurs, did not figure in aggregate savings. In the *Treatise*, Keynes does indeed admit the possibility of an imbalance between investment and household savings, expressed precisely in the profits or losses of entrepreneurs, depending on whether savings are lower or higher than investment (Keynes, 1930: 126). The only identity in the *Treatise* is that between income and production costs, i.e. the cost of factors, the entrepreneur's normal profits being themselves part of the production costs.

In the *Treatise*, it is the independence of the markets for consumer goods and investment goods that is the basis for the rejection of the classical theory of the interest rate, according to which the interest rate determines the equality between non-consumption and investment. For Keynes, not only do the savings market and the investment market not depend on the same variables, but in a market economy there is no guarantee that the composition of expenditure coincides with the composition of output (Meltzer, 1988: 64). This is why Keynes excludes profits from the composition of income because he would otherwise be obliged to recognise the equality of investment and savings (Lutz, 1938: 612). But savings are only partly transferred to the investment market through the purchase of securities.

When Keynes finally included profits in savings, it would be to make savings not equal but identical to investment. By establishing this identity, Keynes frees the interest rate from the responsibility of equalising savings and investment (Lutz, 1938: 612) and thus makes it available for his theory of liquidity preference (Tily, 2007: 157). However, it is hard to believe that Keynes should have untied the link between the interest rate and savings so as to free investment from its dependence on savings. The main reason why Keynes rejects the classical theory of the interest rate is precisely the uncertain result of a change in the interest rate on the amount of aggregate savings (Chick, 1983: 183). This is because savings do not consist of a sum of goods awaiting consumption, but of hoarded cash, and above all of shares and bonds, whose value changes with a change in the interest rate. Thus, a change in interest rate does modify the propensity to save, but it also modifies in the opposite direction the value of savings already constituted: thus, there is a price or substitution effect on savings flows and an inverse wealth effect on stocks, which leaves the effect of the interest rate on overall savings undetermined. What disrupts the savings function in Keynes's work, and what justifies his break with the classics, is the preponderance of financial assets in wealth, the role of financial markets in the constitution of agents' savings and the influence of monetary policy on the dynamics of these markets. Keynes is thus the thinker of the era of financial capital, of the financialisation of wealth, and all his efforts are directed towards the possibility of subjecting this monstrous product of the credit system to the conditions of full employment of resources through monetary policy.

But the very existence of financial markets implies a deeper transformation in the structure of production relations around the job-creating enterprise: the separation between the ownership of capital, represented in the company's shareholders, and the management of the enterprise itself, embodied by the figure of the entrepreneur. It is only with this separation that the divorce between savings and investment is consummated: henceforth, investment is determined by factors independent of existing savings, and the interest rate is determined by factors independent of the "rate of return expected from devoting real resources to a project to enhance future income" (Chick, 1983: 185). But separation is not enough to reverse the causal relationship between savings and investment as long as existing savings are the only source of borrowing for investment. For causality to be reversed, credit itself must be freed from existing savings and determined exclusively by investment demand. At that point, it is savings that become the result of investment. But this reversal changes the very nature of the terms in question, because as soon as savings cease to be the source of investment, they lose their status as a financial variable and become the non-consumed part of income. Thus, the interest rate no longer determines the amount of the non-consumed part of the income since the interest rate is itself determined by the income, which is, in turn, determined by the amount of the investment. Rather, the interest rate determines the nature of the investment of this non-consumed part of the income: whether as cash or securities. However, as soon as the interest rate determines the demand for financial assets, as it did for Keynes, it comes to determine not only the prices of the newly created assets, but above all the prices of assets already accumulated on the markets (Snippe, 1985: 130). And the more the financialisation process develops through the accumulation of household wealth and the profits of enterprise, the more insignificant the share of newly created savings becomes relative to the existing stock of savings; therefore, the more the demand for financial assets becomes independent of the flow of newly created savings, the more the interest rate becomes independent of the supply of and demand for savings and the more it appears as a purely financial variable: "In liquidity preference theory, households demand liquidity for their stocks of wealth; while in the classical model, households supply a flow of saving" (Tily, 2007: 193). For Keynes, the normal interest rate, according to which speculators anticipate a fall or rise in the interest rate, is a purely subjective rate, unrelated to the different rates of profit realised in the sphere of production. Classical theory undoubtedly reduces the capitalist economy to a barter economy in which money fulfils only limited functions of measurement and circulation. But, as we have seen, the dichotomous approach nevertheless preserves the relationship between the rate of interest and the rate of profit, between the price of money and the rate of return on productive capital. Keynes undoubtedly has the merit of having re-defined the capitalist economy as a monetary economy of production. But because of the independence of the rate of interest from the rate of profit, the relations of production – in spite of the presence of the costs of production in the fundamental equations of the *Treatise* – do not enter anywhere into the laws governing the monetary relations, neither in the traditional monetary functions, dedicated to the sphere of consumption, nor in the monetary function of speculation, dedicated to the financial sphere. For sure, it is precisely because he got rid of the natural interest rate of the Classics (of Wicksell) that Keynes was able to conceive a possible equilibrium for each interest rate, and thus a multitude of sub-employment equilibria according to effective demand (Bibow, 2000a: 813). But since the incentive to invest is itself dependent on the current interest rate, it is, under the assumption that the money supply is given, the liquidity preference as determined by the opinion of the financial markets that overdetermines the level of effective demand, i.e. the incentive to invest. By determining the demand for financial assets in this way, Keynes transformed the interest rate into a mainly financial variable. The liquidity preference is a money demand function not for itself but for the markets, and the uncertainty on which this preference depends is only the uncertainty about the evolution of interest rates, whatever the degree of robustness of the fundamental variables of economic activity.

3.3 From the *Treatise* to the *General Theory*: the genesis of the money-asset

The concept of liquidity itself, which for Keynes defines money, is itself a financial concept that classifies the different assets according to the ease with which they convert into each other. Keynes thus proposes to distinguish money from any other debt instrument by the length of time an asset can be held or converted, the limit of which varies according to the nature of the economic problem involved in holding these different assets (Keynes, 1936: 167, n. 1), with the interest rate representing the set of different interest rates for debts of different maturities (Keynes, 1936: 167, n. 2).

For Keynes, the motive of speculation is not only distinguished by the fact that speculation depends on the interest rate, while the other motives would depend on income. In fact, the motive of speculation involves an entirely different kind of money; or, rather, money here fulfils a function neither as a measure of value nor as a means of exchange, nor even a function as money-capital or interest-bearing capital – the general form of value that is valorised by exchange for productive capital. From the point of view of transactions and precautionary motives, money just serves to guarantee the balance of payments and incomes or to meet unforeseen expenses. Speculative money, however, is demanded as a financial asset and presents itself from the outset as financial capital (M-M′).

"Keynes regarded the demand for money as a decision concerning the form in which wealth is kept; the immediate alternative to holding money is to hold wealth in the form of financial assets" (Sardoni, 1998: 280). This is where the confusion with the loanable funds theory comes from: in the loanable funds theory, money is demanded as a medium of exchange whose price is equal to the real return on capital. In the liquidity preference theory, it is a financial asset whose price is determined by the liquidity preference. In the first case, the financial market evolves according to the profit rate of capital. In the second case, the market is the place of purely conventional expectations on the interest rate. In both cases, there is a demand for money, but in the first case it is a demand for new savings flows, given the real capital stock and its average return: it is a demand for a stock of money, given the existing stock of wealth in both money and securities, i.e. fictitious capital. And the confusion between real and fictitious capital is all the more easy to fall into since Keynes, like the Classics, defines the price of real capital as the sum of expected income discounted at the current interest rate (Keynes, 1930: 139). Hence the very confused relationship between the interest rate and the marginal efficiency of capital, the latter assuming that the interest rate is actually known (Keynes, 1936: 135). Money does play a role in the level of activity, but indirectly, through the valuation of companies' securities on the financial market. The demand for money depends on the state of the financial markets, that is to say, given the state of expectations, on the price of securities. Once again, it is not the same money that circulates in the sphere of trade as that which circulates in the financial sphere. One cannot even say that speculative money is a store of value, since this function is expressly reserved by Keynes for the precautionary motive: the desire "to hold an asset of which the value is fixed in terms of money to meet a subsequent liability fixed in terms of money" (Keynes, 1936: 196). Money hoarded for speculative purposes is not a store of value, but a store of liquid assets.

In the *Treatise*'s fundamental equations,

$$P = E / O + (I' - S) / R$$

and

$$\Pi = E / O + (I - S) / O,$$

prices are determined by two quite distinct factors, namely incomes on the one hand, and profits on the other. In the first equation, the profits referred to are the profits of the consumer goods sector; in the second, the profits of both sectors combined. Profits are therefore not part of incomes. The influence of profits on prices is not exercised directly through their purchasing power on the goods sold on the market in these two sectors. In the first case, profits result from an excess of investment over savings; in the second case, from an excess of the market price of investment goods over savings. The difference between the two, i.e. $I - I'$, is therefore just equal to the excess of the market price over the production cost of investment goods. However, the price of investment goods is set on the financial markets, through the liquidity preference of households and the interest rate set by banks. In other words, the price of investment goods does not depend on incomes as is the case for the price of consumption goods (first equation). In the *Treatise*, the liquidity preference is expressed by the trade-off between real capital and money + bonds, whereas in the *General Theory*, there will be a trade-off between money and bonds. But in reality, in the *Treatise*, real capital (fixed capital) is confused with fictitious capital (securities) (Meltzer, 1988: 75). Moreover, in the preface to the Japanese edition, Keynes states that the price of investment goods is indeed dependent on the price of securities and thus on the liquidity preference (Meltzer, 1988: 66). In fact, the interest rate has a much greater effect on investment than on savings, because the price of investment depends as much on the market rate that is expected or anticipated by investors and banks (Keynes, 1930: 180; Meltzer, 1988: 67–68)[2] as it does on the real rate of profit. Keynes wanted to free investment from existing savings, but only in order to chain it back to the financial market. No doubt he hoped that the banking system would have an effect on the markets that it could not have on the propensity to save, or, what amounts to the same thing, on the households' propensity to consume. But this is after recognising that the supply of money in general was itself dependent on conventions in the financial markets (Tily, 2007: 193).

Profits in the capital goods sector meant, for Keynes, that the value of production, given in the price of securities on the financial markets, was higher than the cost of producing the capital goods. This increase in value is the result of the decline in the public's liquidity preference to the benefit of securities. There is thus a transfer of purchasing power to entrepreneurs via the securities market. Conversely, losses in the productive goods sector require entrepreneurs to sell securities or use their bank deposits to compensate for these losses (Keynes, 1930: 131). In the consumer goods sector, profits come from the investment goods sector: a decrease in savings which results in an increased difference between I' and S. But what happens to these monetary profits? They are transferred to the investment goods sector by a purchase of securities on the markets, which increases the price of securities and thus of investment goods. Thus, not only do the profits of the investment goods sector originate from the rise in the price of securities, itself caused by an increase in the demand for securities by savers (entrepreneurs take advantage of the rise to raise more funds and buy investment goods), but the profits of the consumer goods sector, which generally originate from an increase in the expenditure of entrepreneurs (capitalists earn what they spend), but which can also result from the profits of the investment goods sector, represent for Keynes a dissaving or indirect investment. They come from the capitalists' expenditure as made possible either by raising funds on the markets or by bank credit (forced saving).

Kahn sees this as evidence that prices in the two sectors are not independent (Marcuzzo, 2001: 94). But this is a special case where the purchase of securities follows the rise in prices in the consumer goods sector. Kahn fails to see that these are two markets of a different nature, where the variation of securities prices depends not on the profits of the consumer goods sector, but on the propensity of capitalists in this sector to save, as well as their liquidity preference. On the one hand, Keynes assumes that part of the profits already made in the investment goods sector are directed towards the purchase of consumer goods (Keynes, 1930: 125). On the other hand, the assumptions of full factor employment suggest that profits in the consumer goods sector are not reinvested in new investment goods but in the purchase of securities, because, as Keynes repeats, we are not here talking about income with purchasing power over goods but rather of purchasing power transferred to the securities market: "however much of their profits entrepreneurs spend on consumption, their increment of wealth belonging to the entrepreneurs remains the same as before" (Keynes, 1930: 125). For sure, the profits of the investment goods sector do form purchasing power over goods when they are consumed. But they should be seen more as a source of forced savings for income holders whose purchasing power has fallen with the rise in the price of consumer goods, rather than as income in their own right. The proof is that, at the macroeconomic level, profits are not consumed, since the money spent in this way returns to the securities market and thus to the markets for investment goods: it is in this sense that capitalists earn what they spend (de Boyer, 1982: 63).

If, on the contrary, there are losses in the consumer goods sector, this means that the propensity to save has increased. Again, these losses have to be compensated by selling securities or reducing deposits. But on the consumer side, the excess savings go into deposits and/or financial markets in an amount just equal to the losses in the consumer goods sector. Thus, the imbalances between projected savings and investment are always compensated by profits and losses, and this is the case insofar as profits and losses constitute in all cases the non-consumed part of incomes.[3] Through monetary profits, money operates by extraction, or by capture; not by exchange, by equivalence or by transaction. Capitalists earn what they spend. But this money, even if it passes through an "exchange" of goods, not only does not depend on incomes but indeed never constitutes them. Its action results from its existence as a financial asset.

Profits resulting from the difference between selling prices and production costs are therefore not considered by Keynes as a form of income (Keynes, 1930: 112) but as "an increase in the accumulated wealth of entrepreneurs" which is not converted into means of circulation, and which is not exchanged on the commodity market. It was in order to equate this particular saving with household saving that Hicks (1937) and the IS-LM theorists transformed the identity between saving and investment into an equilibrium condition, thus interpreting the Keynesian model as a particular version of the loanable funds theory – or rather, we might say, they mistakenly interpreted the Keynesian model as if savings consisted only of household savings and thus of the unconsumed part of their income, intended for the purchase by borrowers of investment goods.

But why does Keynes not consider profits as a form of income? Given that they can be used to make new investments, and thus to buy labour power and productive goods, why don't they also constitute purchasing power?

Let us take the case where consumption expenditure is insufficient in relation to the income distributed for the production of consumer goods. Households therefore accumulate savings. However, these savings have no purchasing power with respect to consumer goods that have all been sold at market prices below factor costs (in the *General Theory*, where prices are rigid, there would be stock formation which represents capital, i.e. investment). There is therefore a loss on the side of the producers of these goods. These newly formed savings only allow the purchase of investment goods, and only by entrepreneurs. Households must therefore transfer this purchasing power with respect to these goods to entrepreneurs, either in the form of bank deposits that may be used by the banks, or directly in the form of purchases of securities. This is precisely what the loanable funds theory says, which sees the flow of household savings as the source of new investment by entrepreneurs. But, for Keynes, to choose to hold either money or securities is not the same thing, and it is this choice that determines the interest rate. Further, by determining the interest rate, it is also this choice that determines the price of securities on the financial markets. For Keynes, it is the price of securities that determines the value of the investment and justifies that this value should be established independently of the price of consumer goods. This is where the legacy of the Austrian positive capital theory comes in, according to which the value of a productive good is determined by the sum of future incomes from the exploitation of this good discounted at the interest rate (Keynes, 1936: 149). Keynes does not differentiate between the price of securities traded on the markets and the value of investment goods bought and sold in the industrial sphere. Indeed, it is by buying securities that savers transfer to entrepreneurs the quantity of money that enables them to acquire these additional investment goods. The price of goods and the price of securities both result from the transfer of purchasing power over investment goods to the financial market (de Boyer, 1982: 60). It is the difference between this price and the costs of production that determines the amount of entrepreneurs' profits and losses (de Boyer, 1982: 56). Consequently, even if entrepreneurs prove themselves to have poorly anticipated changes in the consumer goods sector, this is not reflected in the market for investment goods, whose value varies according to the interest rate and the households' liquidity preference. Capital is therefore not born as a result of saved consumer goods; it is not the result of abstinence: saving is not the intended result of virtuous decisions of abstinence but rather, insofar as it results from constituted income, the result of bold decisions of investment (Poulon, 2016).

This is where the role of the banks comes in, a role that Keynes does not mention in the *General Theory*. For it is through the banking system that some of this purchasing power passes into the hands of entrepreneurs, notably through open market operations. This is how the central bank acts on the interest rate, leading Keynes to say that

> The price level of investments as a whole, and hence of new investments, is that price level at which the desire of the public to hold savings deposits

> is equal to the amount of savings deposits which the banking system is willing and able to create.
>
> *(Keynes, 1930: 129)*

But for both savers and the banking system, the money that is used to effect these transfers of purchasing power does not function as a means of circulation, but as a financial asset. Of course, as Chick says, "Banks create deposits also when they buy financial assets" (Chick, 1983: 235). But this does not result in the same money as that given to enterprises. All the controversy about the liquidity preference and the role of banks in financial intermediation stems from the fact that it is not the same money that is lent to enterprises and through which the banking system acts on the liquidity preference – that is, the preference between credit money and asset money, between the issue of means of circulation or payment and the issue of liquid assets.

> For Keynes, after consumption, income holders no longer have any purchasing power that can be lent but they do have the power to determine the value of investment, given the money creation policy followed by the banks; this is the liquidity preference theory. The money Keynes theorises is not circulating money but held money.
>
> *(de Boyer, 1982: 64)*

But the nature of the money held changes through the very function it performs. Thus in the liquidity preference theory, the interest rate no longer represents the price of money considered as a flow of savings, but rather as a stock of wealth, as a stock of liquid assets existing alongside less liquid assets:

> Liquidity preference is the decision about the degree of liquidity at which savings should be held. Furthermore, it is a decision concerning the stock of savings – wealth – at any point in time rather than any new flow of savings alone. The rate of interest is hence not determined by the supply of and demand for of saving (flows), but by the supply of and demand for assets into which holdings of of wealth can be placed (stocks).
>
> *(Tily, 2007: 185)*

In reality, not only is the interest rate not determined by the amount saved, but on the contrary the interest rate determines saving twice, once by influencing the allocation of savings between money and securities, and a second time by changing the value of existing savings as represented in the price of securities:

> Since saving – marginal additions to financial wealth – is fairly small in relation to the stock of wealth over a shortish period of time, and since the whole of the stock of wealth must be allocated, saving is trivial by comparison.
>
> *(Chick, 1983: 186)*

And even when new savings increase, the effect on the interest rate remains undetermined until the liquidity preference of not only savers but also the banking system is known, so that an increase in savings might correspond to an increase in the interest rate (Bibow, 2000a: 796–97).

But what determines the level of the interest rate if the choice is between a multitude of assets with different interest rates? No doubt this level will be set when the supply of and demand for money are equal, but what determines the price of this equality? Since, for speculative reasons, the liquidity preference is based on uncertainty about the future of interest rates, the current interest rate represents a fundamentally speculative variable:

> a given M2 [the quantity of money held to satisfy the speculative motive] will not have a definitive quantitative relationship to a given rate of interest of *r*; – what matters is not the absolute level of *r* but the degree of divergence from what is considered a fairly safe level of *r*, having regard to those calculations of probability which are being relied on.
>
> *(Keynes, 1936: 201)*

And since this rate considered normal is itself subjective, the demand for money for speculative purposes is inherently volatile (Chick, 1983: 207). Thus, the liquidity preference curve depends basically on the interest rate as expected in the future, or rather on the difference between the current rate and the expected rate in the future. This is why Robertson criticised Keynes's theory for leaving the interest rate as an indeterminacy that only the loanable funds theory can remove (Johnson, 1951: 101). Thus, the price of assets and thus of investment goods is determined solely by their expected future price and is independent of current supply and demand for that asset, provided that these supply and demand flows remain insignificant relative to the stock of already existing assets. Thus, current supply and demand influence prices only indirectly, through their influence on the expected future price. Therefore, these expected future prices are much more important than the marginal growth in demand for financial assets. For a given state of monetary policy, therefore, it is the expected prices of securities that decide the current price and thus the price of investment goods (Erturk, 2007: 457–58).

3.4 The finance motive and the two monies

By adding, after the publication of the *General Theory*, the finance motive to the three motives of transaction, precaution and speculation, Keynes (1937a; 1937b) seemed to return to the loanable funds theory (Carvalho, 1996: 319–320). For insofar as the finance motive was a demand for money to finance investment, this demand precedes investment and thus the constitution of income brought about by investment (Chick, 1983: 198). What Ohlin and Robertson object to is that, unlike the transaction motive, the demand for finance implies prior saving to satisfy that demand, "for investment and saving to be there ex post, the money needs to be found to finance them ex ante" (Bibow, 2000a: 819). And since bank credit is subject to reserve requirements, a set ratio of debts to claims, etc., the creation of money via credit alters the supply of money and thus influences the interest rate, as Keynes himself admits (Keynes, 1973b: 220). Even when the demand for money for financing is met by bank credit, the savings created on the occasion of the new investment will have to be used to pay back the bank loan (Asimakopulos, 1991: 113).[4]

And since under these conditions the demand for money depends on the planned expenditure and also on the propensity to save, insofar as these propensities affect the demand for money for transaction purposes and the supply depends on both the stock of existing money and the net creation of credit money, the difference between the theory of loanable funds and the theory of the liquidity preference disappears. This is why Tsiang (1956), like Davidson (1972) later, classifies the finance motive as a transaction motive, but in order to make the supply and demand of loanable funds the general theory of the interest rate. For only this theory incorporates both the demand for credit and the demand for money for all transaction motives (Cardim de Carvalho, 1996: 319–20). Moreover, when money is demanded for transaction purposes, on the one hand the interest rate on other securities no longer determines this demand, and on the other hand this demand, extended to include financial purposes, is no longer dependent on income alone but on investment and consumption expenditure in general. And insofar as these expenditures are determined by the expected rate of profit and by the propensity to consume or save, the interest rate once again becomes dependent on the "productivity and thrift" of the loanable funds theory (Bibow, 1995: 651).

For post-Keynesians, Keynes had conceded too much to the loanable funds theory, in particular by admitting that the demand for money for financial purposes put pressure on the interest rate (Graziani, 1987). However, when it is satisfied by the overdraft system, the problem of the demand for money for financial reasons is reduced to technical issues that can have no influence on the money market, provided that the level of investment remains more or less constant (Chick, 1983: 199). The only difference between the demand for money for financial purposes and for transaction purposes lies in the degree to which these demands fluctuate over the business cycle. More fundamentally, since the demand for money for financial reasons is a demand for credit money offered by banks, its effect on the interest rate will depend solely on the banks' willingness to satisfy this demand at the current interest rate and thus on the banks' liquidity preference (Rochon, 1997: 288). Thus, the whole difference between the two theories comes down to their different approach to banks (Cardim de Carvalho, 1996: 325): the loanable funds theory defines the banking system as a financial intermediary between savers and borrowers, whereas the liquidity preference theory makes banks the issuers of money.

But with this objection the very meaning of "liquidity preference" becomes uncertain. For it is no longer as a price for giving up liquidity that we must understand the interest rate that banks set as issuers of money. And on the demand side, it is no longer as a liquid asset that money is demanded, but as a general equivalent, as a general medium of exchange, and insofar as it is kept for future expenditure, as a general form of value. In short, it is as money-capital and not as finance-capital that money is demanded for investment purposes. Despite the formal similarity of the money uses that these motives imply, the finance motive has therefore nothing to do with the demand for transactional money for the income expenditure. In one case, money has been borrowed; in the other case, it has been earned (or rather exchanged for living labour); in one case money is advanced, in the other case it is spent. And when money is demanded for speculation, it is indeed a demand for money as capital, but this too differs in kind from the demand for money for finance. In the first case, it is a stock of reserve value, that is to say, for Keynes, liquid assets; in the second case, it is a flow of means of payment. In the first case, the money supply is determined by the level of existing savings; in the second case, it is decided by the banks. In the first case, an increase in the demand for money necessarily leads to an increase in the interest rate; in the second case, it does not. This is because in the first case supply is inelastic, whereas in the second case it is perfectly elastic to demand. And all these differences express a deeper difference that has gone unnoticed by commentators: when demanded as money-capital, credit money fulfils traditional monetary functions within industrial circulation (including that of a store of value); when demanded as financial capital, money appears as an asset that almost never leaves financial circulation.

The debate on the finance motive not only polarises the loanable funds theory and the liquidity preference theory around the role of savings in the financing of investment and thus in the determination of the interest rate, but it also launches the debate between post-Keynesians on the role of the liquidity preference itself in the determination of the interest rate (Moore, 1988; Palley, 2013). And this controversy has its direct source in Keynes's ambiguities about the banking system, which on the one hand is supposed to determine the interest rate provided that it satisfies the public's liquidity preference,[5] and on the other hand has its own liquidity preference determined by market rates.[6] But above all, by including the finance motive in his money demand function, Keynes conflates the demands for two kinds for money whose prices are determined in an entirely different way: a general equivalent money for the expenditure motive and an asset money for the speculation motive (Keynes, 1930: 127).[7] Now, through its trading of securities, the bank acts less on the economic cycle through its credit than through its action on the interest rate. For Keynes, therefore, the value of investment (which is equal to the price of securities) depends both on the behaviour of banks and on public opinion (liquidity preference). But it does not depend on the difference between income E and consumption C. It is linked to the valuation of all financial capital, i.e. the stock of financial assets accumulated over time, and is not constrained by the flow of savings in the period. Here, therefore, money is a pure financial asset. In the *Treatise*, Keynes not only reverses the direction of causality between income and the interest rate as it was envisaged by the Classics, but, by considering the interest rate to be the variable determining the level of activity, he lays down financial conditions as the ultimate determining cause of the demand for consumer goods (Erturk, 2007: 456). It is therefore through its influence on the equilibrium of the financial market that bank money plays a role in economic activity. In Keynes's view, the money market and the securities market are inseparable: on the one hand, the demand for securities by households is linked to the demand for money, and on the other hand, the demand for securities by banks is linked to their supply of money.

3.5 Conclusion on the Keynesian debates

It is true that Marshall, Pigou and Lavington suggested before Keynes that money is also demanded for its own sake (Bridel, 1987: 28). But by confusing stocks and flows in their money demand functions, they failed to define this demand in terms of portfolio optimisation. This is because their confusion between stocks and flows of wealth derives from their conception of money as a mere medium of exchange, or, what amounts to the same thing, as wealth awaiting goods to be exchanged for. With Keynes, for the first time, the relationship between the demand for money and existing accumulated wealth is established, by the fact that here money is not seen as the monetary form of income, but as a form of wealth in its own right (Bridel, 1987: 129–30).

Keynes tried to go beyond the dichotomous framework of quantity theory by introducing, in addition to the real balance effect, a demand for money distinct from income money (transaction and precaution). With liquidity preference, money is no longer neutral because the interest rate is no longer the price that equalises the supply of savings and the demand for investment. But in so doing, he has only transposed the dichotomy into the demand for money itself. For it is not the same money that is demanded as income and that is demanded as an alternative to securities. Robertson criticised Keynes for limiting the demand for idle money almost exclusively to speculation:

> Mr. Keynes was so taken up with the fact that people sometimes acquire money in order to *hold* it that he had apparently all but entirely forgotten the more familiar fact that they often acquire it in order to *use* it.
>
> *(Quoted by Sardoni, 1998: 281)*

This is because for all other motives, money is demanded as a potential means of circulation. Only the speculation motive determines the specifically monetary character of the interest rate, but insofar as this rate relates to money as an asset, it is imposed as an essentially financial variable. Thus, all the contradictions of the monetary economy of production, which we have seen are ultimately based on the general equivalent character of money, are now concentrated on the relationship between money holders and entrepreneurs, or, what amounts to the same thing, between the interest rate and the marginal efficiency of capital, between financial markets and the market for goods and services. However, within the productive sphere, money continues to fulfil the simple functions of unit of account and means of exchange, while within the banking and financial system it is only a financial wealth. From there, we will see how the so-called horizontalist post-Keynesians have evacuated the liquidity preference from Keynesian theory by untying the links between the banking system and the financial markets. Under these conditions, the interest rate becomes a mere political variable, free of any relation to the state of market expectations. Following the theory of the circuit from which it is inspired, horizontalism only involves the markets in the last place, as a savings market, once the credits have been granted and the deposits created.

The intention was undoubtedly to separate the two markets by determining them through different variables: incomes on the one hand, interest rates on the other; propensity to consume on the one hand, liquidity preference on the other. But he does not succeed in effecting this separation without also confusing productive capital with fictitious capital, real assets with securities. In Keynes's world, there is only one kind of commodity whose price is based on value: consumer goods. Neither labour power nor investment goods measure their value in labour time: the former because it has only an economic existence as an income flow, the latter because they depend on a fictitious and conventional rate. This is what the *General Theory* will enshrine by assuming only one sector: the consumer goods sector, and by assuming rigid money wages.

Followers of Keynes have pointed out the difficulty of distinguishing between precautionary and speculative motives in the *General Theory*, since one form of precaution is to hold liquidity so as to avoid the capital losses which would be possible if all savings were invested in securities (Robinson, 1951; Kahn, 1954). But the distinction in question does not refer to the nature of the events feared, but to the nature of the money involved. Money held for precautionary reasons is essentially circulating money, i.e. money dedicated to circulation. Hicks (1937) was able to reinterpret Keynesian theory on the basis of the IS-LM model, in which the market for money as a stock (LM) is related to a market for flows (IS), because he did not see the difference between money as demanded for speculation and money as demanded for productive investment (Hicks, 1939: 92). For their part, Viner and Robertson do not understand what makes Keynes so convinced that he has refuted the loanable funds theory, because they both reason as if transaction money and reserve money were the same money and acted in the same way on the interest rate (Backhouse, 1999: 204–09).[8]

It is this confusion between transaction and reserve money that, by reviving the loanable funds theory, gave rise to Tobin's portfolio choice theory. Here, arbitrage between securities reflects behaviour against the risks associated with the expected returns on securities. This theory is itself based a theory of probability relied on the history of market prices of securities, rather than on the uncertainty of interest rates. Similarly, it is because he does not see money as a financial asset but as a mere store of value that Davidson, following Hicks (1939: 106), interprets uncertainty in terms of events in industry rather than the vagaries of financial markets and interest rates (Davidson, 1972: 104), and directs the problems of liquidity preference towards credit rather than wealth. And although he defines money as one asset among others, we will see in the next chapter that Friedman conceives the demand for money only as a demand for transactions. A Keynes scholar has pointed out that Marx's monetary theory combined aspects of the loanable funds theory in which the interest rate is determined by the supply of and demand for loans, with aspects of the liquidity preference theory in which the interest rate equals the supply of and demand for money (Sardoni, 1998: 280). This ambivalence stems from the fact that in Keynes's case, the interest rate refers to money as a private form of social wealth, whereas in Robertson's case, money is seen as a private fund for social production. Probably nothing better expresses the paradoxical role of the two modes of being of money in the debate between Keynes and the Classics than the fact that it is the loanable *funds* theory that promotes money in its function as a means of circulation or payment, whereas the *liquidity* preference theory considers money precisely in its private form as a store of value.

Notes

1 The notion of desired cash is found successively in Walras (1900: 305), Menger (Monetary need 1892: 239), Wicksell (1898: 53), Fisher (Average time of turnover [1911: 351]), Marshall (1923: 38–40) and, of course, Keynes with his liquidity preference (1936).

2 Minsky is in a way the only one to have taken the measure of the fundamentally speculative nature of the price of investment goods in Keynes, by considering that any acquisition of assets, whether financial or real, is fundamentally speculative because it involves an uncertain future (1975: 86).

3 Keynes excludes profits from income because otherwise he would be confirming the loanable funds theory in which profits in the market for consumer goods would be equal to the additional savings offered in the loanable funds market. Profits play in the *Treatise* what inventory changes play in the *General Theory*, this difference merely expressing the fact that in the *Treatise* it is prices that vary, whereas in the *General Theory* it is the level of output. Profits and inventories are both equal to the difference between ex ante savings and investment. In the *Treatise*, profits induce entrepreneurs to invest; in the *General Theory*, changes in inventories induce production in such a way that the flow of savings newly created by the new level of income equals I and S.

4 The paradox, which is only apparent, is that both Keynes and Ohlin rely on the fact that it is in fact a demand for credit to demonstrate, first, that there is no link between this demand for money and existing savings, and second, that this demand implies precisely the existence of these savings.

5 "Authorities make [the] rate what they like by allowing the public to be as liquid as they wish" (CW, XXVII, p. 392).

6 The difficulty in grasping the theory of liquidity preference lies in the fact that the interest rate, which determines the terms of borrowing and thus the issuance of money, is the result of the supply of and demand for money that has already been created (see Chick and Tily, 2014: 691).

7 Rochon interprets this difference as a demand for flow-money and a demand for stock-money, respectively (Rochon, 1997: 281). But as Goux (1987) has already observed, the demand for credit is as much a demand for reserves (stock) as a demand for means of payment. Curiously, however, he distinguishes between finance balances and transaction balances, even though Keynes defines part of finance cash as a demand "due to the time-lags between the receipt and the disposal of income by the public and also between the receipt by entrepreneurs of their sale-proceeds and the payment by them of wages, etc." (Keynes, 1938: 319).

8 "Money, it is well known, serves two principal purposes. By acting as a money of account it facilitates exchanges without its being necessary that it should ever come into the picture as a substantive object. In this respect it is a convenience which is devoid of significance or real influence. In the second place it is a store of wealth [...] The significance of this characteristic of money has usually been overlooked; and in so far as it has been noticed, the essential nature of the phenomenon has been misdescribed" (Keynes, 1973b: 115–16).

4

THE IMPOSSIBLE DEMAND FOR MONEY OF THE CLASSICS AND FRIEDMAN'S KEYNESIANISM

4.1 The Cambridge school or the demand for purchasing power

Let us return to the basic assumptions of quantity theory: the ex ante equality of savings and investments, the former necessarily being converted into the latter since money is not demanded for its own sake; and the dichotomy principle. These assumptions gave rise to the three postulates of the quantitative formula to which Fisher (1911) gave its classic expression: MV = PT. The formula implies that (1) the direction of causality is from MV to PT; (2) V and T are attributable to non-monetary factors; (3) the nominal money-stock must be determined exogenously. For Fisher, there is indeed a demand for money, but since this demand depends solely on the overall level of transactions, it is presented as a demand for means of payment, a demand for money-flow, not a demand for money for its own sake, a demand for money-stock. A demand function for money as a store of value would imply that it depends not on the exchanges to be made but on the income to be distributed.

Thus, after Marshall, the Cambridge economists modified the quantity formula by suggesting a cash approach in the form M = *k* PY. Where Fisher's equation expressed a demand for PT/V goods, the Cambridge equation expresses a demand for money representing "the amount of commodities over which people [...] keep command in a ready form" (Laidler, 1991: 59). Cambridge's *k* may well be interpreted as being identical to Fisher's 1/V (Blaug, 1997: 617). But in the first formulation, it is as a store of value that money manifests itself, whereas in the second, it is as a means of circulation. But above all, with the introduction of *k*, monetary equilibrium and the price level no longer depend exclusively on the quantity of money, but on the behaviour of agents, on their desire for cash. For a given quantity of money, there will be as many equilibrium price levels as there are desired cash levels: the price level decreases or increases according to whether

DOI: 10.4324/9780429261299-7

the desire for cash increases or decreases. And since the magnitude of *k* depends on the price of assets as well as on the price of goods (Marshall, 1923: 44–45), the concept of money demand collides with the automatisms of quantity theory: not only does a change in the quantity of money lead to a change in the price of assets in addition to a change in the price of goods, but any change in the price of assets leads to a change in the level of income and thus in the demand for money.

However, *k* does not get us out of the dichotomy between the real and the monetary if agents are not supposed to be victims of a money illusion, i.e. if their demand for money is a demand for real cash independent of the general price level. And, like Fisher, the Cambridge school remains convinced that in the long run, "money is only a mechanism by which a gigantic system of barter is carried out" (Marshall, 1996: 115) and considers the behaviour of the price level as the central problem of monetary economics (Laidler, 1991: 64). Patinkin has clearly seen that this absence of a money illusion causes the Cantabrigians to confuse money prices, on which the demand for money depends, and relative prices, on which the demand for goods depends (Shafir, Diamond and Tversky, 1997). Now, depending on whether one approaches the problem in terms of the demand for money or the demand for goods, the price level is sometimes determined and sometimes undetermined. In the case of a change in the price level, there is a variation in the demand for cash, which leads to a variation in the price level until equilibrium is reached. The general price level is therefore well determined. However, from the point of view of the demand for goods, this variation in prices does not affect the demand for goods, by virtue of the homogeneity postulate according to which the supply of and demand for goods are insensitive to the absolute price level and react only to changes in relative prices. And since the real demand for money also falls within this postulate, the change in the price level does not alter the general equilibrium. Here, the general price level remains undetermined.

4.2 The general equilibrium models or the demand for unjustifiable power

For Patinkin, a genuine demand for cash must be able to affect both the relative prices and the absolute price level (Fellner, 1956). Only then can the store of value function ensure the integration of money in the real economy. Assuming the absence of monetary illusion, the Cambridge school postulated that changes in the quantity of money will lead to equi-proportional changes in all monetary prices.[1] However, only supply and demand functions that depend both on real money balances and on relative prices can distinguish a real money economy from a barter economy.

Let us assume that an agent holds any amount of money balances and that the price level falls. This results in an increase in the real value of these balances. The agent will therefore have a larger stock of money in real terms but not in nominal terms, which will lead him to spend more, until prices return to their initial equilibrium. But in the meantime, variations in the general price level will have modified the level of agents' real balances and this modification will continue until equilibrium is restored. This adjustment therefore assumes that the demand for goods reacts to a change in the price level. Contrary to the Cantabrigians, Patinkin shows that a change in the price level or even in the money supply causes a wealth effect on the demand for money and goods, with a resulting change in the real cash balance. Thus, the stock of real balances determines the demand for goods: the money demand function is inseparable from the goods demand function. The real money effect both breaks with the dichotomous principle and preserves the quantity principle according to which the real equilibrium is not affected by the quantity of money (Patinkin, 1989: 17–21).

But what justifies the introduction of this demand for money if it is assumed that market equilibrium can be achieved without money, and if therefore the absence of money does not prevent the formation of equilibrium prices from the aggregation of supplies and demands for goods? This is Hahn's (1965) famous objection to Patinkin's model, namely that he didn't demonstrate the existence of an $n-1$ positive-priced market equilibrium in which the price of money, good n, is positive. His model always includes an a-monetary solution where the purchasing power of money is zero. But why would anyone demand a good with no purchasing power?[2]

This was already the problem posed by Walras, who had tried to integrate money as a store of value into his general equilibrium model, after admitting that money was "a practical simplification and a theoretical complication, which is why, once we have defined its role, we will very often ignore it in the scientific study of the phenomena of economic life" (Walras, 1988: 544). For the very hypotheses of the model (a currency chosen arbitrarily from among the goods exchanged; an auctioneer centralising the supplies and demands of the trading agents; absence of exchange prior to the determination of equilibrium prices) render superfluous the presence of a kind of money whose functions imply the decentralisation of exchanges and the exchange process itself prior to any possible equilibrium (Bridel, 2002: 268). But even if money is introduced into exchange, Walras gives no justification for why there should be this demand for money once the period of production and circulation is over. Since money has no other use than to facilitate exchange, the service function of supply, as Walras defines money, remains entirely subject to the requirements of exchange, which, once completed, does not justify individuals holding liquid cash between maturities when they could hold interest-bearing assets instead (Hicks, 1935; Patinkin, 1965: 591). Since assets are as liquid as money when prices are in equilibrium, the only way to incorporate it into the economic agent's utility function is to force him to hold it for technological reasons. This is how Walras ended up integrating money in the last version of his model (1900). Since agents know in advance that there will be delays between the time they plan to buy goods and their income, the exchange system forces them to hold money and to pay the price for the delay between income and expenditure, and this price is the interest rate. In the utility function, the demand for money is a function of the amount of future transactions and the interest rate to be paid for these transactions. But

> [b]y introducing money after he had completed his theory of exchange, Walras clearly made monetary phenomena an optional add-on [...]. Further, it was an add-on that would be valued for its own sake rather than as a component enhancing the performance of the rest of the system.
>
> *(Ostroy, 1987: 188)*

Compared to Walras, Patinkin made no progress on the problem of the integration of money by introducing the constraint of uncertainty about maturities or imperfections in the credit market.[3] In fact, all solutions to Hahn's problem, where they do not introduce ad hoc constraints in the manner of Patinkin (Clower, 1967;[4] Grandmont and Younes, 1972; Wallace, 1983), consist in presupposing decentralised exchanges, sometimes to revive the problem of the double coincidence of needs born of the barter economy, sometimes to associate transaction costs with the exchange process.

It is true that, more recently, the search models (Starr, 1972; Kiyotaki and Wright, 1989) have succeeded in bringing out money from a social process of selection of a good that responds to the problem of non-coincidence of needs. In a Mengerian way, the emergence of a unique medium of exchange depends on the degree of probability that exchangers attribute to the ability of a good to be accepted by all. But just as Patinkin and Clower posed a constraint external to individual agents, the value of the probability that a good will be accepted by all is itself exogenously given (Bridel, 2014) and overdetermines the choice of a general equivalent. From this point of view, models based on transaction costs determine the emergence of money from properties of the market economy where, by definition, there is a lack of information on the quality and availability of goods, usual prices, purchases by other agents, etc. Money would result from the choice of a general equivalent and from the search for a good whose transaction costs would be almost zero (Niehans, 1987) or whose properties are well known (Brunner and Meltzer, 1971). But by assuming a decentralised and uncertain market, the search and transaction cost models assume the existence of a good that already has all the properties of money, which also requires the search for a means of exchange accepted by all.[5]

Why would a particular good be considered more reliable or exchangeable than others, if not because it is imposed because of its objective properties, which make it either a widely consumed use value or a good with the appropriate characteristics for its existence as an exchange value (precious metals), or because it is imposed by a sovereign authority? In all cases, the market or institutional process overdetermines the choice of agents even more than the choice of money as a means of exchange, which only responds to criteria of convenience that can give rise to the most varied monetary forms. Nor can money be explained by substituting the extreme subjectivism of constrained choices with the extreme objectivism of the institutions of the developed market economy.

When the hypotheses of the general equilibrium model are retained, it is as a store of value that we seek to integrate money; when these hypotheses are lifted (Fisher, 1983), it is as a general medium of exchange that we seek to justify its existence. But we have seen that general equilibrium models only justify the value reserve function on the basis of imperfections in money circulation. Whatever the hypotheses, therefore, the existence of money is justified as a form of general exchangeability only. And as soon as money separates itself from its function as a measure of value or unit of account, and thus from cash, the functions of a means of circulation or even a store of value can be realised in the most varied forms of existence.

4.3 Friedman or the demand for social power

By reformulating quantity theory after Keynes had relegated it to sterile speculation about the long term, Friedman gave money an ambiguous status. In a sense, he goes further than Keynes himself by defining it from the outset as a financial asset among the multitude of assets among which agents' wealth is distributed: shares, bonds, durable and semi-durable goods, human and physical capital, etc. And the demand for money itself is entirely determined by optimisation behaviour in the choice of portfolio according to individual preferences, of which money forms a component. Thus, in the 1960s, there was an odd convergence between monetarists and Keynesians on the fundamental properties of money:

> In recent years, there has been broad agreement between the proponents of quantitative monetary theory and Keynesian monetary theory on the following points: 1) money has utility as a store of value in an uncertain world; 2) the demand for money is part of a theory of asset preference; and 3) the main determinants of the demand for money are wealth, income and the interest rate.
>
> *(Thorn, 1971: 63)*

In another sense, however, Friedman analyses the effects of the quantity of money supplied on prices as if money only fulfilled a function as a medium of exchange and its utility was entirely dependent on this function. What allows Friedman to assume this ambiguity is the stability of the demand for money which neutralises the effect of its asset function on the price level and which makes him say that

> there is perhaps no other empirical relation in economics that has been observed to recur so uniformly under so wide a variety of circumstances as the relation between substantial changes over short periods in the stock of money and in prices; the one is invariably linked with the other and is in

> the same direction; this uniformity is, I suspect, of the same order as many of the uniformities that form the basis of the physical sciences.
>
> *(Friedman, 1956: 20–21)*

This is why Friedman's quantity formula is a kind of synthesis of Fisher and Marshall: MV = P*y*.[6]

But it is precisely because he generalises the liquidity preference by comparing money with all assets that Friedman can draw conclusions contrary to those of Keynes. Keynes had made the different motives for money demand depend on income and the interest rate alone. Now Friedman intended to determine this demand through the whole range of available assets. Under these conditions, short-term variations in the interest rate hardly affect a demand for money that is a function of all the long-term assets that make up the individual's permanent income (Friedman, 1959: 332–33). Thus, the difference in nature between consumer demand for money and business demand for money disappears. From now on, all goods, services and assets are part of a single utility function, the maximisation of which consists of equalising the implicit or explicit returns on these different resources possessed by the economic agent. Moreover, for Friedman, it is the rate of inflation that determines the rate of return on money, not the interest rate.[7] Thus, from being a financial variable, money regains its traditional function as a medium of exchange, which allows Friedman to revive the Humean mechanism whereby any increase or decrease in the quantity of money leads to a proportional variation in the price level, via the re-establishment of the desired cash level.

No doubt in the short term, agents are victims of monetary illusion. With an increase in the money supply, for example, as long as it results in an increase in nominal income, spending will increase because this increase will be interpreted as an increase in real income. But soon the increase in asset prices, the decrease in the interest rate and the resulting increase in the prices of goods and services will, in turn, modify behaviour through the mechanism of adaptive expectations to re-establish the initial equilibrium in the more-or-less long term. The difference between Friedman and Keynes lies in the nature of the transmission process: for Friedman, Keynes, who makes prices an institutional variable, conceives of nothing other than the interest rate as a channel for the transmission of monetary policy, whereas it would be necessary to include not only all assets, but all goods and services whose market prices change with the quantity of money.

This is why Friedman does not believe in a liquidity trap that would block the desired effects of monetary policy (1956: 17). Besides the interest rate channel, there are all sorts of assets through which the central bank implements its policy: exchange rates, the stock market, real estate prices, etc. (1956: 9–10). It is only after the fact that the nominal interest rate adjusts to these assets, and it is only afterwards that the nominal interest rate adjusts to these price developments.[8] Thus, where the IS/LM model separates consumption and savings decisions from portfolio decisions, Friedman combines them into a single utility function: variables affecting consumption implicitly affect portfolio decisions and vice versa: money demand is a stable function of a number of determined variables. For Friedman, Keynes did not challenge the quantity theory, he just claimed, by limiting the effects of money demand to only a few variables, that it was very unstable under conditions of underemployment (1956: 17).

Therefore, Friedman defines money as a financial asset in a completely different sense than for Keynes: as a store of purchasing power and therefore as a store of social power. Hence the claim for a monetary policy entirely dedicated to the stability of the price level, i.e. to the stability of the social power of the liquidity holders. And this social power is all the more intangible as resources, preferences, tastes and yields are fixed in the real sphere independently of the entry of money into the agents' utility function. Friedman starts from the Keynesian definition of money as an asset, but through the construction of his demand function he restores the general equivalent character of money: as a financial asset, money is a store of purchasing power and the stability of the demand function means the stability of the privileges of the holders of the various financial assets that make up their wealth (Friedman, 1992: 23). In a sense, Friedman articulates money more closely than Keynes via the dynamics of economic relations, because for him money defined as a general medium of exchange cannot be separated from the power it gives as a store of value. But no more than his quantitativist predecessors, Friedman does not deduce the function of the store of value from the nature of money itself. Under this function, money defines a patrimonial asset that is distinguished from other assets for reasons that Friedman himself describes as arbitrary (Friedman, 1961: 93). And as soon as it comes about that only the function of medium of exchange defines money in its own right, the choice of this or that asset to "provide a provisional guarantee of general purchasing power" (Friedman, 1961: 92) for him becomes just as contingent as the existence of holders of social power of money: they should be considered as facts.

4.4 Note on institutionalism's monetary orthodoxy

The institutionalist theory of money differs from search models only in its attempt to overcome the dichotomy of the real and the monetary through the very process of selecting money among the various candidates. In the French institutionalism of Aglietta and Orléan (2002), for instance, value does not pre-exist money as it does in neoclassical theory, and as indeed it does in Marx's labour-value theory through his curious substantialist interpretation of abstract labour (Orléan, 2011: 29–30).[9] But value is equal to money and is based on "the intense attraction that money exerts on all minds". This is because, unlike the search models, the search process is not driven by the practical need to overcome the problem of the double coincidence of needs or to reduce transaction costs, but by the desire to hold liquid wealth. This desire is sometimes explained by a kind of mimetic rivalry between traders (Aglietta and Orléan, 1982), sometimes by the search for security in the face of market uncertainty (Aglietta and Orléan, 2002). But in all cases, money emerges from a spontaneous and haphazard process that is directly inspired by Hayek as "the common goal of everyone's relentless efforts" (Lordon and Orléan, 2006: 5). It is thus a subjective theory of value that owes more to Simmel than to Walras, with exchange resulting not from the utility of commodities but from the veneration of the wealth par excellence, namely money. Before being a means of facilitating exchange, money is the institution through which goods possess value provided that they are exchanged for it.

But as money, for Aglietta and Orléan, emerges from a process of search which itself goes through exchange (2002: 31), a quantitative relationship between the goods exchanged must be established before money appears, and this relationship is therefore a value relation. Moreover, the search for liquidity presupposes that the trader can acquire the liquid good in exchange for his own goods. And why would someone else give him liquidity, if not to satisfy a need quite different from the desire to possess liquidity? The search for liquidity at the origin of the institution of money presupposes the exchange of products as commodities and therefore the need to obtain through exchange the goods necessary to satisfy needs. And since all individuals are driven by the same desire to possess wealth, which has the property that it can be exchanged for any good, it is necessary to assume all the conditions governing the market society, in which all the traders' products of labour are exchanged for money, in other words, are presented as commodities. Orléan refuses to use the myth of barter to analyse and determine the nature and properties of money, but the hypothesis, even theoretical, of a developed market economy without money is not only contrary to his own presupposition that there is no market economy without money, but also deprives him of the possibility of determining the genesis and the nature of the relationship between traders that will subsequently lead them to frantically seek money and thus to objectify their social link in it. More generally, the conception of social relations that makes this genesis possible already presupposes the atomisation of society, the antagonism of individual interests, the struggle of all against all for wealth – in short, a vision of human relations that is bogged down in a view of society as it is at present. It is therefore not surprising that money should emerge from this frenetic and anxious quest for liquidity. All the conditions were there in advance. Like the 18th-century philosophers of the social contract, institutionalists, like search theorists, saturate their models with anthropological or psychological presuppositions whose characteristics are specific to the very form of social organisation whose institutions they are trying to analyse.[10]

Through this account of the genesis of money, Orléan aims to construct an economy of relations where the theories of value had only made an economy of magnitudes (Orléan, 2011: 22). But what determines the magnitude of values within this framework? He does mention the case where the value of money is not contested, where the unit of account is therefore considered stable and where price formation is essentially based on fundamentals (Orléan, 2011: 173). But we will have to go back to our old treatises on value-substance to get an idea of these fundamentals. For Orléan, money is necessary because it is the absolute desirability that determines the commensurability and exchangeability of goods. But insofar as he thus confuses the economic value of money with the value of the desire for money, exchange relations remain quantitatively indeterminate. The genesis of money is not even a genesis of money as a general form of value, but as a mere form of abstract wealth. Orléan does not want value without money, but it is a money with no fixed value that is generated by the universal desire for wealth for its own sake, and thus, as a consequence, a money without value. And in an article co-authored with a Spinozist-inspired economist, he goes so far as to relegate the problem of price formation, under which money functions as a unit of account and means of circulation, to the theory of competition. Although they assure us that it is "futile to try to think of price as the expression of a magnitude that would pre-exist it and of which it would only be the expression" (Lordon and Orléan, 2006: 26–27), Lordon and Orléan lose interest in the question of "the commodity form of conative power" at precisely the moment when, in order to "persevere in their commodity being" (2006: 12), the "wealth-candidates" ask: how much?

Notes

1 This homogeneity postulate is illustrated by an equilateral hyperbola-shaped money demand function.

2 When money has purchasing power, the problem of the vicious circle of value-utility applied to money arises, as stated by Helfferich (1927) and expressed in the fact that money has a utility which depends on its value.

3 He would eventually acknowledge in the preface to the second edition of his *Money, Interest, and Prices* (1989) that in his model money is simply assumed to exist and to perform the function of an exclusive medium of exchange.

4 Clower's famous constraint is stated as follows: "goods buy money, money buys goods but goods do not buy goods".

5 "The logic behind recent non-Walrasian models attempting to provide a rationale to a positively valued fiat money is shown to rely purely on exogenous *ad hoc* qualities attributed to money (qualities other goods do not have). Money is introduced to account for co-ordination failures foreign to the very nature of Walrasian equilibrium theory" (Bridel, 2002: 269).

6 Therefore, not all transactions are affected, but only the income of the period. However, unlike Marshall, since V is stable in the medium term, the relationship between money and the price level is not mediated by a demand for cash, so only M causes a change in P*y*.

7 Friedman distinguishes between money and credit by their respective prices and not by their mode of issue or their status and role in monetary circulation. Thus, the price of money is the inverse of the price level, while the price of credit is the interest rate. It is a cost–benefit logic, so the cost of holding money is the inflation rate, while the cost of credit is the interest rate. From the creditor's point of view, the benefit of money is its purchasing power and the benefit of credit is the interest rate.

8 In fact, Keynes basically emphasises the market's expectations of the appropriate level of interest rates. He believes that the market may not follow the intended consequences of monetary policy if it believes that they are inappropriate, given the economic circumstances influencing market conditions. For example, if the market believes that rates are too low relative to long-term expectations, then it will believe that these rates are unsafe and the liquidity preference will increase.

9 For Marx, each society is defined by a specific way of organising social labour and thus ensuring the participation of individuals in social consumption. In commodity production, the individual's labour becomes social labour (abstract labour) only through the mediation of the exchange of the labour products as commodities, or, what amounts to exactly the same thing, because social labour takes the form of commodity value. Abstract labour under these conditions forms the substance of value, but not in the manner of a material, technical or physiological reality incorporated into the product or commodity; rather, it is the act by which the individual reproduces himself by reproducing the social conditions of his existence, by which he thus participates in the reproduction of society. It is therefore a social substance and it is in this capacity that value is both revealed and created by exchange, as Rubin noted with embarrassment (1926–28: 759). It is revealed because the exchange precisely concerns the product of the individuals' productive activity, but it is created by exchange because the individual's labour gets its property of social labour only through the mediation of the exchange of her labour's product against the product of the others' labour. In the neoclassical theory, utility represents value only in relation to the needs of the individual; in Marx, labour represents value only in relation to the others' labour; in the first case, it is the use which establishes the market value of a good; in the second case, it is the relation in which it is exchanged for the others' labour. In the first case, it is the natural substance that determines its value; in the second case, it is the social substance.

10 This anthropological-institutional doublet leads to Aglietta and Orléan attributing to traders of the pre-money era the psychology and reasoning of the great merchant who has in mind only the exchange value for himself, and to which he sacrifices even his essential needs. Thus, with the desire for money firmly implanted in his body, individual A will prefer to postpone the exchange with B, who is nevertheless in possession of the good he desires, in order to exchange directly with an owner of goods deemed more liquid (Aglietta and Orléan, 2002: 73).

5

MONEY-FLOW AND MONEY-STOCK IN POST-KEYNESIAN THEORY

5.1 The slopes of the debate between structuralists and horizontalists

In terms of financial practice, Kaldor objects to Keynes that safe short-term securities have replaced money as liquid assets in the markets. Therefore, an increase in the liquidity preference of speculators does not translate into an increase in the demand for money but rather into the purchase of safe and liquid securities against less liquid ones (Sardoni, 2017: 214). More fundamentally, according to Kaldor, liquidity does not distinguish money from other assets, except in degree. For to compare money and securities in terms of liquidity is to regard money as a security as well as securities as quasi-money. As Hicks says, one is thus reasoning in a circle, since liquidity results precisely from the fact that money is money, i.e. it is the form of general exchangeability (Hicks, 1989, p. 42). But from the fact that liquidity refers to the exchangeability form of money, he deduced that the store of value function does not belong to money itself, i.e. that it does not define money, because he sees a contradiction with the liquidity function of money. This is because Hicks does not define money as a general equivalent, i.e. also as a general form of value. If he had defined it as the sole representative of the value of all goods, then the store of value function would have seemed to him to be indissolubly linked to its function of exchangeability. But since, sticking to the characteristics of the system of unconvertible credit money, he defines money as an instrument of debt, he derives the monetary character of money solely from its function as a unit of account (Hicks, 1989: 104). Thus, money is distinguished from all other assets by the fact that, as the medium of the unit of account, it is the most liquid asset (running asset). But in normal times, money assets serve only the transaction purpose, the reserve value function being performed by short-term securities (reserve assets). This is

DOI: 10.4324/9780429261299-8

why, like Kaldor, Hicks distinguishes the demand for money from the demand for reserves, so that the liquidity preference is motivated only by transaction or precautionary needs. What distinguishes safe securities from money is therefore only that they cannot be used as a means of payment but must first be converted into money itself (cash, deposits) before serving this purpose (Kaldor, 1960: 63). We have seen that money is specific in that as a measure of value or unit of account it is the instrument in which all other assets are valued. Therefore, in his equations on money and assets, Kaldor prefers to express the liquidity premium as the inverse of the risk premium, money being not so much the most liquid asset as the asset that is entirely risk free: its price does not change in terms of itself; there is therefore no uncertainty as to the future price of money; and above all, as a general medium of exchange, it is always and everywhere exchangeable.

From this approach, Kaldor derives a whole theory of interest intended to demonstrate that the interest rate of money determines the interest rate of all other assets and thus the rate of profit of productive capital (Kaldor, 1960: 70–71). But what is important here is that this interest rate does not designate the price of giving up liquidity, following a financial logic of portfolio choice, but rather the commodity yield, which defines money not as a financial asset but, insofar as it is a unit of account and a medium of exchange, as a form of general exchangeability.[1]

By assuming the money supply as a given in the *General Theory*, Keynes, it is true, seems to contradict his complex analysis of the role of banks developed in the *Treatise*, where the money supply depended on the variable conditions of industrial and financial circulation. And we shall see that, insofar as it is based on this exogenous supply, the liquidity preference theory does not fit well with the theory of endogenous money. But from the point of view of the role of money in the economic process, there is a profound continuity between the two works. Or rather, the *General Theory* draws all the consequences of the role that Keynes gives to money in the *Treatise*. This continuity has been all the more obscured since the *Treatise* is remembered for Keynes's chartalist lineage, which defines money as a unit of account decided by the state power (Keynes, 1930: 4). And no doubt Keynes needed Knapp in order to rid himself of the commodity conception of money. But it was not chartalism that inspired his new conception of money in the *Treatise*, but the Cambridge quantity equation, of which he had already proposed his own version in the *Tract*. We have seen that the novelty of the Cambridge equation compared to the quantitativists is that it no longer defines money only as a medium of exchange, but as the object of a demand for cash. And we have seen how the *Treatise* draws the implications of this conception, by separating the demand for money for industrial needs, which is a demand for credit, from the demand for money for financial investments, which is a demand for liquid assets. The whole theory of the liquidity preference draws its source from this financial conception of money by making the motive of speculation the mainspring of the demand for money. Thus, the *General Theory* systematises the division made in the *Treatise* between money as a general medium of exchange and money as a store of value. But the theory of liquidity preference, which replaces the excess bearish factor of the *Treatise* (Bibow, 2000b: 551), also endorses another conclusion of the *Treatise*: the conventional nature of the interest rate.

By freeing investment spending from the constraints of savings, Keynes had at the same time left the interest rate in a vacuum, for if investment is not limited by the level of savings, which is on the contrary determined by it, by what is it limited? Keynes answers: by the desire to hold wealth in liquid form rather than in the form of productive resources or illiquid securities. And this desire is expressed in the interest rate, which equates the attractiveness of holding liquidity with the attractiveness of holding securities (Keynes, 1936: 167). The analysis of the *Treatise* has shown us the conventional nature of the interest rate. In reality, the deep ambiguity of the interest rate in Keynes stems from the fact that it is both a conventional and a monetary phenomenon: as a convention, the interest rate is subject to the interplay of power relations between the different social classes which determines the orientation of monetary policy. But as a monetary phenomenon, the interest rate refers to the uncertain nature of the monetary economy of production against which money serves as a shelter. It is from this ambiguity that the debate between horizontalists and structuralists on the determination of the interest rate was born (Pollin, 1991). Both currents agree that money creation is endogenous to the demand for credit. The question which sets them in opposition is whether the money supply is perfectly elastic to the interest rate as set by the Central Bank, or whether the interest rate increases with the increase in the demand for money because of the limited availability of reserves provided by the Central Bank. For the former, the interest rate is exogenous, for the latter, it is endogenous, but this disagreement actually leads to two different understandings of the interest rate: for the horizontalists, it is the conventional nature of the interest rate that justifies the power of the Central Bank to set the short-term interest rate. But what the structuralists oppose is precisely the monetary character of the interest rate, according to which it is determined by the agents' liquidity preference (Pollin, 1991: 369–70). And these different conceptions lead, in turn, to the different conceptions of the banks which are the source of their debate: for the horizontalists, the bank is an institution issuing means of payment at a given rate of interest, while the structuralists see it as a financial institution where money represents only one element in the management of its liabilities, thus contributing to making the interest rate an endogenous variable of the markets.[2]

In this sense, horizontalism prefers to talk about animal spirits rather than liquidity preference to describe the behaviour of banks (Lavoie, 1996: 292). But doesn't it amount to the same thing to say that banks have weak animal spirits and that the preference for liquidity is high? It is only a difference in emphasis that distinguishes these two expressions, one referring to the product, sales and aggregates, the other to asset prices and interest rates (*Ibidem*). But these different emphases express deeply different visions of the role of banks: in the first case, the bank fulfils a function of lending money to enterprises; in the second case, it has a function as an operator on the financial markets. This is where the misunderstanding comes from: for the horizontalists, commercial banking is part of a banking system whose function is to meet the investment needs of companies, so that from this point of view, the activity of a commercial bank hardly differs from that of the central bank. This is why they like to recall Keynes's remark that there is no limit to bank credit as long as the banks are moving forward "in step" (Bibow, 2000b; Rossi, 2005). For the structuralists, the bank does not escape competition on the markets and in this sense functions like a joint-stock company whose liquidity constraints are imposed through its loans/equity ratio and therefore depend on the liquidity preference of the markets themselves (Pilkington, 2014).

This is not to say that horizontalists ignore the role of uncertainty in the lending policy of banks, but it is initially manifested only through the volume of credit that it grants to borrowers on the basis of the interest rate set by the central bank. In other words, uncertainty no longer determines interest rates (Rochon, 2001: 48). Since they assume that the demand for money comes mainly from productive enterprises, horizontalists ignore the impact of banking practice on financial markets and thus on securities prices and the interest rate. The role of banks in financial stability can be expressed by the fact that, in situations of increased market uncertainty, banks agree to increase their balance sheets by buying stocks and bonds. In this case, the money supply has indeed increased but without any direct impact on the real economy (Jespersen, 2009: 30). Conversely, by ignoring the effect of the markets themselves on bank behaviour and thus on the bank interest rate (Palley, 2008: 13), they wrongly assume that the short-term rate of interest determines the whole term structure of interest rates (Smithin, 2007: 284; Bibow, 2007: 340).

5.2 The problem of the long-term interest rate control by the central bank

Once the banks' liquidity preference is accepted, the question is what effect it has on monetary policy. Certainly, as the provider of ultimate liquidity, the central bank acts directly on the behaviour of banks through the key interest rate (the Fed's federal funds rate, the ECB's overnight rates). But for Keynes, the essential problem was to influence the behaviour of the banks themselves in order to influence the long-term interest rate, on which the term structure of interest rates mainly depends (Bibow, 2000a: 796). Moreover, it is on the long-term interest rate that the incentive for enterprises to invest depends (de Boyer, 1998). Kahn has shown that open-market operations involve an increase in the number of securities held by banks in order to lower the interest rate (Kahn, 1958: 146–47). However, this support from banks is by no means a foregone conclusion. Like non-bank operators, banks are not forced to follow the trend desired by the monetary authorities.

Like them, the profit motive (Keynes, 1930 320) determines their arbitrages on securities if the central bank seeks to lower rates. However, since the interest rate is a conventional variable based on expectations, a host of factors outside the control of the central bank influence market expectations, regardless of the level of credibility of the monetary authorities.

> Because market expectations play such an important role in the response of long-term rates to monetary policy, however, the connection between policy actions and long-term rates is likely to be more variable than suggested by the standard view of the monetary transmission mechanism.
>
> *(Roley and Sellon, 1995: 85–86)*

It is well known that one of the conditions that led to the 2008 crisis was the Fed's ineffectiveness in raising long-term interest rates, which Fed Governor Greenspan described as a "conundrum". In reality, however, it was from the end of the 1980s onwards that the gradual loss of monetary policy control over long-term interest rates (Cömert, 2012) can be observed, which was essentially due to the growth of the financial markets, in relation to which the effects of the Fed's action were weakening. It is true, however, that between 1957 and 1995 the interest rate on 10-year Treasury bills followed the evolution of the federal funds rate (Mehra, 1996). But this correlation was mainly due to the fact that "the bond rate automatically moves with trend inflation (the Fisher relation) and the Federal Reserve (Fed) keeps the level of funds rate in line with the going trend rate of inflation (the long-run Fed reaction function)" (Mehar, 1996: 28). As soon as inflation was under control and, above all, monetary policy was able to anchor inflation expectations, the link between the Fed rate and long rates loosened (Thornton, 2012: 8). This is because even when monetary policy persists in a particular stance and gains market confidence, market perceptions change over the business cycle, so that the variability in the relationship between movements in long rates and monetary policy reflects other developments in the financial and non-financial determinants of those rates (Akhtar, 1995). Nevertheless, Lavoie (1996) argues that markets cannot play against the central bank indefinitely and that a deviation of market rates from the base rate would only be temporary. Similarly, long rates cannot deviate from short rates forever, because if they were much higher than the base rate, for example, the markets would borrow short-term to lend long-term, which would lower the yield on long-term securities (Lavoie, 1996: 295). Lavoie here neglects the pressure that the increase in short-term borrowing would exert on the credit market and thus on the base rate of the Central Bank. But his horizontalist vision precludes imagining this consequence, and to neutralise it in advance he takes refuge behind Keynes and his critique of Wicksell's natural rate of interest (*Ibidem*). For Keynes, it is not the rate of interest that conforms to the so-called equilibrium rate of profit, but, on the contrary, given that there is a multitude of equilibrium rates of interest, it is the rate of profit that aligns itself with the rate of interest as determined in the financial sphere. But since there is no natural rate of interest and therefore the rate of interest can lock the rate of profit in an underemployment equilibrium, it does not follow that the conventional long-term interest rate is aligned with the short-term rate. While Keynes only freed the theory of the interest rate from the so-called real variables of Classical theory, Lavoie turns it into a financial law according to which in the long run the short-term interest rate always determines the long-term rate.

We have already highlighted how structuralists argue for liability management in contrast to the horizontalist view of money supply.[3] But the liquidity preference of banks in the markets is manifested mainly through asset management, which thus counteracts the monetary policy stance (Bibow, 2007: 336).[4] For monetary policy to come up against a liquidity trap, it is sufficient for banks, which follow the state of the market, merely to anticipate a rise in rates. And such a trap can occur at any interest rate level (Bibow, 1998: 242–43), i.e. as soon as the selling pressure of security holders fully compensates for the upward pressure on prices caused by the open-market operation. This selling pressure occurs as soon as the markets, for whatever reason, become convinced that the central bank will not be able to lower market rates further. Then, the central bank comes up against the banks' liquidity preference and the liquidity it provides them with is immediately solidified in the form of reserves (Bibow, 2000b: 557).

Will it nevertheless be said that, since short-term rates are under the control of the central bank, the latter determines the borrowing conditions of enterprises, taking into account the banks' liquidity preference? Indeed, it is through the control of the federal funds rate that the Fed acts on all other short-term rates through banks arbitrating between certificates of deposit, Treasury bills, etc. Yet, Moore, the most resolute defender of horizontalism, acknowledges that, as far as the discount rate is concerned, "the Fed sets it with some delay, which means that it follows the rise or fall of the market rate".

> The reason, [Moore argues], is the Fed's reluctance to acknowledge its power to set the level of short-term interest rates. As a governmental body not emanating from a popular vote, it has no legitimate authority to set short-term interest rates; paradoxically, it has legitimate authority to set the growth rate of monetary aggregates, which it is unable to exercise. This paradox explains why it tries to hide its power to set short-term interest rates.
>
> *(Moore, 2003: 47)*

Why, then, should the Fed be unabashed about its power to set the federal funds rate and embarrassed about the discount rate? The reason why the Fed lags behind market rates is precisely because it does not have the power to control the market rate, even through the federal funds rate. Post-Keynesian horizontalist theory is adamant that, although money is endogenous, the interest rate remains a discretionary instrument of the central bank. Earlier, however, Moore stated that the level of the interest rate "depends only on the response of the central bank" to market forces. This then leads him to claim that the Fed "is acting in very bad faith when it claims only to follow market rates that would be determined by other factors (such as the phase of the cycle, inflation expectations, or the size of the federal deficit, etc.)" (Moore, 2003: 47–48). Why would it not be in bad faith to state that it does not control the supply of money, which depends on other factors determining the demand for money? Moore claims that the argument for the federal funds rate is the degree of reserve constraint it imposes on the system (p. 48). But why should the discount rate, on which banks' reserves are directly dependent, not be formally conditioned on this degree of constraint? Moore himself admits that the interest rates under the control of the central bank are not completely exogenous when he states: "the federal funds rate is predetermined within a small range, ordinarily within fifty or sixty basis points. It is not directly set by the Fed" (Moore, 1988: 124). And to reduce the scope of this statement by adding that these rates are not determined by market forces, because the market actually anticipates the behaviour of the central bank, does not mitigate the fact that these rates depend on the supply of and demand for reserves (Eichner, 1987) and that in the dynamics of this relationship, the behaviour of the central bank, as taken into account by the market, is itself a market force.

Very early on, horizontalists tried to integrate the objections of structuralists for whom the preference for liquidity necessarily implies an upward curve in the money supply. Lavoie concedes the existence of such an ascending curve, but only if it is interpreted as a succession of ever higher horizontal curves (1996: 280), eventually adopting the most orthodox assumptions about liquidity preference in his Cohesive Stock Flow (CSF) models (Godley and Lavoie, 2007). But a few years later Moore returned to the defence of horizontalism by stating that the money supply "can be viewed as horizontal over the market period", which extends between two Federal Open Market Committee meetings – i.e. about a month! (Moore, 2001: 14). Later, Lavoie will also give in on the banks' liquidity preference, which he would henceforth express as the spread between the base rate and the rates charged by commercial banks. No doubt the supply curve remains horizontal, as a change in the liquidity preference only entails a change in the level of the supply curve (Howells, 2007: 157). But with this ultimate retreat, the exogenous nature of the base interest rate becomes an empty abstraction that Moore himself admits is empirically unprovable, so much so that the central bank sets its rates according to movements in market rates (Moore, 2001: 15). Moreover, the expanded use of repos at the expense of open-market operations not only weakens the link between the base rate and bank rates but also determines the market interest rate on the basis of the all-agents' liquidity preference, including banks (Chick and Dow, 2002: 602–5).

5.3 The nature of money in the post-Keynesian theory

For horizontalists, the liquidity preference claimed by structuralists restores the loanable funds theory by reintroducing scarcity into the money supply. However, the debate does not concern the supply of money but rather the supply of credit, which, for structuralists, is assimilated to a financial investment without being considered as a concomitant creation of bank money as a means of payment. For horizontalists, who consider lending to enterprises as the banking activity par excellence, the preference for liquidity is manifested only in the conditions of credit supply: interest rates on loans, tightening of solvency criteria, increase in the reserve/lending ratio. But as long as horizontalism focuses banking activity on lending to enterprises, and thus on the corresponding means of payment supply (deposits), its supply curve remains horizontal, with any change in the liquidity preference resulting in a change in the level of the curve (Lavoie, 1996). Thus, each of the dimensions of the interest rate, one promoted by the horizontalists, the other by the structuralists, presupposes a specific conception of money: as a means of payment on the one hand, as a store of value on the other (Sardoni, 2017).

Thus, when post-Keynesians of all trends state that money is endogenous to demand, it is not the same money that is demanded by horizontalists and structuralists. For the former, and more generally for the circuit theorists, where the bank essentially fulfils a function of lending to enterprises, the demand for credit is a demand for availability for investment expenditure. Structuralists do not ignore lending to firms, but we have seen how bank credit is confused with the assets between which the bank arbitrates and remains dependent on its liquidity preference. For horizontalists, therefore, there is no demand for money for its own sake. Deposits created in the course of credit demand only serve to pay the factors necessary for production – that is, essentially wages – which, in turn, use them to purchase consumer goods and services. Depositors may decide to save part of their incomes, but either they convert their deposits into financial securities, in which case the means of payment flows back to the firms to be returned to the banks as repayment of their loan (final finance); or they are kept in liquid form and constitute a block in the circuit (Parguez, 2003: 165–66), which only perpetuates the cross-debt relationships between banks, firms and households, because "it is clear that from the point of view of the economy as a whole, money does not represent wealth" (Realfonzo, 2007: 109–10). But this blockage is presented as an anomaly of the system, and money is distinguished from credit precisely by the fact that theoretically there can be no demand for it: "demand for credit is always positive even though production is constant, but the demand for money can be nil: households may choose to hold all of their saving as financial saving, or have no saving whatsoever" (Rochon, 2001: 56). Thus, money is only justified by the existence of wage-labour and, more generally, of commodity circulation (Parguez, 2003).

But what gives the deposit the monetary quality that makes it a general means of payment and a potential store of value for wage earners? For if money defines nothing more than a promise of payment, i.e. a debt instrument, each credit buyer would in principle be able to appropriate without equivalent a sum of value: "[i]f a simple promise of payment could perform the role of final payment, buyers would be endowed with a seigniorage privilege, namely with a right of withdrawing goods from the market without giving anything in exchange" (Graziani, 2003: 60). Now, on the basis of credit relations, this means of final settlement can only come from two instances: either an institution whose promise to pay is accepted by all because of the guarantees it offers to the holders of the debt instruments issued, or an authority whose power of constraint encourages economic agents to hold and seek out the debt instruments issued by this institution. In other words, either the bank or the State. It is in this sense that, in the chartalist theory, decreeing a unit of account is not enough; it is also necessary that the State itself determines the material supports of this unit of account which will be considered as final means of settlement and thus sought for themselves by the agents. Thus, Smithin recognises the need for the final means of settlement to combine the functions of unit of account and means of payment, but he sees it as a mere logical prerequisite for the running of the monetary production (Smithin, 2000: 6). Similarly, Rossi sees it as a means of maintaining stability and promoting the efficiency of the financial system, which, in turn, improves resource allocation, supports growth and increases social welfare (Rossi, 2005: 143). For in credit relationships, the means of circulation function can be fulfilled by any form of promise of payment issued in exchange for goods and services in circulation. "The conflation of bank credit with deposits follows from a desire to concentrate on the medium-of-exchange or purchasing-power attribute and to play down the store-of-value or wealth function" (Chick and Dow, 2013: 6–7). But only money as a general equivalent can fulfil the function of a means of final settlement of a purchased good or service. It is only the fact that bank deposits belong to the payment system and are therefore de jure convertible into the ultimate means of payment, i.e. into the monetary base, that gives them their quality as means of payment. This monetary quality comes from its place in the hierarchical structure of the payment system and is not immanent to the creation of credit money. All the confusion between money and credit in the circuit theory that the horizontalist approach claims (Graziani, 2003) stems from the hybrid status of the deposit, which is both private bank money and a general means of payment – and therefore a potential store of value at the source of the credit block. In post-Keynesian theory in general, the need for money as a general equivalent is only functional: it is required by the necessary unification of the payment system by the central bank and makes possible the control of monetary policy, in particular by the exogenous setting of the interest rate. With the end of the gold standard, private banking monies are jointly settled by the inconvertible central bank money which, as a general equivalent, organises the solvency of the banking system (de Brunhoff, 1979: 67).

In post-Keynesian theory, the necessity of money is a de facto necessity: it is because wage-labour exists as a relation of monetary production and commodity circulation as monetary circulation, in a word, it is because the monetary economy of production exists that money arises from the credit relation and it is only through credit that money is integrated into production. This is why the entire monetary constraint is deferred to the banking relationship, because once the bank agrees to advance means of payment, these pre-validate future production and only fulfil the means of circulation function. Hence the resistance of circuitists to admitting a demand for money for its own sake – for why should it be demanded if firms only ask for money to produce and sell and workers to buy the goods necessary for their consumption? Even the banks' liquidity preference is only reflected by the horizontalists and circuitists in more restrictive solvency criteria, not in the search for more liquid assets. With the liquidity preference, money presents itself as a store of value, and we shall see immediately that the embarrassment of post-Keynesians faced with the need to reconcile endogenous money and the liquidity preference stems from the fact that it is not the same money that is presupposed in both cases. In turn, the difficulty in articulating the functions of means of exchange and store of value stems from the fact that they give rise to money from credit, i.e. from a relationship in which the means of circulating debt and the means of settling it are confused.

5.4 The historical genesis of endogenous money

This confusion undoubtedly stems from the nature of the banking system itself, and insofar as the entire history of banking is presented as the history of the means by which banks increase their capacity to provide credit (Dow, 1997: 48), these means are also those by which money becomes confused with credit. In the history of this confusion, two stages were decisive: the first, which occurs early in banking practice, is when, as a result of the integration of banks into a unified payment system, deposits are used as means of payment (Chick, 1986). But it is when banks are no longer constrained by a given volume of their reserves that money creation becomes entirely endogenous to credit. From that moment on, the monetary system is entirely based on credit money, the supply of which depends on the issuing institution. This is the meaning of Wicksell's "pure credit economy" wherein the interest rate becomes the instrument – if not the only one, then at least the main one – by means of which to regulate the money supply.[5] It is then that the Central Bank, in order to maintain confidence in the banking system, assumes its role of lender of last resort. For on this new basis the banks were no longer content to respond passively to the demand for credit from non-banking agents; they developed an active management of their balance sheets through competition for deposits and speculation on the wholesale market, the Eurodollar market (Wojnilower, 1980). Thus, the endogenous character of money results not from the demand for credit by non-banks but from the supply by banks (Keynes, 1930: 174) as determined by trade-offs between the categories of assets and liabilities available on the different markets.

With an integrated and centralised payment system, on the one hand, the means of circulation as deposits merge with the means of payment, and, on the other hand, bank credit, guaranteed by the reserves of the central bank, merges with money. Then bank money presents itself as a general equivalent:

> It is the general acceptability of bank deposits, gained through years of the evolutionary development of banking, that allows banks to guarantee

> to pay their clients' bills, in effect substituting their name for that of their clients, without anyone refusing to accept either checks on empty accounts, honored by the banks under overdraft agreements, or the deposits that result when these checks clear.
>
> *(Chick and Dow, 2013: 7)*

We will see later how MMT draws absurd consequences from this transformation, but we can already appreciate the attempts of its representatives (Wray, 1990: 58) to show us that money has always been confused with debt. According to this interpretation, banks began to issue short-term liabilities that would have circulated in connection with loans to finance circulating capital expenditures. Gradually, these banknotes would have been used to pay wages and even consumer goods, until they were finally accepted as means of payment in their own right. Thus, money would have originated in bank debt. Yet the whole history of the bill of exchange, which forms the basis of the credit system and the initial object of banking activity, shows that the wider circulation of banknotes was only possible in exchange for the guarantee that these notes, unlike bills of exchange, were at all times convertible into cash (de Roover, 1953). Wray criticises orthodoxy for reversing the order of events and so claiming that banks would have first attracted savings from depositors and then extended credit to borrowers. However, this order would imply that the public had already entered into the banking habit, which would imply, in turn, that it had experienced the short-term commitments of banks. But why would the public accept these short-term commitments in exchange for a loan requested from the banks? Presumably because of the banks' ability to extend credit. If borrowers agree to make use of banknotes, cheques, etc., it can only be for two reasons: (1) because these notes, etc., circulate between account holders at the issuing bank, so that their circulation is identified with simple account-to-account transfers held by the same bank; or (2) because these means of circulation enjoy a good reputation among the sellers of the goods purchased by the borrower. Without a unified payments system, this good reputation can only be based on the ability of the issuing bank to redeem these notes for cash. In both cases, these means of circulation presuppose the existence of money separate from them and only possess this quality because they rely entirely on their convertibility into it.

5.5 Keynes and the aporia of the endogenous money theory

But the source of the confusion between money and credit is deeper, and lies in the very project of a theory of endogenous money that Palley calls a pillar of post-Keynesianism (2008). Let us return to the general formula of capital, M–C–M′, which Keynes takes from Marx to define the monetary economy of production and distinguish it from the barter economy of the Classics. It is true that money appears as the concern and goal of capitalist production. But in this formula, as interpreted by Keynes, money does not arise from the circulation of money as it does in the long version of the formula: M–C...P...C′–M′, but from a credit relationship between the banker and the entrepreneur. In its full form, the formula of capital not only expresses the presence of money as a condition and goal of capitalist production, but also illustrates the necessity for the commodity to be converted into money for the capital–money cycle to succeed. In other words, it illustrates the fact that the buying and selling of commodities are separate acts whose unity conditions the completion of the capital cycle. But for Keynes the demand for money does not derive its condition of possibility from the fact that the value of the commodity must necessarily be embodied in money as a separate thing representing the general form of value. For Keynes, the whole monetary constraint is the credit relationship in which the borrowing interest rate expresses the investors' liquidity preference. Hence the debate between horizontalists and structuralists on the banks' liquidity preference and the way it is expressed. But this also explains the persistence of the debate on the money supply curve, insofar as each of these curves is based on one of the two money modes of being that Keynes had initially separated: the form of general exchangeability on which the whole horizontalist vision of the demand for money is based, and the general form of value which conditions the theory of preference for liquidity. Indeed, from a horizontalist point of view, how can we explain that the supply and demand of money may not be equal, given that the supply of money is entirely endogenous to the demand, according to the adage: credits make deposits and deposits make reserves (Deleidi, 2020)? But conversely, how can the endogeneity of money be maintained if the interest rate is determined by the liquidity preference, i.e. by the demand for money as a store of value? Horizontalists are right to believe that they are more consistent with the principles of endogenous money by assuming a perfectly elastic supply curve at a given interest rate. But structuralists are right to oppose them by saying that endogenous money does not prevent reserve constraints and credit risks from affecting the interest rate and thus the money supply conditions (Wray, 1992: 1160–61). This is because horizontalists see the money thus created simply as a flow of means of payment to finance productive expenditures by borrowers deemed creditworthy by the bank. Structuralists see money primarily as a reserve asset whose demand and supply depend on market risks and uncertainties (Palley, 2008: 6–7).

Here lies Keynes's dichotomous background and his debt to Classical theory, which he tries to resolve by means of the liquidity preference. What Keynes seeks to underline through the general formula of capital is not so much the monetary constraint of capitalist production as the profound uncertainty of its destiny, given that in a monetary economy investment decisions are decentralised and based on anticipated demand. In this sense, the circuit theorists were right to point out, against the structuralists, that uncertainty does not explain the existence of money, since it would remain as a general medium of exchange even in a stationary equilibrium state (Parguez and Seccareccia, 2000: 117). Rather, the uncertainty would have the effect of paralysing the system of bank commitments that ensure the circulation of money. But they should have added that it is, on the contrary, money, as it arises from a decentralised system of production and distribution of resources, that explains the uncertainty.

However, what concerns Keynes in a fundamentally uncertain economy is precisely the demand anticipated by entrepreneurs, i.e. the incentive to invest. Because only this incentive can reduce the rentier-investors' liquidity preference (Keynes, 1936: 375). However, as Keynes does not see the function of the store of value as a result of the separation of the sale and purchase of goods in the movement of circulation, the demand for money for its own sake can only arise where it no longer fulfils the function of a medium of exchange, but where it is presented as a financial asset among other less liquid assets. Thus Keynes only considers the financial consequences of an increase in the demand for money, i.e. its effect on the interest rate. For Keynes, the impact on production of an increase in the demand for money is indirect; it is not related to the monetary character of production, but to the constraints of credit to production: it is as a financial asset that money affects production, through the effect that the demand for and supply of money produces on the interest rate. Hence the resistance of horizontalism to give in on the exogenous character of the interest rate, without which it would be left to the structural uncertainties of the market economy. To put it more simply, for Keynes, it is through the monetary character of the interest rate and not the monetary character of production that money affects the capital cycle.

It is nevertheless true, as we have seen, that the store of value function comes from the liquid character of money, and thus from its general exchangeability. But in the Keynesian tradition, the general exchangeability, in turn, does not come from circulation but from the unit of account function as it is posited by an authority external to circulation: the state. For Keynes indeed, the unit of account is the only function that conditions money both in its existence as a means of payment and as a liquid asset. But in this way money is out of circulation. As a means of payment, it puts an end to the circulation of debts; as a liquid asset, it is kept as a store of value. We will see in the next chapter the consequences of the view that money defines a unit of account issued by the state and which derives its binding force from its use for the payment of taxes: Modern Monetary Theory. But in the meantime we still have to draw some consequences from the circuitist conception that money is issued by banks exclusively for the financing of social production.

5.6 The problem of profits in the circuit theory

The problem of monetary profit in the circuit theory in general is of interest to us only insofar as it directly reveals the limit of a theory which conceives of bank money as Ricardo conceived of capital, i.e. as a creation ex nihilo, and which reduces the capitalist production relation to the monetary relation between banks, capitalists and wage earners. In other words, the limits of a theory which assumes that labour constitutes, at the macroeconomic level, the only factor of production, and therefore that bank credit constitutes the starting point of the process of capital valorisation. Let us recall the problem statement: how, if new production is entirely financed by bank credit, can firms recover, in the form of profits, a quantity of money greater than that advanced by the banks and thus not only repay their loans but pay interest on these loans (Seccareccia, 1996: 405–06)? Reduced to its purest expression: how can more money be recovered than was advanced by the banks if the money issued is exclusively the result of credits needed for firms' investment expenditures? "How does M become M'" (Rochon, 2009: 57)? Or, to bring us a little closer to the real nature of the problem at stake: how can we explain the existence of monetary profits if all the money issued is spent by firms on workers' wages (Febrero, 2008: 111)? If we start from the assumption most often adopted by circuitists that the bank finances production and not investment in investment goods, and that this financing is limited to the payment of wages, the profits of the consumer goods sector are easily explained – assuming that the profits are gross, i.e. including the value of production goods consumed and therefore to be replaced – since they come from the wages of the production goods sector which are thus converted into consumption goods produced beyond the goods needed for the workers' consumption of the latter sector (Robinson, 1956: 75). The proceeds of this sale will be spent on the purchase of investment goods representing the value of the necessary labour of that sector, i.e. the value representing the wages of that sector. But how are the profits of the investment goods sector realised? Several solutions have been suggested: the introduction of an external sector such as the state or exports (Parguez, 1981); the inclusion of profits in wages as Schmitt would have it, with profits resulting from the difference between the market price set by firms and the supply price (Nell, 1986); while a third solution would be to assume an overlap of particular money circuits, with the wages of some serving to realise the profits of others (Seccareccia, 1996). But except for Schmitt's solution, which presupposes what is being explained, namely the formation of profits (Gnos, 2003), these solutions either introduce an external agent to complete the circuit between banks, firms and employees (Cesaratto, 2017: 247), or take refuge in microeconomic subtleties that do not solve the macroeconomic problem of how more money can be created if it is assumed that only the money needed for production costs is advanced by banks? Thus, Lavoie (1987), for example, suggests a sequential model in which aggregate production is divided into sub-sectors between which purchases and sales of consumer and investment goods are decomposed. In this model, where each firm produced first without a means of production, the circuit is started by the firm producing consumer goods, then the firm producing investment goods for the consumer goods sector, and so on. But in the end there is always a sub-sector that is unable to buy production goods to start its own production. It was therefore necessary to assume the existence of a sub-sector where the purchase of investment goods would not be necessary and which would produce investment goods with its own goods (Nell, 2002).

Should we not at least assume that banks do not only finance production but also investment, i.e. the purchase of investment goods themselves (Seccareccia, 2003; Febrero, 2008)? Thus, the investment goods sector would have sold not only the equivalent of the wages of its sector to the consumer goods sector but also the investment goods necessary for the production of this sector. To this money should be added the money circulating within the investment goods sector, between the producers of the different investment goods. Provided that firms only gradually repay the money advanced by the banks for the purchase of production goods, they hold enough money to make their profits and pay the interest on their loans (Seccareccia, 2003; Rochon, 2005: 134–35). But even if we exclude this permissive condition, the banks, by financing the purchase of the firm's investment goods, have financed the profits of the investment goods sector and thus also the interest on the loans made by this sector (Rochon, 2009: 73).[6]

If we assume with some post-Keynesians that it is the bank itself which finances the profit and therefore the interest on its own credits (Parguez and Seccareccia, 2000), then the banking sector plays exactly the role of an agent external to capital which, for Rosa Luxemburg, explained the realisation of profit and therefore the incentive to capital accumulation. Now, through this new function, the bank can no longer define itself as a simple financial intermediary but, insofar as it is itself a source of demand external to industrial and commercial enterprises, it internalises its own exteriority, it folds the exterior into the interior by inserting it into the circuit of capital. In the same way, by this function, nothing distinguishes it from the State except this: the bank issues money in exchange for credit, while the State issues money in exchange for taxes; the acceptability of bank money rests on its credit, whereas that of State money rests on its force. But the mere prior existence of the banking institution, as the origin and starting point of the circulation of capital, but also as the necessary source of demand, shows us once again that capital always and necessarily arises from conditions outside its own process. Both the ability of the bank to issue generally acceptable means of circulation and its ability to appropriate a part of the product without any other equivalent than its own money presuppose the supply of money and means of production prior to capitalist production. (Thus, savings are by no means the residue of the system or the mere result of the process of capital circulation, as the post-Kenesians conceive it [Rochon, 2005: 130].) If one assumes that only wages are financed by banking credit, then the internal circulation of the investment goods sector can only take place by means of the credit that firms grant to each other. As Marx discovered when analysing the reproduction of capital, money plays here only a purely formal role of unit of account and "this would be conceptually identical to a situation in which firms undertake barter within their sector since they do not rely on any bank-created circulating medium to settle their accounts" (Seccareccia, 1996: 407).

The circuit theory systematically stumbles on the fact that it explains neither the formation and existence of the banks at the origin of the credits made to firms, nor the prior existence of means of production and a free labour force for the purchase of these credits. The problem of the formation of profit is nothing more than the technical expression of the deeper problem of the origin of money and capital.

5.7 The circuit theory or the quantum cancellation of money

Bank money is special in that it is a debt that is never paid, a promise of payment that is never fulfilled:

> Issued for the sole purpose of being taken back, the promise does not derive its force from the thing promised (which we would be unable to find today after the disappearance of the gold standard), but is pressed 'forward' on itself.
>
> *(Schmitt, 1975: 247)*

The entire work of Bernard Schmitt and his school is directed against the idea that the issuance of money by banks is an ex nihilo creation of a net asset existing alongside the wealth produced by social production. This would be an illusion that the vision of commodity money as a thing maintains among post-Keynesians despite all its attacks against the barter myth. Post-Keynesians have not taken the measure of the banking revolution that their circuit theory intends to account for and according to which money creation becomes a pure bookkeeping operation based on the principle of double-entry accounting. The banking principle, Keynes recalled in his Clearing Union project, consists simply in "the necessary equality of credits and debits" (Keynes, 1942: 171). According to this principle, the credit that a bank grants to a firm is both an asset of the bank vis-à-vis the firm and, insofar as the credit gives rise to the formation of deposits, an asset of the depositors vis-à-vis the bank (Cencini, 2003: 212). And yet this explanation is too sequential and justifies the Classical confusion in circuit theory between the credit granted by banks and the money that the credit operation creates in the form of deposits. However, as long as no payment is made, the bank has not created any money in the strict sense of the word, nor has it granted the slightest loan; bank credit remains a "vehicle without charge" (Rachline, 1982: 463) which only creates the condition of possibility of production, the only real object of the credit relationship. As a pure monetary virtuality, bank credit only becomes money through its purchasing power over production.

Now, the only exchange by which these units without value issued by banks get their existence as money is the exchange with the only factor creating new value, i.e. labour. This is because the payment of labour is the only one which does not require the expenditure of an already existing purchasing power, the payment of the factor at the origin of the new production immediately transforming the money into income. It is indeed through the payment of wages that money is associated with the product of labour and is transformed into new incomes. It is not therefore by issuing money in exchange for credit to firms that banks create the purchasing power of money, as the post-Keynesians imagine according to their formula "Credits make deposits and deposits make reserves". But the purchasing power of money comes into being as soon as the firm, through the bank, pays wages, because it is only "produced by the workers and measured by the remuneration of their activity" (Bradley, Piégay and Rossi, 2003: 237). Through the formation of incomes, the payment of wages alone monetises production by giving it a numerical form (Cencini, 2003: 215), while the product gives money its content (Cencini, 1995: 15). Through the work it commands, money envelops the product by giving it its measure and, by giving it a monetary value, gives itself a value. Firms do not spend any pre-existing purchasing power, since only production actually forms the purchasing power of money. And just as the purchase of the product by the workers realises this purchasing power, it is the consumption of the product that destroys it. Money is therefore invested with purchasing power by production and disinvested by consumption.

Born of monetary income, this identity of workers' income, which arises from monetary income, requires nevertheless the interposition of the bank between the firm and the workers: the firm went into debt to the bank in order to get on the labour market the production conditions for a product that it sold on the goods market; for their part, the workers too get on the labour market their own product in the form of a deposit. Thus, the worker has given in the form of the product what he has received in the form of wages, while the firm has given in the form of wages what it has given in the form of the product (Schmitt, 1984: 347). Now, this bilateral relationship translates at the bank level into a debt of the firm towards the bank which pays the wages on its behalf and into a debt of the workers towards the bank. The exchange between the firm and the workers is undoubtedly based on credit relations with the bank which is successively creditor of the firm and debtor of the workers. But we should not confuse the bank as a credit institution and this same bank as an issuer of money. And it is for confusing these two qualities that "classical" circuit theorists confuse money with credit. As an issuer of money, the bank is neither a creditor nor a debtor to the economy, since it is simultaneously debited and credited with the number of units of money it issues. By paying wages, the bank is instantly creditor to the firm and debtor to the worker for the amount of the units of wages it issues.

> Any 'circulation of money' is a figment of the imagination. Money, especially bank money, never circulates; each unit of money issued by a bank (secondary or central) returns instantaneously to its source, so that the only money movements that actually exist are 'circles'.
>
> *(Schmitt, 2003: 204)*

In this sense, the payment of wages represents only an asset-liability of the bank that never leaves its place of issuance (Rossi, 2007: 123–24).

Where money is issued by banks as a passive asset whose creation coincides with its destruction, income is produced by production and destroyed by consumption at two chronologically distinct moments of a circular flow coinciding with the acquisition and loss of purchasing power. But can we not acknowledge that between the payment of wages and the final purchase of consumer goods by workers, money does constitute a stock in the form of bank deposits? Not only does this stock not pre-exist the issuance of money by the bank, but since the deposit fills the period of time between the moment of payment of wages and the final purchase of goods, it is no longer money but income (Cencini, 2017: 9). Therefore, by virtue of the identity of income and product established above, the deposit constitutes nothing other than its product in the form of units of wages: it is a stock of product made necessary by the fact that the worker does not immediately consume her own product and that she lends it to the firm, which disposes of it materially until it is sold on the market. According to the principle of double-entry bookkeeping, these two moments of credit define the same quantum and last only for an instant: the monetary issue is simultaneously a loan from the depositors to the firms and an expenditure by the workers for the final purchase of goods and services. Bank deposits may remain between the two, notably in the form of financial securities, but money had already been extinguished in the flow-reflux of payments: "Stricto sensu, money comprises only units of account with which banks simultaneously debit and credit their accounts. It may in no way be identified with bank deposits, which are financial assets" (Gnos, 2006: 27).

This leads to an important consequence for the circuitist approach to money: money really exists only in the form of payment flows, never in the form of stocks (Cencini, 2003: 215). This is how the confusion between money and credit is avoided. According to Schmitt, post-Keynesians and classical circuitists confused money (income payment flows) with credit (deposits lent by income holders) because they wrongly assumed that banks create deposits which they lend to firms and which the latter transfer to workers. And this confusion is caused by the fact that credit itself has as its object the means of payment that the bank makes available to the borrower: the deposit would be both a claim of the depositor and the object of that same claim. But the deepest reason for this confusion is that post-Keynesians call money what is in reality the product deposited in the accounts of wage earners, as if this money could exist alongside the product stored in the firms (a confusion between claim and object of the claim). So they give both too much and too little to bank credit: too much because they imagine that the bank is capable of creating ex nihilo a monetary wealth capable of financing any expenditure; not enough because they still make this credit depend on the creation of bank deposits.

Yet, Schmitt readily admits that although money is a dimensionless number, the instantaneous circle it describes nevertheless implies a production time that transforms inputs into output. Production is indeed a process that extends over time. But since the circle can only be defined by the instantaneous identity of the product of the "factors" (at the input) and of this same product (at the output), production time is, through the monetary issue, "quantised", concentrated in a single instant (Schmitt, 1984: 40). Since only labour creates the product and only money makes the heterogeneous products of labour commensurable, the payment of wages and production are, from an economic point of view, one and the same instantaneous operation that quantifies the continuous production time into a finite and indivisible unit of time. It is in this sense that the theory of the money circuit is a quantum theory of emissions rather than a mechanical theory of circulation.

Thus, the numerical form that money gives to production expresses production time, the time of work done by direct producers in exchange for the payment of wages. This is how Schmitt finds the labour-value behind the pure number, since labour-time is the only content of a number that relates the labour factor (in the form of wage units) to the product of labour. If money transforms input and output into homogeneous quantities, the labour factor and the product of labour, it is by translating wages and the product into labour-time expressed in monetary units. Schmitt uses money like Smith uses wheat: he makes it the common unit of measurement for labour and the product of labour. In the same way that Smith reduced labour to a quantity of wheat necessary for the maintenance of the worker, Schmitt reduces the labour factor to a sum of units of purchasing power on the production of wage goods. And for both, profit arises from the difference between the number of monetary units paid to the employee and the number of monetary units measuring the value of the labour product. This is how Schmitt returns to the theory of commanded labour-value from the point of view of value. By instantaneously homogenising the whole space of production and circulation of capital in dimensionless monetary units, the circuit theory in general reduces the capital–labour relation to a pure distributional relation of the real product mediated by money. The circuit theory calls for a theory of endogenous money which makes production prevail over exchange, which breaks with the primacy of exchange proper to theories of exogenous money, but by confusing value with money, by reducing units of value to units of money, it reduces the production of value to the exchange of monetary values, it confuses the production relation with the distribution relation mediated by the creation and circulation of money.

Thus the real asset of banks, the object of their credit, is the product of firms, just as the means of payment and store of value (the savings of depositors) functions do not mobilise any object created by banks but only the goods produced in the economy. From this point of view, money is well integrated into the economy since the payment of income and the consequent formation of savings are not related to two distinct objects, monetary assets on the one hand and goods on the other, but to a single real object, the goods that wage earners receive in the form of money units and save in the form of bank deposits (Bailly and Gnos, 2003: 255). Production gives substance to money and money gives form to production, so that the real object of exchange is the unity of form and substance that constitutes the product. Since mere units of account cannot interfere with real transactions, except by measuring them, it must be concluded that wage earners are only really paid by means of their own product. "Output is exchanged against itself via an absolute exchange defining its deposit into money" (Schmitt, 2012b: 37). And this is the nature of the exchange relation between capital and labour, which is nothing other than an exchange of dead labour, materialised in the monetary wage representing the value of wage goods, and the living labour creating these same goods. Thus, in a system of credit money, money represents only the purely numerical form of the product, the real object of payment. Basically, there is only one real object in a system of endogenous money, the product of labour, and one cannot even say that the means of payment and store of value functions are functions fulfilled by money. Money reveals itself through the interplay of relations between the bank, the firm and the wage earner, to be what for circuit theory it has always been: a pure unit of account serving to homogenise the products of capital and to circulate promises of payment in a money that does not exist (Schmitt, 1975: 248; Cencini, 1995: 17–21). By the very way he manages to integrate money into the economy, Schmitt demonstrates the failure of circuit theory in general to give credit money a status different from the status of money in neoclassical theory. For all currents agree at least on the fundamental characteristic of credit money, namely that the payment of factors of production with money borrowed from banks "constitutes a mere advance on the receipts from the sale of the goods produced" (Bailly and Gnos, 2003: 250). As soon as entrepreneurs finance the purchase of the production factors by the sale of the goods produced, "payment in money would constitute only a transitory stage, the true or final payment being made in the goods produced" (p. 250). And if the production process were an instantaneous operation, firms would pay their workers directly with their product, assuming that they produce the very object of their consumption (Gnos, 2007). The whole financial relationship between the bank, the firm and the worker derives exclusively from the fact that the firm must ask the worker to give it credit for the time it takes to sell its product on the market:

> Monetary payments, which banks may effectively make by means of units of account because the object of the monetary transaction is nothing other than the real goods produced, ratify the firms' commitment to deliver goods to their workers later on.
>
> *(Gnos, 2007: 94)*

Through the diversions of credit, money finally fulfils only classical functions justified by the very reasons that flowed from the neoclassical barter fable: "the homogeneity and convertibility of bank monies allow the development of a complex network of transactions allowing every worker and his dependants to buy whichever goods best meet their needs, regardless of the particular goods the worker actually produced" (Gnos, 2007: 94–95). The Schmittians reproach the classical circuitists for having confused money and credit, the flow of units issued by banks and the stock of deposits of wage earners and firms, but they eliminate the confusion by abolishing the monetary object itself, dissolving it into the numerical form of the product and income. They thus substitute a "production theory of money" for Keynes's "monetary theory of production" (Chick, 2000): "The monetary issue is in fact an issue of information" (p. 238) and "the national output, which is initially formed 'in money', is simultaneously transformed into real income, 'in kind'" (Schmitt, 2012a: 85). The only object of payment is the product expressed in units of money: as soon as these units are recorded in the assets of the depositors, the income is immediately converted into the product.

Notes

1 This convenience yield depends on the ratio of the quantity of money in circulation to the volume of monetary payments. It can therefore fall to zero above a certain stock of money: this is the case with inflation. This quantity depends, in turn, on the interest rate that the central bank wants to achieve, so that the money supply forms an endogenous variable determined by the demand for credit and therefore incidentally by the rate targeted by the central bank. Thus, the interest rate depends on the relationship between the supply of money and the demand for money, but the supply of money depends indirectly on the rate set by the central bank. But how could the money supply exceed the volume of money payments if it is endogenous?

2 Structuralists are so trapped in the financial vision of banks that they exclude a priori the use of the discount window (borrowed reserves) to compensate for the limitation of non-borrowed reserves caused by open-market operations (Pollin, 1991: 373).

3 On liability management, it is never clear whether structuralists mean strategies of increasing reserves or, on the contrary, decreasing them. This ambiguity is not accidental and stems from the fact that for structuralists, the search for liquid funds by banks aims at optimising their assets. In an unpublished paper, Rafferty (2009) rightly observed that even when liability management increases the funds available to banks, these funds are used less to build up reserves than to expand banks' assets.

4 Thus, Smithin points out that the preference for liquidity of banks, which manifests itself through their liability management, is contradictory to the principle of endogenous money according to which credit is always available (2007: 283–84). On the one hand, Smithin confuses the availability of credit for banks with their willingness to grant credit to third parties (banks or firms), and, on the other hand, the endogenous character of money is entirely independent of the banks' liquidity preference as manifested by their operations on the securities markets.

5 This is the empirical basis of the horizontalist theory of the interest rate, according to which the interest rate becomes a political variable whose level is determined by the balance of power between the different classes in society (Parguez, 1999). It is worth noting here the proximity of Wicksell's theory of the pure credit economy to the horizontalist theory: in both cases, it is a theory of endogenous money in which the money supply is perfectly elastic to the interest rate as controlled by the central bank. It is true that in Wicksell's case, the monetary interest rate must be aligned with the natural interest rate, which is determined by real variables. But for him, as for the horizontalists, monetary policy is able, through the interest rate, to aim at full employment of resources. Finally, it should be noted that after having directly controlled the quantity of money supplied, the Fed returned to the interest rate as an instrument for controlling monetary growth in 1981 (Howells, 2007: 54).

6 They also finance, as before, the part of the profits of the consumer goods sector corresponding to the wages of the producer goods sector.

6

THE UTOPIAN IMPERIALISM OF MODERN MONETARY THEORY

6.1 Historical context and theoretical framework

After Keynes, Modern Monetary Theory (MMT) returns to chartalism by defining money as a debt issued by a sovereign state whose character as a general means of payment lies in the obligation to pay taxes by means of this money itself (Wray, 2000). Insofar as this definition shares a certain number of characteristics with that developed by the theory of the circuit, we may take the opportunity to examine the relationship that MMT has with this theory by showing how they agree on a *political theory of value* as opposed to economic theories of value. But before addressing the first point, a word is needed on the historical context and the theoretical framework of MMT. The end of the gold exchange standard and the reinforced hegemony of the dollar from the 1980s onwards led to the return of the concept of money as a debt issued by a sovereign state, whose character as a general means of payment lies in the obligation to pay taxes with the money itself. On the theoretical level, Keynes had given the impetus to this conception by refuting the theory of loanable funds, which made investment, and therefore the credit granted by banks to firms, depend on savings previously accumulated and deposited in the banks (Keynes, 1936; Bertocco, 2013). Thanks to bank credit, Keynes objected to the classical theory, it is investment expenditure that, on the contrary, determines the level of savings, understood as the difference between the income created by investment and the consumption expenditure of the holders of this income. On the basis of this principle, money is presented as a debt issue that is fundamentally endogenous to economic activity and hence this reverses the traditional causality between credit and savings. As the post-Keynesians have made their credo, loans make deposits, deposits make reserves and the demand for money induces the supply of money (Lavoie, 2014). But the experience of the US' "deficits without tears" has pushed monetary heterodoxy to be bolder.

DOI: 10.4324/9780429261299-9

Since modern bank credit relies on a fiat money payment system that is entirely free of its metallic base, why impose artificial liquidity constraints on banks if the government, whose legal tender is money, can issue unlimited money, since it is assured that its debt will be financed by taxation and that it satisfies the desire of private agents for cash? Thus, MMT has resurrected Knapp's old chartalist theory according to which, since money is a creature of the law, only the state determines, by fixing the unit of account and describing its material support, the "valuableness as one" of money (Ellis, 1934: 15).[1] But above all, since the State has always intervened to regulate the units of measurement, to coin the precious metal and to guarantee their weight and fineness, neo-chartalism, like most monetary theories since the formation of modern States, has confused the value-measuring function of money as it arises from trade with the unit of account as it results from the State's fixing of the price standard. Now these two functions must be distinguished, even in a regime of inconvertible state money.

6.2 The confusion between value-measurement measure and unit of account

In its first function, money has a variable value like any other commodity and there is no need to go back over the history of precious metals and the differences between the market price and the official price of gold and silver to illustrate this aspect. It is enough to observe the continual variation of exchange rates to be convinced that the variability of the value of currencies has never prevented them from fulfilling their monetary functions. But even if we disregard the foreign exchange market, the exchange value of money considered as a simple unit of account varies constantly with the value of all goods whose price is expressed in this unit. As Marx says, "Gold is a measure of values because its value is variable; it is the standard of prices because it has been established as an invariable unit of weight" (Marx, 1859: 309). Ingham claims to prove the historical validity of the nominalist approach to money by quoting Keynes who, in the *Treatise*, declared that

> it was not necessary for the talents and shekels to be minted as coin for them to be money. Rather, the state need only define what weight and fineness of silver would constitute a payment expressed in the money of account of talents or shekels.
>
> *(Keynes, 1930: 51)*

But what does this prove, except that the shekel and the talent as units of account each represented a certain quantity of silver metal? Prices were indeed expressed in shekels and talents, but their magnitude was determined by their exchange value, which was represented in a certain quantity of precious metal broken down into shekels and talents. And what mattered for transactions was the amount of metal contained in the talent or shekel, fixed by law, not the name of the account itself or the number of talents or shekels represented in the price. As units of account, the shekel or talent serve to express quantities of money, but it is money as a measure of value that determines the price of various goods. The law is necessary here because it is imperative that the same amount of fine silver used as a unit of measurement remain invariable, and thus that the shekel or talent always represent the same weight of metal. But this money can only serve as a measure of value because, like all the goods for which it is exchanged, its value can vary. Moreover, as soon as it comes to the exchange rate of money, i.e. the external value of money, chartalism abandons its principles and sticks to a strictly commodity conception of money:

> In open capitalist economies under a floating exchange regime, the attempt to manipulate a currency's external exchange rate is a more prevalent means of altering the domestic value (purchasing power) of money. This may be pursued by the central banks' buying and selling on the foreign exchange markets, or by base interest rate changes to attract or deter buyers of currency. In this regard, the value of money is affected by its status as a commodity, and, consequently, it can largely be explained in terms of supply and demand.
>
> *(Ingham, 2004a: 83)*

But where Knapp had confined himself to state the principle of a hierarchy of means of payment for an inconvertible money system, we will see in the next chapter how MMT pretends to discover the state origin of money in all periods of history. Whatever the role of the State in the birth and functioning of the market, it is immediately clear that, as the organised power of society, it must be based on the prior existence of equivalence relations. Even if we retain Weber's hypothesis that the origin of money lies in the wergild, the pricing of obligations or reparations already implies a system of equivalences that makes it possible to evaluate the nature and amount of compensation in the event of damage. But if one assumes that the market in which these equivalence relations arise does not pre-date the legally fixed unit of account, by what channel would state money enter into circulation?

Either the function of unit of account refers to a currency that is already circulating in society and fulfils its function of measuring values; or, if we make the MMT assumption that the currencies in circulation are instruments of debt, this unit represents an accounting unit that serves to record the claims and debts between the state and merchants or between the merchants themselves. In both cases, exchange values have been converted into prices that presuppose equivalence relations between heterogeneous goods. Or let's suppose that the state issues the monetary supports for the fixed unit of account. It would still have to create the monetary relationship through which to bring them in before recovering them through taxation. And this would not be enough, for since this money derives its character of legal representative from the obligation to pay taxes with it, it is still necessary to suppose that all those subject to the tax manage to obtain the quantity of monetary units required to honour their obligations, and thus participate in some way in the monetary circulation. Moreover, the determination of the amount of the tax presupposes a monetary evaluation of the wealth and income of the taxable members of society, and thus again the existence of market relations. If they were forced to enter into these relationships, they would determine the value of the unit of account, regardless of the amount of tax set by the state and the method of calculation of this amount (percentage, fixed amount, etc.). It is true, however, that one of the modalities of colonial domination was to impose by force the use of the means of circulation of the conquering nation, thus transforming the traditional economy of the colony into a market economy. But these practices already presupposed not only the existence of money but also the trade and banking institutions of the colonising country (Narsey, 2016).

The carelessness with which MMT treats the relationship between the state and the market stems from its definition of the nature of money. According to MMT, the social nature of money lies not in its function as a representative of social wealth, nor even in its function as a means of circulation, but in its function as a promise of payment that has arisen from a debt relationship: money is a "claim" or "credit" that is constituted by social relations that exist independently of the production and exchange of commodities (Ingham, 2004a: 12). MMT conceives any society as a multitude of personal obligations, of debt relations, of which market relations are only the generalised and systematic form. The idea is that, in order to appear, the market requires a universally accepted means of settling the debts contracted by individuals. But since the market itself cannot be at the origin of debt relations but rather presupposes them, only an authority that is both sovereign and external to the market can impose a debt instrument as the final means of settlement. Hence the role of the State in setting a unit of account and in choosing the material medium representing this unit in transactions. The confusion that this conception causes between debt and money, or what is the same thing, between money and credit, comes from the fact that money is defined both as an instrument of debt and, as a general means of payment, as a means of settling debts. Ingham states:

> Money is a 'promise' to pay – in other words, a 'social' relationship. Over the centuries, money has taken a multitude of forms determined by the state of technology: clay tablets, coins, paper, writing sets, plastic cards, electronic messages. However, all these forms of money, including precious metals, only really became money when they were expressed in relation to an abstract unit of account.
>
> *(2002: 143)*

However, even if the unit of account is to be distinguished from all forms of money in circulation as well as from all forms of credit, credit is distinguished from money by the fact that payment in money defines not a promise of repayment but the unwinding of a debt relationship. But Ingham, like all MMT magicians, confuses money with the promise of payment, because in contemporary societies there are two forms of debt that combine these opposite qualities. Either the State issues fiat money to finance its expenditures and decrees that this money will be accepted in payment of taxes: it then constitutes both a means of purchase (of expenditures) and a debt instrument, a promise of payment that is extinguished by the payment of taxes with itself. By issuing money, the state redeems its debts by accepting them as a means of payment of its claims. As one of the most fervent followers of MMT puts it, "money is a creature of the state and a tax credit for extinguishing this debt" (Tcherneva, 2007: 69). Or it is the bank that issues bills or cheques in exchange for the credit granted to the borrower with the promise to accept them in settlement of the debt thus contracted by the borrower. In these conditions, bank money is indeed a means of purchasing goods in circulation and a debt owed by the bank to itself.

6.3 The role of the confusion between money and credit in MMT

In both cases, the confusion between money and credit stems from the fact that government money and bank money both represent a debt on oneself issued on the occasion in exchange for a claim against one's debtor, a debt on oneself that a creditor issues in order to assign it to his debtor. "Contrary to usual financial assets, credit money is not supposed to constitute a claim to anything lent by the bearer and due to him: money and claims to money are supposedly one and the same thing" (Gnos, 2006: 25). Money is a debt with which the creditor pays his debtor. It thus forms both a means of payment between buyers and sellers of goods and a promise of payment which, unlike the bill of exchange, is drawn on the creditor himself, who undertakes to accept it in order to extinguish the debt of his debtor. This is why, as Parguez and Seccarecia point out, "it would be wrong to conceive holders of bank liability as bank creditors" (Parguez and Seccareccia, 2000: 105–6). And since in a banking economy all social production is financed by credit money and the payment system is based entirely on fiat money, all economic agents are involved in debt relationships between which IOUs circulate as means of payment, debt-monies. Victoria Chick notes that the mystery of modern banking lies in the fact that "expenditure against a bank credit agreement gives rise to deposits, which transforms a bilateral contract into a liquid, multilaterally accepted, asset" (Chick, 2000: 131). It is equally mysterious from this point of view that this credit relationship leads to the mere issuance of bank bills and that this gives rise to a multilateral monetary relationship. The deposit is in fact only a developed form of means of circulation issued by the bank. In reality, the real mystery of contemporary banking practice is not that a monetary relation is based on a credit relation but, as is also the case with the State, that the creditor assigns to his debtor a debt on himself. And this mystery, like Chick's, dissipates as soon as we understand that the bank and the State are the only economic agents whose debt holds for money.

Nevertheless, behind the apparent similarity of their forms (Lavoie, 2019: 100), the debt relations described by bank money and state money actually hide major differences in their role and functions in monetary circulation. Consider first bank credit money. A bank makes a loan to a firm and, in so doing, creates monetary facilities to carry out the firm's investment expenditures. These means of circulation cover deposits as well as cheques and banknotes. For simplicity, let us assume that the bank issues only banknotes. These notes, which form a debt owed by the bank to itself, circulate as a means of purchase between buyers and sellers of goods until, at the end of the loan period, they flow back to the creditor bank. From that moment onwards, the debt relation is undone: the firm has repaid its loan with the bills that the bank has advanced as a promise of payment. But what kind of payment? In a system of pure credit money, payment is made in units of account equal to the amount lent by the bank itself. As Schmitt and his followers have clearly shown, the debt relationship is here reduced to a pure game of bookkeeping entries between the bank and itself, mediated by a currency fulfilling a simple circulatory function. Here, money regains its role of "great wheel of circulation" that Smith had assigned to it. It is in this sense that Schmitt's circuit theory forms the very essence of any demand-based approach to endogenous money. For in reality, the entire operation is reduced to a distribution of the product among the various parties involved in the debt relationship (Schmitt, 1982). Money is not demanded for its own sake, either by the firm, for which it is only a debt repayable in itself, or by the bank, for which it is only a debt issued against itself.

Let us now turn to the State's money. Here, it is the State itself that, by hypothesis, issues its own banknotes through the intermediary of the central bank, in order to finance its own expenditures. Unlike the bank, therefore, the state does not lend the money it creates directly, but instead buys goods and services from the producers themselves. The latter, in turn, use it to make purchases among themselves and thus to make their investments as well as to satisfy their consumption needs. These banknotes therefore function here as a means of circulation. But they were issued with the promise of being accepted in payment of taxes. Here again, therefore, money is only demanded for its own sake in order to pay taxes. But for the State, it ensues from the money flowing back that it finances its expenditures without equivalent. There is a demand for money by the state because it is thanks to the money it creates that its needs are satisfied (unlike the firm, which satisfies its needs only by borrowing). The State directly creates the purchasing power on the appropriate goods without equivalent; moreover, it creates the market itself – if by hypothesis it creates all the money in circulation.

In the case of bank debt, money is advanced as a means of financing, as money-capital; in the case of state debt, money is spent as a means of purchase, as anticipated income; in the first case, the bank merely interposes itself between the firm and the worker (the employee) and takes in the form of interest a part of the product realised by the worker without an equivalent; in the second case, the state confronts society as a whole and directly appropriates part of the social product. In the first case, money is issued as credit money before flowing back as a means of payment; in the second case, it is advanced as a general equivalent before flowing back as a means of settlement. For sure, in both cases, money is issued on the basis of a prior debt relationship (bank loan on the one hand, tax obligation on the other). But in the first case, the bank issues a debt on itself that it transfers to its debtor; in the second case, the State issues a claim directly on its debtor. It is in this sense that, in a fiat money payment system, the general-equivalent character of money results from taxation:

> A dollar of money is a dollar, not because of the material of which it is made, but because of the dollar of tax which is imposed to redeem it. In other words, what 'stands behind' the state's currency is the tax system, and the state's obligation to accept its currency in tax payment. There is sovereign power behind state money – the power to impose fees, fines, tithes, or, ultimately, taxes.
>
> *(Wray, 2010: 44–45. See also Heinsohn and Steiger, 2000: 92)*

What places state money at the top of the payment system, then, is that the state resorts only to itself to repay itself:

> To settle debts, all economic agents except one, the state, are always required to deliver a third party's IOU, or something outside the credit–debt relationship. Since only the sovereign can deliver its own IOU to settle debts, its promise sits at the top of the pyramid. The only thing the state is 'liable for' is to accept its own IOU at public pay offices.
>
> *(Wray, 2003: 146 n. 9)*

But MMT, which focuses solely on the debt-form, confuses bank debt with state debt and, in so doing, transforms the banking system purely into a transmission mechanism for state expenditure and tax collection:

> In modern economies, the banking system operates as an agent of government, as almost all government payments and tax receipts flow through banks. In a floating rate regime, the government that issues the currency spends by crediting bank accounts. Tax payments result in debits to bank accounts. Deficit spending by government takes the form of net credits to bank accounts.
>
> *(Wray, 2006: 277)*

It could be said that MMT simply systematises the practice of the central bank, which also consists of issuing general-equivalent debt-money. But, as the Bank of the Banks, it must precisely limit itself to converting the private money of commercial banks into the ultimate means of payment, and the whole debate about its function as lender of last resort concerns the boundary between the creation of money without equivalent and the creation of money that ensures the unity of a payments system that is not initiated by the central bank.

Yet for MMT, the separation of monetary and fiscal functions and the formal independence of the central bank from the Treasury are denied in practice by the various mechanisms through which money creation is akin to the financing of government spending (Tymoigne, 2014: 657) and which they observe at different periods in the history of the Fed and the Treasury (Wray, 2014a). From there, it would only be a step to the actual consolidation of their status and functions. Lavoie (2013a) rightly noted that with consolidation, the debt relationship between the Treasury and the central bank would be transformed into a mere internal transaction. In fact, all appearance of exchange would disappear since the issuance of central bank money would no longer be distinguished from government spending through money creation: the latter, which the central bank would carry out on behalf of the government, would be equivalent to issuing zero-coupon government bills, and only the obligation to pay taxes in central bank money would distinguish these bills from government debt securities. With consolidation, the financial system would fulfil an exclusively functional role, at the service of the public policies of the issuing state: "Functional finance can be implemented in any country in which the government provides the domestic currency" (Wray, 2003: 145). Thus, the issuance of Treasury bills would no longer constitute a loan intended to finance government expenditures, but a means of regulating the interest rate by absorbing the excess reserves created by the government itself: it would no longer be an instrument of fiscal policy, but of monetary policy (Wray, 2007: 8). Conversely, monetary policy would be transformed into fiscal policy: the state would become the main employer (Mosler, 1997; Mitchell, 1998) and the general equivalence of its currency would no longer derive solely from the obligation to pay taxes into it, but from the fact that all social labour would be directly paid by it (Tcherneva, 2007: 82; Kregel, 2019: 93). As Skidelsky has rightly noted, the state would here simply issue "receipts (tokens of liability) for goods it commandeers. Coins (with the head of the ruler on them) are stamped tokens of state debt" (Skidelsky, 2018: 25–26).

Under these conditions and against all the lessons of history, unemployment would be interpreted as a lack of means of payment issued by the state:

> 'unemployment' is in a certain sense created by government. From the point of view of households, unemployment is evidence of someone wanting but not being able to obtain the currency. Recall that the tax that creates demand for the currency immediately creates unemployment. The population is required to fulfill a nonreciprocal obligation with currency it does not have. The source of that currency is the government. Thus, the private sector provides real goods and services (labor) to the government in exchange for that currency. The tax creates a demand for government-issued money by creating unemployment in that currency (that is, labor which seeks remuneration). It is therefore incumbent on the monopoly issuer to provide its currency in a manner that is consistent with the objectives of full employment and price stability.
>
> *(Tcherneva, 2016: 21)*

Furthermore, as the employer of last resort, the state would itself set the price of labour power (Tcherneva, 2007: 82). Thus, consolidation would transform the state itself into the sole owner of the means of production and the Central bank into a planning agency for social production.

6.4 The political theory of value versus the economic theory of value

Compared to the circuit theory, the chartalism of MMT restores to the monetary system its hierarchical character, but it does so by providing monetary policy with the conditions for its greatest possible influence on economic activity. For MMT, as for the circuit theory, money is fundamentally credit money, a debt instrument, but among these instruments state money enjoys a special status that places it at the top of the pyramid of the payments system. The circuit theory confined itself to placing the central bank at the top of the pyramid of the payments system and the central bank money as the ultimate means of payment. The merit of MMT is that it clarified the conditions for issuing this general equivalent and, more generally, the relationship between the State and the central bank. Not only does the state set the legal unit of account in which all debt instruments are denominated, but the currency issued by the state is the only one that is universally accepted because it is the means of tax settlement (Lavoie, 2019: 97). But in reality, MMT simply draws radical conclusions from what money has always been for post-Keynesian theory, namely a social relationship of indebtedness based on state power, and in which this power is embodied by the central bank (Parguez and Seccareccia, 2000: 105–6; Forstater, 2006: 230). And from this point of view, we note how Wray became progressively closer to the post-Keynesian horizontalist current, after having begun to defend a structuralist approach to the money supply and the interest rate. What Wray now shares with post-Keynesian horizontalism, despite the structuralist inspiration of his beginnings, is not so much the endogenous character of the money supply as the exogenous character of the interest rate (Wray, 2006: 271), as well as the perfect elasticity of the supply of reserves from the central bank at this interest rate (Wray, 2006: 273): it is this presupposition that authorises him to substitute the Treasury for the central bank in the supply of reserves to private banks. But it is also by virtue of this conception that money becomes the stake of a political balance of power rather than the expression of production relations (Tcherneva, 2018: 238).

> Control over the monetary instruments and the monetary institutions which operate them, becomes one of the main 'contested terrains' in the struggle for political control and supremacy in the society. In the contemporary era of electronic money, these points should be even more clear than formerly.
>
> *(Smithin, 2000: 6)*

Since, according to this theory, money enters circulation without value and that value of money can only be derived from the value of the goods and services for which it is exchanged, the setting of a price standard or unit of account is presented as a discretionary operation, and the only institution for which discretion characterises the very essence of its actions and decisions is the sovereign authority (Ingham, 2004a: 49). Thus, money in MMT is separated from the market twice: not only has money not arisen from market relations, but there is no money without the state. This is why, in the absence of a theory of economic value, MMT – but this is also true of theories of endogenous money with exogenous interest rate – has developed a political theory of value according to which the price of money and goods results from the conflict between the only social classes recognised by this theory, namely debtors and creditors, issuing institutions and economic agents considered as a heterogeneous whole, but whose elements relate univocally to these institutions, which are the State and the banking system. This conflict finds its privileged expression in the interest rate set by the central bank:

> the most structurally fundamental struggle in capitalism is not that between productive capital and labor, but rather between debtor (producers and consumers goods) and creditor (producers and controllers of money) classes and centers on two rates of interest – the long and the short. [...] Rates of interest represent benchmarks, or terms of reference, for 'settlements' between conflicting groups. The central banks are the main mediators of these struggles, and all the recent changes in their organization and operation express the resurgence of money-capitalist creditor power.
>
> *(Ingham, 2004a: 150)*

In the same way, according to this conception, all the contradictions between the State and the banks themselves, or rather between the State and financial capital, and which stem from the fact that there are debt relations between them, are eliminated in favour of the quasi-fusion of the State and the banks.

6.5 The liquidity preference in MMT

We noted above that, in neo-chartalism, the demand for money was motivated only by the obligation to pay taxes. This means that this demand only arises when the government has made its expenditures and the money spent has not yet been returned to it by taxpayers. This deficit therefore takes the form of claims on the government, which differ from holding Treasury bills only in that these liquid claims do not earn interest:

> Governments issue money to buy what they need; they tax to generate a demand for that money; and then they accept the money in payment of the tax. If a deficit results, that simply indicates that the population

> wishes to hoard some of the money. The deficit is of no consequence to the government; it merely allows the population to save in the form of government money. If the government wants to, it can let the population trade the money for interest-earning government bonds, but the government never needs to borrow its own money from the public. Taxes and bonds, therefore, have nothing to do with financing a government's spending. They necessarily follow spending rather than precede it.
>
> *(Wray, 2000: 62)*

But why would the government seek to substitute one debt for another by paying interest if it is said that it does not need to borrow to finance its spending? Here is Wray's answer:

> the purpose of government bond sales is not to borrow reserves – a liability of the government – but is instead designed to offer an interest-earning alternative to undesired non-interest-earning bank reserves that would otherwise drive the Fed funds' (overnight) rate toward zero.
>
> *(Wray, 2004: 257–58)*

Thus the government issues government debt in order not to drive the interest rate to zero. "Bond sales are not really a borrowing operation but are instead an interest rate maintenance operation" (Wray, 2004: 258). But why would the state not let the interest rate continue to fall if MMT proclaims full employment as the primary mission of the issuing state and the zero interest rate as the preferred instrument of its policy?

> There may well be economic or political reasons for keeping the overnight rate above zero (which means the interest rate paid on securities will also be above zero). But it is incorrect to argue that the size of a sovereign government deficit affects the interest rate paid on securities. Not understanding this, treasuries sometimes try to 'play the yield curve,' issuing longer maturities when interest rates are low on them, or reversing course and issuing short maturities when the yield curve is steep. While it is perhaps true that market forces of 'supply and demand' enter into maturity spreads, if treasuries understood that the purpose of bond sales is to drain excess reserves so that the central bank can hit its overnight interest rate target, they would not issue long maturity debt at all. Indeed, paying interest on reserves is an adequate substitute for treasury debt issue – as the overnight rate cannot fall below the interest rate on reserves.
>
> *(Wray, 2007: 9)*

The sale of Treasury bills is therefore not intended to borrow but to help the central bank in its interest rate policy. It is an instrument of monetary policy and not of fiscal policy. And Wray goes so far as to claim that it is because Treasuries do not understand that Treasury bills are an instrument for draining excess money reserves or, on the contrary, for injecting money into circulation, that they imagine they can influence long-term market rates. The government would be better off paying interest directly on reserves rather than issuing Treasury bills. But why doesn't it do so?

Whenever he is forced to be consistent with himself, Wray backs off by invoking political forces to explain either that the interest rate cannot fall below a certain level, or that Treasuries are deluding themselves about the real function of their debt. He evades the consequences of his model because without a positive interest rate, money would no longer be demanded for its own sake and would only fulfil its basic functions as a medium of exchange and a means of settling taxes, and would follow a circuit that would only differ from the banking circuit in that the state would be the final purchaser of the products of social labour and the sole creator of society's net wealth (Wray, 2011: 7).

Wray had already cleared the theoretical way for this evasion because for him the demand for money, which is a demand for credit money for spending purposes, is distinct from the liquidity preference that his structuralism retains within a model that excludes it in principle. Indeed, the liquidity preference is not a demand for money (Dow, 1997: 51) but a demand for liquid assets determined by portfolio choices. Even when he states the constraints on the supply of money by banks (risk perception, reserve requirements, etc.), he limits the impact to the interest rate, since with a higher rate, reserves that had previously been hoarded would enter the credit market. However, he admits that the motive of finance, as long as it is a request for cash, has practically no influence on the interest rate in the current conditions of the banking and financial system where the funds remain in their accounts, not to mention methods such as overdraft facilities that do not require any cash advance.

In a sense, MMT draws the consequences of Keynes's own confusions: on the one hand, he does not separate the demand for money from liquidity preference; on the other hand, he conceives of money for speculative purposes as a financial asset distinct from money fulfilling its classical functions. But while for Keynes the speculation motive expresses a form of contradiction immanent to the monetary economy of production, that is, the contradiction between the holders of liquidity and the entrepreneurs (between the owners and the managers of capital) and which manifests itself in the gap between the interest rate and the marginal efficiency of capital, for Wray and in MMT the preference for liquidity is summed up in regulatory constraints, in maturity spreads, in portfolio choices between assets that differ from each other only in their maturities and their returns. MMT criticises circuit theorists for neglecting uncertainty and therefore the liquidity preference, but it only includes it as a variable in an economic system that, because it is based on credit, is fundamentally forward-looking. Hence the possibility for the state, whose capacity to issue money is unlimited, to remove uncertainty by anchoring expectations with objectives of full employment, low interest rates and low inflation. MMT says that it is ready to achieve the euthanasia of the rentier that Keynes dreamed of, but by removing, with the same stroke of the pen as the banker's credit, all the obstacles that stand in the way of this achievement: the incentive to invest, the liquidity preference beyond a certain interest rate floor, etc. Under these conditions, the exogenous nature of the horizontal interest rate would be verified (Wray, 2007: 14). Although it makes debt relations the essence of economic relations in general, MMT evacuates the only debt relation that had fuelled Keynes's pessimism about the future of capitalism, namely the relation between holders of liquidity and entrepreneurs. Keynes had kept monetary and fiscal policies separate because, in his view, the interest rate did not merely indicate the level of credit scarcity, but expressed a social relationship of production that the state could not overcome by means of any monetary policy. Hence the necessity of a public works policy requiring the socialisation of the strategic means of production of society. But MMT wants to do less and more than Keynes: to preserve existing property relations while aligning interest rates below the marginal efficiency of capital. Since, for MMT, all economic relations are debt relations and all power relations are reduced to the power to incur debt, there are no longer any obstacles to merging monetary policy and fiscal policy, to making the central bank's money issue the sole manifestation of the state's fiscal policy. Since all these obstacles to the full use of resources are summed up in the desire of banks to lend and the incentive of entrepreneurs to invest, it is sufficient for the state, insofar as it possesses both an unlimited capacity to issue money and a sense of the general interest, to substitute itself for the private sector and to become, through the public deficit, the source of all the net wealth of society. In this way, surplus value would be transformed into a claim by society on the state (Wray, 2011: 7). The state would become not only the employer of last resort, but the sole employer of first resort. The prophets of MMT repeat: the only limits of a sovereign money society are the real existing resources such as technology, skills, population, etc. As MMT guru Stephanie Kelton brazenly claims, "If the deficit has to be 4.7 percent of GDP to create the economy we want, with full employment, low inflation, and poverty going down", who cares? "If we can create the economy we want with a deficit of 2.1 percent, that's fine too. The budget outcome isn't the thing that matters, it's the real economic conditions" (quoted in Epstein, 2020: 27). Thus, once the state has injected as much money as it needs to use all of these resources, money, the starting and ending point of the monetary economy of production, will be reduced to what it has always been in the eyes of MMT, i.e. a pure unit of account fixed by the sovereign authority. Then the financial system will be transformed into a functional tool à la Lerner intended to regulate the price level, stabilise the interest rate, etc.

6.6 The monetary imperialism of MMT

MMT has often been criticised for neglecting the international constraints that, in an economy open to the outside world, would weigh on its deficit policy through money creation, even under a flexible exchange rate regime: imported inflation, flight from money, etc. (Palley, 2019). Add to this the total lack of consideration of the effects of this policy on developing countries (Epstein, 2019: 6), and MMT reveals its profound monetary imperialism by attributing to the modern currency all the exorbitant privileges attached to the dollar: deficits indefinitely financed by international savings, indifference to depreciation or appreciation, the former stimulating trade and income from abroad, the latter facilitating foreign investment itself, etc. A close look at the nature of these different constraints shows us that they actually affect the dollar either in its relationship to other currencies or in its role as a reserve asset, i.e. the currency as a commodity. This is what Ingham admits with embarrassment when he observes that in its determination of external value, the commodity character of money regains its rights:

> In open capitalist economies under a floating exchange regime, the attempt to manipulate a currency's external exchange rate is a more prevalent means of altering the domestic value (purchasing power) of money. This may be pursued by the central banks' buying and selling on the foreign exchange markets, or by base interest rate changes to attract or deter buyers of currency. In this regard, the value of money is affected by its status as a commodity, and, consequently, it can largely be explained in terms of supply and demand.
>
> *(Ingham, 2004a: 83)*

Now, since the only social relation that MMT considers is the relation between debtor and creditor, the only market quality that it is supposed to attribute to money is the interest rate. And since it neutralises the binding force of this quality by positing the exogenous nature of the interest rate, the definition of money as a mere IOU allows MMT to evacuate any market constraint from the borders of its monetary zone and thus to found the possibility of an unlimited budget deficit, through the mere play of money issue and taxation (Wray, 2014a: 29). Contrary to Conally's statement to the cranky Europeans, the dollar is not MMT's currency but it is their problem. This is because on the foreign exchange market and in the savers' portfolios, money immediately presents itself as a general form of value and, in the case of the dollar, as the universal equivalent, in other words, as the equivalent of all commodities, including other currencies. The paradox of all theories of credit money is that, while they conceive of money directly in the form of money-capital, they interpret the supply of and demand for money, insofar as it is presented as credit money, i.e. as a supply of and demand for simple means of circulation.

Note

1 Valuableness is thus to be distinguished from its value.

7

NEITHER BARTER NOR CHARTALISM

7.1 The particular equivalent of beings and the general equivalent of things

The theory of debt-money is a new transhistoricism and a new determinism, behind the apparent infinite variety of monetary forms and experiences identified in history. For the corollary to defining money as an instrument of debt is to postulate the universality of the monetary fact. Money as a universal fact is the principle of the new monetary institutionalism (Servet, Théret and Yildirim, 2008: 175). Sometimes, this universalism is explained by the universality of fetishism: in paleo-currencies, money takes the form of persons, where the monetary market relationship transforms the relationship between persons into a relationship between things. But in both cases, money is "a relationship of collective faith between the members of a society and the representation of the whole of this society, which is itself the result of this trust" (Aglietta, 2007: 20). Sometimes, money is defined, through its universal functions as a unit of account and a means of payment, as a "totalisation operator unifying the system of debts" (Théret, 2007: 21). And the anthropological root of the formation of units of account by modern states is thought to be found in the infinite debt of human beings to divinities, which is posited to be at the origin of all debt relationships.

However, the universality of the monetary fact implies first of all that debt in primitive societies is a form of exchange, a means of exchange that would be proper to a society that relied basically on exchanges. We know that Mauss left open the question of whether debt is primary in relation to exchange or whether it is merely a mode of exchange (Mauss, 1990: 41–42). But suppose that it is only a mode of exchange (Mauss, 1990: 41–42). If exchange is the basis of all relations, then just as Deleuze and Guattari ask why the gift and counter-gift should not look like an exchange, why should debt itself not look like an exchange? (Deleuze

DOI: 10.4324/9780429261299-10

and Guattari, 1983: 185). The answer is because the primitive market proceeds by bargaining rather than by fixing an equivalent (Sahlins, 2017: 176–77). Institutionalism in this sense "does nothing more than hypostatize the principles of an exchangist psychology to account for institutions that on the other hand are recognized to be nonexchangist" (Deleuze and Guattari, 1983: 186). Moreover, the idea that paleo-currencies are primitive forms of equivalence postulates a kind of price equilibrium, commensurability or equality, against which inequalities or imbalances are measured. However, everything in the organisation of prestations and counter-prestations demonstrates, on the contrary, the existence of open systems in contradiction with the idea of trust associated with the closure of prestation (and counter-prestation) cycles. Institutionalism claims to be opposed to standard economics, but in reality, just like standard economics, it understands the conditions of social reproduction based on phenomena observed in the sphere of circulation.

But it is above all through the notion of debt itself that institutionalism actually universalises the money of state societies. If there is a monetary universality, say the institutionalists, then, in view of the historical variations in the role, uses and functions of money across societies, it can only be anthropological (Servet, Théret and Yildirim, 2008: 184). Thus, commercial exchange presupposes the existence of money, but money would find its origin in sacrificial payments, i.e. in debts generated not by horizontal exchanges governed by the principle of reciprocity, but by vertical "exchanges" between humans and supposedly sovereign powers. Thus, money would proceed from debt in relation to sovereignty and thus from a hierarchy of value (sovereign money): the obligation of the living being to redeem, during their lifetime, this vital power of which they have been made the depositary (Aglietta and Orléan, 1998: 21–22). But if taxes are only a measure of our debt to the society that created us, how can we explain that such an infinite life debt can be converted into money when money is the means of measuring and comparing the value of different things? How do we move from the infinite debt we owe to the gods to the finite debt we owe to our fellow human beings? In reality, infinite debt belongs essentially to state societies and belongs only to them. For while there are primitive societies without debts, there are hardly any states without money. But it is with money and the State, and with the circulation of money in State society, that debt becomes truly infinite.

> The infinite creditor and infinite credit have replaced the blocks of mobile and finite debts. There is always a monotheism on the horizon of despotism: the debt becomes a *debt of existence*, a debt of the existence of the subjects themselves. A time will come when the creditor has not yet lent while the debtor never quits.
>
> *(Deleuze and Guattari, 1983: 197)*

But this neocolonialism of anthropological thought does not just extrapolate to all monetary forms in history money's role as the exclusive social bond of labour in capitalist societies. To put it in other words, this extrapolation does not take place without a reversal, an inversion of values. Bloch and Parry have clearly shown the impasse of monetary ethnographies that attempt to understand social orders on the basis of the nature, role and functions of monies circulating in traditional societies (Parry and Bloch, 1989: 21). As long as economic relations in the broad sense remain intertwined with family, tribal, symbolic or religious relations, it is not money that contains within itself the relationship of individuals or groups to the social or cosmic totality; on the contrary, it is the consideration of this totality that assigns to money the particular meaning and role that it possesses within this totality.

But could we not at least acknowledge the universality of the debt as a life debt contracted by everyone with society? Even though there may be societies without currencies, could the debt of life not form the common denominator of societies where monies do circulate? But here too there is a break in the historical continuity between egalitarian societies and societies of power, which consists precisely in the reversal of their debt relationships. Clastres has made this break clear in Sahlins's analysis of the leader's obligation of generosity towards the members of his community (Clastres, 1980: 136–42). Here, the flow is not from the members of the society to the representatives of power, but on the contrary from the chief to the rest of the society, in exchange for the prestige he enjoys. In egalitarian societies, it is not society as a distinct entity that gives life to individuals in exchange for money; it is the living society of individuals that gives prestige to power in exchange for goods: it is power that works for society, not society for social power. And this direction of flow is the sign that we are dealing with a society in which power is folded into the homogeneous social body, in which the separation of power and society, the division between the dominant and the dominated, does not take place. Conversely, as soon as the social body is indebted to power or to the representative of the cosmic order, we are dealing with a society where power has separated from the rest of the social body: a society with a state. In this sense, sovereign money belongs only to modern societies: there is no universality of sovereign money. The money of the sovereign has not always been sovereign money.

It is true that institutionalists admit that market money breaks with the historical continuity and anthropological universality of money (Aglietta and Orléan, 1998: 15), but when we study primitive societies, it is not the separation of the economy from the rest of social relations that introduces the major differences, as Polanyi would have it, but the separation of power from the rest of society. Yet, pre-state societies reveal not only an inverted debt relationship in relation to power societies, but a disconnection of debt and money or of non-monetary debt relationships. As Testart says, credit logically and historically precedes money, and as long as money is not invented, the economy remains caught up in the interplay of personal relations (Testart, 2001: 48–49). And it cannot even be said that a pure credit system is necessarily more limited than a monetary credit system. Once again, this is a difference in nature, not in form. In egalitarian societies, debt is not a form of exchange; it is a unit of alliance (Deleuze and Guattari,

1983: 185). Furthermore, between the debt-money of traditional societies and the credit-money of capitalist societies, there are also differences that do not belong to the same history and are not subsumed under the universality of the monetary fact. Crump has set out the restrictive conditions for studying the monetary phenomenon:

> Two such restrictions prove to be essential for a consistent treatment of the phenomenology of money. The first is that a true money must of its nature be capable of circulating indefinitely among those who use it, and the second is that a true money has a distinctive identity as such, so that it has no significant use for non-monetary purposes.
>
> *(Crump, 1981: 3)*

It is clear that these conditions exclude all the so-called primitive currencies whose circulation between the parties involved in the exchange is not indefinite, but also whose uses are never strictly monetary. Thus, the difference between the market and the Wergild distinguishes money entirely from these primitive means of settlement, and even those who agree to include the Wergild in the great history of money recognise this:

> Wergild expressed two fundamental elements of social structure: the utilitarian and the moral evaluation of social roles and positions. The indemnity schemes of the wergild aimed to compensate for functional impairment, but also expressed society's normative order. The scale of fines and tariffs were related to both injuries and insults.
>
> *(Ingham, 2004b: 183)*

This intertwining of utilitarian and moral aspects in the use of primitive money prevents us from analysing the primitive function of means of payment as if it were first in the order of modern functions of money. For the supposed anteriority of the means of payment over the other functions of money just means that primitive money did not animate a market economy, but honoured services or compensated for damages. This is the function par excellence of non-market societies.

> Historically, Weber writes, the oldest function [of money] is that which makes it an imposed means of payment. At this stage, money is a currency without the capacity for exchange; this is a property that is made possible by the fact that an economy that ignores exchange nevertheless experiences economy-to-economy services, which are not based on exchange but nevertheless require a means of payment: tributes, chieftain's gifts, the price of girls to be married, dowries, wergeld, fines, sanctions: so many payment situations that must be honoured with typical means of payment.
>
> *(Weber, 1950: 236)*[1]

These monies represent means of payment for the reparation of a damage or an offence, for a woman, for some debt, but in no case means of exchange of goods or services exchanged as commodities. Moreover, when money exists as a unit of account and as a means of payment, it is most often embodied in different objects, mainly because the specific nature of the payments to be made required different currencies.

> In this stage of development, money in the unitary sense of today is not to be thought of; rather in each economic zone different sorts of services rendered correspond to specific sorts of goods which mediate the payment function, so that different species of money exist side by side. For example, never and nowhere could a man buy a wife for shells, but only for cattle, while in small transactions the shells were accepted because they were available in small denominations. Money which develops in this way in connection with intra-group payments we call internal money.
>
> *(Weber, 1950: 237)*

The fact that in most cases different currencies according to the type of service coexist in a particular sphere of exchange would be enough to clearly distinguish primitive monies or paleo-monies from the money of merchant societies, whose essential characteristic is to represent a general equivalent to the different goods in circulation. But what distinguishes paleo-monies more radically is that, in each of these spheres, they relate not to goods but to people. As Testart puts it, "The particularity of all the goods purchased by primitive money is that they are goods associated with the person" (Testart, 2001: 41; see also Weber, 1950: 237). In primitive societies, money as a means of payment does not concern the settlement of debts on goods but on persons. It is a particular equivalent of beings.

Yet does not the dissociation between money as a unit of account and the variety of currencies in circulation observed in many ancient or primitive societies at least prove that money is an instrument of credit resulting from debt relationships expressed in units of account? It is on this premise that Graeber has traced 5,000 years of the history of debt and for which he provides illustrations taken up by the inspirers of Modern Monetary Theory. Thus, he refers to Mitchell Innes, who reports that Newfoundland fishermen

> sold their catch to the traders at the market price in pounds, shillings and pence, and obtained in return a credit on their books, with which they paid for their supplies. Balances due by the traders were paid for by drafts on England or France.
>
> *(Quoted in Graeber, 2011: 38)*

Now these balances occur at the end of all buying and selling operations and function as credits on the fishermen's account with the European banks. Similarly, the example of the nails with which the workers paid their bills at the local pub (*Ibidem*) shows that these nails were distributed by their employers and functioned as a means of circulation replacing the official currency. What Graeber describes is not the creation of credit relations immanent to monetary relations, but the dissociation between money as a unit of account and money as a means of exchange or circulation. In these examples, individuals are not improvising credit systems in view of the scarcity of money (Graeber, 2011: 38), but rather creating alternative means of circulation to commodity money that served as a measure of value and a price standard. Graeber seeks at all costs to encompass the most rudimentary exchange relationships within the concept of debt, which he sees in barter.

He sees barter as "a kind of accidental byproduct of the use of coinage or paper money" (Graeber, 2011: 40). Thus for Graeber, there is no money without credit and no barter without money, but assuming that barter presupposes money, this proves nothing other than that the primary monetary function is to measure the values of the things exchanged and thus to represent a commodity-standard. In fact, the examples Graeber mobilises to challenge the barter fable are cases where money exists at least in the form of a unit of account and which, because of its scarcity, is replaced by alternative means of circulation or a record of debits and credits. These examples only prove that credit presupposes money and that the existence of money, even in the form of a simple unit of account, implies, in turn, the comparison of exchanged things. Graeber wants to go back to the real sources of money but introduces it in a form presupposing the process of exchange itself from which a good, i.e. a thing that will serve as a unit of account, emerges. He always confuses money as a measure of value, which emerges from exchange, with the function of money as a unit of account, which reduces it to an abstract and purely conventional unit. To put it another way, as whenever a kind of wealth fixed as a measure of value is transformed into a unit of account, and this transformation is always made by custom or decree, Graeber and all institutionalists imagine that money itself is a pure convention that serves to calculate the debits and credits of the exchangers. Graeber notes as an objection to theories of barter that, when it does occur, "it takes place between strangers, even enemies" (2011: 29). But this is precisely where the birth of anonymous commodity relations takes place. When exchanges take place within a community, they necessarily take on more complex forms in which a host of aspects, issues and relationships are intertwined, far from strictly economic equivalence relationships. (See Bohannan, 1955 and also Dalton, 1965. On the complexity of transactions in wampum, see Desmedt, 2008: 279.)

7.2 The sovereignty of money against the sovereign money

Neo-chartalism developed in opposition to the neoclassical myth of barter, but it shares its subjective foundations: the debt relationship for the former, the preference relationship for the latter. It is true that neo-chartalism insists on the function of objective representative of value in settlement of debts, while the neoclassicals need the means of exchange function to ensure the allocation of resources according to individual preferences, but for the neoclassicals at least, money arises from the market relation, although it has no necessity, neither as a unit of account, since this function measures utilities and can therefore be assumed by any kind of money, nor as a medium of exchange, since this function arises only from the practical needs of the agents. For neo-chartalists, money does not arise from market circulation, since its sole purpose is to settle debts, which do not necessarily result from a commercial relationship: "money – as a social institution – is produced by non-market agencies and does not obey the economic 'laws' of the production and exchange of commodities" (Ingham, 2002: 22). Money is only necessary when it is imposed by a sovereign authority outside the market both as a unit of account and as a means of payment (and thus as a store of value) (Ingham, 2000: 21–22). Neo-chartalists denounce the inability of neoclassicals to explain the existence of a generally accepted means of payment, but they themselves only explain it by a state decree against the background of already existing market circulation. The state may impose a means of payment that was not previously in use, but this can only be by replacing means of payment already in circulation and born of market relations between individuals subject to the authority of the issuing state. Yet, Ingham, one of the most accomplished theorists of sovereign debt-money, himself asserts that bank money originated from the circulation of bills of exchange between merchants and that it only became money proper (general equivalent) with the merger of state and bank money. He thus accepts that credit-money emerged with the development of trade and that the circulation of bills of exchange was based on a generally accepted means of settlement; and thus that the store of value function developed with the circulation of goods and the credit relations it gives rise to. As for the wergeld system, not only does it involve a list of rates or at least a prior estimate of the value of the goods transferred in compensation for damages, but Wray himself makes it clear that the compensation rates were based on commonly available goods (Wray, 2014b: 9). Thus in the wergeld, damage and contempt are already valued as goods.

The confusion between the function of value measurement, which arises from the relationship between goods, and the function of the unit of account, which is fixed by decree, maintains the illusion that money as a unit of account is suddenly created by a sovereign authority and imposed on traders who have not yet exchanged any goods (since credit theorists deny the existence of the barter economy). This is because, as a unit of account, money has only an abstract existence which can be assumed by any unit arbitrarily fixed by the sovereign authority. Yet, there is no historical or archaeological record of this kind of fiat (Davies, 1994: 28). And it has been made clear that this power actually presupposes not only the circulation of money within the space of sovereignty, but foreign trade from which the sovereign takes advantage through the obligation for merchants to exchange foreign currency for local currency (Le Rider, 2001: 81). More generally, Le Rider notes that signed and minted money has always been based on the search for a gain from the difference between the value of the currencies already in circulation and the newly issued money. For his part, Weber noted that the first mints did not come from public authority, but from large merchant families or guilds of merchants:

> In the form of coinage, money first appears in the 7th century before Christ. The oldest mints were located in Lydia, probably on the coast, and arose out of the cooperation of the Lydian king and the Greek colonists. A forerunner of coined money was precious metal in bars privately stamped by merchants, which appear in Indian commerce and later in Babylonia and in China. The shekel is nothing but a piece of silver with the stamp of a certain mercantile family, which was recognized for conscientiousness in weighing. The Chinese tael is similarly a piece of bar silver stamped by the mercantile guilds. Not until later did the political power take over the coinage, and shortly afterwards assume a monopoly of the activity.
>
> *(Weber, 1950: 241–42)*

But let's assume that money is first of all just a standard for any price. Graeber asks what this standard measures and answers: debt. A coin is therefore only an acknowledgement of debt. First of all, if money is related to debt, it does not measure the debt itself but the value or amount of the debt. Secondly, once the value of what is owed has been measured, the debt can be settled either in the standard commodity or in any other commodity of equivalent value. Most often money, when it measures a debt, also serves as a means of payment to the detriment of its function as a means of circulation. Certainly as a means of circulation, it does not matter whether money is a nickel coin, a silver dollar, a digital datum, etc., but as a means of settling debts, these differences are of great importance. Yet, Graeber argues that, "A gold coin is a promise to pay something else of equivalent value to a gold coin. After all, a gold coin is not actually useful in itself. One only accepts it because one assumes other people will" (Graeber, 2011: 47). It is accepted because it is the final means of settlement of the transaction; for, a few pages later, Graeber himself states:

> This is probably why coins - pieces of silver or gold that are already valuable commodities in themselves, but that, being stamped with the emblem of a local political authority, became even more valuable - still sit in our heads as the quintessential form of money.
>
> *(Graeber, 2011: 75)*

If an individual incurs a debt, it is precisely because he or she does not directly have the means to pay for what he or she buys. In debt, money functions not only as a unit of account but as a means of payment. But Graeber concludes from the diversity of means of circulation that these means are indifferent in their monetary function in general. Either money only fulfils the unit of account function and discussion of the other functions of money is useless, or money is also a means of payment and this function must be distinguished from its role as a simple means of circulation. Graeber constantly shifts between these different functions to demonstrate that money is nothing more than an instrument of debt.

And this is what is important to him, insofar as this basic function would lead to the birth of money from politics, i.e. sovereignty (Graeber, 2011: 57). By associating the creation of money with the necessities of debt relations between individuals, Graeber slips from money to credit to identify circulating money with credit-money. And since most of the means of circulation have always been embodied in the most diverse and distant forms of account money (coins, banknotes, etc.), they become mere acknowledgements of debt passing from hand to hand between debtors and creditors of the debt system on which all monetary circulation is based. However, since circulating money represents nothing more than an acknowledgement of debt for a value expressed in purely figurative and abstract units of account, only trust guarantees the validity of money (the Geltung of Simmel and Knapp). Thus, the value of money problem, which had so concerned the monetary theorists of the 19th and early 20th centuries, is replaced by that of its validity, its legitimacy, and thus the conditions of trust in money and its issuer. And thus Graeber welcomes the fact that the value of a monetary unit no longer measures the value of an object: it measures "one's trust in other human beings" (Graber, 2011: 47). When money is fixed by the state, trust is guaranteed by the acceptability of the money for tax payment.

Yet, all the cases Graeber cites in favour of chartalism sound, on the contrary, like objections to this approach: while Charlemagne's empire was dislocated, he recalls,

> the monetary system he created continued to be used, for keeping accounts, within his former territories for more than 800 years. It was referred to, in the sixteenth century, quite explicitly as 'imaginary money,' and derniers and livres were only completely abandoned, as units of account, around the time of the French Revolution.
>
> *(Graber, 2011: 48)*

This example actually shows that the role of the state in monetary circulation is here limited to setting the price standard and that without political power this standard can continue to prevail in the world of exchange where many different means of circulation circulate. Similarly, the example of the silver coins given to the soldiers before requiring the families of the kingdom to pay their taxes in silver proves that the political power has not only created a unit of account, but has also thrown into circulation the metallic money with which the tax must be paid. Here money functions simultaneously as a unit of account, a means of circulation and a means of payment. Wray uses the circulation of state-stamped coins whose face value does not represent their material content to prove that the means of exchange did not originate in retail trade but in the issue of symbols of state debt. But in this way he confuses money with the forms of money which, in circulation, adopt the most diverse modes of existence insofar as they are convertible into money proper.

7.3 The dumb money of ancient empires

But for Graeber, not only does money make debt possible, but debt and money enter the scene at exactly the same time, like the cause with its effect. For what distinguishes debt from any other form of obligation is that it is "precisely quantified" (2011: 21). Among the evidence that archaeology provides for this consubstantial relationship of debt and money, Graeber naturally cites ancient Mesopotamia. Archaeological research would tell us that some of the earliest writings that have come down to us are Mesopotamian tablets that record credits and debits, rations distributed by the temples, rents due for the leasing of temple lands (Graeber, 2011: 21). These traces only mean that the debts were recorded in tablets, not that these debts entered the market circulation at the same time as the money. Moreover, the temple administrators had no reason to record any immediate transactions that animated the social life around these exchange centres. As a specialist in this civilisation aptly puts it:

> Thousands of tablets have been found, but they are only part of the archives of the state services and not those of private individuals. After the fall of the Ur empire, from the beginning of the 2nd millennium BC, the documentation bears witness to a significant private initiative, the intensity of which varies according to place and time.
>
> *(Grandpierre, 2010: 223–24)*

Rejecting with horror the idea that any trace of cash payments could be found outside our cold and inhuman market economies, institutionalists have generally been misled by the role of money in the keeping of accounts by Mesopotamian temple officials. Since the weight units of the precious metal only played a role as a unit of account in the calculation of debits and credits, they concluded that money itself was only an instrument of debt. In reality, money served as a medium of exchange, but it was customary to substitute all sorts of equivalent goods, such as barley, in the circulation process as final settlement for sums expressed in money (Renger, 2011: 25).

Thus, the account books in Mesopotamia are proof less of credit relations between merchants than of an organisation keeping accounts of purchases and sales or of taxes to be paid. The fact that money was used to pay taxes did not make it a debt economy. Graeber sees the Sumerian accounting system, based on the shekel, whose weight in silver was equivalent to a bushel of barley (gur), as a means not to develop commercial transactions but "to keep track of resources and move things back and forth between departments" (Graber, 2011: 39). What is moving things between services if not the result of a commercial transaction?

And what is keeping track of resources if not giving the value of the things exchanged a tangible, fixed and uniform form of existence, precisely in the shekel? The fact that the shekel was primarily a unit of account does not change the nature of transactions valued in shekels, and the fact that temple officials collected taxes does not mean that the monetary economy was a debt economy, any more than the payment of taxes today means that the euro is basically used to pay debts. Graeber takes advantage of the fact that money does not serve to pay the debts calculated in it to demonstrate that it only serves to incur debts: "Peasants who owed money to the Temple or Palace, or to some Temple or Palace official, seem to have settled their debts mostly in barley" (Graeber, 2011: 39). But also in goats, furniture, lapis lazuli. But this only shows that money played the role of a unit of account in the levying of taxes and, above all, that the currency in which taxes were to be paid was not issued by the state, contrary to what Chartalism claims. Moreover, Graeber states a little further on: "Merchants (who sometimes worked for the temples, sometimes operated independently) were among the few people who really and often used money in transactions" (Graeber, 2011: 39–40). Yet it is the market sphere that interests us if we want to determine the functions of money and the nature of monetary relations: how can we affirm that money does not exist without debt if money "often" serves as a means of immediate transaction between merchants, producers and consumers? Moreover, Graeber forgets to mention that the temple officials did not only levy taxes but also lent money to merchants, especially for their distant expeditions (Jursa, 2010: 776).

Archaeologists have always warned against extrapolating from the discovery of tablets written by the administrators of the temples and palaces of ancient Mesopotamia. In a civilisation where writing was not widespread, the chatty trade is lost in the silence of past acts. "The problem of cuneiform records in a nutshell: nearly everything that was obvious to them was not written down" (Powell, 1996: 234. And for Egypt, see Moreno Garcià, 2014: 19). Yet, it is on the basis of these few thousand tablets – and what basis do they provide to judge a civilisation lasting 6,000 years and stretching over an area of 3,50,000 km^2? – that the modern theory of money has built its conception of money as an instrument of debt created by the State. It is true that Polanyi (1957) affirms them in this conception by defining Mesopotamian society as an economy of redistribution organised by the State through its temples and palaces as centres of exchange. But already in 1972, Veenhof (1972) had used Kanish texts to reveal that the merchants were not officials of temples or palaces but private entrepreneurs engaging in market trade and using money.

The temples and palaces were of course important centres of trade, transactions and debt contracts, but the mere existence of barley as a unit of account, not to mention money, could suggest that the bulk of trade took place elsewhere, or at the very least that money could not be reduced to settling debts registered in the accounts of institutional trade. However, by opening the doors of the temples, the latest discoveries have given us a glimpse of the animated landscape of this silent trade. For what the latest finds reveal first and foremost is the very great importance of cash exchanges compared to the debt contracts recorded in the tablets of the state institutions. And in this immediate trade, two commodities come up again and again: barley and silver. This was already evident in the tablets, where barley and silver were used as units of account for the calculation of debts and claims. But why two units of account – indeed there are others – and why not one, if, as the neo-chartalists claim, all debts were reduced to a set of writings? This is because they each had their functions in distinct circuits of exchange and in different amounts. Because of its high value and the technical difficulties of dividing it into small quantities (Powell, 1996: 229), silver was used primarily for large transactions (Seaford, 2004) and, because it was easily preserved, often for distant trade. Barley, a more flexible but also less durable unit of measurement, was used for smaller transactions and rarely went beyond the local sphere. Thus barley fulfilled all the functions of money except that of a store of value (Renger, 1995: 286–87). But what profoundly united them was their commodity character, so that before constituting units of account, barley and silver fulfilled the function of measuring values. Thus, it has recently been pointed out that, although most written records do not mention it until the first millennium, concern for the quality of the silver and its weight predominated over counting it. "The history of money in Mesopotamia is intimately bound up with weighing and measuring, and the bond between weighing and money persevered in the Near East until relatively recent times" (Powell, 1996: 246). The Akkadian language has left a trace of this, since the term *pay* literally means to weigh (Seaford, 2004: 321). But, however, barley and silver as units of measurement are prominent in mathematical texts on monetary issues in ancient Babylon (Powell, 1996: 227). In other words, the unit of measurement function of silver was entirely dependent on the value of the metal. More generally, there is little evidence of abstract units of account or symbolic money (Powell, 1996: 227; Seaford, 2004: 337) apart from notes circulating between private traders, and the astonishing stability of prices over very long periods of time is essentially explained by the market basis of all measures of value in Mesopotamian society. Since neo-chartalism conceives of money only in its form as a state-decreed unit of account, it ignores the forms of monetisation that, in both Egypt and Mesopotamia, existed long before the coinage of money or the fixing of units of account (Manning, 2013: 4574). Moreover, the conditions for the penetration of money relations within institutional trade are exactly the opposite of what neo-chartalists claim. It was in fact the administrators of the temples and palaces who, for their own needs related to distant trade (Jursa, 2010: 776), gradually imposed the generalised use of money on the urban elite who, in private trade, were accustomed to make extensive use of banknotes as a substitute for precious metal. But these needs, in turn, resulted from the importance of long-distance trade shipments. The long-distance trade

> was feasible and profitable thanks to the differences between the exchange value of the goods traded in Assur and Anatolia. Silver, rich in supply in Anatolia, once shipped to Assur allowed the Assyrians to buy there tin and

> textiles, which in Anatolia could again be sold for two (tin) to four times (textiles) as much silver as they had cost in Assur.
>
> *(Veenhof, 1999: 56)*

This is why it has been said that the penetration of money into the internal exchange relations of the temple or palace essentially distinguished these from the domestic economy of the home and made it risky to extrapolate the mode of functioning of one from the other (Jursa, 2010: 564).

> Probably the main reason why the temples seem keen to acquire silver, demanding substantial amounts of it from their personnel as house rent and for offerings at the entrance gate of the sanctuary, is simply that large amounts of silver were required to keep the organizations going. [...] We can distinguish four different purposes for which the temple needed silver: the crown; payments to temple personnel (prebendary income and food rations in addition to hired labour); commercial activities, i.e. the purchase of basic materials, finished products, animals and sometimes land or houses; and silver for the repair and the manufacture of the jewellery and utensils of the gods.
>
> *(Bongenaar, 1999: 167)*

Thus institutional trade, far from initiating the form and conditions of exchange and distribution of goods and services, appears as the refractive index of the intensity and rich variety of private trade.

Nevertheless, although barley and especially silver fulfil all the traditional functions of money, none of them constitutes a general equivalent. This is because in reality barley and silver emerged against the background of an intense barter economy (Jursa, 2010: 472) in which a multitude of particular equivalents (oil, cotton, but also other cheap metals such as copper and bronze) circulated. Moreover, the silver good remained limited, as the vast majority did not use silver as a medium of exchange (Bongenaar, 1999: 162). And since each of these particular equivalents has a varying degree of exchangeability (Renger, 1995: 318), barley and silver enter these different spheres of exchange sometimes as one of several equivalents, sometimes as a commodity for which one of these particular equivalents is exchanged (Seaford, 2004: 323). And this phenomenon is explained precisely by the fact that the Mesopotamian state is not a chartalist state: neither barley nor silver owes its existence as money to any forces other than those of trade itself. There is no record of any decree or law fixing silver or barley as a general means of compulsory settlement of goods purchased or debts incurred:

> silver is in the Old Babylonian period predominant over all other commodities as a measure of value. But it is neither the only measure of value nor clearly predominant in any of the other money functions. Nor has it ceased to be a commodity.
>
> *(Seaford, 2004: 325)*

So with the multiplicity of measures of value and the changing role of the same commodity in different spheres of exchange, barter is only with difficulty to be distinguished from monetary exchange (Seaford, 2004: 335), with the outcome that the oldest monetary civilisation provides us with an example of the genesis of money that belies both the myth of the chartalist money and the orthodox's myth of barter.

The discovery of several means of exchange in Egypt (Bogoslovsky, 1987) also overturned the widespread idea of a cashless society based on a large public sector ensuring the redistribution of wealth (Moreno Garcià, 2014: 19). Without written evidence, the archaeological record leaves little doubt that there was a much larger sphere of private exchange than previously assumed and, above all, a large circulation of precious metals.

> The evidence of precious metals used in trade, as well as the payments of gold and silver to the tax authorities by merchants, farmers, fishermen and craftsmen, all point to the existence of markets where metals circulated, also on the fringes of the institutions and transactions, redistribution networks and reward systems that they fed.
>
> *(Moreno Garcià, 2014: 19)*

As in Mesopotamia, the need for money was also motivated by trade with the Levant, where not only luxury goods were exchanged, but a large number of everyday goods (Moreno Garcià, 2014: 25). If we add to these different factors the presence of nomadic populations that also participated in the production and distribution of metals (Moreno Garcià, 2014: 26), the recent discoveries reveal the existence of spheres of exchange that escaped institutional circuits (Moreno Garcià, 2014: 27). Henry (2004: 95) believes that the Egyptian *deben* is a unit of account created from scratch by a minority in power in order to capture the population in a system of obligations, as in the Corinth of Cypselos. However, the only unit of value that Egypt ever created was the *shat*, which was in reality only a monetary standard based on gold and whose origin was probably a gold ring of regular weight (Daumas, 1977: 426). The *deben* did not originate in Egypt but probably in Babylon (Pulak, 2000) and was in fact an international silver standard measure of the Middle East in use since the second millennium (Daumas, 1977: 428). However, from Ramses II onwards, the *shat* disappeared in favour of the *deben* and the *qite* which, as a silver standard, were used both as units of value and as units of weight (Daumas, 1977: 429). Not only were the units of value derived from the units of weight of precious metals, but in several papyri it is observed that the standard of value, the monetary values and the weights of metals are often confused in the description of transactions (Weill, 1925: 67). The question that Egyptologists still ask today is not what the unit of account was or what the social motives for its creation were, but why the Egyptians never minted money even though all the material and institutional conditions were met.

Yet, Egyptologists find it strange that from Rameses II onwards, when gold was abundant in Egypt, a silver standard was used for domestic trade. "A conversion from one to the other would have seemed simpler for foreign trade than a change of base metal for the monetary standard" (Daumas, 1977: 435–36). This is undoubtedly because, alongside grain, which formed the great majority of transactions (Davies, 1994: 52), internal trade had already been penetrated by silver metal, forcing the state to adapt to the habits of its merchants. Here, no more than in Mesopotamia, it was not the dominant minority that forced the vast majority to measure their obligations to the Egyptian state in a unit of account created from scratch (Henry, 2004: 95–96. See also Semenova and Wray, 2015), but the intense ferment of production and exchange among the variegated majority that forced the power to let its unit of account be represented in the monetary forms required by the suppliers of the state's centres of redistribution. So much so that from the first millennium BC onwards, temples in the Near East, as in Egypt, were the scrupulous guarantors of the value of silver metal (Manning, 2013: 4574).

Note

1 Testart writes: "The great characteristic of primitive monies is that they are means of payment without serving as means of exchange" (2001: 38).

PART 3
The dollar policy

8

THE INTER-ROLE OF THE DOLLAR

8.1 Introduction

The formation of the dollar as a universal equivalent is not the creation of a concerted imperial project of the US (Panitch and Gindin, 2012). It is, given the economic relations that emerged from the First World War, the natural fruit of the world market that was formed in the aftermath of the war, with the US as the leading commercial power but also as the leading world creditor. The history of this formation is undoubtedly marked by vigorous actions by the US authorities to consolidate the role, defend the position and extend the influence of the dollar in the world. But we shall also see that the forms of this influence were partly beyond their control and could go against their immediate national interests. And the unilateral withdrawal from the Bretton Woods system, which is probably the most resounding episode of US hegemonic power, will reveal that it was aimed at a retreat to their national economic objectives at the expense of the hegemonic position of the dollar.

The global market for money-capital has always implied the existence of a universal equivalent. But the novelty of the Bretton Woods dollar standard is that this equivalent now represents a credit-money issued by a particular state, the US. And since the issuance of this credit currency is at the discretion of the US monetary authorities, the entire history of the IMF from Bretton Woods onwards is marked by a permanent contradiction between the dollar as a general form of value – which requires the stability of its value and therefore of world prices expressed in it – and the dollar as a form of general exchangeability – which requires that it be issued in sufficient quantity to ensure world liquidity. We shall see that Triffin's dilemma (1960) and its metamorphoses up to the present day (Farhi, Gourinchas and Rey, 2011; Obstfeld, 2011) express in the form of the conflict between the international role and the national

DOI: 10.4324/9780429261299-12

character of the dollar, the expression of this contradiction between these modes of being of money.

Triffin's dilemma – according to which the conversion of the dollar into gold is increasingly compromised by the increase in its issuance – does not disappear with the demonetisation of gold declared by Nixon in 1971. It takes the form of the contradiction between the growing balance of payments deficits needed to provide dollar liquidity for the rest of the world and the US fiscal capacity to issue debt (Obstfeld, 2011: 19) – Treasury bonds – to guarantee the dollar's function as a store of value. This is because the end of the Bretton Woods system did not remove the market basis of the dollar. It replaced gold with the Treasury bond or, to put it another way, it substituted a particular commodity, the product of a particular labour, with social wealth levied by taxation and broken down into small coupons circulating on the public bond markets. In the absence of a metallic base, the currencies issued by the central banks of the dominant states rely entirely on trust in these institutions, which is directly proportional to the tax revenues of the Treasury (Bordo, 1993: 51). This confidence takes the form of an assurance for the debt holder to receive interest at the stipulated maturity. It is in this sense that Treasury bills replace the precious metal as the ultimate support of the monetary relationship (Jiang, Krishnamurthy and Lustig, 2020).

Since then, the growing imbalance between the key role of the dollar and the growing twin deficits in the US has regularly prompted calls for reform of the international monetary system (Guttmann, 2022). However, the constantly announced decline of the dollar has never prevented it from penetrating ever more deeply into economic and financial relations outside the US. Yet, the same explanations for this paradox are repeated over and over again: the political and cultural links of the US with the major capitalist powers, its military might, the role of its multinational firms and of course its liquid and deep markets, which are like those of no other country. But sometimes these explanations over-politicise the conditions of the persistent hegemony of the dollar, whereas its emergence is based on economic causes (Kirshner, 2014; Helleiner, 2016); sometimes, on the contrary, the hegemony of the US itself is explained by the international functions of the dollar, whereas the question is precisely that of explaining why those functions are maintained despite everything (Cohen, 2013; Norrlof, 2014). All this literature on the hegemony and structural power of the US appeared at the very moment when the US was in industrial decline relative to Germany and Japan. In the meantime, with the emergence of the Eurodollar market, we were witnessing a process of what I call the relative autonomy of the dollar in relation to the national economy of the US, a process that should be distinguished from the process of formation of the dollar as a universal currency: it is not the same story, nor are the mechanisms the same, and we shall see that we can date quite precisely the moment when the dollar ceases to replicate in a larger way what the pound sterling had been, so as to inaugurate a new era for which there is no precedent in the history of capitalism.

In the same way that the dollar became a universal equivalent with the reconstitution of the world market, the Treasury bond, insofar as it represents a negotiable security on the public debt market, became the safe asset of financial globalisation (Gorton, 2017).[1] The whole history of the formation of the dollar as a universal currency is presented as an accelerated passage through the three successive stages of the constitution of the world market: first, the international market for goods and services (Marshall Plan), then the multinational market for oligopolistic production (Eurodollar market), and finally the global market for financial capital (integrated financial markets) (Michalet, 2002). And each of these stages requires the universal equivalent to have its appropriate monetary function: as a general medium of exchange for the exchange of goods and services, as a means of payment and store of value for the financing of multinational enterprises, and as a unit of account for the issuance of debt instruments negotiable on the financial markets. The systematic confusion between money and debt that we have analysed in contemporary monetary theories cannot be explained other than by the role to which the dollar and money in general are reduced at the stage of globalisation where the financial circulation of dollar-denominated debt instruments largely replaces and entirely determines the monetary circulation of the dollar itself (Pozsar, 2015: 4).

8.2 The gold standard–sterling system

It is now well known that the classical period of the gold standard system was never based on the respect of the "rules of the game", according to which external adjustments between surplus and deficit countries are carried out by the movements of domestic prices (de Cecco, 1975). Central banks were always ready to use expedients to neutralise the effects that the ebb and flow of precious metals would have on domestic prices and incomes. In fact, the system owed its smooth functioning to capital movements rather than to price, income or employment movements (Triffin, 1964; Cohen, 1977: 79–80; Gallarotti, 1995: 35). And Nurkse, who assessed the gold standard system while the bombs of the Second World War were still falling, went so far as to claim that a gold standard with fixed exchange rates would only really be possible if there were international mobility of labour, migrating between the world's economic zones according to the prosperity and decline of the moment (Nurkse, 1944: 218). But this mechanism of adjustment by capital was basically true for the capital-exporting countries, with England in the first place, the other countries being subject to the conditions of the creditor countries (Triffin, 1964: 7). Thus, the balance of payments was favourable to England thanks to the income from its investments abroad, although its trade balance was in deficit. The deficits of the countries entering the world market more recently were financed for 50 years by foreign capital. For England, for example, it was enough to raise the discount rate to reduce the outflow of capital in the event of a balance of payments deficit.

> The Golden Age, therefore, was really limited only to the 'core' of advanced nations of Europe and the so-called 'regions of recent settlement'

> (including North America, Australasia, South Africa, and Argentina). Elsewhere, the gold standard was far less successful in preserving payments stability or avoiding policy conflict.
>
> *(Cohen, 1977: 80)*

The instrument through which the Bank of England's discount policy exercised its control over capital flows was the bill of exchange, which, together with precious metals, formed the main private and public store of value in the 19th century.[2] One of the advantages of the bill of exchange was that it was interest-bearing and therefore had lower opportunity costs than gold. But the bill of exchange also fulfilled a function as a medium of exchange which, at the beginning of the 19th century, rivalled the banknote in the monetary circulation of the UK (Gallarotti, 1995: 29). This is because even before its classical period, between 1899 and 1914, the pound sterling, through bills of exchange and sterling balances, dominated international monetary circulation, due to the commercial importance of England, and especially due to the London market and the British banking system (de Cecco, 1975: 103–4).[3] According to Triffin, by 1872 the world's expanding money supply consisted of 95% bank money and only 5% gold and silver combined, so that by the eve of the First World War, gold money already constituted only 10% of the world's money supply (Triffin, 1968: 41). Thus, at its peak, the gold standard was already primarily based on a credit-money system. Even as a store of value and a means of payment, credit-money in the form of foreign exchange reserves fulfilled all the functions of precious metals during the classical gold standard period:

> Equilibration of exchange rates which reached the gold points was more often achieved through private transactions in foreign exchange markets than through gold arbitrage. International payments systematically began clearing with the transfer of foreign exchange holdings: gold was normally the last thing to move when imbalances developed between nations.
>
> *(Gallarotti, 1995: 29)*

Even before the gold exchange standard, central bank operations consisted of a mix of gold and foreign exchange reserves (D'Arista, 2009: 637).[4] With the withdrawal from domestic circulation of the remaining gold coins, which allowed the metal reserves necessary for the growth of world production and trade to be swelled (Eichengreen, 1990: 240–41), gold would soon be used only for transactions between central banks, allowing them to ensure the free convertibility of fiat currencies between them and the smooth functioning of international payments (Triffin, 1968: 38). But by 1914, the suspension of convertibility and free export of gold revealed an international monetary system whose mechanisms were all based, to varying degrees, on a hierarchy of national fiat currencies.

8.3 The era of central banks

In terms of its form, the post-war gold exchange standard system continued and accelerated the tendencies of the classical gold standard system to reduce the monetary role of the precious metal to its function as a store of value which guaranteed the commodity basis of the fiduciary monies in circulation. These trends, which resumed with the disorderly return to the gold standard, ended "in the 1920s and early 1930' with the universal disappearance of gold (and full-bodied silver coinage) from active monetary circulation and even from the cash reserves of commercial or deposit banks" (Triffin, 1968: 38). But in terms of its content, the ounce of gold was now counted in dollars: the war had transformed the US from a net debtor to the world's largest creditor in a few years: it accounted for 45% of the world's industrial output and, above all, had established a Federal Reserve System that provided the stability and liquidity necessary for the international functions of the dollar that the war had expanded. As Paul Warburg, who was to the Federal reserve system what Taylor was to Scientific Management, claimed: "In order to make our paper part and parcel of the means of the world's international exchange, it needs, however, as a preliminary condition, to become the foundation on which our own financial edifice is erected" (quoted by Broz, 1999: 61).

Whereas at Versailles, the US, which was the creditor of all the belligerents, had been magnanimous towards Germany in the face of the angry and chauvinistic demands of Britain and France, at the Brussels Conference in 1920 it fiercely defended its national dollar in the face of the recommendations of the League's Commission on Currency and Exchange, to which Keynes's Bretton Woods plan owed almost everything, and which consisted in creating an international credit bank backed by a clearing house. "Until Allied debts to the United States were properly scheduled, private, short-term lending from the United States was the method for dealing with European financial needs approved by Washington" (Bordo, Edelstein and Rockoff, 1999: 10). Instead, private cooperation between central banks was encouraged and, to this end, they were created wherever they were still lacking, even if it meant sending Money Doctors to teach the best practices for managing a gold standard system.[5]

It was at the Genoa Conference in 1922 that a compromise was reached between the US, whose possession of 40% of the world's gold reserves demanded a return to the gold standard, and the UK, whose small gold reserves were insufficient to meet its sterling commitments abroad. The tensions in the interwar gold standard system were not caused by a shortage of gold relative to liquidity needs (Eichengreen and Flandreau, 1997: 12), but by a disproportionate distribution between the US and France on the one hand, and the rest of the world on the other (Eichengreen, 1990: 241). The Conference had in fact led to two measures leading to the gold exchange standard: the elimination of gold coins from domestic circulation first – this is the meaning of the transition from the gold *coin* standard to the gold *bullion* standard – and the agreement at the end of the Genoa Conference to supplement the gold reserves of the central banks with foreign exchange reserves which would rise to more than 40% on the eve of the system's collapse – this is the meaning of the transition from the gold *bullion* standard to the gold *exchange* standard itself. The financing of the war through money issue and credit had led to a rise in the general price level that was no longer compatible with the existing gold reserves, which had hardly increased since 1915 (Eichengreen and Flandreau, 2009: 383). Rather than forcing a deflation to return to a price level compatible with gold reserves and, above all, to increase the price of gold in order to stimulate further extraction of the precious metal necessary for the expansion of economic activity in the longer term, it was therefore decided to supplement gold reserves with foreign exchange reserves in the main financial centres where these reserve assets are freely convertible into gold, i.e. mainly in dollars and pounds. In this way, foreign exchange increased from about 20% of total central bank and government reserves in 1913 to 42% in 1927–28, i.e. at the height of the interwar gold exchange standard. In fact, except for the pound reserves held by the Commonwealth's trading partners in London, these were almost exclusively dollar reserves, so that by the mid-1920s the dollar dominated central bank reserves (Eichengreen and Flandreau, 2009: 379).[6]

To the extent that price stability was added to the exchange rate objectives, Rothbard, whose defence of the gold standard went so far as to convince him that the Depression had resulted from the violation of its rules, saw this *managed* gold standard (Boyce, 1987: 41) as the beginning of the era of central banks (Eichengreen, 1990: 291–92; Rothbard, 1998: 134). For gold reserves would now be used to protect against external shocks instead of playing the balancing role on exchange rates and balance of payments that they had in the classical gold standard era (Fenstein, Temin and Toniolo, 2008: 51).[7] This meant that central banks and the states behind them would no longer be willing to sacrifice their internal equilibrium for external (exchange rate) stability. This is where Triffin's dilemma comes in, i.e. the contradictions that key-currency countries were facing between the domestic functions of money and its functions as a reserve and means of international payment (Triffin, 1968: 38). From then on, key currencies would be at the mercy of speculative attacks as their liabilities increased relative to their gold reserves (Bordo, Edelstein and Rockoff, 1999: 3–4 n.).

All scholars of the interwar period agree that the downward rigidity of wages was the novelty of the gold exchange standard compared to the classical gold standard period. And this downward rigidity would refer to the growing political role of trade unions and labour in general, with the proletarian revolution in Russia in the background. Thus Bernanke, for example, bases his entire interpretation of the Great Depression on the imbalance between wage rigidity and the deflationary tendencies of the gold standard (Nurkse, 1944: 25; Eichengreen, 1990: 291–92; Bernanke, 1995: 7–8; Feinstein, Temin and Toniolo, 2008: 114–15). But it should be recalled that the stability of domestic prices, which condition the stability of the exchange rate, was itself dependent on the stability of wages. This is because the role of labour in the reproduction cycle of capital had changed.

> A brief survey of the new labor-market conditions allows us to understand the impact of unemployment on the daily life of the most affected individuals and communities, as well as to intuitively perceive what difference it made to be unemployed in western Europe and North America instead of in less developed, predominantly agrarian societies.
>
> *(Feinstein, Temin and Toniolo, 2008: 113)*

In the interwar period, it was not only labour that entered the parliaments, but also states that entered the workers' homes. Before Keynes, it was the capitalist world that became Keynesian by integrating the proletariat into the monetary circuits of demand. From that moment on, social reproduction is conditioned to the overall reproduction of capital; and hence from that moment the state relies on the two main pillars of its action on society: the management of money and the management of labour power (de Brunhoff, 1978). And what gives state action its formal unity is a profound change in the way the state relates to labour.

8.4 Labour or life: a critique of biopower

Against sovereignist and repressive approaches to the state, we know how much Foucault insists on the immanence of power relations to economic, epistemic, sexual, etc., relations, and the directly productive role of these relations (Foucault, 1998: 92–93). Thus, the molar power of the state operates less by radiation from a central point than as the global effect of molecular relations of force running through the entire social body (Foucault, 1998: 94). In reality, Foucault does not modify the classical conception of the state as a molar and global power over the social body, but he reverses the direction of its genesis, by relating its condition of possibility to capillary relations of force that induce states of power. But by reducing state power to the hegemonic effects of local powers, Foucault deprives this power of its specific positivity, which makes the mode of state intervention irreducible to local relations of force, i.e. both immanent and external to them. His approach to power no longer accounts for the relative autonomy of the political instance, even when this instance is presented as productive and not only repressive. Yet relative autonomy implies not only a political instance distinct from the economic one, but above all an economic instance that is not reduced to a set of power relations. However, when it comes to identifying certain global strategies of power and thinking about state power, Foucault does refer to society as a determined mode of production, notably by using the notions of bourgeoisie and proletariat (Foucault, 1998: 120–22). But he does so in order to reduce the capitalist production relation to relations of force: yet capitalism also has a positivity which implies constraints required for its reproduction that only a central power is able to manage, to relax and to guarantee at the same time.

The capitalist relation of production does imply a class power but, precisely as a relation of production, it presents determinations which are not defined as relations of power. Without a state, there is no money, but it does not mean that money is an emanation of the political; it implies relations of production and circulation of exchange values which differ from relations of power. By immersing the instances of society in relations of power, Foucault makes politics an instance without Power and the economy an instance without Production.

It is true, however, that the era of biopower, which Foucault defines as state power from the 18th century onwards, is explicitly associated with the development of capitalism (Foucault, 1998: 140–41). But the issue of this new political power is not the proper object of political economy. Foucault refers to political economy as the science of the relationships between population, territory and wealth, but these relationships were of no concern to the Physiocrats, whose specific object was the reproduction of the different classes of agricultural society in the Kingdom of France, nor to Smith, for whom the wealth of nations depended on the conditions of the division of labour between the classes of society no less than within the class of workers. No doubt biopower in its form of population discipline and regulation "would not have been possible without the controlled insertion of bodies into the machinery of production and the adjustment of the population to economic processes" (Foucault, 1998: 141). No doubt, too, that it also required more than this: the growth of both the former and the latter; reinforcement at the same time as usability and docility; the methods of power likely to increase forces, aptitudes and life in general without making them more difficult to subjugate.

> The adjustment to the accumulation of men to that of capital, the joining of the growth of human groups to the expansion of productive forces and the differential allocation of profit, were made possible in part by the exercise of bio-power in its many forms and modes of application.
>
> *(Foucault, 1998: 141)*

Foucault describes the action of the state in exactly the same way as Ford advocated and applied in Rouge River or even Dr. Ure in his *Philosophy of Manufactures*. It does not matter that the state is no longer understood as the only instance of power exercising its constraint on society from outside if its immanent action and function adopt the conception according to which it guarantees, by amplifying them, the relations of power that are established at the level of the factory, the school, the army, the asylum and the family. For Foucault, the only difference between the family, the enterprise and the state was the difference in scale and the amplitude of action. The great state regulations do nothing more than complete the disciplinary micro-powers by forming with them the extremities of the same continuum of body technologies (Foucault, 1998: 143–44; 2008: 118–19). But the Fordist or Keynesian state precisely develops a very specific technology that only it can implement. For what characterises it, unlike the family and the firm, is the reduction of the body, its forces, its faculties, its maintenance, its reproduction, etc., to purely quantitative flows by means of a set of interventions operating essentially at the level of these very flows.

If we define a capitalist society for what it is, namely a market society based on wage labour, then we can no longer be satisfied with defining political action as a biopolitics applied indifferently to all members of the population of a given territory. For the capitalist relation of production requires a very specific mode of intervention and forms of action. Moreover, its development over time implies very different modes of state integration in economic activity according to the stages of this development. The capitalist state of the 20th century does not differ from the state of the 18th century by its degree of governmentalisation, but by the very structure of its organisation, by the object and content of its intervention, by its role in the reproduction of capital, in short by the very field of its positivity. Biopolitics as state policy is both separated from society by the nature of its object and separated from history by the specific content of its action.

We know the great repressive or regulatory functions of the state in the genesis of capitalism and the first phases of its development: the functions of primitive accumulation and the function of regulating labour time. But in the period known as the Great Transformation, between the 1930s and 1945, two decisive phenomena occurred which are ignored by Polanyi himself: the constitution of workers as a fully fledged working class (i.e. when labour power establishes a collective class relationship with capital) and the development of the credit system freed from its direct link with commodity money, i.e. gold and silver. Both call for two new functions of the state which form the two joint pillars of what will be called economic policy. These two functions are the state management of labour power and the state management of money. This is what profoundly defines the so-called Keynesian state; this is the Great Transformation that is undergone by the state power in capitalist society. The change that takes place in the relationship of the state to capitalist society is that the state now refers to labour power as a single wage mass, as a great flow of monetary income. This is the Keynesian revolution: not the new role attributed to demand in growth, nor the theory of involuntary unemployment, but the inclusion of the working class as an economic subject in a circuit of flows which assimilates quanta of labour to money wages and quanta of money to sources of income. What we call economic policy in the Fordist era refers to a new function of the state and a new conception of society: First, a new function of the State, through the loosening of some market constraints by its intervention (between the sale of labour power and income due to social benefits and allowances; between income and expenditure due to the credit system) which requires maintaining control over labour power and money. Second, a new conception of society which evacuates the labour-value in order to consider labour only as determined behaviour expressed in monetary flows. At the level of state practice, Suzanne de Brunhoff insists, economic policy operates simultaneously on the two fronts of money and labour power, which, with the development of capitalism, "must in a way be treated as homogeneous flows, able to merge with each other" (de Brunhoff, 1978: 8). This is because the capacity of money to function as a means of payment depends first of all on the transformation of bank credits into wage payments, which are themselves spent on consumer goods; and conversely, wages as "strategic" income are fed by bank financing. The function of the state is precisely to unify the diversity of these flows and to anchor them politically. But if we want to understand the actual movement of this unification, we cannot presuppose the unity of a state that would manipulate and adjust diverse and fragmented flows; any theory of the modern state must instead start from state interventions in order to deduce the form of the state that results from them at each phase of capitalism. This is the approach that Foucault called for in the study of governmentality, but here the interventions from which the form of the state derives concern objects that are entirely specific to the mode of production for which state action ensures regulation and development. In reality, the state management of labour power and the state management of money are presented as constituent parts of a whole in which neither is privileged in relation to the central object of economic policy, and this central object is not bare life, it is not the control of the population in general; rather, this central object is the capitalist control of the labour market (de Brunhoff, 1978: 26).

8.5 The crisis of the 1930s: the dollar as general equivalent and the gold as universal equivalent

Doesn't the UK's return to the gold standard mean the sacrifice of the European countries' domestic goals to the impossible requirements of the external stability of currencies pegged to the precious metal? Since Temin (1989) substituted the international viewpoint for Friedman and Schwartz's narrow American framework on the Great Depression, the gold standard has become the ultimate cause of contraction and deflation in the interwar period, and the ideology of the gold standard the source of all the mistakes in monetary policy (Hamilton, 1988; Bernanke and Carey 1996; Eichengreen and Temin, 2000). Although the data and facts on which their analyses are based contradict their conclusions, they just transpose to the international monetary system as a whole the monetarist views that Friedman had applied to the Federal Reserve System:

> The length and depth of the deflation during the late 1920s and early 1930s strongly suggest a monetary origin, and the close correspondence (across both space and time) between deflation and nations' adherence to the gold standard shows the power of that system to transmit contractionary monetary shocks.
>
> *(Bernanke and James, 1991: 33)*

Indeed, they show us that the failure of the system lies not in the adherence to the rules of the gold standard but in its disorderly disregard. Kindleberger said that the tragedy of the interwar period was that the UK was no longer able to exercise its hegemony over the world, while the US did not want to exercise it (Kindleberger, 1973: 11). The truth is that the UK was unable to return to the pre-war gold standard, while the US, which had not left it, was reluctant to abide by its rules. For while Britain chased its pre-war parity at the cost of a deflationary policy reinforcing stagnation, the US neutralised its gold inflows to avoid inflationary pressures:

> While the United States, as a surplus and creditor country, defended its internal equilibrium to the detriment of the external equilibrium, Britain sacrificed its internal equilibrium to the external equilibrium. But in these contradictory policies both countries were aiming at the same goal: the defence of the international role of their currency.
>
> *(Niveau and Crozet, 2010: 410)*

However, even Churchill saw in this defence the predicted ruin of the British economy. Contrary to what Keynes denounced in his pamphlet against Churchill's policy, Churchill had remained to the end very sceptical about restoring the old parity, both for imperialist reasons and out of economic foresight. The City's concerns were not the only ones that mattered concerning the gold standard: "The merchant, the manufacturer, the workman and the consumer have interests which, though largely common, do not by any means coincide either with each other or with the financial and currency interests" (quoted by Boyce, 2009: 74). Churchill, who even invoked Keynes's analysis to resist pressure from the City and from Montagu Norman, the Governor of the Bank of England (Boyce, 2009: 151), finally gave in. But from then on, he made their weekly meetings "an occasion for tirades against his advice and 'the evil effects of the Gold Standard'" (Boyce, 1987: 135). Not only would Keynes have been more fair in calling his pamphlet "Mr Norman's Economic Consequences", but he fiercely defended the gold standard when it came to being abandoned. Faced with Lord Bevin, who sought to put the brakes on the City's gold disaster as quickly as possible, Keynes resisted in the name of the interests of the rentier class. While it was true that prices had fallen since the return to gold in 1925, "the decision had been taken, and he could not believe any responsible person would seriously advocate breaking faith with creditors by going back on it: 'the consequences of that might be too appalling to contemplate'. The cost of devaluing, according to Keynes, would be prohibitive, not only because of the loss on foreign investments – 10% of £2,500 million or £250 million – and the moral obligation to compensate all bona fide holders of short-term funds in London – amounting to another £50 million – but more important, because of the great and enduring damage to Britain's credit. At all events, 'the powers that be were simply not prepared to listen to such advice'" (Boyce, 2009: 282). As long as they did not affect the gold standard, Keynes envisaged all sorts of solutions, including those he condemned ex cathedra in his books: a general fall in all incomes; trade protectionism, which would lower real wages and restore profits in the sheltered sectors; or a reduction in reserve requirements to stimulate credit and investment. Faced with Keynes's stubborn defence of the "barbarian relic", Bevin exclaimed: "In all our discussions we seem quite willing to face an industrial upheaval or a decrease of wages; but we are simply terror-stricken at touching the rentier, or the value of the pound" (quoted in Boyce, 1987: 293).

In reality, the return to the gold standard in the UK had to imply, in order to ease the pain, the return of inflation in the US and consequently the resumption of British exports (Rothbard, 1998: 114–15). For until it responded to Norman's urgent demands to ease monetary policy to facilitate the inflow of gold to London, Strong's Fed had a policy at odds with its surplus status: instead of gold inflows easing money supply conditions as the rules of the game would have required, the Fed, except during short periods of recession, maintained a restrictive policy until 1927 (Bordo and Landon-Lane, 2010), both to avoid the credit glut that accommodative conditions would have caused but also to make use of the precious metal without its export disrupting domestic credit conditions (Drummond, 1987: 36; Eichengreen and Temin, 2000: 195). The result was a net surplus financed by unilateral transfers, capital exports and gold receipts from abroad (Blair, 1961: 171). But despite the sterilisation measures, prices had not fallen enough to return to pre-war levels[8] and the fall in rates launched speculation in the bond and property markets. Thus, Strong's Fed raised the discount rate in August 1927 (Boyce, 2009: 161). Yet, the increase proved modest in relation to the massive diversion of funds normally directed overseas. This, together with the inflow of foreign speculative funds, led to a decline in net capital exports from the second half of 1929 onwards, i.e. when short-term interest rates exceeded long-term rates (Boyce, 2009: 217–18). And the onset of the crisis "more or less completely cut off the flow of US credit that had kept the rickety international financial system going through the 1920s" (Panitch and Gindin, 2012: 52). It was the withdrawal of US capital, especially from Germany, to feed speculation on Wall Street that pushed the central banks into deflationary policies, in search of what remained the universal equivalent despite the diversifications provided by the gold exchange standard: the yellow metal.[9]

Wall Street speculation contributed much more to deflation in Europe than the rigours of the gold standard. The New York stock exchange, which offered up to 20% interest (Boyce, 1987: 189), attracted not only dollars but also gold reserves, so that between 1928 and 1929, foreign loans, which made up 40% of the resources of German banks, fell by half. The shortage of gold caused by this speculative fever was compounded by France's decision to unwind its forward exchange contracts and convert its dollars into gold (Boyce, 1987: 186), just as it did in 1966 when US balance of payments deficits cast doubt on the dollar. However, France had to limit its demands for conversion, fearing that a devaluation of the dollar would flood European markets with US exports at a time when the recovery was still in its infancy. It feared especially that the devaluation would lead to financial instability which would also affect French trade (Eichengreen, 1992: 294). These fears expressed the recognition of both the US as the world's leading economic power and the dollar as the pivotal currency of the international monetary system. More generally, the flight from the dollar hardly threatened to lower the level of reserves to the point of leaving the system. The drain never reached the minimum gold cover of the currency in circulation. Admittedly, this level was preserved by the fact that the Fed did not conduct aggressive open-market operations to increase the quantity of money. Eichengreen himself admits that the recovery was a problem of demand, not supply of liquidity (Eichengreen and Flandreau, 2009: 389).

No doubt the devaluation of the pound, which led to significant losses in central banks' foreign exchange reserves, provoked a new flight from the dollar, whose devaluation was feared (D'Arista, 2009: 638; Ghosh and Qureshi, 2017: 5). But this liquidation of dollar reserves was undertaken only by Belgium and some Eastern European countries (Eichengreen, 1990: 306–7). In fact, the US retained its position as a net recipient of long-term capital at a time when it was facing a liquidation of its short-term foreign liabilities (Feinstein, Temin and Toniolo, 2008: 79). Half of the dollar sale that followed the liquidation of foreign exchange reserves in pounds was carried out by France (D'Arista, 2009: 638) and led to an increase in the bank rate from 1.5% to 3.5%. It has been argued that this increase deepened the Depression in the US and the rest of the world (Kindleberger, 1984), but how else can this effect be explained except by the fact that the dollar was already the currency of global investment finance?

The role of the Fed in the Depression, through the tightening of its money supply conditions after the crisis and the slowness of its response for fear of a resumption of speculation, may be the only episode in economic history where Keynesians and monetarists agree (Galbraith, 1955; Friedman and Schwartz, 1963; DeLong, 1990; Calomiris and Wheelock, 1998; Meltzer, 2002). Yet Eichengreen notes that the monetary tightening after 1929 was modest compared to the fall in output in the US (Eichengreen, 2004: 2) but also in the rest of the world. And above all, the fall in production outside the US had already started before the Fed's reaction (Eichengreen, 2004: 3). In fact, the US rate hike had provoked a vigorous response from other central banks, required by investors' growing doubts about their willingness to ensure exchange rate stability and to subordinate their domestic objectives to external stability. Thus, by 1929, monetary tightening was stronger in Europe and Latin America than in the US (Eichengreen, 2004: 4). It was the fall in demand that first hit the US economy through the decline in its exports to Europe in particular. This drop in demand was all the more marked as the rise in US interest rates had attracted capital from Europe, causing the downturn in the cycle before it occurred in the US.

The gold rush that began in Europe with the bankruptcy of the Credit-Anstalt in Austria and the devaluation of the pound in 1931 was a rush for the universal equivalent whose accumulation in the US and France had made it scarce in the rest of the world. The spiral of rising high interest rates, falling prices, output and employment, but also debt deflation (Fisher, 1933) which further aggravated the reduction in spending, was not due to the return to a pure gold standard

(Eichengreen and Temin, 2000: 200) but to the movement by which the rush to the universal equivalent abolished all forms of money other than gold to fulfil the various functions of money. Under the gold exchange standard, gold served only as a store of value, with the dollar providing, far ahead of the pound and the franc, the bulk of global liquidity through the loans and foreign direct investment that its huge trade surpluses made possible. Except in the case of the pound, whose forced return to the gold standard was solely a response to the demands of City bankers in the face of competition from the freely convertible dollar,[10] global deflation was above all the result of factors determining the level at which the dollar met global liquidity needs. For without a lender of last resort such as the Fed would be after the Second World War, the flight to quality was naturally and exclusively to gold, which the gold exchange standard had maintained as the universal equivalent.

Eichengreen notes that with the abandonment of convertibility by some 20 countries, the gold standard as a global system was history (Eichengreen, 1996: 82–83). But the US did not abandon it until 1933, and then only for six months. The Fed may have encouraged the Depression by keeping its interest rate high and reducing its bond purchases, but this does not mean that the Fed "had chosen international stability over domestic prosperity" (Fenstein, Temin and Toniolo, 2008: 151), even if its options were limited by the choice to preserve the convertibility of the dollar (Epstein and Ferguson, 1984). In fact, threats of devaluation quickly dissipated after the first measures, while demands for currency put pressure on the Fed's reserves. However, they were never severe enough to make the authorities devalue or suspend convertibility. The devaluation and the short suspension of 1933 were strictly domestic concerns, coming on the heels of cascading bank runs and, to end them, the week-long Bank Holiday of March 1933 (Edwards, 2017). In reality, the problem was not the demand for conversion into gold but the conversion of bank deposits into currency. The Fed did raise the discount rate, but to limit domestic credit and thus replenish the monetary base of its fractional reserve system. However, credit decreased but not the monetary base, which even increased due to the demand for reserves that banks nevertheless brought to the Fed's discount window (Hamilton, 1988: 79). But the decrease in the credit of the reserve banks was enough to stabilise the gold reserves (Eichengreen, 1992: 295). This is why there was no monetary crisis in the US, but a banking crisis caused not by the conversion of dollars into gold, but by the conversion of deposits into hard dollars. While the currency crisis in Europe caused by the gold rush was a crisis of the universal equivalent, the banking crisis in the US was a crisis of the hierarchical system of payments in which the dollar issued by the Fed served as the general equivalent. This began a decade of competitive devaluations, exchange restrictions, capital controls and trade barriers to attract the little gold in circulation. Panitch and Gindin see the root cause of deflation in the attempt to "compensate for capital loss of confidence in the absolute commitment of governments to monetary stability and the protection of bondholders"

(Panitch and Gindin, 2012: 53). But the protection of bondholders implies the protection of the industry on the basis of which dividends are distributed and taxes levied, while monetary stability implies the stability of the exchange rate and thus the defence of the currency's peg to gold. It was not the ideology of the gold standard that was responsible for the Great Depression (Eichengreen and Temin, 2000) but the very real absence of an alternative to gold with the withdrawal of the dollar from the channels of global liquidity.

The depth and duration of the Great Depression came from the in-between roles of the dollar: the dollar was not only the currency in which capital was exported from the US to support European reconstruction in the form of loans or foreign direct investment. But on the basis of the gold standard and insofar as the US current account remained in constant surplus, the crisis of 1929 reminded us that it remained a national currency against which only gold retained its status as a universal equivalent. It was because the dollar acted as a universal equivalent that speculation and the 1929 crisis, by causing dollar liquidity to dry up, led the world into deflation. But it was because it remained a particular equivalent to gold that the dollar could not prevent the world from falling into depression.

Notes

1 The current monetary policy responds to two principles which, depending on the situation, are either interdependent or contradictory. While the "traditional" monetarist objective of breaking inflation helps to stifle workers' demands for the distribution of added value, however, it is the duty of the major central banks to guarantee the conditions for financial circulation (Chesnais, 2011: 88–90). The first of these two principles conditions the other, as the return on securities is based on limited nominal wage increases. Indeed, the valuation of fictitious capital is in principle dependent on the expectation of future profits.

2 The bill of exchange was first used to finance international trade and functioned as a "postdated check". It was in effect a debt contract between an importer and an exporter whereby the former undertook to pay a certain sum to the latter at a future date, usually three months after the bill was issued (Gallarotti, 1995: 29).

3 The return to a stricter gold standard was due to a loss of confidence in the system caused both by growing political tensions between states (the Boer War) and financial crises (the US crisis of 1907) (de Cecco, 1975: 125).

4 Since 1885, the Scandinavian countries have used their currencies for mutual settlement (D'Arista, 2009: 637).

5 These principles can be summarised as follows:

> to balance national budgets and stop inflation; to direct the flow of long term capital to countries financially and economically disorganized by the war and to safeguard that capital; to generalize and develop the institution of central banking and safeguard the independence of central banks; to adopt measures of gold economy; to reach a settlement of past debts.
>
> *(Brown, 1940: 346)*

6 After 1931, sterling reserves regained the top spot but on the basis of the sterling bloc formed by the Commonwealth countries.

7 "Gold and foreign exchange reserves thus came to play the role of 'buffer', 'shock absorber' or 'insulator' instead of the 'transmitter' service required by the rules of the gold standard" (Nurkse, 1944: 119).

8 Eichengreen himself admits, relying on more recent data than those he used for his major book on the gold standard, that the price level in the US in 1925 was 40% higher than in 1913 and that the US had never returned to its pre-war level. The dollar was therefore undervalued relative to European currencies (Eichengreen and Flandreau, 2009: 388). But, curiously, Eichengreen uses this data to demonstrate that there was no shortage of gold but a misallocation between countries, and not, as he should have urged, that the cause of global deflation was not the Fed's monetary policy.

9 Capital flows from creditor countries amounted to

> perhaps between $10 and $11 billion. Almost 60 percent of this sum came from the United States; about 15 percent each came from the United Kingdom and France; and the balance, on a much smaller scale, came from the other European creditors: Switzerland, the Netherlands, Czechoslovakia, and Sweden. About one-third of this massive outflow was invested in Germany, and a further one-fourth was invested in the other European countries.
>
> *(Feinstein, Temin and Toniolo, 2008: 77–78)*

10 This competition was expressed in the fierce struggle between New York and London for short-term and long-term international loans.

9

THE DOLLAR AND ITS RELATIVE AUTONOMY

9.1 The Triffin dilemma and its challenges

When the dollar was at the height of its role as a universal credit currency, Robert Triffin (1960) saw in this provision of world liquidity by a particular state a contradiction which placed the US in a dilemma: either the US provides the volume of dollars necessary for the growth of international trade, but by eroding the confidence of foreign economic agents in the convertibility of these dollars into gold whose stock remains inelastic to this growing demand, or the US limits its dollar issues to guarantee convertibility, but by sacrificing trade and world economic prosperity (Triffin, 1960: 63). Thus, the gold exchange standard mechanism of the Bretton Woods system carried within it "the seeds of its own destruction" and could only lead "sooner or later, either to a sudden collapse à la 1931 or to a gradual tapering off of the reserve increases necessary to sustain feasible rates of growth in world trade and production" (Triffin, 1968: 102). Triffin's thinking thus referred to the experience of the interwar period and the transformation of the role of gold reserves from preserving central bank liquidity to financing short-term external deficits (Triffin, 1960: 31). In the gold exchange standard, gold was no longer used as a general medium of exchange but as a means of ultimate settlement. From that time onwards, and even more so after the Second World War, liquidity needs were met by foreign exchange reserves in sterling and to a lesser extent in dollars, which Triffin in 1960 feared would reproduce the fate of the pound. The British currency was indeed exposed to capital movements as a result of changes in interest rates or exchange rate expectations, and above all to the massive conversions into gold that had precipitated the end of the gold standard, or rather the sterling exchange standard (Maes, 2013: 1138–39).[1]

In fact, Triffin's dilemma was already expressed in the dollar itself at the end of the First World War and was embodied in the rivalry between the factions of

DOI: 10.4324/9780429261299-13

the US bourgeoisie at that time: on the one hand, Wall Street sought to extend its influence through stabilisation loans to the collapsed economies of Central and Eastern Europe, including the huge $1.4 billion loan to Germany (Guttmann, 1994: 79). This was because the US banking system was defending free trade, reconstruction aid and the US world leadership. But, however, Congress, driven by powerful isolationist instincts, obstructed this trend, first by blocking the country's membership of the League of Nations, then, with the short but brutal depression of 1920–21, by raising import tariffs under pressure from domestic industry. Yet, these contradictory trends were far more responsible for European tensions than the terms of the Treaty of Versailles. The Allies, unable to rely on their exports to the US to pay off their debts, compensated by pressuring Germany to extract huge reparations. Congress, for its part, rejected the US bankers' own demands for debt cancellation on the grounds that it would result in loss of government revenue (Guttmann, 1994: 78–79). In reality, the US was replaying the Currency School–Banking School debate, but with the fate of an entire continent at stake: Wall Street supported the dollar in its function as an international vehicle currency, while Congress, through its pressure on foreign governments, sought to defend the dollar in its function as a store of value.

The loss of confidence in the dollar has been interpreted as a consequence of the fact that its global function implied a deficit in the US current account, i.e. a growing trade deficit (Bordo, 1993: 55). Yet, not only did Triffin state his dilemma at a time when the US still dominated trade (except for the year 1959, its trade balance would remain in surplus until 1971 (Eichengreen, 2007: 12) but he "did not make any reference to the US current account deficit, but to the capital exports that lead to a deficit on the balance of payments" (Barredo-Zuriarrain, 2016: 27). In fact, the US government itself insisted that, as part of the Marshall Plan, the Europeans devalue their currencies sharply, without imagining that European catching up could affect them right down to their balance of payments (Denizet, 1985: 51). "Aid recipients were urged by the United States to expand their exports to the dollar area, and the devaluations of 1949 were a part of this effort" (Solomon, 1982: 15).

> Countries receiving Marshall Plan assistance were encouraged not to spend it all for imports but to hold a portion of the dollars so as to rebuild their depleted reserves. In other words, pursuit of balance-of-payments surpluses was established as a laudable objective.
>
> *(Eichengreen, 2007: 16)*

But above all, faced with the dollar shortage, the US encouraged domestic companies to invest in Europe, either by opening subsidiaries or by buying existing companies, in the same way that the US banks were encouraged to lend to European companies and to organise issues in their favour. "Extraordinary was the mothering of Europe by the United States during the 1950s, the excess of their attention and precautions" (Denizet, 1985: 53). Extraordinary above all was the fear of the power and influence of Soviet Russia and Communist China on the masses (Steil, 2021).

The nature of the deficits feared by Triffin was thus related to the universal equivalent function of the dollar and not to a lack of competitiveness or dynamism of the US economy vis-à-vis its German and Japanese competitors. Although the loss of power was real, from the 1960s onwards, the mistrust of central banks could certainly not be about the US ability to pay, nor about the decline of the dollar or of US industry. On the contrary, these deficits expressed the financial power of the US and the strength of its industry. It could therefore only concern the convertibility of the dollar into gold, and thus the very foundations of the international monetary system, while it had been known since the interwar period that gold alone could not meet the needs of world liquidity. Speculation against the dollar may have begun in 1961 and again in 1968, but this was entirely a matter of circumstance, in one case because of the expectation that Kennedy's programme would depreciate the dollar, in the other case because of the expectation that the price of gold in dollars would rise after the devaluation of the pound in 1967. In reality, there was no doubt about the ability of the US to pay; on the contrary, it was feared: it was the "exorbitant privilege" of the dollar that explained France's exit from the gold pool and its demands for conversion to gold in 1965, not the loss of confidence in the dollar (Bordo, 2018: 9). What worried Triffin, therefore, despite the widening balance of payments deficit, was the ability of the dollar to fulfil its function as a store of value as its function as a universal medium of exchange expanded on a steadily narrower metallic basis. With the loss of confidence in the dollar as a reserve asset, its function as a medium of exchange itself would be threatened, leading to a shortage of liquidity and thus a new Great Depression (Triffin, 1960: 70).

> [B]y granting credits to foreign governments and throughout direct investments abroad, the United States provided increasing liquidity in dollars to foreign agents without deterioration in its current account; however, deterioration of the ratio between its official reserves and external liabilities could not be avoided.
>
> *(Barredo-Zuriarrain, 2016: 41)*

As a solution, Triffin proposed the creation of a truly international reserve instrument that would fulfil the same role as gold in the interwar period. This credit mechanism would do on an international scale what the banking system had already done on a national scale by substituting credit instruments for gold (Padoa-Schioppa, 2010). But Triffin did not take into account the fact that gold had been replaced only as a means of circulation, not as a universal equivalent, i.e. as a general form of value, even if gold no longer came out of the central bank's vaults. But what Triffin proposed was not just a medium of international exchange, but a purely fiduciary reserve instrument. Doesn't the creation of an international reserve currency contradict the reserve function of money as money capital? The plan proposed by Keynes during the Bretton Woods negotiations, directly inspired by Triffin, provided for the creation of an international currency, the bancor, which central banks would buy to settle their respective balances. The exchange rate of the various currencies against the bancor would be fixed and the gold in the official reserves could be converted into bancor in order to increase the credit of central banks. But conversely, the bancor was not convertible into gold. In fact, bancors could only be used for transfers to the clearing accounts of other central banks. Through this mechanism, Keynes wanted his international clearing bank to be "a tool for encouraging the growth of money in circulation globally, and for putting up barriers against monetary contraction" (Steil, 2013: 143). But just as the national monetary policy was to lead to the rentier's euthanasia, the international clearing bank and its currency, the bancor, were to abolish money as a store of value of the wealth of nations. As Adolf Berle, then Roosevelt's economic adviser and Morgenthau's assistant, gently objected, the bancor, "which was not to be redeemable for gold, would never be a credible store of value for a creditor country like the United States" (Steil, 2013: 161). Just as with Gesell's melting currency, it was a matter of "to use it or to lose it". If creditor nations did not wish to spend their surpluses on imports, then they would be required to make them available to other countries struggling to pay for their imports and requiring time and resources before they could adjust. But the bancor would not simply have represented the international equivalent of national currencies, but also the surplus value contained in these surpluses, resulting from the process of valuing the productive capital of surplus nations. What the Keynes Plan amounted to, which was opposed not only by the US but also by the Bank of England party (Dostaler, 2009: 393), was a monetary system in which the surplus value itself in its general form of store of value, as a form of private appropriation of social wealth, would actually disappear.

Triffin had begun to express his concern about the fate of the dollar when, with the return of external convertibility of European currencies in 1958, the central banks of Europe sought to reduce their surplus dollar reserves by converting them into gold (Cohen, 1977: 99). We had moved from dollar shortage to dollar glut. But it is forgotten that this external convertibility led to an increased role for the dollar on the foreign exchange market because of its function as a vehicle currency (Battilossi, 2020: 283). Above all, the return of external convertibility coincided with and stimulated the emergence of a new market that would bring the dollar closer to its pre-war status as a universal currency without borders and remove it from the control of its issuing bank, the Fed, and from the circumstances of the country in which it officially circulated, the US. For while the public demand for dollars weakened with the demand for conversion of official reserves into gold, the private demand for dollars spread throughout the world.[2]

9.2 The bewitched currency: the Eurodollar market

The story of the formation of the Eurodollar market is the story of a bewitchment (Sartre, 1960: 173). For until the US decided to do something about it, it seemed as if whatever they did would have the opposite result to that expected or hoped for. This is why one cannot understand this story if one tries to trace it according to the logic of the interests at work, even if it is obvious that the City found in it the opportunity for its resurrection and that the US industry and banking sectors found in it the living source of their prosperity and their world domination. But the whole process of its formation makes the US national interests the plaything of the higher laws of money in its role as universal equivalent and the manager of its contradictions. This submission was undoubtedly voluntary, as the Marshall Plan and the export of dollars to Europe responded to the need to accelerate post-war reconstruction and thus ensure prosperity for the masses seduced by the success of the Soviet model. But it was precisely the export of dollars that assumed its role as a universal equivalent, and the Marshall Plan actually played only a minor role in the reconstruction of Europe. Industrial production in Europe had already reached its pre-war level by the time the first convoys arrived from across the Atlantic, and the Plan represented only a tiny fraction of the GDP of the individual recipients, with the exception of Austria (Hitchcock, 2010: 159–60). What the Marshall Plan actually provided were the dollars needed to purchase products and raw materials on not only the US but foreign markets. The shortage of dollars, in fact, "threatened to halt Europe's recovery, and it was with this fairly narrow problem in mind that American planners in the State Department framed the idea of a large American aid program to Europe" (Hitchcock, 2010: 160). It was not, therefore, the Marshall Plan that allowed the US to impose the dollar as a universal currency, but it was because the dollar was already the international invoicing currency that the Plan allowed the reconstruction of Europe to be completed through the world market.

In order to transform the dollar gap into a dollar glut, it is true that the US had not only exported dollars: it had also provoked its future deficits, by pushing Europeans to devalue their currencies in 1949, by increasing their spending from 1950 onwards, by making foreign US aid permanent (de Cecco, 1982: 6–7), and by pushing its firms to make direct foreign investments in dollars, either for the purchase of existing firms or for the creation of new ones.[3] However, the US very quickly became captive to the very conditions of the globalisation of production and finance that it had initiated with the all-out spread of the dollar.

This is because the offshore dollar market did not arise from the US use of US dollars in Europe, but from the placement of foreign dollars with European banks. And the irony of history is that, among these foreigners, the communists were the pioneers. For it was China which, fearing the US reprisals following the 1949 revolution, decided to keep its dollar assets in the Soviet bank in Paris, whose cable name, Eurobank, gave its name to the market for dollars placed in Europe (Markham, 2002: 328). But it was also Russia itself that, for the same reasons, preferred to keep the dollars earned from its exports of luxury goods – caviar, vodka, canned crab – in banks in London. Even as the Cold War took hold, the dollar transcended the boundaries of the "free world" and crossed geopolitical divides. Nevertheless, it was the pound crisis in 1957,[4] which heralded the decisive crisis of 1967 and for which the Eurodollar market was directly responsible (Denizet, 1985: 99–100), that established the market in London: the crisis had in fact prompted the Macmillan government to prohibit British banks from lending sterling to finance trade between countries outside the sterling zone (de Cecco, 1982: 8). It was at this point that these banks began to accept dollar deposits and to finance international trade with them. The return of the convertibility of the pound for non-residents stimulated transactions in unregulated currencies before Thatcher removed all foreign exchange controls in 1979 (Palan, 1998: 632–33).[5]

The dollar had been the real world currency since at least the First World War, but only for central banks. Yet, the accumulation of foreign currency deposits in London banks was not new, the practice being common in the interwar period (Schenk, 1998: 221). Only with exchange controls, imposed from the Great Depression onwards, were deposits immediately returned to the Bank of England or deposited in the US accounts of domestic banks. The novelty of the Eurodollar market is that these deposits can be used for loans to third parties in the UK and elsewhere (Schenk, 1998: 221). What makes the Eurodollar market the great monetary event of the 20th century is that for the first time since the formation of modern states, a national fiat currency became a global private currency whose supply would be brought under the control of the market (Burn, 2006: 4).

Eurodollars are, literally, nothing more than dollar-denominated time deposits that are not subject to the US banking regulation because they are issued by a non-US commercial bank or a non-US branch of a commercial bank. The expansion of these deposits occurs when a Eurobank re-deposits Eurodollar funds that have been deposited with it. Each re-deposit creates a deposit liability on the Eurobank's balance sheet; the total Eurodollars created can therefore be several times the original claim on the Eurobank (Greenberg, 1983: 1495). These are time deposits (or certificates of deposit, see below) which cannot be used as a means of exchange to settle debts. On the one hand, and unlike bank deposits, there is no ex nihilo issuance of dollars on this market since here credit in Eurodollars is conditional on an initial deposit in a New York bank. Moreover, it is not possible to draw cheques on these deposits, for example, and thus to bring these deposits into commercial circulation other than by converting them into cash. But on the other hand, these deposits, whose maturity varies between one day and five years but mostly between one week and six months (Murau, 2018: 18), are permanently replicated: "Once money is raised, then without a reserve requirement it can be loaned, deposited, re-loaned, re-deposited, re-loaned, and so on in offshore markets without limits imposed by the banking system" (Allen, 2016: 4). This is what inspired Friedman to say that Eurodollars only come from the bookkeeper's pen.[6]

As rightly noted by Jean Denizet, probably the best post-war French specialist on the international monetary system, it was the velocity of circulation of existing dollars that increased and was responsible for part of the inflation of 1965–75 (Denizet, 1977: 108–09). But Denizet neglects the fact that in the absence of a regulatory framework, particularly in terms of reserve requirements, banking practice in the Eurodollar market also increased the quantity of money in circulation.

> Similarly to other money market innovations of the period (such as repurchase agreements and money market funds), Eurodollar deposits allowed investors to place funds outside the domestic banking system without limiting its capacity to generate deposits. Being free from reserve requirements (which had been introduced in 1969 but lifted in 1974, since they were easily circumvented), Eurodollars, by decreasing the effective reserve ratio, provided an additional 'avenue for the growth' of credit not directly constrained by the supply of federal reserves. [B]y then the volume of external dollar claims vis-à-vis nonbanks – a measure of the credit generated by the Eurodollar market – was already equivalent to more than 10% of the US money stock as measured by M3.
>
> *(Battilossi, 2020: 305–06)*

The fictitious nature of these short-term claims is proven by their growth, which between 1970 and 1985 rose from 20% to 80% of trade in goods and, after a drop to around 40% in the second half of the 1980s, reached 120% in 2007 (Battilossi, 2020: 280–81). And although a large proportion of Eurodollar transactions were linked to foreign exchange transactions (liquid funds were converted into dollars and the exchange rate risk was hedged by forward contracts), the bulk of Eurodollars was decoupled from international trade and resulted from interbank transactions whose multiplication formed a "deposit pyramiding" (Mehrling, 2002). But while the Eurodollar market had uncertain effects on the quantity of money outside the US (de Cecco, 1982: 37), it was responsible for inflation through the extravagant interest rates that the Fed's monetary policy imposed on the whole of Europe from 1965 to 1969 and especially between 1972 and 1974 (Denizet, 1985: 53 and 66). It is through them that inflation was permanently established by feeding the price–interest–low profit–price spiral (Denizet, 1985: 54).[7]

If with the emergence of the Eurodollar market, neoliberalism was reborn before its time (and we shall see that the neoliberal project indeed goes back much further), this is because that market developed, from the 1950s, from the measures of liberalisation and deregulation of the monetary and financial system elaborated at Bretton Woods: relaxation of the rules compelling banks and companies to hand over their dollar surpluses to their respective central banks; external convertibility of European currencies in 1958, i.e. convertibility for non-residents having invested in local currency; relaxation of exchange controls (Burn, 2006: 23). In this early attack on the Bretton Woods system, the Bank of England, entirely dedicated to the interests of the City, was probably the first to launch hostilities. While the Swiss and German authorities blocked the entry of Eurodollars, fearing both upward pressure on their currencies and the inflationary pressures that an increased supply of money would provoke, the Bank of England, which sought, as it did after the First World War, to save the former prestige of the pound, and above all to revive a City rendered anaemic by Wall Street, lobbied for an early return to external convertibility of the pound, the removal of exchange controls and other restrictions, with a view to re-establishing the pound as a vehicle and reserve currency, thereby re-establishing the City as the leading financial centre (Burn, 2006: 97).[8] The City bankers had already written off the British nation to save the pound, so all they had to do was sacrifice the pound to the dollar and act as stockbrokers for their former colony. Financial globalisation was not the result of a concerted expansion of US finance (Konings, 2009; Panitch and Gindin, 2009), nor of the attempt of banks and markets to escape the control of national states (Green, 2016), but of the requirements of the universal role of the dollar in the monetary and financial circulation of the world market. No doubt, Green rightly observes, American finance could never have become global without the City perpetuating its role as a warehouse of global liquidity (Green, 2016: 431). But the Anglo-American axis was decisive in this development insofar as the new universal currency found in the structures of the old one the institutions adequate to the nature of its functions. And when the US institutions were sufficiently mature to allow the dollar to fulfil these same functions, the Fed, through President Volcker, called in its troops.[9]

Once the market was established, any binding rule imposed on the official markets immediately led to an influx of new liquidity: for example, the prohibition by the West German, Swiss and later French monetary authorities of interest payments on balances held by foreigners (Burn, 2006: 23). But the central banks, and especially the Bank for International Settlements (BIS), did more than give up some of their capital and exchange controls. They were, along with multinational firms, the most important source of funds for the market in its early days (Scott-Quinn, 1975). As the European recovery took hold, the central banks of surplus countries supplied their dollar surpluses to the market, sometimes directly, sometimes through the BIS, and sometimes via swap agreements with their commercial banks (Schenk, 1998: 232). But they were not only feeding the market, they were also borrowing dollars from it. In both cases, the intention was to maintain the Bretton Woods parity of their currencies and to control the national money supply. By encouraging private recipients of dollars to hold on to them, the market prevented dollars from entering the official reserves but, more importantly, helped prevent a further reduction in the US gold reserves, despite the cooperation of the central banks. It was primarily for the latter reason that the US took advantage of a market that had completely eluded them in the first place (Burn, 2006: 135). Thus, while in 1960 almost the entire US deficit of $3.9 billion had been financed by gold sales and increased foreign official dollar holdings, in 1961 only half of the $2.5 billion deficit was financed in this way, the rest being held in private dollar assets. But the windfall of the market for central banks actually meant the loss of their foreign exchange control. For

> [t]he flows of hot money unleashed by the Eurodollar market destabilised sterling and the dollar during the 1960s and 1970s. By increasing the

> exposure of these two key currencies to speculative attacks, the Eurodollar market played a central role in the collapse of fixed exchange rates. But, paradoxically, the Euromarkets entrenched the hegemony of the dollar, ensuring its international supremacy even after its fixed convertibility to gold was terminated.
>
> *(Green, 2016: 430)*[10]

The Eurodollar market thus shifted the Bretton Woods system to an offshore dollar standard even before its official collapse; to put it more exactly, it shifted the system of exchange rates between different units of account to a system of exchange at par between onshore and offshore dollars from a common unit of account (Murau, Rini and Haas, 2020: 772).

However, from 1960 onwards, everything the US authorities did to curb the outflow of dollars only accelerated the growth of this market. Since the New Deal, the US banking system had been regulated by Regulation Q, which imposed reserve requirements and, above all, gave the Fed the power to set interest rate ceilings on savings accounts and time deposits, the aim being to reduce competition for deposits and limit banks' investments in risky securities (Friedman, 1975). As soon as monetary policy tightened and interest rates rose above these ceilings, commercial firms and institutional investors shifted their liquidity from banks to alternative money market instruments (Baxter, 1968). Banks responded to this competition first by issuing certificates of deposit, for which an active secondary market was soon organised in New York.[11] But the Fed reacted by also imposing ceilings on these certificates of deposit. It was then that the US banks found in the opening of branches in London and soon also in other offshore locations the means to fully exploit their competitive advantage in the Eurodollar market (Sylla, 2002), occasionally introducing certificates of deposit in the City (Green, 2016: 445). While the Kennedy administration initially authorised the issuance of these new financial instruments precisely to improve the balance of payments by attracting capital to the US markets, their development led to a strengthening of the Eurodollar market (Burn, 2006: 169). Thus, since their introduction in 1966, the circulation of Eurodollar certificates of deposit has increased steadily, reaching $50 billion in 1980 and $130 billion in the late 1990s (Goodfriend, 1998: 51). Even the tensions of the Cold War contributed to the growth of the market when, following the Cuban missile crisis, the Soviet Union's state bank transferred its foreign dollar reserves to London, fearing that the US authorities would freeze its accounts.

With increased government spending on bombs in Vietnam and butter in the US (Johnson's Great Society project), the Federal Reserve, fearing overheating, tightened monetary policy in 1966 (and again in 1968 and 1969), by reducing the interest rate payable on certificates of deposit, thereby increasing the interest premium offered on Treasury bills. Their intention was to attract investors and reduce the money supply in circulation. But their strategy backfired. First, the certificates of deposit were cashed in to redirect funds to the Eurodollar market, attracted by its even higher interest rates. More importantly, these funds were then repatriated to the US as New York banks, seeking to replenish their reserves, began to borrow via the interbank market from their own foreign branches in Europe and other Eurodollar areas. This influx led to increased lending by New York banks, precisely the opposite of what the Fed had hoped for (Burn, 2006: 139).

Not only were foreign dollar holders now discouraged from depositing their dollars in the US money market, but at the same time, the US companies were no longer willing to repatriate capital earned abroad. In fact, they began to cut themselves off from their domestic money markets, depositing their foreign earnings and obtaining the short- and long-term financing needed by their foreign branches in the Euromarkets. The deeper effect of these changes was to create a powerful link between the US, the Eurodollar and European financial markets, and to make European markets more exposed to changes in the US domestic and monetary policy (Dosoo and Gallant, 1992: 17–18).

We have seen above that the deterioration of the US national accounts was due to nothing other than the international role of its currency; that the US civilian and military aid and capital outflows coincided with a trade surplus. However, it soon became clear that foreign trade owed its surpluses to this foreign aid and capital investment: without the purchases of US products induced by these exported dollars, trade would be in deficit (Denizet, 1985: 73). In order to improve the balance of payments without reducing these exports, Kennedy and then Johnson created the Interest Equalization Tax, which imposed a tax on the US residents (banks or security holders) lending to non-resident borrowers or issuers of securities.[12] It may have had beneficial effects on current accounts, but by accelerating the opening of subsidiaries of US banks, it intensified the activity of the Eurodollar market (Markham, 2002: 328) and thus favoured the recovery of the US deficit after 1966. For it was not the balance of payments deficit that drove the Eurodollar market, even if the US multinationals helped it through the direct export of capital without repatriation of profits; through the reduction of exports due to relocation; through increased competition from European industry, stimulated by the transfer of technology and management techniques; and through industrial concentration resulting from competition from the US firms themselves (Junne, 1973: 76). Above all, it was the Eurodollar market itself that stimulated private demand for dollars in the form of time deposits and Treasury bills. "New 'non-European' bond issues in Europe increased from less than $200 million in 1962 to nearly $1.5 billion in 1966" (Allen, 2016: 13). From 1965 onwards, it was because capital from the rest of the world fled to the US that the balance of payments deficit widened. But in 1969 the interest rate war began between the US, whose rates, which had been high until then, were lowered from that year onwards, and Germany, which raised its rates to contain the threat of inflation. And as the US took measures to discourage banks from borrowing from their foreign subsidiaries, there was an influx of capital into the Eurodollar market, but also massive conversions of dollars into deutsche marks (Allen, 2016: 18). On the eve of the *Nixon shokku*,[13] everyone in the US agreed that the dollar was overvalued against the mark, the yen and the Canadian dollar. The disagreement was about the method of rebalancing, between the supporters of diplomacy and the Nixon administration. Charles Coombs, for example, then director of the New York Fed, suggested a revaluation of the three currencies through negotiation, while Nixon's entourage relied on the Benign Neglect method to encourage speculation against the dollar (Helleiner, 1994: 112–13). In either case, the hope was that the desired result would be achieved because either the central banks would absorb the dollars pouring into the markets to maintain parity at all costs, thereby forcing a monetary expansion that would lead to an appreciation; or they would allow the dollar to fall, only to be pressured by the exporting sector into an expansionary policy (Coombs, 1976: 209). The former would rely on Bretton Woods principles, the latter on the US market power. But in both cases, the Benign Neglect relied entirely on the strength of the Eurodollar market, i.e. on dollar movements outside the Fed's control. Coombs lamented that he had been totally excluded from discussions on the measures to be taken, but only the existence of a dollar market outside the jurisdictional borders of the US could explain this political quirk. The whole operation was based on the interest rate differential between the US and the offshore market, without which the pressure on European currencies would never have reached the speed and magnitude the Nixon administration had hoped for. The first Nixon shock did not come in August 1971 but in January 1970 when, at the inauguration ceremony of the new Fed Chairman Arthur Burns, Nixon said to him, with a smile on his face: "Dr. Burns, please, give us some money" (Coombs, 1976: 206). In Nixon's mind, the Fed was also the central banker of the offshore market, through which money would flow to the London foreign exchange market.[14]

No doubt Nixon's primary goal was re-election in 1972, for which he intended to reduce unemployment and boost activity (Bordo, 2018: 14). But the poise with which he pressured Burns to change the direction of policy while removing the monetary authorities from the discussions also leaves no doubt about the international effects of this reorientation: Connally's words – the dollar is our currency but it is your problem – already inspired Nixon's address to Burns. And Nixon could all the more easily decide to suspend the convertibility of the dollar into gold and practice the policy of Benign Neglect because there was no real alternative to the dollar standard, with or without gold. No one, not even France, could seriously contemplate returning to a gold standard system when the Eurodollar market was booming and liquidity needs were pressing. And neither Germany nor Japan was willing to give up its trade advantage to make its currency the world's reserve asset (Guttmann, 1994: 146–47). Of course, the US had an interest in keeping the dollar as the backbone of the system and acted vigorously to do so. But just as individual economic agents are the bearers of social relations of production, the US acted as the conscious force of the autonomous and contradictory development of the universal equivalent.

It was thus through the offshore dollar market, entirely outside the US jurisdiction until the creation of the International Banking Facilities[15] in 1981, that the US benefited from the issuance of universal currency. And it was through the growth of this market that the interest rates of the currencies of the major capitalist powers aligned with each other to form, with LIBOR, a true single interest rate for the world money market. For the past 60 years or so, the Eurodollar Interbank Offered Rate (LIBOR), which is an average of the rates offered by the largest banks on the London market, has in effect acted as the "true global cost of money" (Stigum and Crescenzi, 2007: 240). Throughout this period, the LIBOR rate has provided a kind of structural premium over comparable national deposits and other US money market rates. Today, the markets are so closely integrated that it would be futile to establish unidirectional causal relationships between the two markets, as they "are merely competing segments of the total market for dollar-denominated credit" (Giddy, Dufey and Min, 1979: 51). However, an extensive empirical analysis has shown that not only was there no cointegration between the US interest rate and the Eurodollar rate prior to 1992, i.e. the start of truly global financial market integration, but that prior to that date and from at least 1983 onwards, causality ran from the Eurodollar rate to the federal funds rate (Yang, Shin and Khan, 2007: 142–43). Since 1992 and until 2002, however, while the two rates appear to be more co-determined, "the strength of causality from the Eurodollar rate to the US CD [Certificate of deposit] rate is more conspicuous than the other way around" (*Ibidem*).

However, it is well known that from the 1980s onwards, the market declined with the rise of financial innovations that reduced the traditional intermediation activity of banks in favour of securitisation and off-balance sheet activities (Logan et al., 1986: 540; Battilossi, 2020: 279). With banks both competing on both sides of their balance sheets with non-bank financial institutions and under pressure (see Logan et al., 1986: 539–40; Guttmann, 2014: 63), the market lost its privileged position in global capital flows at this time. But it had first acted as a cocoon before it became the chrysalis of global finance, for not only was it the originator of the international money market, but the Eurobanks experimented with the instruments of offshore finance before anyone else (Green, 2016: 445).

9.3 Dollar defence and "Nixon shokku"

We have examined how the first tensions on the dollar arose with the return of external convertibility of European currencies. By reducing dependence on the dollar for trade finance, the dollar shortage suddenly became a dollar glut, leading to massive demands for convertibility that quadrupled between 1958 and 1960 (Guttmann, 1994: 138). As early as 1961, the Kennedy administration reacted with measures aimed at preventing foreign governments from converting their dollars into gold: raising interest rates on the US government securities held in foreign official reserves, and exempting them from taxes on interest payments (Seabrooke, 2001: 58). But after the establishment of the gold pool in 1961, the first real crisis of confidence occurred in 1968, when inflation accelerated in the US and the pound gave in to speculation through devaluation. After first measures to control foreign direct investment by the US firms, the US replaced the gold pool with a two-tier system allowing the private market to coexist with an official market where gold continued to trade at $35 per ounce (Bordo, 2018: 13). In the same month, the 25% gold cover requirement for the domestic currency supply was removed, freeing up reserves for convertibility claims. More importantly, Special Drawing Rights (SDRs) were introduced in the same month, a currency created from scratch and backed by IMF gold reserves, which surplus countries agreed between 1970 and 1972 to exchange for their own currency in order to supply their debtors with it (Eichengreen, 2007: 10). In fact, as early as 1968, the US stopped paying back the dollars accumulated abroad in gold and adopted the Benign Neglect policy. The only way to speculate against the dollar would be to exchange it for other currencies, thus placing the entire burden of speculation on foreign central banks.

But from the early 1960s onwards, the Fed entered into bilateral or standby swap agreements to get short-term credit in case of a speculative surge (McCauley and Schenk, 2020). And the US had already created Roosa bonds,[16] medium-term bonds denominated in foreign currency that allowed central banks to convert their dollars into assets denominated in their own currency. Their sale peaked in 1965 (Triffin, 1968: 36), at the same time as the Eurodollar market allowed central banks to invest their reserves in dollars (Klopstock, 1968). But 1968 was the year of withdrawal: withdrawal of the class struggle into itself with the student revolts marking the great movement of subjectivisation of social contradictions (the student in solidarity with the worker, the establishment of Maoist militants in the factories), but it was also the withdrawal of the power of the US, which, with the policy of détente, ceased to worry about international communism. Thus, Nixon extended through dollar diplomacy what he had begun through political diplomacy: a movement of relative withdrawal from the great external projections of US power. But it was the withdrawal of a country sure of its victory and the signs of its power, namely its currency as well as its military bases:

> President Richard M. Nixon declared in his inaugural address on January 20, 1969, that 'after a period of confrontation, we are entering an era of negotiations' with the Soviet Union. Privately, he told the Soviet foreign minister, Andrei Gromyko, that in the United States 'whenever elections approached, political leaders were tempted to take a belligerent anti-Communist line,' but that Nixon himself 'did not consider such an approach to be in the interests of world peace or of Soviet-American relations'.
>
> *(Schulzinger, 2010: 373)*

In 1968, with the creation of the two-tier gold market, the US stopped converting official dollar reserves presented to the Fed into gold.

It has been said that after the devaluation of 1971, the Nixon administration set out to eliminate any potential competitors to the dollar: through the demonetisation of gold and the veto of a new SDR issue, among other things

(Guttmann, 1994: 146–47). However, the US would soon put pressure on Germany and Japan to replace the dollar as the international reserve currency with the deutsche mark or yen. Not only had gold already been demonetised since 1968, but nobody believed that SDRs could replace the dollar. These measures were mainly aimed at preserving the US gold reserves (Bordo, 2018: 8). Moreover, Burns did not hesitate to persevere with his accommodating monetary policy, nor did the Treasury falter in the expansion of its budget deficit (Guttmann, 1994: 147). In any case, the ensuing surge in commodity prices was the result of the combined effect of devaluation, domestic inflation and monetary expansion. From then onwards, floating exchange rates could not be resisted for long: after the Smithsonian agreement on new parities in December 1971, which Nixon said was "the most significant monetary arrangement in the history of the world", the dollar was devalued by a further 10% in February 1973 and, after massive but unsuccessful interventions to stabilise exchange rates, the price of gold was allowed to float freely on the market and the industrialised countries soon abandoned their currencies to the generalised float (Ghosh and Qureshi, 2017: 13).

9.4 The Volcker shock and financial inflation

The dollar crisis of 1978 came as a punishment for the years of stagflation that followed the Nixon shock and the move to floating exchange rates. Not only had the dollar continued to depreciate, especially against gold, but stagflation had plunged financial markets into their worst decade since the 1929 crash (Wigmore, 1997: 367). Prior to Volcker's mandate in 1979, the Fed took vigorous action against inflation, including raising "the discount rate a full percentage point to 9.5 percent" (Solomon, 1982: 350), its highest level for 45 years (Markham, 2002b: 71). It was seen as the end of the era of Benign Neglect: "November 1, 1978, came to be viewed as a turning point in US policy. Henceforth, it was widely believed, US policy makers would be more sensitive to the external value of the dollar" (Solomon, 1982: 350). But soon Volcker "both tightened monetary policy and changed the operating procedures of the Federal Reserve System" (Solomon, 1982: 353). These measures would lead to interest rate levels from which Europeans would suffer bitterly, not because they would lead to deflation, but because, with the rise in the dollar exchange rate that these levels led to, the prices of goods invoiced in dollars, primarily oil, rose. To mitigate the depreciation of their currencies, they also had to raise their interest rates even as they suffered from ever higher unemployment (Solomon, 1982: 356–57).

But since the US owed its economic power to the international role of the dollar (Norrlof, 2020), every effort was made to free up the financial circulation of the dollar wherever possible. The question of whether the US pushed for the lifting of capital controls first in the OECD countries (Helleiner, 1995: 328), and then in the emerging countries hit by the crisis, for its own interest or that of the global financial oligarchy (Gowan, 1999: 33), is historically irrelevant if we consider the place of the dollar on the eve of the great wave of financial liberalisation. This is because at that time the US no longer had to impose the dollar. All they had to do was to let it impose itself, which meant letting its own financial markets impose themselves, which were more liquid, deeper and more "productive":

> US officials predicted accurately that internationally mobile funds would be attracted by the unique depth of US financial markets and the international role of the dollar, as well as by the high US interest rates which emerged out of the combination of tight monetary policy and loose fiscal policy in the Reagan years.
>
> *(Helleiner, 1995: 329)*

Then, the hegemonic power of the US would become a "structural" power, i.e. based on market requirements (Helleiner, 1995: 323). All that was needed was to take measures to free capital from financial repression and, above all, from state control of central banks: the abolition of capital account controls in 1974, before the UK and, a little later, the other OECD countries followed suit; the abolition of the ceiling on the amount of loans granted by a bank to an individual borrower; and the Treasury's guarantee of the banks' credit risks (Gowan, 1999: 22). But the Treasury became not only an international lender of last resort but also an international borrower of first resort when, in 1984, after the US abolished the withholding tax on foreign ownership of US bonds, it issued Treasury bills directly on the Eurodollar market for the first time (Helleiner, 1995: 329). Externally, the Eurodollar market again served as a platform for the spread of the dollar, through the recycling of petrodollars accumulated during inflation by oil-producing countries, which the US had ensured were channelled through the private international banking system and not through the IMF (Helleiner, 1995: 323). Once again, it does not matter whether this price increase was intended precisely for this purpose or whether all the conditions were already in place for such a development: the dollar was more than ever the universal invoicing currency, means of settlement and reserve instrument. But from then onwards, the stability of exchange rates, which, apart from the fixed exchange rate system, were based above all on the mechanisms for rebalancing deficits with the help of the IMF and surplus countries, depended entirely on the markets' opinion of the "fundamentals" of the deficit states with regard to their exchange rates.

The expression "Volcker shock" probably reflected the effect of the Fed's first measures on speculators on the Tokyo Stock Exchange in October 1979, but it does not do justice to the effect on the US industrial workers. For Paul Volcker's policy was less a brutal shock than a long series of blows delivered with a relentlessness that only ceased in 1982, once the proletariat was on its knees and the US economy in recession. It has been said that after Volcker and the concentration of the Board's powers, the Fed's communication took on an unprecedented importance in the conduct of monetary policy (Akhtar and Howe, 1991). But the Fed's first major message was not to Congress in the form of a speech by its chairman, but to the world's investors through the only language they universally shared: that of the key interest rate figures which, on the eve of the recession, had reached 20%, whereas the unemployment rate was close to 11% (Markham, 2002: 73). Volcker did not disappoint: he had been appointed to "reassure the financial markets, to buy back legitimacy and to reassure our major partners and our partners in the international financial markets" (Vice-President Mondale quoted in Helleiner, 1994: 133).

Because of this new distribution of added value in favour of financial income, the Volcker shock has been hastily characterised as the launch of neoliberalism (Duménil and Lévy, 2004). In reality, the very project of fighting inflation, whatever the socio-economic costs, presupposed the opening up of liberalised financial markets both inside and outside the US. Above all, it presupposed the international role of the dollar, and the challenge was precisely to consolidate its existence as a universal equivalent. By returning to low inflation and anchoring inflationary expectations, the Fed's monetary policy gave back to the dollar the stability required by an international unit of account and to Treasury bills the status of a safe asset par excellence (Aquanno, 2009: 126–27). But above all, by making price stability the fundamental objective of monetary policy, including disconnecting interest rate policy from domestic growth and employment requirements, Volcker transformed the Fed into a bank for financing international markets and its key interest rate into the single interest rate of the international financial system. This is because the new procedures for controlling bank reserves to reduce the money supply did not reduce the demand for credit. They shifted it from the industrial sector to the financial sector. Moreover, the rise in long-term interest rates and the instability of short-term rates that resulted directly from Volcker's decisions stimulated the demand for credit from banks and financial institutions:

> the Volcker shock arguably increased the demand for credit within the financial sector, where financial institutions of all kinds, though particularly banks, suddenly needed to rapidly revolve instruments based on short-term liabilities, in order not to have to call in long-term loans. The resultant 'innovation', all of which was and remains ultimately dollar-based, was phenomenal.
>
> *(Newstadt, 2009: 100–01)*

More generally, the control of the money supply came at the same time as the proliferation of financial instruments (Panitch and Gindin, 2009: 31) which, as quasi-currencies, multiplied both the forms of store of value and the means of financial circulation. In fact, apart from the new reserve rules, Volcker did not take any measures against the use of these new financial techniques, allowing banks easier access to reserve funds (Greider, 1987), so that the Volcker shock shifted inflation from the goods market to the assets market:

> international bond placements grew exponentially, driven by growth in all of the market's primary segments. From 1980 to 1990, the total foreign ownership of US public debt securities increased from US$129.7 billion to US$458.4 billion [...] Further, the international arm of the US market received a boost from the globalization of US corporate securities: foreign purchases of US corporate bonds increased from $2.9 billion in 1980 to $39.8 billion in 1985 (US Census Bureau 1998). New issue volume in the Eurobond market was even more pronounced, increasing in volume from approximately US$18.8 billion in 1980 to over US$210 billion by the end of the decade.
>
> *(Aquanno, 2009: 127)*

And while he was concerned about the consequences of the Eurodollar market growth on his policy of restricting the money supply (Aquanno, 2009: 135), Volcker readily accepted the creation of the International Banking Facility which, by attracting Eurodollars to the New York market, would "undermine domestic policy" by "creating additional opportunities for monetary leakage" (Richard Dale quoted in Helleiner, 1994: 139).[17]

As a result, by 1982, monetarism had disappeared from the monetary authorities' analytical framework. As Greenspan admitted:

> Increasingly since 1982 we have been setting the funds rate directly ... in the current state of our knowledge, money demand has become too difficult to predict .... As the historic relationship between measured money supply and spending deteriorated, policymaking, seeing no alternative, turned more eclectic and discretionary.
>
> *(Greenspan, 1997)*

The interest rate once again became the sole instrument of inflation control for the entire dollar-anchored world economy. But the main goal had been achieved: workers' aspirations and capacity for collective action had been broken, so that Volcker confided some years later that "the most important single action of the administration in helping the anti-inflation fight was defeating the air traffic controllers strike" (quoted in Taylor, 1995: 778).[18]

But with the financial liberalisation measures, even the interest rate policy made the Fed dependent on foreign markets. The interest rate cuts that followed the Volcker shock were basically due to the deregulated influx of foreign capital. And this influx was further fuelled by the Reagan administration's deepening of the budget deficit through tax cuts and military spending, giving attractive interest rates on Treasury bonds (Allen, 2016: 32).[19] The influx of cheap foreign dollars was the material for the "debt factory" in the US: the savings rate of US residents fell from 8% to 4% by the mid-1980s and in 1985 the US became, for the first time since 1914, a net debtor to the rest of the world (Allen, 2016: 33).

Faced with the contradiction in the functions of the dollar posed by the dilemma, we have seen how Kennedy's US worked to defend the dollar in its value reserve function, until the demonetisation of gold from 1968 onwards left the dollar without a serious alternative: creation of a gold pool guaranteeing a sufficient supply of the precious metal by central banks, General Arrangements to Borrow (GAB) allowing the IMF to use funds in the event of a speculative attack against the dollar or any other currency (McDowell, 2017: 47), swap agreements between central banks allowing mainly the Fed to defend the dollar in the foreign exchange market (McDowell, 2017: 54), Roosa bonds converting Treasury bills held by foreign central banks into long-term US Treasury bonds denominated in foreign currency, and finally, from 1968 onwards, the creation of SDRs to finance part of the US balance of payments deficit (Grin, 1999: 379–80). But since there was no question of letting the deficits grow indefinitely, we have seen how, once the de facto demonetisation of gold had taken place with the creation of the dual gold market, Nixon used Benign Neglect, the sole purpose of which was to shift the burden of balance of payments adjustment onto the surplus countries.

The demonetisation of gold, caused by this pressure from foreign central banks, explains the structure of the balance of payments disequilibrium after Bretton Woods. This is because it removed any objective limit to the accumulation of US external liabilities, making it depend solely on confidence in the dollar and the downward pressure that a loss of confidence would necessarily bring.[20] But what keeps the system stable is the safe asset nature of these liabilities in times of crisis.[21] After the demonetisation of gold, it was the US Treasury bills that would form the objective market base of the dollar. For even as gold disappeared from public circulation, the market for the US bonds was becoming more international, especially for Treasury securities, whose foreign ownership rose from 10% to 21% between 1970 and 1980. With the price and exchange rate volatility resulting from the Nixon shock, Treasuries became the main safe asset for international investors "who recognised the depth and liquidity of the US bond market despite all the hand-wringing about declining US power and economic strength" (Panitch and Gindin, 2012: 151).

9.5 The US Treasury security: the universal equivalent of finance capital

9.5.1 From the dollar-gold standard to the dollar-Treasury bill standard

The superiority of public credit over private credit from companies or consumers is due to the guarantee that the state has inexhaustible sources of revenue, thanks to its tax system and its assets. This is not the case for private borrowers whose income depends on profits and wages which are by nature uncertain in a market economy. No doubt, taxes and customs tariffs are also subject to the vagaries of the economic climate, social conflicts, war and epidemics. But it is a structural superiority that underpins the elasticity of the borrowing capacity of states and the anchoring role of interest rates on public debt in the financial markets. This is why Ricardo entitled his great work *On the Principles of Political Economy and Taxation* (Ricardo, 1821: 265). The fact that it offers the investor a regular income without having to go through productive investment makes government securities the safe asset par excellence.

> All modern finance, the whole of the banking business, is interwoven in the closest fashion with public credit. A part of their business capital is necessarily invested and put out at interest in quickly convertible public funds. Their deposits, the capital placed at their disposal and distributed by them among merchants and industrialists, are partly derived from the dividends of holders of government securities.
>
> *(Marx, 1852: 171)*

But the more the development of capitalism itself increases the liquid wealth of its agents (uninvested profits, unconsumed wages, unspent annuities), the more the demand for these safe assets grows relative to their supply and makes Treasuries the backbone of the entire credit system (Gorton, 2017: 548). This is why the very people who give lessons in sobriety and frugality to overextended states urge them to return to the public debt market when, as in the case of the US federal government at the end of the technology boom, its primary surpluses signalled the outright extinction of its current debt (Stiglitz, 2003: 79).[22]

It is during periods of market tension, and especially during financial crises, that the flight to quality melts into government securities as if they were the salvation of the stock markets. The character of public debt as a safe asset has become so much a part of the consciousness of financial agents and financial market specialists that they forget that it is first and foremost a levy on social wealth and therefore a transfer of income to the benefit of holders of liquid wealth. Since the states manage crises and refinance speculators anyway, we might as well prevent crises by issuing as many Treasury bills as ordinary market speculation requires (Pozsar, 2014: 42). This is because in financial circulation, government securities are to private securities what money is to bills of exchange and credit instruments in industrial circulation: the Treasury bill is the currency of the financial markets (Krishnamurthy and Vissing-Jorgensen, 2012).

But does not the currency of the states itself owe its modern development precisely to the role of government securities as a reserve asset? Wasn't the Bank of England itself born out of the right of its shareholders to issue money by pledging it on government securities held alongside precious metals?

> The Bank of England began with lending its money to the Government at 8%; at the same time it was empowered by Parliament to coin money out of the same capital, by lending it again to the public in the form of banknotes.

> [...] It was not long ere this credit money, made by the bank itself, became the coin in which the Bank of England made its loans to the State, and paid, on account of the State, the interest on the public debt.
>
> *(Marx, 1867a: 743)*

It was no different in the US. A century after the creation of the Bank of England, Alexander Hamilton proposed to Congress the creation of a national bank, the Bank of United States, which was established in 1791.

> Under the plan, the federal government took a 20-percent stake in the bank, paid for with a loan from the bank itself and to be repaid in annual installments over ten years. Private investors were offered the remaining 80 percent of the bank's shares, payable one fourth in specie and three fourths with U.S. 6% bonds. This design meant that the national bank would support the national debt, and vice versa. It had the effect of raising the market values of bank shares and public debt securities.
>
> *(Sylla, 2012: 4)*

And later, during the Civil War, the federal banking system required national banks to back their banknote issues with government securities (Konings, 2009: 52). As this system ensured a constant demand for government debt, these securities played a central role in the New York money market (Myers, 1931: 243–44), before, with the entry of the US into the war, the Fed rediscounted government securities at preferential rates and encouraged banks to extend their credit to the public in order to promote the purchase of Treasury securities (Konings, 2009: 53). But the modern role of Treasuries in the Fed's monetary policy dates from 1932, when the Glass–Steagall Act authorised the inclusion of Treasuries among the securities eligible to be held as reserves to back up its note issue. From that moment onwards, the Fed became responsible for the stability of the Treasury bond market but also for keeping the yield curve as flat as possible, so as to favour the long-term financing of the US economy (Marie, 2009: 41–42). Carter Glass and Henry Steagall are famous for having passed the following year the homonymous law providing for the separation of investment banks from commercial banks and Regulation Q as part of Roosevelt's New Deal. But the Act of 1932, voted under Hoover, through the expansionary open market operations it made possible, not only transformed the Fed into a Treasury bank at the service of the New Deal, but also signed the retrospective birth certificate of the dollar-Treasury bill standard that would be imposed after Bretton Woods.

Meanwhile, the New Deal that subordinated the Fed to the Treasury, together with the short suspension of the gold standard in 1933 (Sarai, 2009: 75), stimulated further purchases of US debt by the banking system and thus the expansion of the Treasury market until 1951, when it was agreed with the Treasury that interest rates would be determined by the market (Seabrooke, 2001: 75). Thus, the Fed's permanent support of public debt coupled with a deep and liquid debt market encouraged central banks under Bretton Woods to convert their dollars into US securities rather than gold, thus helping to make the dollar a reserve currency "as good as gold", and even better than gold since it gave interest (Michie, 2006: 17).

No doubt the demand for safe assets such as Treasuries goes back at least to the end of the convertibility of the dollar into gold, when central banks decided to convert their cash into the US Treasury securities (Hudson, 2003: 17). But the Treasuries only acquired their status as a truly universal safe asset with financial globalisation, where its functions were broadened (Seabrooke, 2001: 102). Conversely, it was the character of the reserve asset acquired during the Bretton Woods period from the central banks that made this globalisation possible and placed it under the aegis of the US. Its Treasury market indeed "was at the very centre of the process of financialization and tended to give a unique advantage to US financial firms that developed linkages to this market" (Sarai, 2009: 80). Today, a safe asset is defined as an asset with a commodity return, which is invisible by definition and actually refers to the liquid quality of the asset, with money being the most liquid asset here, and thus having the highest commodity return (Gorton, 2017: 548). We now need to look at the factors behind the convenience yield of the Treasuries.

By the late 1980s, the US Treasury market had become the largest single-asset capital market in the world (Allen, 2016: 2). But this market became universal not so much in size as in the granting of primary dealer certification to foreign firms. As a result, in 2016, about two-thirds of the 20 trillion securities in circulation were sold outside the US (Allen, 2016: 3). And insofar as the Treasuries are the Fed's main operating tool, foreign financial firms also directly influence the US monetary policy.

But with securitisation, the process of universalising the US Treasury bond marks a new stage in the new role of the US Treasury itself. This is because the rise of securitisation actually concerns two entirely separate markets that developed almost simultaneously: the public debt of emerging countries and the private debt of US households. In the first case, the creation of Brady Bonds, named after the Treasury Secretary from 1988 to 1993, not only transformed the immense debt contracted by emerging countries from the late 1970s onwards into marketable securities in exchange for relief, but investors were assured of protection against the risk of default on their principal collateralised by the US Treasury bonds (see Buchanan, 2017 and Gumbau-Brisa and Mann, 2009). After Bretton Woods, therefore, the US bond was no longer just the reserve asset of central banks, but the investment asset of foreign firms and the collateral asset of foreign public debt.

In the domestic sphere too, the new financial techniques developed by the banks have made the Treasury bill the pivot of the entire onshore and offshore payment system in dollars.

We have seen how the growth of the Eurodollar market led to the multinationalisation of commercial banking and the development of risk and liquidity management techniques (Battilossi, 2000: 30). The development of these financial techniques and therefore of the markets where the various assets on the banks' balance sheets are traded (ABCP, options, futures, etc.), but also the recycling of petrodollars, have anchored the dollar in the international financial system to a much greater extent than at the time of Bretton Woods. But now the dollar is imposed not in the form of deposits and thus liquidity that can escape from the market, but in the form of tradable securities denominated in dollars (Konings, 2011: 123). "Although big commercial banks had been the primary driver behind the expansion of global finance in the 1970s and early 1980s, it was global portfolio investment that exploded in the 1990s" (McDowell, 2017: 78). Thus, between 1990 and 1994, approximately $670 billion of foreign capital flowed to Asian and Latin American countries as investors from around the world began to place their funds in the stock and bond markets of emerging market economies (Calvo, Leiderman and Reinhart, 1996: 123). The governments of these host countries, once dependent on commercial banks, began to rely more heavily on the issuance of debt securities (bonds) in international credit markets.

With the development of offshore banking, the growth of cross-border capital flows (Prasad, 2014: xii–xiii) and the financialisation of the banking system, safe assets now condition banks' access to money itself, insofar as borrowing against collateral on money markets has replaced demand deposits. Banks' balance sheet management techniques have therefore also affected their liabilities, in particular through the repo market (liability management). In a sense, a repo contract is just a particular form of loan against collateral, except that the collateral consists of the sale of a security or a portfolio of securities, with an agreement to repurchase the security or portfolio at a specified future date and at a price agreed in advance. But compared to an unsecured deposit, for example, "the safety of the repo derives from the marketability of the collateral and the terms of the standard repo contract". Indeed, the repo is over-collateralised since the contract provides for a difference called a haircut between the amount lent and the market value of the collateral as well as a margin call in case of a decline in the value of the collateral (Sissoko, 2019: 321). In fact, the Fed has been using this market at least since the First World War, initially to lend to banks and later to other market participants (O'Malley, 2015: 131). After a long decline in activity between the Great Depression and the 1950s, the market came back to life with the opening by some large US banks of offices specialising in repurchase agreements on the Eurodollar market (*Ibidem*: 131). But it was with the inflation of the 1970s that the market took off, when banks began to borrow liquidity from the money market funds that had been draining savings too weakly remunerated by bank deposits because of the interest cap imposed by Regulation Q (Mullin, 2020: 14). A real take-off followed in the 1990s and 2000s. In the US, the volume of outstanding contracts rose from $833 billion in 1990 to $4,498 billion in 2007; and in Europe, the market grew from €2,157 billion in 2001 to €6,382 billion in 2007 (Wansleben, 2020: 196). And on the supply side, the enormous liquidity generated by firms since the late 1970s against the backdrop of a declining wage share in income, coupled with the limitation of deposit insurance to $250,000 in the US, explains the growing demand for alternative forms of investment such as money market funds or repos (Pozsar, 2015). Not only do interest rates on government securities provide the anchor for other rates and thus also the means to protect against interest rate risks, but the status of these securities as a reference asset on the money market and the repo market make them a real substitute for bank deposits.

And just as the Treasury bond underwrites securitised foreign public debt, it underwrites the drawdown of domestic private debt, supporting the entire domestic housing market debt. Regulation Q and the interest rate cap in the context of rising inflation and interest rates in the 1960s had diverted savings from the low interest deposits of banks and S&Ls to the securities market, where by 1966 they had moved en masse. In 1966, the Fed had raised its key interest rate, both to reduce the demand for foreign goods by making money more expensive and to attract foreign investors to the federal bond market. The aim was to bring dollars back to the US from the Eurodollar market by attracting foreign investors (Hyman, 2010: 129). Since the Fed had dried up the mortgage market, Congress passed the Housing Act in 1968, which authorised the creation of MBSs, the first of which was issued in 1970 by the Government National Mortgage Association (Ginnie Mae) with the Federal National Mortgage Association (Fannie Mae), followed the next year by the Federal Home Loan Mortgage Association (Freddie Mac) (Gerardi, Rosen and Willen, 2010: 336). The secondary market for MBS was guaranteed by the federal government. The private mortgage securitisation market did not appear until 1977, from Salomon Brothers and Bank of America (Ranieri, 1996), but it was not until the reforms of the 1980s, such as the change in accounting rules (Mason, 2004), the elimination of Regulation Q, the expansion of mortgage products and, above all, the Secondary Mortgage Market Improvement Act of 1984, that it became a market attracting capital from all over the world. Because "[d]ue to their relatively high yield compared to US Treasury securities, MBS soon became of interest to global investors. In terms of the US capital account, it received a boost due to this new-found flow of foreign investment" (Buchanan, 2017: 71). Yet, it was precisely the federal guarantee that led to the prosperity of the secondary market:

> The challenge with all mortgages had always been that every loan was in some sense as unique as the house that the money was being lent against. The FHA and FNMA had overcome this challenge through federal guarantees and standards. All loans that were not federally insured, so-called 'conventional mortgages', had no such secondary market.
>
> *(Hyman, 2010: 136)*

As a result, from the 1980s onwards, not only foreign capital but also monetary authorities began to buy both Treasury securities and mortgage bonds from foreign government agencies (Duncan, 2005: 106–07; Krippner, 2011: 101–02). In addition to its status as a reserve asset since the creation of its banking system, the Treasury bond had already been the investment asset of the US nation's savings since the issuance of Liberty bonds, mentioned in the Introduction. But with repos and mortgage agencies, it complements its status as a safe asset by its role as a guarantee for domestic private debt.

Thus, the end of Bretton Woods did not leave the dollar without its market base, but rather moved the system from the gold-dollar standard to the dollar-Treasury bill standard: it had transformed the sterile and immobile market base into a marketable one. The financial globalisation whose emergence we have traced requires an asset as secure as gold in monetary circulation. This is how the US Treasury bill gradually became the truly universal safe asset. However, as soon as the dollar-Treasury bill standard was introduced, the balance of payments deficit ceased to be the major economic problem of the US; it even ceased to be a problem at all (Gowan, 1999; Konings, 2011: 123). This is because the development of the secondary market for dollar-denominated bonds stimulated by financial innovations (Moran, 1991) allowed the federal government to substitute the creation of public debt securities for the constitution of foreign exchange reserves (Panitch and Gindin, 2009: 32). Moreover, as an international quasi-currency, they became the safe asset during periods of crisis and financial instability (Schinasi et al., 2001).

9.5.2 The US security in the management of the great financial crisis

In 1865, Marx, who was so quick to anticipate the most remote developments in capitalism, wrote that one would have to be mad to imagine "that it is the duty and power of [central] banks to transform all bankrupt swindlers into solvent and respectable capitalists by means of pieces of paper" (Marx, 1894: 513). Yet, this is what the Fed blithely did after the onset of the 2008 crisis. With the end of the gold standard and thus of the convertibility of central bank notes, the problem is not to understand why the Fed governor transformed this crazy claim into a moral requirement in the space of a few months: this is an exercise that is within the reach of anyone who sees the links between the monetary authorities and the interests of the big banks and financial institutions. The problem is to understand by what means the Fed has been able to attribute to itself the power to achieve this transubstantiation. For the Fed has expanded its modalities of action to a point that makes its crisis management one of the main features distinguishing the current crisis from that of 1929. In its function as a lender of last resort, the central bank had until now always limited itself to using the traditional tools of monetary policy: intervention in the money market (open market), lowering the amount of reserve requirements for banks or opening the discount window to eligible banks. It is true that its open market operations in general were not limited to buying and selling short-term public debt securities but also covered private securities, including mortgage securities, commercial paper and bankers' acceptances (Beckhart, 1972: 490–92). Through these expedients, the central bank increased and facilitated its supply of money, but in no way intervened directly in the rescue of banks or financial companies that became insolvent.

Through the various modalities of its unconventional policy by which it broadened the assets and actors eligible for its rescue plans (Term Auction Facility in 2007, Term Securities Lending Facility and Primary Credit Dealers Facility in 2008), the Fed transformed not so much its role as a lender of last resort as the status of the Treasury bond and the economic function of the US Treasury itself. More profoundly than the loosening of the conditions of its liquidity provision, it is the widespread use of the Treasury bond in its expanded scope of action that is the novelty of the Great Recession: by exchanging illiquid securities for government debt, the Fed not only metamorphosed claims on dubious future securities into securities pledged against the nation's own revenues, but it also endorsed the role of the Treasury bond as a pillar of the international financial system.

With its new prerogatives and with the support of the Treasury, the Fed was fulfilling the mission that Proudhon had assigned to his People's Bank: it provided free financing to the entire economy (Proudhon, 1849).[23] "By replacing the entire financial system that had failed to finance the economy", Aglietta and Rigot acknowledge,

> the Fed was taking on credit risks that it could not assume without the support of the Treasury. At the zero interest rate, monetary policy and fiscal policy are one and the same. There is therefore no longer any basis for central bank independence.
>
> *(Aglietta and Rigot, 2009: 108–9)*

Through its management of the crisis, the Fed has proved less its independence than a complete reversal of the direction of its relationship with the Treasury that had prevailed during Bretton Woods. While previously the Fed, through its issuing and discounting policy, financed investments made under the aegis of the Treasury, it is now the latter that, through the over-issuing of public debt, supports the central bank in its mission to save the centres of speculation that the big banks, insurance companies and financial agencies have become. In reality, the central role of safe assets in the interbank market has removed from the Fed any illusion of independence. In addition to the traditional functions of price stability and liquidity provision, there is now the financial stability that only Treasury-issued securities can provide.

It is indeed since the unconventional monetary policies for managing the 2008 crisis that the repo market has inaugurated a new era in the international monetary and financial system. By expanding the collateral eligible for liquidity lent on the repo market, but also the actors eligible for its operations (insurance companies, pension funds, non-financial companies), the Fed, but also the ECB and the BoE, have become collateral factories for the shadow banking sector (Gabor, 2016: 2). The reason is that by providing liquidity to investment funds and shadow banks, the central bank directly finances speculation:

> repos effectively fund the working capital needs of levered bond portfolios in order to fund short-term financial economy transactions, that is trades, in the form of levered bets on the direction of interest rates,

> foreign exchange rates and credit spreads with an aim to satisfy retail and institutional investors' wealth aspirations by delivering financial goods in the form of excess return.
>
> *(Pozsar, 2015: 12; see also Bezhanidze, 2020: 40)*

And since after the crisis Quantitative Easing had created excess reserves that were pulling the interest rate below the target rate, the Fed introduced the Overnight Reverse Repo Program, which allows banks to lend their excess reserves through repo transactions while ensuring that the repo rates are at or above the overnight rate (Mullin, 2020: 16). In doing so, the Fed expanded the institutions eligible for its open market operations: money market funds, banks, government-sponsored enterprises, etc. But with the COVID crisis, the Fed went further, creating the Standing Repo Facility (SRF), which consists of offering facilities at a rate slightly above the market, and thus in a way widening its discount window while making it less stigmatising (Cheng and Wessel, 2020: 6). However, here only Treasury bills and government agency securities are accepted as collateral, the aim being to set a ceiling on the federal funds interest rate.

In reality, the Fed not only guarantees the liquidity of the repo market, but also provides the safest collateral on the market: the US Treasury bonds "backed by the full faith and credit of the U.S. government" (Fleming, 2000: 224–25). It claims to be independent of political power, but requires the Treasury to issue in abundance the assets with which it believes it should conduct its monetary policy:

> In the Committee on the Global Financial System, central banks [argued in 1999] that financial stability in modern financial systems required global safe assets, issued in liquid government markets, 'lubricated' by free repo markets. In so doing, the central banking community recognised that sovereign bonds had become the cornerstone of modern financial markets, used as benchmark for pricing assets, for hedging, as collateral in private repo markets and central banks' repo operations.
>
> *(Gabor, 2016: 5)*

We have seen how the announced repayment of the Treasury's floating debt had worried Wall Street. The Office of Management and Budget even projected a total repayment for 2012 (Fleming, 2000: 221). However, it was at this point that the Fed broadened the range of eligible collateral on the repo market to include structured products such as ABS and MBS, until Congress voted in 2005 for the "safe harbour exemption" for these securities on the repo market (Gabor, 2016: 988). Thus, the Fed contributed less to the subprime crisis through its low interest rates than through its active support of shadow banking and its manufacture of "safe assets". It is therefore not only the central bank that is abandoning its function as lender of last resort to banks to become a "shadow central bank" guaranteeing market liquidity (Gabor, 2016: 22); it is the state itself that, by mortgaging the wealth of nations against speculative loans, has turned into the market maker of last resort. Moreover, as governments increasingly turn to the repos market to finance their spending and as such increase their demand for Treasuries as collateral (Gabor, 2016: 974), the Treasury bill becomes the universal equivalent of financial circulation and the US Treasury the Bank of the rest of the world.

The quasi-money status of securities issued by the US Treasury is a direct result of the fact that, with the reduction in the range of safe assets following the 2008 crisis, the Treasury and government agencies have become the quasi-exclusive issuers of safe assets in the US. Hence the very low interest rates on these securities (Gourinchas and Rey, 2007); hence also, because of the historical size and depth of the US government securities markets, their very high liquidity (Bordo and James, 2009: 179). And their quasi-money status is all the more important as they directly determine the exchange rate of the dollar itself, whose supply and demand now depend on "the expected value of all future interest rate differences and convenience yields less the value of all future currency risk premia" (Jiang, Krishnamurthy and Lustig, 2020: 3). This would explain the persistent violation of the principle of uncovered interest rate parity.[24]

9.5.3 The US Treasury bond and the new Triffin dilemma

We have seen how the demonetisation of gold has loosened the US constraint on its external deficits. However, it did not make Triffin's dilemma disappear. It only transformed the terms and the stakes. The convertibility of the dollar into gold has been transformed into the fiscal capacity of the US to issue public debt to meet the growing demand for safe assets, even as its share of GDP in the world economy continues to decline (Obstfeld, 2011). However, in the various formulations of the new Triffin dilemma (Gourinchas and Rey, 2007), the role of the US is no longer to provide global liquidity but to reassure speculators and guarantee global financial stability. With the universal dollarisation of integrated financial markets, the US has moved from being the "world banker" (Kindleberger, 1973) to the "venture capitalist of the world" on the assets side of the balance sheet, FDI and securities have replaced long-term loans, while liabilities are composed mainly of safe, low-yielding assets (Gourinchas and Rey, 2007: 10). It is therefore no longer as an issuer of ultimate liquidity but as a market maker of last resort that the US is called upon to act for the international monetary system: "the sheer size of the gross liquid external debt of the U.S. may be threatening at some point the ability of the U.S. to act as a world banker or insurer" (Gourinchas, Rey and Sauzet, 2019: 34). Hence the exchange rate risk replacing the convertibility risk that Triffin had feared (Gourinchas and Rey, 2007: 24–25). But insofar as public debt securities remain rights on a fraction of the US fiscal reserves, it is all the social wealth from which the revenues are taken that, in the form of a store of value, is pledged on the financial markets.

It is true, however, that in their formulation of the dilemma, Jiang, Krishnamurthy and Lustig (2020) return to the traditional role of the US as a provider of liquidity, but in a context where the growing demand for dollars is pushing both foreign and US firms to issue dollar debt. For foreign firms, this practice increases the risk of currency mismatch when their revenues are denominated in domestic currency. In these circumstances, the risk is not the exchange rate itself, but the asymmetric financial spillover between the US and foreign firms. But unlike Triffin's dilemma, the supply of dollar assets is no longer limited by the US GDP growth but by world GDP growth, as all dollarised firms, including foreign ones, are likely to offer dollar assets. However, on the one hand, like all versions of the new Triffin dilemma, this interpretation confuses the supply of dollars with the supply of dollar assets, and on the other hand, the supply of dollar assets can only meet this growing demand by being convertible into hard dollars. For both Jiang et al. and the fiscal interpretations of the dilemma, the financial role of the US presupposes an international monetary and financial system in which the dollar has already become autonomous from its issuing country.

9.5.4 The US Treasury bond and Bretton Woods II

The current exchange rate system, in which South East Asian countries in particular effectively peg their currencies to the US dollar, has been called Bretton Woods II. Since, through this peg, these countries accumulate dollar reserves through their exports that they immediately reinvest in the US Treasury bills, they would artificially maintain an exchange rate favourable to their exports and reminiscent of the fixed exchange rate system under Bretton Woods (Dooley, Folkerts-Landau and Garber, 2003; 2004). Against this overly mercantilist view, the protection of emerging countries from the capital volatility that caused so much ruin in the 1997 crisis has been highlighted (Eichengreen, 2007: 5; Prasad, 2014: 12). But dollar funds had not just flowed in and out of Asian financial markets. They had penetrated deep into the region's financial circulation channels. This is why McKinnon recalled that the exchange rate stability sought through reserve accumulation was primarily the result of the size of the private sector's dollar assets and liabilities, but also the role of the dollar in non-US trade relations. This is where the "fear of floating" (Calvo and Reinhart, 2002) comes from. An appreciation of the domestic currency would not only lead to capital losses for holders of dollar assets, but to a loss of competitiveness vis-à-vis the region's trading partners and a risk of recession and deflation. By collectively pegging their currencies to the dollar, South East Asian countries are expanding the dollar zone by enhancing their domestic price stability. Thus, the huge transfer of capital to the US induces an exchange rate risk largely borne by the Asian creditor countries. But it is the dominant role of the dollar that allows the US to get "a virtually unlimited line of credit with the rest of the world" (McKinnon, 2013: 85). The centre–periphery relationship of the Bretton Woods II theory, according to which it is the mercantilist policy of the South Asian countries that feeds the US deficits, must therefore be reversed. On the contrary, it is the asymmetrical role of the dollar that allows the US to increase its deficits without tears.

And even if the mercantilist hypothesis were to be taken on, it should be pointed out that this policy is directly opposed to the interests of workers in emerging countries whose living conditions are sacrificed for the benefit of consumption in advanced countries, in the same way that the investment of accumulated reserves in dollars sacrifices domestic investment because of the weakness of their financial markets (El-Gamal and Jaffe, 2010: 128–29 and 131). Bretton Woods owes its revival less to the return of neo-mercantilism in Southeast Asia than to the dollarisation of global investment. For the region's central banks, the dollar is no longer simply, as it was for Federal Germany and Japan under Bretton Woods, the currency of the world's largest market: it is the financing currency of their own currency area.

9.6 The relative autonomy of the dollar

We left the Eurodollar market at a time when, due to financial innovations and the first loosening of the regulatory framework for global finance, its role in international banking was declining. From the 1990s onwards, the market was revived but under new conditions that blurred the differences between the domestic and foreign markets for the dollar. The purely offshore market has now given way to round-tripping by European banks (He and McCauley, 2012), which consists of borrowing dollars from the US residents through money market funds in particular (Baba, McCauley and Ramaswamy, 2009) in order to reinvest them in structured products such as ABS (Shin, 2012). These dollar flows were motivated by regulatory arbitrage, as European banks, like the US securities firms, were not subject to regulations on reserve requirements, capital/asset ratios and minimum risk-weighted capital/asset ratios, etc. However, these dollar loans were sometimes made on the Eurodollar market or other offshore markets (Battilossi, 2020: 291) and sometimes and more widely on the US markets themselves by their local branches (He and McCauley, 2012: 40). Round-tripping dissolves the distinction between the onshore and the offshore markets, between the dollar market and the Eurodollar market. From this period onwards, there is only one global dollar market whose financing and investment channels are determined exclusively by the opportunities offered by regulatory differentials. If the Eurodollar market contributed to the subprime crisis, it was only insofar as it provided a relay for the speculative orgy of European banks on these structured products.[25]

But soon banks no longer needed to use their foreign subsidiaries to take on dollar liabilities. As the share of dollars raised in the US by European and non-European banks declined, these banks took on more and more dollar debt in their own jurisdictions. In 2018, more than 50% of these dollar liabilities were incurred in the country of origin (Aldasoro and Ehlers, 2018: 20). However, not only is a significant proportion of this debt matched by the US residents themselves, whose liquidity flows into offshore markets, but they are now also able to borrow from their own central banks. This is why recent developments in the offshore dollar market have prompted analysts to move away from the traditional view of the international monetary system that "a state's territory, the decision-making area and the monetary area are identical" (Avdjiev, McCauley and Shin, 2015). Today,

> the international monetary system is built on money creation that is substantially de-coupled from the nation state. Not only is the vast majority of credit money created by private institutions, but the core of the system also relies upon credit money created outside of a state's decision-making area.
> *(Murau, Rini and Haas, 2020: 769)*

Not only does the dollar dominate as much as it did in the early Bretton Woods era as the world's reserve currency, but its role has increased since the collapse of the ruble in the 1990s (Ilzetzki, Reinhart and Rogoff, 2017: 4–5).

Consider the three roles through which an international currency exercises its hegemony according to Cohen (2013): trade, official reserves and financial markets. In trade, more than 40% of traded goods and services remain invoiced in dollars, five times the US share of global imports and exports (Gopinath and Stein, 2018: 2), while the share in global product is only 20% (Bergstein, 2013: 17). In central banks' vaults, almost 60% of their reserves are declared in dollars and these figures are believed to underestimate the reality of the phenomenon (IMF Data, 2021). Moreover, 60% of countries effectively peg their currencies to the dollar and the percentage of global GDP pegged to the dollar has probably never been higher (Ilzetzki, Reinhart and Rogoff, 2017: 52). Through this universal anchorage, which the foreign exchange market expresses through the use of the dollar in almost 90% of its transactions (Bertaut, Curcuru and von Beschwitz, 2021), the dollar enjoys "privileged insularity" (Gopinath, 2015) in that it is protected from inflation resulting from exchange rate changes.[26] And we will see how a change in the value of the dollar affects the overall volume of international trade, even among countries that are not partners of the US (Boz, Gopinath and Plagborg-Møller, 2017).

But this is just a reminder of the traditional role of a reference currency, which differs only in magnitude from the role that sterling played until the interwar period. It is as a currency of international credit that the dollar has opened a new phase of monetary history since the appearance of the Eurodollar market. It is as a global financing currency that the dollar expresses the relatively autonomous development of its growth and functions. Today indeed, the majority of international credit in dollars is created outside the borders of the US, primarily on the Eurodollar market (Maurau, Rini and Haas, 2020: 771), so that in 2015 two-thirds of the dollars issued circulated outside the US (Bernanke, 2015: 40). Moreover, "much of the non-US activity occurs directly between non-US entities and does not flow through the US banking system" (CGFS, 2020: 5). Dollar deposits in non-US banks are at least as large as those held by the US banks (Shin, 2012) and dollar borrowing by non-US firms accounts for 60% of their borrowing.

With the dollar as the global financing currency, all the traditional laws of international trade are reversed (Avdjiev et al., 2019). A fall in the dollar, for example, not only improves the US trade balance, but insofar as it facilitates dollar borrowing conditions, global trade in general (Bruno and Shin, 2020), in the same way that a fall in the US interest rate stimulates investment and trade in the rest of the world. As an invoicing currency, the dollar affects world trade through changes in the price of traded goods caused by fluctuations in its exchange rate (Boz, Gopinath and Plagborg-Møller, 2017: 58). Thus, the bilateral exchange rate of any currency with the dollar directly determines the prices and quantities of imported goods, regardless of the source of those goods (Casas et al., 2016). But as a financing currency, the dollar directly affects the production conditions of goods produced for world trade. Thus, it is the totality of the phases of the capital cycle that the dollar determines through its commercial and financial hegemony. Moreover, the dollarisation of global investment finance is such that the financial impact of a change in the exchange rate dominates its trade impact (Avdjiev et al., 2019: 4).

Like cross-border lending, about half of international debt securities are denominated in dollars (CGFS, 2020: 4–5) and the combined size of all US debt markets measured by the value of bonds issued by different layers of government and private firms in 2012 was larger than the debt markets of the Euro area, Japan, Switzerland and the UK combined (Prasad, 2014: 25). But it is not only the US government and corporations that issue dollar debt, and while the universal role of the dollar is evidenced by its role as a reserve instrument, its autonomy is illustrated by the fact that holdings of dollar bonds issued by non-US states, agencies and organisations are three times higher than holdings of securities issued by the US corporations (McCauley, 2019: 12). The US treasury securities would in fact account for only half of the dollar reserves of non-US central banks (McCauley, 2019: 12–13).

Among the measures taken by the Fed in 2008 to rescue the financial system, much attention has been paid to the swap line agreements with foreign central banks, as opposed to the more traditional last resort lending operations of the Term Auction Facility, the Term Securities Lending Facility and the Commercial Paper Funding Facility (Bordo, Humpage and Schwartz, 2014). And it is true that through these agreements, what was at issue was no longer supporting the dollar standard on the foreign exchange market, but a fully dollarised international banking and financial system. And through these agreements, foreign central banks, which were responsible for providing dollar liquidity to their own banking institutions (Carré and Le Maux, 2018), became mere regional branches of the Fed, which was itself responsible for issuing dollars to the rest of the world (Baba, McCauley and Ramaswamy, 2009). Through these swap lines concluded with 14 central banks (Broz, 2015), the Fed ratified the existence of a unified global dollar market.[27] And since the aim was "to extend its reach into the offshore USD segment and safeguard the structures of financial globalization" (Murau, Rini and Haas, 2020: 775), here too the Fed assumed, through its function as international lender of last resort, the role of a world bank, whose intervention conditioned the resumption of global investment in general.[28] But on the one hand, these agreements were mainly aimed at enabling foreign banks to meet their obligations to the US banks and money markets: they therefore fall within the traditional functions of lender of last resort (McDowell, 2017: 155). On the other hand, it is forgotten that domestic measures were already fulfilling an international function. This is because they were largely intended for the local branches of foreign institutions, in particular European banks (McDowell, 2017: 144), whose decisive role in the formation of the speculative bubble in the subprime market we have recalled.[29]

9.7 Dollar hegemony and US structural power

Insofar as it appeared at the moment when the US began its economic decline (Hobson and Seabrooke, 2009: 291; Desai, 2013: 324–25), the whole project of reflection on the US hegemony is based on what Strange defined as the structural power of the US, the power "to shape how things shall be done, the power to shape frameworks, within which states relate to each other, relate to people, or relate to corporate enterprises" (Strange, 1989: 24–25). And the US owes this indirect power over structures to the dollar, which irrigates all channels of the international monetary system (McKinnon, 2013: 21).[30] Through its currency, the US remains able to extract wealth from foreign nations, to finance its deficit without assignable limits, and to impose its macroeconomic preferences on the world as needed (Helleiner, 2005: 5). The structural power of the US thus defines an indirect (Gill and Law, 1993) or even unintentional (Guzzini, 1993) power to shape and control the monetary environment within which other nations and economic zones must operate. This structural power implies a whole geography of money that is based neither on a physical space nor on a space of transactions as such, but on what Cohen calls an authoritative domain, which is presented as a field of forces between the state and the market (Cohen, 1998: 24). This new conception of geography undoubtedly has the merit of putting an end to the triple coincidence of space, money and residence, and of reducing capitalist power relations to inter-state relations. But it is not certain that it will help us understand the nature of the relationship between the hegemonic state and its currency, nor the nature of the hegemony of the dollar itself, nor even the nature of the compromises between nations within the same monetary force field. On the one hand, Cohen's approach understands the state as a homogeneous bloc representing the interests of a given nation as a whole; on the other hand, market forces are understood as what drives the dollar out of the space of US sovereignty, as a force eroding the domain of authority of a currency. No doubt, this new geography accounts for the hierarchical relationships between currencies, and between transactional spaces in which market forces erode the authoritative domain of one currency to the benefit of another. But these relationships are overdetermined by politics, i.e. by the power of the states issuing these different currencies. Even though Cohen distinguishes the authoritative domain of a state from the transactional domain of money, the hierarchy of currencies remains symmetrical to the hierarchy of states, so that market forces enter into hierarchical relationships only insofar as the pyramid of currencies they invest expresses the hierarchy of states (Cohen, 1998: 26).[31] As the hierarchy of currencies is overdetermined by the political power of states, Cohen's followers are surprised that the hegemony of the dollar is maintained despite the decline of the US, and they exhaust themselves in circular explanations to understand this apparent paradox:

> The divergence of the two trends seems puzzling. If the United States is fading as a world power, how is the dollar able to retain its decades-old supremacy in financial affairs? Conversely, if the greenback still dominates the global monetary order, why should US power and the liberal international order be in decline?.
>
> *(Norrlof et al., 2020: 145)*

Similarly, Jonathan Kirshner asks: "If not the dollar, what? At the moment, there remains no satisfactory answer to this question" (Kirshner, 2014: 1014).[32] This is because neither Cohen nor his followers conceive that the market may play a role in the trend of the currency hierarchy.

In this respect, Norrlof's work (2014) well expresses the confusion of the International Political Economy (IPE) School between the two hegemonies. To the question of why the dollar remains hegemonic while the hegemony of the US declines, she answers by trying to show how the US transforms what she calls "monetary capabilities", i.e. in reality the various functions that the dollar fulfils in the world economy as a reference currency, into "currency influence" through various forms of power exercised by the US, ranging from negotiating power to the power to modify the perceptions of the states dependent on the US. But in this way she assumes that what is being explained is given, since currency influence is nothing more than the result of these monetary capabilities. The paradox of Norrlof's analysis is that she tries to account for the coexistence of dollar hegemony and the US decline by explaining the influence of the dollar through the different forms of power exercised by the US itself (Norrlof, 2014: 1045). But not only does she explain the strength of the dollar by the relatively weakened powers of the US, but all the forms of power vindicated to explain the hegemony of the dollar are based precisely on this hegemony. However, by explaining the "currency influence" exerted by the various powers used by the American state, she confuses the economic power of the currency with the power of its issuing state. Thus, on the one hand, the dollar derives its hegemony from the fact that it is the reference currency for oil, but on the other hand, she explains this link between oil and the dollar by the US military power and the role of the US as an offshore police force, particularly in the Middle East. This mania for translating the slightest economic relationship into a power relationship leads her to explain the hegemonic role of the dollar by the need to get dollars in order to get oil invoiced in dollars. But just because oil is billed in dollars does not mean that only dollars can buy oil, and one would not understand the oil shocks without considering the relative decline of the dollar against other currencies following the end of the dollar's convertibility to gold and the floating of its exchange rate in 1972.[33] Only the protection against exchange rate fluctuations would explain the holding of dollars for the purchase of oil.

More generally, Norrlof sometimes explains the hegemony of the dollar by the power of the US, in particular its military power (Norrlof et al., 2020: 4). Sometimes, on the contrary, the strength of the dollar explains the continued hegemony of the US despite the weakening of its economic power (Norrlof et al., 2020: 6). This confusion stems from the fact that this approach never separates hegemony from the supposed acts of power that condition its existence, even and especially when it refers to the concept of structural power (Keohane, 2000).[34] This is why she misses the conditions of autonomy of monetary hegemony from state hegemony, as they express the independence of the social relation that is money from political power relations.[35]

And since the IPE is permeated by a functional conception of state power, it tends to ignore the counter-finalities of the state's actions on money, i.e. the very exercise of its hegemonic power. It is not enough to stress that structural power is also exercised through the unintentional actions of states. It must also be said that the intentional exercise of power generates counter-finalities that make money a bewitched object with regard to the power of its issuing state. And insofar as one does not see any contradiction between the functions of money, one overlooks the fact that the actions of the state in monetary matters always consist in strengthening the functions of money to the detriment of other functions and that the whole game observed between the state and market forces actually expresses the game of the relationship between the various functions of money.[36] Thus, the Nixon shock aimed to reinforce the function of domestic and international means of payment against its function as a store of value (Benign Neglect),[37] in contrast to the Volcker shock which sought to restore the dollar's function as an international reserve of value against its function as a means of domestic circulation. The end of Bretton Woods was not caused by "the changes in the policy priorities in the US, the imposition of the neoliberal agenda and the retreat of the welfare state" (Vernengo, 2021: 3). It is the opposite. It was primarily to free the welfare state from the constraints of Bretton Woods that Nixon laid the foundations for the neoliberal regime to come. And, like Volcker's policy, Nixon's action entailed a domestic cost that belied the idea that states would compete on the monetary stage as homogeneous blocs of interests: inflation after Nixon's measures, recession after Volcker's tightening. But if the US strengthens its hegemony each time, it is because with each measure taken, the dollar is strengthened in one of its international functions: as a vehicle currency under Nixon, as a store of value under Volcker: in one case as a form of universal exchangeability, in the other as a universal form of value. Hence, each time, a round of negotiations aimed at stabilising the dollar's exchange rate: in one case, market speculation depreciated the dollar; in the other, it appreciated. It could be said that these negotiations were precisely the moment when the US exercised its hegemonic power over the entire capitalist world. But the agreements reached in these negotiations expressed compromises between bourgeoisies on the relationship between the currencies whose hierarchical relationships on the world markets were given. And these hierarchical relations were precisely the relations in which these bourgeoisies prospered and the international capitalist relations of production were reproduced. Moreover, not only was this hierarchy defended by these bourgeoisies, but the US itself militated for a further internationalisation of the deutsche mark and the yen (Frankel, 2012). Similarly, the relationship between states and markets cannot be defined by oppositional relationships. Thus, during the process of transition to floating exchange rates, the US used market forces to provoke speculation on the fall of the dollar in order to make its partners give in to the generalised floating (Denizet, 1977: 130–31). However, if the transition to floating exchange rates appears to be the victory of the market over the state, for the German state it enabled the containment of the inflation that was threatened with the defence of the dollar and the accumulation of foreign exchange reserves, while other European countries were able to free themselves from the defence of their exchange rates in order to increase their money supply and stimulate their growth. And the Plaza Accords, where an orderly decline in the dollar against European currencies and the yen was agreed, were required by the tightness of Volcker's monetary policy on wages and prices. Faced with the strength of the dollar, the Reagan administration demanded, in addition to interventions on the foreign exchange market, the implementation of Keynesian policies to stimulate consumption in Germany and Japan (James, 1996: 436). But negotiations with the German Finance Minister were conducted against the advice of the Bundesbank, for whom price stability remained a priority, and the concerted decline of the dollar against the deutsche mark was frowned upon by German exporters (James, 1996: 438).

Notes

1 Triffin has been criticised for assuming a constant velocity of the dollar and a money multiplier of gold equal to unity, and thus, incidentally, global monetarism with a fixed price system (Serrano, 2003). If, however, we assume an increasing velocity of circulation, the dilemma would disappear. In reality, this velocity cannot increase indefinitely, just as the money multiplier cannot increase without compromising the convertibility of scriptural or fiat dollars. But above all, Serrano fails to understand the nature of the problem expressed in the dilemma. Triffin was not concerned that the dollar could not satisfy global liquidity, but rather that it would satisfy it so well that sooner or later confidence would erode and lead holders of dollar reserves to convert them into gold. The problem of the dilemma was not the dollar in its function as a vehicle currency but the dollar as a store of value and thus as a means of payment.

2 The return to external convertibility

> revived the 'correspondent banking' system, frozen since the 1930s. International institutions (such as the Bank for International Settlements) and the monetary authorities of some European surplus countries (Bundesbank and Bank of Italy) actively encouraged commercial banks to develop their activity in foreign currencies.
>
> *(Battilossi, 2000: 158–59)*

3 Not only are these two different forms of direct investment, but in this difference lies the whole misunderstanding between the US ideologues who, like Kindleberger, pass off the US as a generous world bank that borrows in the short term and lends in the long term (1973: 210), and European sovereigntists who, like General de Gaulle and his advisor Jacques Rueff, see the dollar as the instrument par excellence of US predation on European resources (Grin, 1999: 391).

4 The pound was in fact subject to speculative borrowing which led to a currency crisis that year.

5 "It increased the propensity of capital holders to place their capital in interest-bearing deposits outside their country and accelerated the mobility of international capital. The foreign exchange operations of banks were to expand considerably. The receipt of deposits and the granting of credit in currencies other than the national currency would give rise to a very active market in foreign currencies" (Bekerman, 1997: 10).

6 "Dollar-credits today, just like gold-notes in the Renaissance, can be issued almost without limit, that is, as long as all private parties to the issuance profit from the use of those notes" (Allen, 2016: 7). In an important article, Schularick and Taylor (2012) distinguish two major eras of modern financial history: the first runs from 1870 to 1939 and is characterised by a stable relationship between credit and money and between these and GDP in most developed countries. But from 1945 onwards, a new era began, marked by a growing decoupling of credit and money as well as of credit and GDP.

7 The strange series of coincidences that presided over the inflation of the 1970s (Vietnamese spending in the US, wage demands in Europe, speculation following droughts in Russia, the Sahel and India, but also the bizarre exodus of anchovies from the Pacific coast of South America) finds its lawful explanation in the oligopolistic structure of the markets, including that of raw materials, in particular oil through the formation of OPEC. This structure in fact carries all incomes in the spiral of successive feedbacks from price rises, and "in every new round, industrial prices rise more than wages in the previous round" (Denizet, 1977: 69). So what is the value of monetarism if the most infernal inflationary episode of world capitalism since the end of the war completely contradicts its principles? While the rate of inflation in the US had risen from about 4% to over 12% between 1972 and 1974 (inflation.eu data), from the middle of 1972, the Fed, in addition to its very restrictive reserve policy, raised its key rate (the Fed Funds rate) from 4% to 6% at the end of the year, then to 10.5% in mid-1973, and then to 13% a year later. The rate of growth of the money supply was halved over the period (World Bank data). As Greenspan himself acknowledges, the arrival of emerging countries on the world market did much more to break the inflationary spiral than the Volcker shock of 1979, which responded more to the concerns of the financial community than to those of industry:

> The apparent excess in savings, combined with globalization, technology-driven increases in productivity, and the shift of workforces from centrally planned economies to competitive markets, has helped suppress interest rates both real and nominal and rates of inflation for all developed and virtually all developing nations.
>
> *(Greenspan, 2008: 13)*

8 These measures were neoliberal before their time, not only in fact, but in intent:

> In addition, with arguments eerily prescient of the rhetoric of Thatcherism and the monetarism experiment of the 1980s, it is clear that, even as early as 1960, the Bank viewed 'hot money' flows as almost a mechanism by which the financial markets discipline profligate government.
>
> *(Burn, 2006: 89)*

9 "Between 1978 and 1981, the Euromarkets and offshore banking were central to the interactions between British and American monetary authorities. As banks on

each side of the Atlantic pushed their governments to create regulatory conditions favourable to competing internationally, the existing regulatory orders gradually broke down. These effects continued to erode American financial regulation during the 1980s. Regulatory transformations in the US then fed back into Britain, with the further liberalisation during the 1980s and Thatcher's own 'Big Bang' carried out after British officials had visited the US in order to learn from the American regulatory apparatus" (Burn, 2006: 448).

10 Helleiner (1994: 81), blinded by his hegemonic view of the dollar, interpreted the US government's inducement to go to the Eurodollar market as a way of making the dollar attractive to private operators. But at the same time, the Fed was implementing a restrictive rate policy for domestic borrowing. The only political reason for this inducement was that borrowing in this market encouraged European lenders to rid central banks of their dollars, mitigating their insistent threat to demand the convertibility of their dollars into gold (Denizet, 1971: 70–71). However, after the deterioration of the balance of payments in 1968 and faced with the impossibility of unilaterally devaluing the dollar, everything was done on the contrary to incite private holders of dollars to get rid of them at the central banks, with a view to forcing governments to depreciate the dollar, i.e. to revalue their currencies (Coombs, 1976: 205–8). This is what Germany did, precipitating the 'Nixon shock' and the end of the Bretton Woods fixed exchange rate system.

11 Certificates of deposit, invented in 1961 by the First National City Bank, are negotiable instruments issued by banks with a maturity of up to one year in the short term that allowed banks to tap into the long-term capital market (Palan, 1998: 639).

12 The IET was followed in 1965 by the Voluntary Foreign Credit Restraint Program (VFCR), which voluntarily capped lending to non-residents, and in 1968 by the Foreign Direct Investment Program (FDIP), designed to reduce foreign direct investment by the US companies (Burn, 2006: 139).

13 The expression "Nixon shock" is an invention of the Japanese.

14 de Cecco (1982) traces the mass entry of speculators into the Eurodollar market back to 1964 and the speculation against the pound, reaching its peak precisely in the 1970–71 period. The growing capital flows from 1958 onwards and the Eurodollar market exposed the monetary authorities to ever more intense speculative attacks on currencies whose parities were deemed inadequate. With their arrival, the Eurodollar market grew to serve as a platform for currency speculation (1982: 19). As a result, it was increasingly difficult to keep the currency parity (Cohen, 1977: 101–2).

15 An International Banking Facility (IBF) is a separate account established by a US bank, or a US branch or subsidiary of a foreign bank, that provides banking services to foreign residents and institutions while being exempt from Federal Reserve requirements and some state and local income taxes.

16 Loans issued by the US Treasury on the European financial markets to absorb the dollar balances accumulated in certain creditor countries. They were created by Robert Roosa, the Treasury Undersecretary of the Kennedy administration.

17 It must be said that offshore dollar deposits had long been found within the US itself, so that in reality, "making transactions on the Eurodollar market merely meant using a different desk at one of the New York banks. In practice, the Eurodollar market became just one funding channel next to the onshore Feds Fund market" (Murau, 2018: 20).

18 Similarly, in 1971, the key element of Nixon's New Economic Policy

> was a 90 day wage price freeze. Arthur Burns was successful in overcoming the opposition of Milton Friedman and George Shultz and convincing first Secretary of the Treasury John Connally and then President Nixon that incomes policy would deal with the inflation problem.
>
> *(Bordo, 2018: 21)*

19 Reagan repeated Nixon's strategy, but this time the issue was no longer gold but growth, following a Keynesian rationale:

> Policymakers in the Reagan administration hoped that, as in the past, a falling dollar would not only improve the U.S. trade position but would also encourage foreigners to bear the main burden of adjusting to the U.S. external deficit. By 'talking down the dollar,' they hoped both to devalue the U.S. external debt and indirectly to prompt foreign governments to begin expansionary policies that would help reduce the U.S. deficit without requiring the United States to arrest its growth.
>
> *(Helleiner, 1994: 184)*

20 It is therefore not at all paradoxical that the use of the dollar increased enormously with the end of the dollar's gold parity, just as it is hardly surprising that official dollar reserves increased with floating exchange rates and capital liberalisation (Gourinchas, Rey and Sauzet, 2019: 3–4 and 7).

21 Hence, in the aftermath of the 1997 Asian crisis, the self-insurance policies of developing countries against financial volatility and the lack of a global financial safety net to manage this volatility; hence also, in the aftermath of the 2008 crisis, the rush to the dollar in the aftermath of the crisis, the epicentre of which was located in the issuing country itself (Ocampo, 2017: 31–33).

22 Conversely, some economies benefited from primary surpluses for their role in paying down public debt. For example: "the buoyancy of U.S. capital markets in the 1920s, and perhaps some of their excesses, was due in part to the federal government returning its budget surpluses to the markets via national debt retirements" (Sylla, 2012: 7).

23 It provided financing not only for the US economy but for the whole world economy. Many European financial institutions had borrowed huge amounts of dollars on a short-term basis to speculate on securitised loans. When the interbank market froze, they were unable to refinance their dollar-denominated debt. Dollars had to be injected into the European financial system, but the Fed could not lend them directly to European banks. Bernanke found a solution: he proposed to exchange his dollars for the currencies of the European central banks, which would, in turn, lend these dollars to institutions that requested them. This operation amounted to 500 billion dollars at the end of 2008. The role of the dollar as a universal equivalent explains the paradox that the currency of the country where the crisis broke out appreciated relative to all other currencies.

24 The principle of uncovered interest rate parity is that the difference in the nominal interest rates between two countries is equal to the relative changes in the foreign exchange rate over the same time period.

25 "[T]he BIS international banking statistics reveal that combined US dollar assets of European banks reached approximately $8 trillion in 2008, including retail and corporate lending as well as holdings of US securities: Treasury, agency, and structured products [...]. Of this amount, between $300 billion and $600 billion was financed through foreign exchange swaps, mostly short term, against the pound sterling, euro, and Swiss franc" (James, 2017: 48).

26 But this insularity privilege of the US is not independent of its international role. No doubt it has the freedom to conduct its monetary policy independently of exchange rate fluctuations in order to focus on the price level and the purchasing power of the dollar in terms of goods and services. But by focusing on domestic prices, the Fed performs a nominal anchor function for the international monetary system (McKinnon, 2001: 231). Conversely, the undervaluation of foreign currencies imposed by foreign central banks through their peg to the dollar creates anti-inflationary pressure on the US price level and thus contributes to the stability of the system. Moreover, it is through their respective counter-finalities that the actors of the international monetary system cooperate without rules or agreements.

27 Since 2013, the Fed has made permanent in time and unlimited in volume five of the emergency swap lines that were created in immediate response to the crisis. The partner central banks that form this "C6 swap network" are the ECB, the Bank of England, the Bank of Japan, the Bank of Canada and the Swiss National Bank (Mehrling, 2015). The C6 swap network represents the last defence line against further systemic financial crises in the current version of the US dollar offshore system.

28 "The international US dollar funding network is large, diffuse and interconnected. It consists of a diverse set of borrowers and lenders interacting through a range of intermediaries and a variety of financial instruments. It is geographically dispersed, with a large share of activity occurring outside the United States. It is interconnected, incorporating long and sometimes opaque cross-border and cross-sector linkages transcending regulatory jurisdictions" (CGFS, 2020: 4).

29 The TAF was launched in December 2007, in parallel with the central banks' swap lines. It provided 28- to 84-day loans to commercial banks (deposit-taking institutions) in the domestic market that had difficulty borrowing in the wholesale markets. The TSLF was introduced in March 2008 and was designed to meet the needs of financial institutions (primary dealers) that did not qualify for credit under the TAF, including investment banks (non-depository institutions). Under normal circumstances, these institutions raised funds by offering securities as collateral, including mortgage-backed securities. When the markets for these securities collapsed, the Fed allowed primary dealers to swap toxic securities for the US Treasury securities, which they could then use as collateral to raise funds in the wholesale financial markets. The CPFF was introduced in October 2008 when the commercial paper market dried up.

30 The opposition between the realist current known as the hegemonic stability hypothesis, according to which only the US hegemony has so far guaranteed international order (Kindleberger, 1973; Gilpin, 1987), and the liberal current, for which the sharing of rules, norms and institutions defines an international regime that guarantees the preservation of this order as well (Krasner, 1983; Keohane, 1984), is the theoretical manifestation of the ambivalent role of the US in contemporary capitalism: a mixture of hegemony and cooperation based entirely on the role of the dollar in reproducing the international monetary regime. The realist current has questioned this very 'benevolent' vision of hegemony, which makes the exercise of power look like a global collective good for the benefit of all (Cohen, 2008: 72). But in the monetary order, the role of the hegemon is precisely to provide global liquidity: keeping a relatively open market for imports, providing contracyclic long-term lending and supplying short-term financing in the event of a crisis. The dollar is the true global public good to which the properties of non-excludability and non-rivalry apply. Kindleberger justifies the altruistic nature of his conception of hegemony – or rather 'responsibility', as he likes to call it – by the fact that the US has to constantly adapt its domestic economic objectives to the requirements of the international role of its currency (exchange rate, interest rate, inflation, etc.). This is why each update of his theory has charged the US with a new function: first as a world banker, then as a lender of last resort and finally as a world economic government, through the coordination of exchange rates and macroeconomic policies. The misunderstanding at the root of this controversy is that the particular power of the US is exercised through the universal functions of the dollar, while these functions, in turn, require the US to provide the global public good of the dollar in times of crisis to defend its domestic financial system.

This is evidenced by the fact that both the US Treasury and the Federal Reserve have historically been quite picky about whom they rescue. That is, they have a strong propensity to respond to those economies in crisis where the US financial system is most exposed and tend to ignore those countries where direct risks are minimal. Thus, coincidentally, at the interstate level, US foreign rescues also

> reflect a joint product model where both the US and global financial systems are simultaneously stabilised.
>
> *(McDowell, 2017: 179)*

31 "Monetary hegemony is a political and economic system "organized around a single country with acknowledged responsibilities (and privileges) as leader" in the sphere of money (Cohen, 1977: 9).

32 Another Kirchner attempts to explain the dollar's hegemony in terms of US leadership in security, trade and culture, but without taking into account the decline of US hegemony in relation to the increased international role of the dollar (Kirchner, 2019: 3).

33 See Hartmann who recalls that before 1974, Middle Eastern oil countries invoiced their barrels in dollars but, being members of the Commonwealth, asked to be paid in pounds sterling (Hartmann, 2003: 19).

34 This confusion even leads Norrlof to confess his perplexity: "In the case of the unprecedented US security network, it is not clear whether it is the defense commitment per se, which is important, or, for instance, whether countries 'liking' the United States politically is what triggers currency support" (Norrlof et al., 2020: 21).

35 This actually applies to all approaches to money defining the money as a unit of account as the result of a sovereign act and the privileged form of expression of sovereignty. And even a Marxist like Ivanova remains trapped in the state view of money when she writes:

> [The dollar] is a national fiat currency whose value can never be fully independent from domestic economic conditions and can be manipulated by the policies of the USA state. Still, it is the closest equivalent of world money that the world has known for almost seven decades.
>
> *(Ivanova, 2013: 52)*

36 The sterility of the IPE's analyses stems from the fact that by interpreting all international phenomena in terms of power, it makes the bearer of power par excellence, the state, the central actor. Even the liberal current analyses international regimes primarily as a 'pattern of interstate relations' (Cohen, 2008: 67).

37 This is the deep meaning of its famous formula: "We are all Keynesians now" (Gilpin, 2001: 70). For from a monetary point of view, Keynesianism is a set of economic policies aimed at transforming money into a pure medium of exchange.

10

THE DOLLARISATION OF THE WORLD THROUGH CRISES

10.1 The purchasing power parity and the imparity of the currencies' power

Shortly after the conversion of the international monetary system to floating exchange rates, Rudiger Dornbusch and Paul Krugman wrote: "Under the skin of any international economist lies a deep-seated belief in some variant of the PPP [purchasing power parity] theory of the exchange rate" (Dornbusch and Krugman, 1976: 540). For PPP is like the cipher of universal capitalism, for which only the diversity of units of account circulating on the foreign exchange market would preserve the remains of a time when nations developed at unequal rates and in specific ways. This theory is based on the principle that any monetary unit should be able to be exchanged for the same quantity of good regardless of the country in which the exchange takes place, so that its exchange rate with any foreign currency represents the inverse of the relative price of the good expressed in these two currencies. Thus, purchasing power parity (PPP) means a real exchange rate equal to 1: Real exchange rate = Nominal exchange rate × Domestic price/Foreign price. The theory of PPP therefore considers money exclusively in its general exchangeability form, i.e. as a unit of account and transaction currency. Here the exchange rate is not affected by any other variable than the domestic and foreign price level and only the trade balance determines the stability of exchange rates (Cassel, 1932: 658). PPP therefore discards all influences relating to money as a financial asset (capital flows, speculation) or as a store of value (trade balance). According to the principle of PPP, neither the capital account nor even the balance of payments affects the exchange rate (Einzig, 1962: 269). That this theory considers money as a mere medium of exchange is demonstrated by the fact that its first modern formulations are found in the Salamanca school, in the early Bullionists such as Wheatley and Ricardo, and especially

DOI: 10.4324/9780429261299-14

in the report of the Bullion Committee (Einzig, 1962: 206). In reality, Cassel's theory was born in the same conditions that had inspired Ricardo's quantity theory, except that Cassel, whose thinking developed in the wake of the suspension of gold payments during the First World War, was directly motivated by the search for a new parity of currencies with gold with the prospect of a return to convertibility (Taylor, 2006: 2). In the absence of a generalised peg of national currencies to gold, Cassel was in fact proposing a new monetary policy rule for which the parity of currencies with gold would only be the sign of its right application (Cassel, 1923: 173). He transferred the uniqueness of the universal currency that gold had previously constituted to the price level. Indeed, he believed that PPP reproduced exactly the same mechanisms as the gold standard system when imbalance appeared in the balance of payments. A balance of payments deficit, for example, would cause the exchange rate to depreciate to such an extent that, with the currency undervalued relative to its domestic purchasing power, it would become more attractive for trading partners to buy the undervalued currency. In doing so, the currency would appreciate back to its PPP level. Thus, both the balance of payments and the exchange rate would return to their equilibrium level (Humphrey, 1978: 6).

But with the liberalisation of the foreign exchange market and the capital account, the exchange rate has ceased to reflect the state of the current account and has become dependent on international capital movements and financial transactions based on expectations about the evolution of interest rates and exchange rates themselves: these transactions are a hundred times higher than those related to trade (Plihon, 2017: 41). However, these capital movements do not fulfil the balancing role of the international trade laws: sometimes they compensate for the effect of the current account, while sometimes they aggravate it and thus provoke lasting misalignments of exchange rates: "Gone are the days when a lasting surplus logically allowed a country to see its currency appreciate" (Norel, 1995: 3). And these movements can hardly be relied upon to monitor the evolution of exchange rates. Thus, it has been noticed that some currencies appreciated or stabilised while outflows accelerated (the deutsche mark in 1986 and 1987, the French franc in 1994). Not only does the distinction between residents and non-residents no longer cover capital movements, but more and more currency transactions between residents themselves are weighing on the exchange market (interbank transactions, risk hedging, etc.). And conversely, when non-residents buy domestic assets with funds borrowed from domestic banks, they leave a trace on the capital balance, not on the foreign exchange market (Norel, 1995: 7). Finally, when capital movements influence exchange rates, it is because of the inertia of prices relative to the extreme mobility of speculative capital, to increase their volatility. This is why the financial operators' assessment of the monetary authorities' capacity to maintain a non-inflationary internal policy geared towards the stability of the nominal exchange rate constitutes a much more important determinant of the exchange rate than the competitiveness indicated by the current account balance. Under these conditions, interest in the study of the determinants of the exchange rate grew in inverse proportion to the development of financial globalisation, in which operators gave less credence to fundamental economic variables, which are supposed to influence exchange rates, than to past developments (Frankel, 1984), even and especially when they contradict these variables.

Thus, portfolio choice or exchange rate overshooting models (Dornbusch, 1976; Miles, 1978; McKinnon, 1982) have replaced the old Cassel theory by treating money, like Keynes and Friedman, as a specific financial asset whose exchange rate results from arbitrages between assets with different returns and risks (Drunat, Dufrenot and Mathieu, 1994).[1] However, not only do these models not renounce the principle of PPP, even if it means postponing its application to a distant and uncertain future (Bénassy-Quéré, Béreau and Mignon, 2009), but they retain it as a guide for monetary action in the absence of a fixed exchange rate (Kadochnikov, 2013: 118). But more fundamentally, these models retain from PPP the dichotomous principle of quantity theory according to which the structure of relative prices is given prior to the determination of the price level by the quantity of money thrown into circulation (Cassel, 1916: 62). Although financial models of the exchange rate consider money as a mere financial asset in the short term, as soon as they take into account the long-term effect of this "financial" exchange rate on the market for goods and services, money again appears as a transaction currency and the price level is again determined by the supply of money.

This is because the monetarist conception of the exchange rate validates PPP by over-determining it through its assumptions on the supply and demand of financial assets (Driver and Westaway, 2005). Thus, the assumption of perfect substitutability of domestic and foreign capital, as well as monetary and non-monetary capital, neutralises any effect of the current account on the exchange rate (Frenkel, 1976; Frankel and Rose, 1995; Taylor, 1995). It assumes that the exchange rate is the relative price of two currencies that is determined by supply and demand in the different money markets. Although this principle considers money as an asset, the effect of the supply of money on domestic prices through the interest rate determines this price itself (Taylor and Taylor, 2004). Causality therefore runs from money to domestic prices and the exchange rate (Humphrey, 1978).[2] The variations in the prices of goods compensated on the exchange market by variations in the relative price of currencies are therefore the effects of strictly monetary causes (Taylor and Taylor, 2004: 141).[3]

It has been shown in the analysis of the demand for money in quantity theory how, in spite of its a-monetary character, the formation of relative prices presupposes in fact the existence of a numeraire fulfilling the monetary function of unit of account. But it is at the international level that this presupposition reveals the deep link of quantity theory with the gold standard system and, in default, with the existence of a fiat universal equivalent. Of course, monetarism assumes the existence of n convertible currencies. But there is always one currency that must serve as the unit of account against which the $n - 1$ exchange rates of currencies are established (McKinnon, 2010: 2). In fact, the very existence of international goods presupposes this currency in which the prices of goods are expressed. For not only are these prices determined on international markets by the country with the lowest cost of production, i.e. the one with the highest productivity, but the very existence of a single price presupposes the existence of an international unit of account to which the different currencies relate in order to determine PPP. While under the gold standard the entry and exit points of gold regulated the balance of payments and exchange rate equilibrium, the law of one price ensures this equilibrium in PPP. The assumption of single prices has been criticised for being applied to goods that are in reality not substitutable or perfectly mobile, etc. But these are practical objections to PPP. The problem is theoretical, since the law of one price actually presupposes a single common unit of account in which all national prices coexisting in local markets are expressed (Taylor and Taylor, 2004: 137).[4]

Just as quantity theory makes money superfluous in domestic prices, the monetarist approach to exchange rates makes the diversity of national currencies superfluous in relation to international prices. "Everything happens as if the different currencies were sub-multiples of a single money supply" (de Brunhoff, 1986: 110), except that this supply refers to a reference currency that is never defined in monetarism. Even equilibrium exchange rate models, which no longer seek to explain the exchange rate theoretically but to account for its evolution as a function of fundamental variables supposed to influence the real exchange rate in the medium term (FEER) (Williamson, 1985) or the long term (BEER) (Clark and MacDonald, 1998), presuppose a common unit of account to compare real exchange rates and their evolution, despite the fact that money is absent from these models (Joly, Prigent and Sobczak, 1996). It is probably this presupposition that led Rogoff to say that most economists "instinctively believe in some variant of purchasing power parity as an anchor for long-run real exchange rates" (quoted in Taylor, 2006: 2).

By the time new currency parities were discussed after the Nixon shock, monetarist ideas on exchange rate flexibility had already gained ground with the US authorities. Among these authorities, Treasury Secretary Schultz pretended to be concerned about the exchange rate problem, but everything in their attitude led to the endorsement of a floating exchange rate system. Friedman (1953) argued that exchange rate fluctuations would absorb most of the imbalances between surplus and deficit nations, between those favouring full employment at the cost of inflation and those choosing price stability at the cost of inevitable unemployment if wages were rigidly downwards. Each nation could "pursue the mixture of unemployment and price trend objectives it prefers, consistent with international equilibrium, equilibrium being secured by appreciation of the currencies of 'price stability' countries relative to the currencies of 'full employment' countries" (Johnson, 1969: 18). But we forget that Friedman's model assumed no capital flows (Flanders and Helpman, 1978) and that it inspired the US authorities at the very moment when the major currencies were under incessant speculative attack through the ebb and flow of capital on the Eurodollar market. In this context, even the central bankers of the time were opposed to floating currencies, because "the small number of important banks and multinational corporations that dominated the markets were frequently prone to irrational, bandwagon behavior unrelated to changes in fundamental economic conditions" (Helleiner, 1994: 117). On the basis of capital mobility, any divergent movement of prices or costs from a supposed equilibrium would be immediately sanctioned by an overshooting of exchange rates (Guttmann, 1994: 144–45). Most importantly, flexible exchange rates not only do not protect nations from global financial shocks or cycles (Obstfeld and Taylor, 2017: 17) but they fuel them through changes in exchange rate expectations.

The reason why the US considered that the liberalisation of capital movements could preserve its monetary policy autonomy was that only the country whose currency serves as the international unit of account and the global financing currency could benefit from this regime: when the exchange rate fell, current accounts improved and external revenues increased; when it rose, foreign products became cheaper and thus lowered domestic prices, allowing monetary policy to lower interest rates. For other countries, especially developing countries, a fall in the exchange rate increases the dollar bill, the debt burden and the capital drain, while a rise in the exchange rate not only reduces competitiveness but also exerts inflationary pressure by attracting foreign capital. Here, we can grasp the practical significance of the monetarist presupposition of a common unit of account. For in a regime of inconvertible currencies, the presupposed unit of account is necessarily one of the national currencies in relation to which all other currencies gravitate. Monetarism is to the foreign exchange market what MMT is to monetary policy: it brings to theoretical generalisation the presuppositions specific to the particularity of the dollar as a universal currency.

10.2 The dollar in currency crises

With PPP no longer valid in the short term, the monetary authorities had to be given new criteria for action. Thus, the author of the Washington Consensus, whose effects on the fate of Latin America in the 1990s will be analysed shortly, proposed the so-called theory of exchange rates target zone theory (Williamson, 1986), in which the equilibrium exchange rate is said to be fundamental when, in the medium term, the securities market is assumed to be in equilibrium and wealth (the stock of assets) is considered to be stable.[5] In reality, the writer of the Ten Commandments of financial globalisation was taking note of the fact that for the markets, the equilibrium exchange rate defines nothing more than the rate against which some basic variables such as a balance of payments deficit are considered sustainable, i.e. financeable by external loans. The greater the financial openness of a country, the greater the margin of sustainability of its deficit in the operators' eyes, but also the greater the mobility of capital and with it the risks of currency crises.

However, the source of all the misunderstandings about the exchange rate crises which followed one another from the 1980s onwards lies in the fact that the effects of financial liberalisation were confused with the key role of the dollar in the post–Bretton Woods currency hierarchy. Calvo and Goldstein (1996) pointed out at the time that capital account liberalisation triggers a substitution of foreign assets for domestic assets that increases exposure to exchange rate risk and default risk.[6] Financial globalisation means nothing more in monetary terms than the globalisation of the dollar. But regardless of the fact that the universal role of the dollar was prepared for a long time, the floating exchange rate regime cannot do without a reference currency.[7] Even in the absence of a central currency, a "hierarchical compromise" is established between the need for an international unit of account and the maintenance of the specificity of national currencies. With the liberalisation of the foreign exchange market and therefore international financial competition, this hierarchy is expressed in the level of priority given to the external objectives of low inflation and high remuneration of money over the internal objectives of growth, employment, social protection, etc. It may be said that only the US, as the issuer of the reserve currency, is spared this concern. But the international role of the dollar also requires it to meet the new international standards of finance, even if this means increasing inequalities, reducing real wages and making the labour market as flexible as possible.

Referring to the cycle of international financial crises in the 1990s, Rose said, "Within the profession, we have to admit that we have a poor understanding of what triggers a crisis, especially in the case of currency crises" (Bordo et al., 2001: 75), and even questioned whether these currency crises really have macroeconomic causes (Cartapanis, 2004: 7). This is because, just as exchange rate theories presuppose the existence of a common unit of account in their real exchange rate models, crisis analyses presuppose the existence of key currencies without realising that these currencies do not merely serve as an anchor for secondary currencies: they also perform monetary functions whose modalities give crises their particular forms. What economists have called the three generations of currency crises are not so much generations of models as stages in the growth of the dollar – but also of the deutsche mark in the case of Europe – as a general equivalent at the world or continental level.

10.2.1 The first-generation currency crises: the dollarisation of the Public Treasuries

However, the Mexican crisis of 1982, although it represented the first major exchange rate crisis after the abolition of the fixed exchange rate system, was not caused by the floating of the peso against the dollar. On the contrary, the defence of exchange rate fixity was one of the very factors that caused the crisis. Nor did the crisis owe its brutality and severity to financial liberalisation: Mexico had not yet liberalised its capital account and its public debt was not securitised at that time. But it is the first great crisis of universalisation, not of the dollar as a mere key currency, but of the dollar as money-capital, as universal financial capital issued by the central bank of a particular country guided by its national interests. Thus, after years of massive borrowing on the Eurodollar market, the emerging countries suffered the combined effects of Volcker's rise in the US interest rates and thus their increased level of indebtedness, and the rise in commodity prices on which their trade depended. The Mexican government soon declared that it was suspending payments on its debt (excluding interest). But what turned this external debt crisis into a currency crisis was that Mexico, in order to gain the confidence of foreign investors, had moved to a fixed exchange rate regime with the dollar after years of uncontrolled inflation. The rise of the dollar worsened Mexico's balance of payments, which had already been worsened by the loss of competitiveness of Mexican products and the fall in the price of oil, of which it was a major supplier (Wolfson, 1986: 103). It is fair to say that this balance of payments was mainly worsened by the continuous increase in public spending fuelled by government borrowing in dollars. But this borrowing owed its effects on the balance of payments mainly to the increase in the debt burden caused by the rise in the US interest rates. Similarly, inflation rates close to 100% were certainly Mexico's business, but the rise in these rates was itself fuelled by capital flight accelerated by successive peso devaluations.[8] It is therefore the combination of the rise in interest rates, the value of the dollar and the flight of capital in dollars that gives the Mexican crisis its specific character and explains its magnitude relative to the fundamentals pinpointed by the so-called first-generation models of currency crises (Krugman, 1979; Flood and Garber, 1984). However, although these models explain the triggering of crises by the deterioration of fundamentals such as the current account balance or the budget deficit, Flood and Garber themselves recognised that the crisis depended as much on downward speculation on the peso as on Mexico's fundamentals (Flood and Garber, 1984: 6). Similarly, Krugman admitted that, among the variables responsible for the fall in reserves, portfolio movements provoked by simple expectations on the evolution of prices were decisive (Krugman, 1979: 379).

In these three effects of the dollarisation of Mexican public debt, the contradiction between the dollar acting as financial capital and the peso fulfilling the functions of a means of circulation, i.e. of the equivalent of goods and services sometimes exchanged on the international markets and sometimes spent in the domestic sphere, is actually expressed. In this sense, the 1982 crisis expresses not so much the contradiction between the need to anchor the currency and the mobility of capital, in which Eichengreen sees the ultimate source of the ills of financial globalisation (2008: 1), as the contradiction immanent in borrowing in dollars to finance economic policies applied to a monetary space in which the local currency continues to fulfil the functions of unit of account and medium of exchange. The role of fundamentals in first-generation currency crises is that they are related to transactions and expenditures carried out by the domestic currency where the source of these transactions and expenditures depended on the reference currency of the international monetary system. While the government, although running a capitalist sate, fulfilled its internal public functions through the social functions of the domestic currency, it was dependent on creditors for whom the dollar fulfilled a private function of monetary capital.

However, after the debt crisis triggered by the changes in the US monetary policy, these government bonds were replaced by market instruments such as Brady bonds, at the request of the banks themselves, which were seeking to develop more active management of their portfolios. Thus "successive issues of Brady bonds in the following years created very large markets for dollar-denominated sovereign securities, on the basis of which the financial and secondary markets were able to develop very rapidly" (Sgard, 2002: 22). The consequences of this change were the diversification of investors, the very wide opening of the capital account of emerging countries, exposing them to volatile short-term capital movements, with new issuers such as corporations and commercial banks suddenly accessing international currency markets. These changes led to one of the largest waves of investment into peripheral economies: from $35 billion a year in the 1980s to $280 billion a year between 1995 and 1997 (Sgard, 2002: 22).[9] After offshore banks had dollarised their Treasuries, investors dollarised the financial markets of emerging countries.

10.2.2 The second-generation currency crises: the dollarisation of private markets

The Mexican crisis of 1994 has been described as a second-generation crisis because of its self-fulfilling character, due to the predominance of the financial sector in the dollar debt (Masson, 1999). Unlike the 1982 crisis, therefore, this one is less a solvency crisis than a liquidity crisis provoked by a market reversal (Pesenti and Tille, 2000: 7. See also Jeanne, 2000: 37–38). But it has not been sufficiently emphasised that this change of generation expressed a change in the role of the dollar in the nature of this crisis. Unlike in 1982, indeed, the entire private sector was exposed to the dollar and at the mercy of dollar investors. The financial liberalisation that began after the first crisis and was accelerated by the Washington Consensus actually meant the financial globalisation of the dollar itself. Compared to 1982, the Mexican economy in 1994 was different in that with the deregulation of financial markets and the reprivatisation of banks, not only were markets opened to the issuance and circulation of foreign securities, but banks borrowed massively in dollars to fuel a debauchery of real estate and consumer loans (Musacchio, 2012: 12). While in 1982 this was direct government dollar debt to private banks, 12 years later it is indirect debt, mediated by the capital market in addition to the banks.

Let us recall the context of this new influx of dollars into Mexico. Firstly, depressed activity in the US, Canada and the UK, and the resulting fall in interest rates, whetted investors' appetites for emerging markets with high growth potential (Solomon, 1999: 116). In addition, there was debt deflation in Japan, with falling prices for securities, land and the yen, but also the first Iraq war and the rise in the price of oil (*Ibidem*). Above all, there was the triple financial revolution, endorsed by the Washington Consensus and, in the case of Mexico, the Brady Plan organising the securitisation of Mexican debt: deregulation of the markets, internationalisation of capital, and financial innovations launched by the Brady bonds, among others. The active role of institutional investors, who had free rein to diversify their investments, encouraged the influx of capital from advanced countries, which rose from 65 billion per year in the years 1975–79 to 460 billion in 1989 (Solomon, 1999: 109–10).

This influx was facilitated by the fact that from 1989 onwards, Mexico had gone from being a prodigal child to a model pupil: the budget became in surplus in 1992–93, inflation was reduced to single-digit levels, GDP accelerated and it was less dependent on oil exports than in the early 1980s. This transformation was rewarded by Mexico's entry into the GATT (later WTO) and the OECD, and especially by the signing of free trade agreements with the US and Canada (Solomon, 1999: 120). Nevertheless, the gradual depreciation of the exchange rate[10] did not prevent its real appreciation due to the resumption of inflation after 1990. Yet the resulting current account deficit was easily financed by capital inflows and in fact foreign exchange reserves continued to rise until the first quarter of 1994. But in the meantime interest rates in the US rose: both long rates and the federal funds rate as a result of monetary tightening measures by the Fed (Solomon, 1999: 120–21).

The government was responsible for the resulting inflation only to the extent that it borrowed itself by issuing dollar-denominated Treasury bills (*tesobonos*): on the eve of the crisis, the Mexican economy owed more or less all of its financing to the US dollar. The larger the balance of payments deficit, the more the government borrowed to maintain its exchange rate. Since a simple reversal of capital flows could immediately trigger a devaluation of the exchange rate, the crisis could have been a textbook case of the second-generation model, but political events provided a rational basis for the sudden reversal of capital flows: the assassination of the PRI candidate in the 1994 elections and the unfortunate announcement by his elected replacement of a new team at the Ministry of Finance, combined with the decision to widen the exchange rate band, precipitated the withdrawal of capital and soon the floating of the peso. Not only did these political events justify in hindsight the fears of investors who would have used even more innocuous events as a pretext for the downturn, but the markets reacted sharply to the only action the government had to take in the circumstances, namely to loosen the exchange rate stranglehold on the Mexican economy.[11] One analyst, comparing the 1994 crisis to that of 1982, asked:

> Why then did Mexico not treat these sudden outflows as they treated in 1982 the dollar deposits in Mexican banks? To answer: 'Because to do so would violate the new rules of the game' of what Chairman Greenspan of the Federal Reserve has referred to as 'the internationalized capital markets. The possibility that one might impose exchange controls precludes

> one from access to these capital markets because the last thing that any mutual fund manager can tolerate is the possibility that he or she might not be able to quickly dump a holding and shift elsewhere.
>
> *(Lichtenstein, 1995: 1775)*[12]

Money has no homeland, but neither do its owners: the first peso-to-dollar conversions came from the Mexicans themselves, and an IMF report revealed that the pressure on foreign exchange reserves during 1994 came from Mexican residents, not from foreign investors or from speculative positions taken by those investors (Solomon, 1999: 123).[13]

Frankel and Rose were surprised to discover that neither the current account nor the fiscal deficit "appear to play an important role" (1996: 20) in emerging market currency crises. All of the factors considered, however, involve both a reference currency as a financial asset and the price of that reference currency, i.e. the interest rate. However, given the strangeness of these crises in relation to the traditional variables affecting exchange rates, specialists confined themselves to see the effect of a strategic game between the markets and the authorities and to explain the crisis as the result of a simple self-fulfilling prophecy.

10.2.3. Third-generation crises: the dollarisation of global investment

Dornbusch (2001) has contrasted the "old style crises", which are mainly linked to real exchange rate distortions and unsustainable external imbalances, with the "new style balance sheet crises", whose source lies in banking fragilities. However, third-generation models are usually distinguished by the bank liquidity crisis that goes with the currency crisis (Chang and Velasco, 1998). By doubling the financial crises with banking crises, the third-generation model of currency crises endorsed the presence of the dollar at all stages of financial intermediation in peripheral currency areas. This change is reflected in the fact that the indicator of fragility is no longer expressed by the ratio between the level of foreign exchange reserves and the balance of payments deficit, but by the ratio between these reserves and the amount of short-term external debt (Furman and Stiglitz, 1998: 23–24). The question is therefore not whether the crisis expresses a banking liquidity problem (Chang and Velasco, 1998) or whether it is the inevitable result of deteriorating fundamentals (Corsetti, Pesenti and Roubini, 1999). The question is whether the exchange rate plays a role in both the liquidity crisis and the deterioration of fundamentals.

No doubt the banking crisis coming with the currency crisis reveals an over-indebtedness of banks. But this coupling with the currency crisis would be a coincidence if other indicators did not give the twin crises their specific character: the ratio of banks' external liabilities to GDP, the interest rate of creditor countries or the spreads demanded of emerging country debtors (Kamin, Samuel and Schindler, 2001). However, under a fixed exchange rate regime, banks are not aware that they are taking a foreign exchange risk. By accepting deposits and credits in dollars, any questioning of the parity can only precipitate the banking crisis. Even if the banking system were properly supervised, a change in parity would put all the risks on the banking system because in emerging countries "banks are responsible for a larger share of financial intermediation there than in most advanced countries" (Solomon, 1999: 158). In this case, the causality runs from the currency crisis to the banking crisis and not the other way round, as econometric studies on panel data teach (Boyer, Dehove and Plihon, 2004: 29). They are therefore not collateral effects of banking crises, as Krugman (2001a) thinks, for example (see also Cartapanis, 2004: 21). Pesenti and Tille see in the twin crises the effect of a reciprocal causality between the liquidity crisis and the currency crisis:

> A currency crisis has an adverse effect on the banking sector when banks' liabilities are denominated in a foreign currency. A devaluation suddenly and sharply increases the value, expressed in the domestic currency, of these liabilities. As banks typically lend domestically in the local currency, a devaluation exposes them to a sizable currency mismatch and a deterioration of their balance sheets. In turn, a banking crisis can lead to a currency crisis through the burden it imposes on the fiscal side of the economy.
>
> *(Pesenti and Tille, 2000: 7)*

But the difference between the two causalities is that the banking crisis could not have been caused without the currency crisis.

To justify the insane orgy of short-term foreign currency (dollar) loans made by international banks to Asian banks prior to the 1997 crisis, analysts were quick to condemn governments for implicitly guaranteeing these loans, either directly or indirectly through IMF support programmes, thereby creating moral hazard, i.e. the "apparent neglect of the standards for sound risk assessment" (Corsetti, Pesenti and Roubini, 1999: 8). For example, the ratio of short-term foreign liabilities to foreign exchange reserves was over 100% in Korea, Indonesia and Thailand on the eve of the crisis. With regard to exchange rates, the appreciation of the dollar and the depreciation of the yen led to a loss of competitiveness in the region, particularly vis-à-vis Japan, and more generally to an appreciation of the real exchange rate – albeit unevenly – of currencies pegged to the dollar. But the level of appreciation was modest compared to the appreciation of the peso before the Mexican crisis. In fact, real exchange rate indicators had not changed significantly in South Korea, Thailand and Indonesia. Although current accounts had deteriorated in the region, even the most severe analysts admit that there is little evidence of when current account deficits reach excessive proportions to create expectations of devaluation, speculative withdrawals or financial crises (Corsetti, Pesenti and Roubini, 1999: 312). Moreover, it is admitted that in the case of Asia, GDP growth rates remained remarkably high until the eve of the crisis (investment rates ranged between 30 and 40 in most countries in the region (Corsetti, Pesenti and Roubini, 1999: 316), although the returns on these investments tended to decline). Moreover, the savings rate was roughly equal to the investment rate, so that current account deficits could not be attributed to excessive government spending. Finally, unlike in Mexico, the inflation rate remained relatively low (Corsetti, Pesenti and Roubini, 1999: 322) despite the huge capital inflow, indicating that the real exchange rate appreciation was entirely due to the appreciation of the dollar and the depreciation of the yen.

While Indonesia suffered the largest currency debacle in the region, it was the country with a rigid exchange rate policy against the dollar whose currency experienced less real exchange rate appreciation than the others. More generally, if we look at the estimates proposed by the World Bank, none of the countries hit by the crisis presents a serious problem. Indeed, the debt-to-GDP ratio for many of these countries had remained relatively low and the share of short-term debt in total debt, although increasing, had remained relatively modest (see table 24 in Corsetti, Pesenti and Roubini, 1999). The only worrying indicator was the ratio of external liabilities to foreign assets: domestic banks had borrowed heavily from foreign banks to lend to domestic investors. But

> [i]n normal times a high ratio of foreign liabilities to foreign assets may not cause concern, as short-term foreign debts are easily rolled-over. In the presence of a rapid currency depreciation, however, this imbalance may cause serious financial problems (especially if the foreign borrowing is in foreign currency while the domestic lending is in domestic currency). Foreign lenders may suddenly refuse to roll over short-term lines of credit to domestic banks, precipitating a credit crisis. To a large extent, this is what happened in 1997.
>
> *(Corsetti, Pesenti and Roubini, 1999: 341)*

In fact, the only notable event before the crisis broke was the market euphoria over the investment opportunities offered by Malaysia: its interest rates were too attractive to ignore. As a result, capital inflows exploded in 1996, from $2.4 billion in 1995 to $11.3 billion in 1996, causing property prices to rise by 25% (Corsetti, Pesenti and Roubini, 1999: 347). If the excess borrowing and the resulting crisis are to be explained by the weakness of the banking and financial systems, this weakness does not explain the form in which the crisis hit Asia or the spread of the crisis to countries that were not experiencing excess investment.

> By the end of the summer, the combined effective devaluation of about 30 percent in 3 months for the currencies of Thailand, Indonesia, the Philippines and Malaysia had a strong negative impact on the other currencies in the region. For instance, the Singaporean currency that was formally on a float started to depreciate on the wheel of the sharp deterioration of the ringgit – the currency of its close neighbor and trading partner Malaysia. By the end of September, the Singaporean currency had lost 8 percent of its value relative to the beginning of 1997.
>
> *(Corsetti, Pesenti and Roubini, 1999: 352).*

The large devaluations that followed the first depreciations were due to market reactions to monetary policies aimed at limiting the outflow of capital and especially speculative pressures on the foreign exchange market, in order to avoid too much monetary contraction and too high an interest rate. What does this mean? It means that the authorities had chosen to gradually relax their exchange rate at the same time as they sought to exert control over capital. The only country having resisted a speculative attack on its currency, Hong Kong, did not hesitate to drastically increase its interest rates, no doubt because of the predominance of its financial sector compared to other countries in the region. In any case, it convinced the markets of its commitment to maintain its fixed parity with the dollar (Corsetti, Pesenti and Roubini, 1999: 354). And while all the measures to prevent interest rates from rising had caused market panic and capital flight in Asia, what was able to restore speculators' confidence was... the lowering of interest rates in the US, a sign that the Fed was ensuring the cheap availability of the universal equivalent.[14]

The Asian crisis shows that both a fixed and a floating exchange rate regime would have led to great financial fragility. Thus a floating exchange rate regime would have caused a real appreciation of the exchange rate and a loss of competitiveness of the export sector anyway. As for the fixed exchange rate regime, which prevailed to a variable extent depending on the country, it is at the origin of the financial fragility, i.e. the excess of short-term loans in foreign currencies and the resulting maturity mismatch. Thus, in a fixed exchange rate regime, the pressure on the nominal exchange rate is relieved by the accumulation of reserves by the central bank. However, in order to avoid an excess supply of domestic money and therefore inflation and a real appreciation of the currency, the monetary authorities proceed to sterilisation policies leading to an increase in interest rates. This is what happened in Thailand. But as long as the belief in the currency peg to the dollar lasts, the rise in interest rates causes a shift in the composition of capital inflows to unhedged short-term debt. As a result, banks were exposed to an excess of short-term foreign currency debt. In addition, this inflow of short-term capital stimulates domestic demand and, when the supply of non-tradable goods is less elastic, raises the relative prices of these goods, which encourages investment in the non-tradable sector. Thus, the price of domestic assets rises and encourages speculative bubbles, especially in real estate, while these bubbles, in turn, bring in new capital. Thus the ability of banks to repay their short-term foreign currency debts depends not only on the return on the domestic investments they are financing with these liabilities, but also on the exchange rate between the currency in which their liabilities are denominated and the currency in which their assets are recorded.

10.3 The hierarchical compromise in the European monetary system crisis

So far, the analysis of the crises has shown how the penetration of the dollar into the peripheral economies, through which the process of relative autonomy of the dollar in relation to the US economy was accomplished, was inseparable from the hierarchical compromise between the dollar and the currencies hit by the currency crises. But one would not believe that, conversely, the hierarchical compromise is inseparable from the autonomisation of the currency at the top of this compromise. Just as the hierarchical compromise is not necessarily organised between a key currency and the currencies of developing or emerging countries. This is what the crisis of the European monetary system (EMS) revealed a few years before the creation of the euro. Here again, the role of fundamentals must be put into perspective: even more than in Mexico, the transformation of European currencies into pure and simple financial assets had freed the movement of the foreign exchange market from any fundamental basis and left it to the whims of speculation. Under these conditions, the crisis represents nothing more than the random outcome of a game of influence between the monetary authorities and the markets, where macroeconomic aggregates are reduced to mere variables of strategic choice (Cartapanis, 2004: 11–12). Faced with the sterility of the debate on the role of fundamentals in second generation crises, Obstfeld simply retorts: "The interesting question is not whether the crisis was 'justified' by fundamentals, since everyone agrees the fundamentals play and must play a role, but whether the fundamentals were such as to make the crisis the inevitable and unique outcome" (Comment on Krugman, 1996: 395). Not only do the analyses agree that they were not, but the European crisis reveals that the outcome depended on the place of the different currencies in the hierarchy of the EMS.

Eichengreen (2000) sees the crisis as an expression of the difficulty of anchoring exchange rates in the global context of high capital mobility. And although he does not include the problem of currency hierarchy in his analysis of the crisis, he supports the dollarisation of Latin America, with a view to forming a monetary union with the US. The only other solution that he imagines to be suitable for the current system is a floating exchange rate regime (Eichengreen, 2000: 2). But what happened from 6 September onwards, when the UK asked to leave the EMS? Not only did Italy follow the UK, but all the currencies in the system, except the deutsche mark and the Dutch gulden, which was firmly pegged to the former, were attacked. However, this crisis cannot be considered as a crisis of current account deficits, as before the crisis these deficits were more significant in Germany due to the expenses necessary for reunification. It is true that deficits had increased everywhere to avoid importing the recession to the US and the UK, and the fall in the dollar that the fall in interest rates brought about to cope with this recession weakened the competitiveness of European countries, but there is no justification for comparing the European crisis to the Mexican crisis from the point of view of the nature of the deficits, as Eichengreen suggests. Following this view, he notes the curiosity that in the first case, it was the fall in the US rates that caused the crisis, whereas in the second case, it was the rise in rates that caused Mexico to plunge. The explanation would be that, in the case of Europe, it was a crisis of current account deficits, and therefore of competitiveness, while in the case of Mexico, the capital account was responsible for the crisis (Eichengreen, 2000: 18). But not only was the Mexican crisis the result of a competitiveness crisis linked to the pegging of the peso to a dollar that had appreciated after 1992, but the EMS crisis hit countries that, like France, had comfortable trade surpluses until the eve of the attack. What these two crises have in common, however, is that in both cases the markets doubted the viability of their respective pegs to the reference currency, the dollar in the case of Mexico and the deutsche mark in the case of France. In the case of France, it was the rise in interest rates, demanded by Germany so as not to have to respond to the rise in domestic demand with inflation; that made the markets doubt the survival of the franc in the EMS.[15] Eichengreen himself acknowledges that much of the speculative attacks are poorly explained by the first-generation model of currency crises (competitiveness crisis) (Eichengreen, 2000: 19). No doubt the first attacks had targeted the most fragile countries in the system – those with the highest current account deficits, unemployment rates, public debt and weakest banking systems. But it is also accepted that these fragilities would only be a source of crisis if there was a capital outflow, i.e. a reversal of investor confidence, proving that the crisis was also a capital account crisis as in Mexico.

Eichengreen is surprised that the banking and financial systems were hit to an extent unusual for developed-country crises (Eichengreen, 2000: 39), attributing this strange phenomenon to financial deregulation and capital account liberalisation. But he should have asked why Germany and the Netherlands were spared. Instead, what all the attacked countries had in common was that they had pegged their respective currencies to the deutsche mark, which, despite Germany's budget and trade deficits, high unemployment and inflationary pressures on its domestic products, was a key currency together with the dollar and the yen. Eichengreen calls this crisis the first crisis of financial globalisation (financial deregulation and capital account liberalisation) (Eichengreen, 2000: 45), but it is above all the first crisis in which deregulation and liberalisation are in direct contradiction with the need for peripheral currencies such as the franc, the lira and even the pound sterling to be anchored in a reference currency, even though on the foreign exchange market currencies are treated as perfectly substitutable assets, as stated in the Modern Portfolio Theory. The so-called second-generation crises are distinguished not so much by the minor importance of fundamentals relative to market psychology (self-fulfilling prophecies) as by the importance of the anchoring of peripheral currencies to the key currency in the fate of these fundamentals: interest rate policy, budgetary policy, exchange rate policy. Through the opening of financial markets to foreign capital, all private investment becomes subject to the vagaries of the reference currency and its effects on the exchange rate.

10.4 The dollar zone

The exchange rate crises, and especially the 2008 crisis, have in no way slowed down the financial integration of the world economy or the pegging of currencies to key currencies, despite the diversity of exchange rate regimes. On the contrary, the financial crises have acted as powerful levers for financial integration, banking concentration and the over-determination of exchange rates by reference currencies. Thus, the conflicting centralisation under the aegis of the dollar that Suzanne de Brunhoff observed in the 1980s now delineates a genuine dollar zone alongside the other monetary zones, whether de jure like the euro zone or de facto like the yen zone, and which brings together "economies with currencies that are relatively stable against the dollar" (Ito and McCauley, 2018: 1). Within this zone, cross-border investment and borrowing in dollars imposes a zone bias on investors' portfolio choices: this reduces currency risks relative to more diversified portfolios. Under this approach, the dollar zone would cover 50%–60% of global GDP. In reality, for both the euro and the dollar, the reduction in their respective shares of world GDP has been more than offset by growth in their respective areas (Ito and McCauley, 2018: 8).

On this basis, the US current account deficit should be assessed in relation to the current accounts of the dollar zone, which would be in balance. Thus, an exchange rate crisis within the dollar zone is less likely to occur as the "dollar bias" makes a "sudden stop in response to heightened perception of currency risk less likely" (Ito and McCauley, 2018: 10). Moreover, the dollar zone perspective reveals that, whatever the crisis in the dollar zone (Mexico in 1982, Asia in 1997 or the US in 2007–8), "current accounts tend to redistribute themselves within the dollar zone" (Ito and McCauley, 2018: 11). This is not the case in the euro area, where surpluses in the centre after the 2012 crisis have not been offset by deficits in the periphery (i.e. in European countries that do not belong to the euro area in the strict sense). Therefore, we cannot correlate exchange rates with the current account deficits of the reference-currency-issuing countries or regions, but to the aggregate balance of payments of the currency area in question. Thus, at the same time that investors were becoming wary of Asian deficits (Thailand, Korea), the opposite was happening with the dollar: despite the widening current account deficits, the dollar appreciated in 1997. Solomon acknowledges that the law according to which a current account deficit leads to a depreciation of the exchange rate has no longer applied since the 1990s, neither for the dollar nor for the deutsche mark (Solomon, 1999: 144).[16] And the appreciation of the dollar, despite the huge current account deficit in 2006, is explained as soon as we observe that this deficit is exactly offset by the sum of the surpluses of all the countries in the dollar constellation. In the same way, the surplus of the official euro zone is put into perspective if we take into account the deficits of the countries whose currencies are more or less rigidly anchored to the euro (mainly Central and Eastern Europe). Financial and banking integration, consolidated in particular by the transnational role of the central banks issuing the key currencies, has now reached such a degree that investors exclude the possibility of a 1990s-style currency crisis. Moreover, the financial circuits through which key currencies are spread across borders (international banks, non-financial companies, central banks) completely reverse the traditional relationship between exchange rates and the balance of payments (Bruno and Shin, 2015). Thus, an appreciation of the dollar, for example, while it improves the trade balance of the US' trading partners, increases the cost of borrowing in dollars, depresses investment and worsens the capital account of these same partners.[17] However, with the rigidity of prices of tradable goods invoiced in dollars (Boz, Gopinath and Plagborg-Møller, 2017), this effect now outweighs the trade balance (Avdjiev et al., 2019). As a result, in the exchange rate movement between the dollar and the currencies belonging to the dollar zone, the financial current now dominates the traditional trade current. The dollar so dominates global trade relations that the bilateral exchange rate of a currency with the dollar is the main determinant of the prices and quantities of that country's imports, regardless of those goods' country of origin (Casas et al., 2016). Moreover, the dollar exchange rate has become a key predictor of the overall volume of trade with the rest of the world and of both producer and consumer price inflation (Boz, Gopinath and Plagborg-Møller, 2017: 40). Similar phenomena can be observed for the euro area, albeit to a lesser extent. New contradictions result: no longer the Mundell-Fleming trilemma but the impossible dilemma between monetary policy independence and capital mobility (Rey, 2015). Thus the floating exchange rate regime is by no means sufficient to guarantee this independence, given the impact of US monetary policy on the global financial cycle ("via the endogenous response of leverage and the pro-cyclicality of cross-border credit flows" [Rey, 2015: 22]). This can be seen in the persistent deviations from the principle of covered interest rate parity, as set out by Keynes in his 1923 *Tract*. This is presented as a quasi-economic law according to which the interest rate differential between two currencies on the spot market – i.e. on the interbank market – must be equal to the differential between the forward exchange rate and the spot exchange rate – i.e. between the exchange rate as anticipated by the market and the actual exchange rate. If a difference between these two differentials were to appear, agents' arbitrage would immediately reduce this differential to zero. For example, if the dollar were cheaper in terms of yen on the forward exchange market than the rate stipulated by the covered exchange rate, a dollar borrower on the spot market would take advantage of the situation by selling dollars against yen on the spot market and buying them back later at a cheaper rate on the forward market. As a result of the increased demand for dollars in the forward market, the dollar would appreciate until the spread between the forward rate and the spot rate equalled the borrowing rate in the dollar market. However, since the 2007 crisis, this law of covered parity has ceased to apply to the dollar, as shown by the persistence of the so-called cross-currency basis, which indicates the amount by which the interest paid to borrow one currency against another on the currency swap market differs from the interest paid to borrow that currency directly on the spot market. In other words, the exchange rate of the dollar against the major currencies in the forward market has been consistently maintained at a level such that the spread with the spot foreign exchange market exceeds the spread between the interest rate in the dollar market and the interest rate in the market for other currencies. After trying several explanations, BIS analysts found that only the demand for the dollar as a safe haven, i.e. as a universal equivalent, could explain this persistent deviation (Avdjiev et al., 2019b). A strong dollar, for example, with larger deviations from the covered interest rate parity and a decrease in cross-border dollar lending. Thus, the level of dollar appreciation becomes a proxy for the shadow price of bank leverage. Despite the easing of concerns about bank credit quality and the resumption of wholesale funding in dollars, financial firms are still seeking to hedge their foreign exchange with dollars. And because of the new regulations constraining banks' arbitrage activity between different financial assets (including currencies), this deviation, which in competitive markets should have been cancelled out by arbitrage, is continuing.

In fact, this phenomenon is not new. It had already puzzled observers after the 1982 recession, when the dollar exchange rate should have fallen to compensate for the differential between the US and foreign interest rates (see Solomon, 1999: 12). And they should have fallen all the more so because the US inflation rate was higher than in Germany and Japan and the balance of payments deficit was widening even as the reverse was happening in Germany and Japan. We have seen that the Plaza agreements for concerted intervention in the foreign exchange market put an end to this situation. And the subsequent Louvre Accords, as well as the crash of October 1987, were a direct consequence of these interventions.

10.5 Krugman and Stiglitz: the critique of capitalism in the service of the dollar

Stiglitz blames the IMF in the same way that Proudhon criticised monetary gold: he defends the status of the dollar and Wall Street where Proudhon defended money and commodity production. Thus, in relation to the Asian crisis, he holds the fiscal restraint measures imposed by the IMF responsible for the spread of the crisis, even though the course of the crisis has left us in no doubt as to the role of the foreign exchange market in triggering the crisis, regardless of the fiscal situation of the country affected. And when he acknowledges that no other policy would probably have prevented the crisis, it is to blame the brutality of the capital outflow on the opacity of local banking systems: "Because of the lack of transparency, the market shut off the supply of capital to all firms, or charged all of them a high risk premium, thus exacerbating the downturn" (Furman and Stiglitz, 1998: 71). Similarly, he rails against the IMF's obsession with the balance of payments indicator, even though it is merely a symptom of an excess of private investment over private savings (1998: 34). Is this not because the balance of payments is, in the eyes of the market, an indicator of the sustainability of the exchange rate, which is precisely what the IMF has its eye on?[18] He is therefore surprised by the contradiction of the IMF, which advocates the ideology of the free market except when it comes to the foreign exchange market (Stiglitz, 2002a: 148–49). Yet by defending the exchange rate at all costs, not only does the IMF not encourage companies to protect themselves against exchange rate depreciations (on the derivatives market), but it pushes for higher interest rates, budgetary restrictions, i.e. measures protecting international lenders to the detriment of these same reckless borrowers

(Stiglitz, 2002a: 149). But Stiglitz never asks whether this defence of the exchange rate was not precisely the condition for the inflow of capital that he calls for. The interests of the financial community that he criticised the IMF for defending at all costs expressed nothing other than the very conditions of financial globalisation that he himself defended and wished to strengthen by mitigating its excesses. The man who, a few years earlier, had proposed a model aimed at guaranteeing creditors against the risks of default by over-indebted emerging countries (Eaton, Gersovitz and Stiglitz, 1986) now reproached the IMF for exclusively defending the interests of these same creditors, whereas all the reforms that had conditioned the entry of capital into the emerging countries were carried out precisely to guarantee the security of their investments.

When, following Krugman's good advice to negotiate with the banks instead of taking control of its capital account, Latin America undergoes austerity policies, Stiglitz asks in "Lessons of Argentina" why the countries of the North do exactly the opposite in a crisis. And the Nobel Prize-winning economist replies: "Unfortunately, I can not give [...] a good answer" (Stiglitz, 2002b: 161). Similarly, Stiglitz says he does not understand why Latin America is being forced to liberalise trade while the US is at the same time taking protectionist measures on steel, for example. His solution for Argentina is for the US to open its market to Argentine beef, which would be good for Argentine trade and good for the American consumer. But as he hesitates to advise capital controls, he imagines an ideal world where labour mobility would replace capital mobility (Stiglitz, 2002b: 165).

In "What happened to Asia?" (1998), Krugman calls the Asian crisis a crisis of financial excess (as if that did not describe the Mexican crisis three years earlier), in relation to which the currency and the exchange rate were only ever symptoms of the crisis. Yet, we have seen how the fixed exchange rate system was at the very origin of this "financial excess". But for Krugman, this financial orgy is rooted in a lack of regulation, laxity on the part of the authorities, implicit guarantees by governments, etc. (Krugman, 1998). And when he mentions the symptom of the exchange rate (after all, the Asian crisis is indeed an exchange rate crisis), it is to deplore, in a paper entitled "Analytical afterthoughts on the Asian crisis", the lack of firmness of governments to maintain the fixed exchange rate whatever the cost, before blaming this same fixed exchange rate a few lines further on for the excess of firms' debt in foreign currency (Krugman, 2001a: 252). But the financial excess results from the fact that the authorities have chosen to maintain parity with the dollar at all costs. Yet for Krugman, the Asian crisis can be summed up as the bursting of an asset bubble inflated by excessive debt and institutions "whose liabilities were perceived as having an implicit government guarantee, but were essentially unregulated and therefore subject to severe moral hazard problems" (Krugman, 1998). But when the US economy was in recession in 2001, he commented in the *New York Times* about the housing market: "Most of the credit probably goes to the dogged optimism of American consumers, but the Fed's dramatic interest rate cuts helped keep housing strong even as business investment plunged" (Krugman,

2001b). And while in Asia he blames the authorities for creating these bubbles, in his own country, in the same journal he condemns them for having made them disappear too quickly: "To fight this recession the Fed needs more than a snapback; it needs soaring household spending to offset moribund business investment. And to do that [...] Alan Greenspan needs to create a housing bubble to replace the Nasdaq bubble" (Krugman, 2002).

Krugman fully acknowledges that emerging countries owe their financial crises to excessive short-term foreign currency debt (Krugman, 2000: 95). Not, as the sequence of events suggests, because the fixed exchange rate regime caused the massive influx of capital, but because the fixed exchange rate actually guaranteed firms against possible currency risks. Hence his advice to tax or discourage Asian firms from borrowing in foreign currency. But, even if it means imposing even greater flexibility on them and hence the crises that would necessarily result (Krugman, 2000: 76), it would still be better to dollarise their economies completely than to impose capital controls, as India and China are doing: the risk of discouraging Wall Street speculators is too great (Krugman, 2000: 99–100).[19] Instead of the possibility of capital controls in times of crisis, Krugman prefers a "standstill negotiated with banks" (Krugman, 2000: 89), the draconian conditions of which the latter have imposed on states before any rescheduling, new borrowing, etc. (cite examples). Even if it means borrowing from the big banks or the IMF if necessary, dollarisation is better than the indiscriminate use of the printing press to save financial institutions. But a year after dollarisation, dollarised Argentina plunged into the worst financial crisis in its history: direct investment in the country had almost quadrupled in 1999 compared to the previous year, reaching its highest level since the end of the war (see World Bank graph). As for its exports and imports, indicators of its trade integration, they had respectively more than doubled and more than tripled between 1991 and 2000 (see IMF statistics).[20]

Stiglitz calls for reform of the entire international monetary system, including the mandate and scope of the IMF, but without ever raising the place of the US and the role of the dollar in the functioning of this system (Stiglitz, 2002c). No more than Krugman, Stiglitz does not question the dependence of developing or transition countries on foreign capital or on the dollar as the pivotal currency of the international financial system. Moreover, Krugman and Stiglitz only criticise the fixed exchange rate regime insofar as it contradicts the foreign trade of the country whose currency is pegged to the dollar. For example, Stiglitz advocates opening up the US market to Argentina's agricultural products, which is the only way to justify the dollarisation of the Argentine economy. Thus, they both focus on financial liberalisation and deregulation, in the same way that an epidemiologist would focus on the density of human interaction as the cause of mortality in an epidemic without considering the effect of the virus on the human body. But unlike the epidemiologist, their scotomisation of the dollar within the international monetary and financial system is due to their very function within that system.[21]

Most analyses of the currency crises of the 1990s in emerging countries have denounced the role of capital mobility in financial fragility and the triggering of crises, but without ever drawing the consequences of the fact that capital flight on the eve of crises invariably takes refuge in the reference currency, the dollar – even when this flight takes the form of speculative gambling on the fall of the exchange rate of the peripheral currency under attack. In the same way, there is debate about what exchange rate regimes would prevent the recurrence of these crises, but without recalling that the peg to the dollar, whatever the official exchange rate regime, was the very condition for the inflow of this volatile capital. The profound imperialism of Krugman's and Stiglitz's interventions on these crises stems from the fact that the problem of the dollar's place in the hierarchy of currencies is presupposed but not posed. If it had been posed, all these crises would have appeared immediately for what they are, namely the expression of the contradiction between this hierarchy and the process of forced unification of financial markets under the aegis of the dollar and Wall Street. The role of the banks in the depth of the crisis or the actual state of the fundamentals on the basis of which the markets decide to turn around, or even the level of real appreciation of the exchange rate, matter only insofar as these factors signal the depth to which dollarisation determines the activity of the country hit by the crisis and the channels by which this penetration is achieved.

10.6 Final considerations

Eichengreen sees the succession of financial crises after Bretton Woods as an expression of the contradiction between the need to anchor currencies in some exchange rate regime and the freedom of movement of capital. And it is true that all emerging market crises invariably repeat the same scenario of capital flight coupled with the depletion of foreign exchange reserves. "The only truly common denominator of international financial crises", said Jeanne, "is the concomitance of a foreign exchange crisis and a capital flight in several countries" (2003: 1).

But this flight makes manifest a deeper contradiction in the internationally distributed functions of money: between the universal money-capital function of the dollar and the monetary functions of unit of account and medium of exchange of local currencies. With the liberalisation of the foreign exchange market, all particular currencies have become local means of circulation into which the dollar (or the deutsche mark in the EMS) converts according to the market exchange rate where it is invested as financial capital. It is well known that the phenomenon of dollarisation is measured by the number of functions of the currency fulfilled by the dollar in place of the domestic currency. It begins when dollar reserves replace local currency reserves (asset substitution) and ends once the greenback circulates from hand to hand in domestic transactions (currency substitution) (Rochon and Seccareccia, 2003: 1). But currency crises have shown that domestic currencies do not need to give up any of their functions to be subordinated to a reference currency. As soon as domestic investment or expenditure is financed by funds in dollars, for example, whether these funds are raised by borrowing or by issuing securities, the functions of the currency are redistributed between the dollar, which, as loan capital, occupies a function of reserve of value in the domestic space, and the domestic currency, which is reduced to circulating goods within this space. The three generations of crises are like the three degrees of extension of the dollar's function as a store of value in the monetary and financial space of this local space. And this extension proceeds in a top-down movement: first the state with the external debt crisis; then the markets; finally the banks and companies, until the very laws of international trade are overturned. It is under its general form of value that the dollar has gradually imposed itself as a universal equivalent, dragging the emerging markets open to it into what is now called the dollar zone.

But these currencies do not merely ensure the exchange of goods in their circulation spaces. They also function as money-capital, as investment money that is valued in the very process of production and circulation of goods. Thus, their existence as financial assets on the foreign exchange market depends on their capacity to reproduce themselves as a general equivalent, i.e. on their capacity to represent the universal equivalent through the monetary functions they fulfil in their spheres of exchange. From this point of view, it does not matter whether this capacity is compromised by fundamental macroeconomic variables (first-generation crises) or by irrational market beliefs (second-generation crises). For in all cases, this capacity is verified according to two criteria: the interest rate (the remuneration of money-capital) and foreign exchange reserves (the conversion into universal money-capital).[22] For the foreign exchange market, only these two variables are said to be fundamental, insofar as they are the only ones to indicate to the markets the capacity of domestic currencies to represent the requirements of universal capital.

Notes

1 Aftalion (1927) was one of the first to reverse the causality of the PPP between the exchange rate and prices by pointing out that currencies were sought after not only for their purchasing power but as financial assets and means of speculation.
2 In addition to the orthodox flexible price approach where the PPP applies continuously (Frenkel, 1976), Dornbusch (1976) proposed a variant in which prices are rigid, thus explaining the phenomena of exchange rate overshooting before the PPP is verified in the longer term.
3 "Cassel's references to the stability of price level and of the supply of money as the pre-conditions (additionally to the domestic monetary policy) to the stability of a currency may be regarded as his own version of the quantity theory of money and of the monetary view on exchange rate determination" (Kadochnikov, 2013: 1108).
4 The Balassa-Samuelson effect, which is supposed to express the effect of international prices on the real exchange rate of developing countries through their effect on the real wages of the exposed sector, in fact assumes the law of one price (LooP). For if we look at this law in detail, we notice that (i) in order to determine the relative price between the two goods produced locally and abroad, it is necessary to assume a common unit of account, as we saw in the chapter on the history of monetary thought; and (ii) the single price is fixed by the country with the best production conditions, since the exchange rate evolves precisely as a result of the catching up of the less advanced country as manifested in the evolution of the real wage. It is therefore in relation to the currency of

the advanced country that the real exchange rate of the less advanced country appreciates. It should also be noted that the hypothesis of pure and perfect competition, which implies in particular the perfect mobility of capital, should lead to the establishment of identical production conditions in all the countries producing tradable goods and thus to an alignment of all the corresponding exchange rates, so that we would have only one currency denominated under different account names.

Rainelli (1986) wants to stress that PPP and LooP cannot be confused since PPP does not refer to the prices of individual goods but to the general price level and is based on a demand function for foreign currency. Moreover, Cassel rules out any price index calculated solely on the basis of tradable goods. Thus, the LooP would only lead to PPP if all goods were perfectly tradable and substitutable. But what LooP has in common with PPP is the dichotomous approach: in both cases, we have relative prices without money, or rather relative prices expressed in a common unit of account distinct from the currencies traded in the foreign exchange market.

5 Like the BEER model (Clark and MacDonald, 1998), the FEER model (Williamson, 1985) does not aim to explain the exchange rate theoretically but to account for its evolution, in particular in order to evaluate misalignments of the current exchange rate. In the first model, the source of exchange rate change is the capital account; in the second, the change is the result of the current account. But neither of these models predicts better than the random walk models that predict that tomorrow's exchange rate will be today's exchange rate.

6 Thus, Mishra, Gupta and Sahay (2003), in particular, show that the more a currency crisis is preceded by intense capital flows (of all categories) with foreign countries, the more powerful its depressive effect is when the capital account is liberalised: they estimated that an additional inflow of foreign capital of 10% of GDP induces a relative contraction in growth of between 2.6% and 3.5%, all other things being equal.

7 After 1972, not only did the states not settle their balance of payments, contrary to what the monetarist doctrine suggested with the abolition of fixed exchange rates, but above all the central banks did not get rid of their foreign exchange reserves or their gold reserves (de Brunhoff, 1978: 51–52).

8 The banking system was spared less by emergency aid than by the end of the US recession and the fall in interest rates from the second half of 1982. If we add to these functions a more accommodating monetary policy on the part of the Fed and a counter-cyclical fiscal policy on the part of the US Treasury, the 1982 crisis already shows on a regional scale the role of the global financial cycle of the dollar in the economic and social destinies of emerging countries. In 2003, Jeanne wondered about the relationship between the recent financial crises:

> Wall Street could be not only a vector of propagation, but also a source of shocks. Capital flows to emerging countries are characterised by boom and bust dynamics that are difficult to justify in terms of economic fundamentals, a phenomenon that is seen in many other financial markets. Thus Wall Street could be a source of correlated shocks between countries that have nothing in common other than being in the same risk class.
>
> *(Jeanne, 2003: 6)*

9 Sgard notes that short-term capital movements were not included in the list of reforms promoted by the Williamson's Washington Consensus (1990).

10 Without disturbing the markets, the Mexican authorities had already introduced a floating exchange rate regime in 1989 and set up a system of fluctuation bands in 1992 allowing the gradual depreciation of the peso but setting a ceiling on the exchange rate with the dollar.

11 The banking system recovered more or less quickly from this crisis but with a new look as it became almost entirely controlled by foreign banks: "By 2008 foreign banks controlled about 80% of assets of the commercial banking system, including the largest Mexican banks" (Musacchio, 2012: 23).

12 The author refers to the risk of contagion from the 1982 Mexican crisis to the entire global financial system to explain why the G10 states outside the US participated in the resolution of the crisis, whereas they would have washed their hands of it in 1994. The big difference with the latter crisis, however, was the role of the IMF in the rescue of the country, which was due to the fact that the default involved the Mexican state itself (Vallée, 2016).

13 The current system is certainly more effective and stable "but one that was lending less to the private sector and has some of the most expensive fees and commissions in the world" (Musacchio, 2012: 23).

14 The financial crises in emerging countries are an empirical refutation of the monetary theories based on the notion of trust. These theories assert that distrust of a given payments system undermines hierarchical trust and hence the monetary order as a whole, which, according to this theory, is based on the organic links between money and the state and the sovereignty of the institutions of money, namely the central bank and the government. Thus, ethical trust, the apex of the system of trust in money, would be "the belief that the power of money is not deployed to satisfy arbitrary goals in favour of groups of private actors or partisan political interests" (Aglietta and Valla, 2017: 217). When ethical trust is undermined, legal tender is no longer perceived as legitimate (*Ibidem*). But all the financial crises that have affected emerging countries have occurred at the same time as states have been facing speculative attacks "from groups of private actors" that are particularly voracious and desperate to retain their sovereignty, by maintaining the nominal peg of their currency at the expense of their foreign exchange reserves and fiscal balance. The loss of "ethical trust" was not the result of questioning the sovereignty of the monetary institutions, but rather the impossibility of remaining in a system of monetary subservience to the dollar. In each case, it was the threat of a repossession of their sovereignty that caused the loss of trust in a payments system entirely subject to the dollar standard.

15 Moreover, the dollar, as a reference currency, played a non-negligible role in the speculative attacks on the EMS. If we compare this crisis with the Mexican crisis two years later, we would have to say that the former was caused by the weakening of the dollar and therefore by the loss of competitiveness in Europe, and the latter by the rise in the US interest rates and therefore by the flow of capital back to the US: in the first case, it was only a problem of the balance of payments resulting from the hierarchical relationship between the currencies of the industrialised countries; in the second case, it was a problem of arbitration between securities denominated in pesos and dollars.

16 See Solomon (1999, Figure 6.1) on the evolution of the relationship between the exchange rate and the US current account deficit. See also p. 146 on the embarrassment of economists when misalignments coincide with exchange rate appreciation.

17 The role of the dollar in financing export activities is reflected in the fact that "over 83% of cross-border payments associated with credit-related activity is denominated in US dollars" (Bruno and Shin, 2020: 1). This dependence of exporting firms on international credit is due to the lengthening of value chains and delays in receiving payments.

18 Stiglitz himself is so obsessed by the IMF that he also criticises it for implicitly guaranteeing loans taken out by emerging countries, thus generating moral hazard for borrowers (Stiglitz, 2002a: 201).

19 When it comes to alternative models to market liberalisation and the Washington Consensus, for example, for South East Asian countries to regionalise their relations around Japan, Krugman does not hesitate to compare them to the worst decisions in history (Krugman, 1995: 42).

20 What is striking about Krugman's exchange rate model (1991) is that he introduces the exchange rate into his equations on the macroeconomic equilibrium of a developing country without ever specifying to which foreign currency or monetary standard the domestic currency relates.

21 At the time they were commenting on currency crises, Krugman was a member of the Group of Thirty, composed of leading financiers and central bankers, and Stiglitz was a member of the Council of Economic Advisers under President Clinton, a position he held simultaneously with that of Chief Economist of the World Bank.

22 The banking crisis that goes with the currency crisis comes from the fact that the interest rate is also the price of local investment – and therefore of growth and employment – and that devaluation also means higher dollar borrowing.

11

ORDOMONETARISM

The original neoliberalism

11.1 The gold of early neoliberals

The return to the gold standard after the war presented a new challenge compared to the previous century, when England returned to gold after the Napoleonic Wars: it would be a means of controlling the government whose spending was growing with the rise of the wage-earning class and the political role of the working class. As the banking press of the time promised: "a return to gold would prevent future 'unsound' experiments by Socialist Governments which might divert the English people from the only real solution of their problems – economy and hard work" (quoted in Burn, 2006: 52). And the political force of the gold standard, which expressed nothing more than the essence of money in general, came precisely from the fact that it presented itself as an apolitical force that made class struggle for control of economic policy unnecessary. The scarcity of money artificially created by its metallic anchor would replace the saturation of debate in the House of Commons.

Studies of neoliberalism repeatedly point out that it differs from classical liberalism in that it is not about letting the market develop freely, but about creating the conditions for that freedom: not a market liberalism, but a liberalisation of markets that the states have embedded under the democratic pressure of the organised proletariat. From this point on, and following the analyses of Foucault (2008) in particular, there was a tendency to present neoliberalism as an intellectual project, as an episteme which, through its organisations, techniques and discourses, would have gradually built an institutional framework for the enlargement of the market sphere and the deepening of its logic in the mechanisms of social life (Polanyi, 2001; Harvey, 2005; Krippner, 2011; Dardot and

DOI: 10.4324/9780429261299-15

Laval, 2014). It would be up to the state to fulfil this mission. Here is how David Harvey understands neoliberalism:

> Neoliberalism is in the first instance a theory of political economic practices that proposes that human well-being can best be advanced by liberating individual entrepreneurial freedoms and skills within an institutional framework characterized by strong private property rights, free markets, and free trade. The role of the state is to create and preserve an institutional framework appropriate to such practices. The state has to guarantee, for example, the quality and integrity of money. It must also set up those military, defence, police, and legal structures and functions required to secure private property rights and to guarantee, by force if need be, the proper functioning of markets. Furthermore, if markets do not exist (in areas such as land, water, education, health care, social security, or environmental pollution) then they must be created, by state action if necessary. But beyond these tasks the state should not venture. State interventions in markets (once created) must be kept to a bare minimum because, according to the theory, the state cannot possibly possess enough information to second-guess market signals (prices) and because powerful interest groups will inevitably distort and bias state interventions (particularly in democracies) for their own benefit.
>
> *(Harvey, 2005: 2)*

But it is not enough to set up this institutional framework to make this market logic work everywhere. It is also necessary to add techniques of governmentality by which the members of society mould themselves to this logic, subjectivise its constraints and adhere to the ideal it serves. From this perspective, neoliberalism

> is firstly and fundamentally a rationality, and as such tends to structure and organize not only the action of rulers, but also the conduct of the ruled. The principal characteristic of neoliberal rationality is the generalization of competition as a behavioural norm and of the enterprise as a model of subjectivation.

And here again, it is up to the state to accomplish this task of governing the conduct of individuals within its framework and using its own instruments, so that the individual internalises this conduct: "to govern is not to govern against liberty, or despite it; it is to govern through liberty – that is, to actively exploit the freedom allowed individuals so that they end up conforming to certain norms of their own accord" (Dardot and Laval, 2017: 5). The emergence of this new rationality is explained by the crisis of the Keynesian state and the embedded liberalism of the Bretton Woods era (Harvey, 2005). But our analysis of the dollar and the rise of offshore markets show that the crisis of the Keynesian state was opening up precisely because the state has already been neoliberalised in its external relations: penetration of the Eurodollar market, floating exchange rates, increasing capital mobility. Even before it begins its internal neoliberal transformation, the state already possesses the tools of its social-liberal governmentality. Yet, the neoliberal project was emerging during the very birth of this governmentality and at a time when Keynesian conceptions of the state were almost universal among the governments of capitalist nations (Ruggie, 1982). The misunderstanding of all the genealogies of neoliberalism stems from the systematic confusion between the historical conditions of its intellectual emergence and those of its state practice.

For the first neoliberals, however, the main concern was to free markets from the intrusions of politics, to extract them from the workings of the organising state (Schmelzer, 2020). Neoliberalism does not proceed by deepening the logic of the market in behaviour, but by limiting the possibilities of action; not by adding market axioms, but by removing the market from political regulation. All the domestic reforms and governmental techniques introduced from the 1970s onwards were the result of this withdrawal of the market from state power. And the state itself undoubtedly contributes to its own limitation, by signing treaties, creating supra-state institutions and adopting the principles of new public management, but only because they condition the remains of its sovereignty. And similarly, once turned inwards, the state does add market axioms, but axioms that remove the market from popular resistance.

The neoliberal project is therefore primarily developed on a transnational level, where the institutional order would protect capital and guarantee its freedom of movement throughout the world. From this point of view, the Geneva school, which, compared to the Freiburg neoliberals, intended to extend the principles of ordoliberalism on a global scale, is the conscious organ of transnational capital and the expression of its contradiction with national particularisms: the harmonious synthesis, by means of a global law (Hayek's "same law"), of state imperium and monetary dominium (Schmitt).[1] The Lippmann Colloquium was no different: the protection of the price mechanism was seen as the fundamental criterion of any good society to which all social values and objectives should be subordinated (Schulz-Forberg, 2020, p. 71). To the ordoliberals who placed human dignity or the human person at the top of the list of values, Hayek replied that freedom serves no other end than itself (Schulz-Forberg, 2020: 172). And there was no more monstrous violation of freedom than capital and exchange controls: "It is, in fact, the complete delivery of the individual to the tyranny of the state, the final suppression of all means of escape – not merely for the rich, but for everyone" (Hayek, 2010: 96). Neoliberalism is first and foremost an ordomonetarism.

For against the backdrop of unanimous agreement on the free movement of capital, not everyone at Mont Pèlerin thought that a return to the gold standard would be the only condition for fiscal and monetary discipline in "democratic states". As one early member of the society confided, "the original Pelerins could agree on everything save the subjects of God and Gold" (Davenport, quoted by Schmelzer, 2020: 200). Indeed, from the very first debates, Hayek and the supporters of the gold standard were arguing with the defenders of a floating exchange rate system, among them Frank Graham whose exchange rate system based on a "Commodity Reserve Standard" would directly inspire the model that Friedman would propose in his famous 1953 paper (Schmelzer, 2020: 207).[2] But while the article offered assurances that with flexible exchange rates, states would enjoy monetary autonomy and would be free to choose between full employment and price stability, the pilgrim Friedman asserted, on the contrary, that by handing over the currency to the foreign exchange markets, market discipline would be imposed on monetary and budgetary policies by preventing, in particular, the use of devaluation in the event of loss of competitiveness. Subsequent events would reveal that the article's conclusions were valid only for the US, and we now know the influence that Friedman, Machlup and Haberler had on the Nixon administration's withdrawal from the Bretton Woods agreements (Schmelzer, 2020: 199–200). Nevertheless, the supporters of flexible exchange rates recognised that the gold standard "would have directly removed the discretion of governments and central banks with regard to monetary policy and exchange rates" (Plehwe, 2017: 196). But this discipline was not sufficient in the face of trade union pressure and the weaknesses of the social state. The experience of the interwar period had shown that the gold exchange standard had not prevented protectionism, capital controls and excessive spending. For Haberler, for example, the return to the gold standard would not be sufficient to force governments to give up their monetary autonomy: it would push them to limit capital movements (Schmelzer, 2020: 196). Compared to the flexible exchange rate system, the gold standard still offered too much room for manoeuvre to the "democratic state". Here again, Friedman agreed with Keynes: from the point of view of monetary orthodoxy, gold was a barbaric relic.

Yet, the vicissitudes of gold had themselves presided over Keynes's new monetary conceptions.

> Asked at the height of the 1914 crisis to brief the chancellor of the exchequer as to whether the pound should remain tied to gold, he had come down very strongly in favour of maintaining the link: 'London's position as a monetary centre depends very directly on complete confidence in London's unwavering readiness' to meet its obligations in gold and would be severely damaged if 'at the first sign of emergency' that commitment was suspended.
>
> *(Ahamed, 2009: 275)*[3]

It was later in the *Tract* that he famously argued that credit policy hardly needed this "barbaric relic" to act in a sound and responsible way. For from the point of view of monetary policy, Keynes remained committed to price stability. But what had changed his mind was not so much the constraint that the system itself imposed as the constraint that resulted from the concentration of gold reserves in the US. Indeed, in 1928, three years before Britain's suspension,

> Strong saw gold production at record levels in 1928 and believed that the release of part of the US gold reserves would replenish the stocks of European central banks and provide sufficient quantities of yellow metal for the international monetary system.
>
> *(Mouré, 2006: 175)*

Gold is undoubtedly the currency of the barbarians, but it was primarily because Britain had become a relic of global capitalism that Keynes pleaded for the abandonment of what had made it great in the past and to which it could not return: the gold standard.

For the gold standard in the US had not prevented Strong from pursuing a Keynesian monetary policy before its time, just as the New Deal would not wait for the *General Theory* to revive investment through public spending: before the *Treatise on Money*, Strong had cut the links between gold reserves and credit policy, subordinated external constraints to domestic price stability, and generally replaced the gold standard mechanism with a monetary management that facilitated credit when trade weakened and tightened it when the economy boomed. On the one hand, therefore, the US accumulated gold reserves because of its trade power and the world economic relations in the interwar period; on the other, it prevented the gold standard mechanism from affecting the domestic price level, i.e. from raising the price level. On the one hand, the US defended the gold standard system; on the other, it acted in such a way that Europe could only abandon it. The US limited the role of gold to its function as a store of value, while at the same time preventing it from fulfilling its function as a medium of exchange in Europe. As Keynes rightly notes in his *Tract*: "For the past two years, the US has pretended to maintain a gold standard. In fact it has established a dollar standard" (Keynes, 1923: 155). It was this new dollar standard, which subjected Britain to the whims of the Fed following its own conceptions of monetary policy, that Keynes saw glimmering behind the dull yellow of the barbaric relic.

11.1.1 The BIS and the birth of neoliberalism

In the interwar period, neoliberal practice must be taken literally, i.e. as a return to liberalism, as a new liberalism. And this project was imposed as soon as the bombs of First World War stopped falling, on the initiative of the only class for which liberalism was the right regime for the period: the banker class. "The unique mobility and fungibility of money ensured that policymakers were not faced with the same collective action problems in creating and maintaining an open international financial order that existed in the area of trade" (Helleiner, 1994: 18). Before the return of the gold standard, the Brussels Conference in 1920 and the Genoa Conference in 1922 were the great forums for a concerted call by

Wall Street and the City for the return of balanced budgets, the independence of central banks, the free movement of capital and, above all, the restoration of the international gold standard system (Helleiner, 1994: 26–27). And just as the League of Nations was intended to be the institution of nations free to dispose of themselves, the Bank for International Settlements (BIS), founded by central bankers and consortia of private banks to implement the Young Plan for the payment of reparations to Germany, was intended to be the institution of central banks cooperating freely with each other in order to dispose of each other's money: "a body that was supposed to facilitate central bank cooperation as well as to depoliticize the debt and reparation issues" (Helleiner, 1994: 27). But the crisis of 1931 and the Great Depression embedded this new liberalism: the New Deal in the US and the end of the gold standard in the UK subjected the political economy of central banks to the economic policies of nations (Helleiner, 1994: 27–28).

Yet, no episode in the history of the BIS illustrates the political economy of the banker better than its role in the manoeuvres of Third Reich Germany. With Norman and Strong, but also the Reichsbank Governor Hjamar Schacht, who liked to say that the BIS was his bank (LeBor, 2014: 15), the BIS served until the end of the war as the international branch of the Third Reich Bank. In addition to the foreign exchange transactions it carried out on his behalf, the Bank accepted without question the gold looted by the Nazis, whether it came from the central banks of the occupied countries or from the teeth extracted from deported Jews (LeBor, 2014: 96). Certainly, during the war, monthly meetings were suspended,

> but relations between the BIS staff of the belligerent nations remained cordial, professional, and productive. Nationalities were irrelevant. The overriding loyalty was to international finance. The president, Thomas McKittrick, was an American. Roger Auboin, the general manager, was French. Paul Hechler, the assistant general manager, was a member of the Nazi party and signed his correspondence 'Heil Hitler'. Rafaelle Pilotti, the secretary general, was Italian. Per Jacobssen, the bank's influential economic adviser, was Swedish. His and Pilotti's deputies were British.
>
> *(LeBor, 2014: 16)*

Before one decries the banality of the evil committed by ordinary officials of the Nazi regime, we should recall that the Dulles brothers, one an OSS agent in Bern during the war and a friend of McKittrick, the other a Secretary of State under Eisenhower, arranged to reinstate the great bankers, businessmen and industrialists who had served under Hitler to key positions in the new Federal Republic of Germany. And while the US delegation at Bretton Woods had proposed a resolution to dissolve the BIS, Keynes personally intervened with Morgenthau and threatened to withdraw Britain's participation in the IMF and the World Bank to urge him to give it up. Morgenthau gave in. Keynes had failed to impose his

Bancor and International Clearing Union at Bretton Woods, but he had put all the weight Britain had left into saving the BIS, of which gold was the God, free capital the law, and Norman, Strong and Schacht its prophets. But this unnatural brotherhood was nothing compared to the one that money sealed through the BIS. For money was not only stateless, but enforced the bonds between warring nations and converted their hatred into love. It was with the BIS that the fraternisation of impossibilities (Marx, 1844: 210) was extended to the level of the peoples themselves. By Nazi Germany's continuing to pay interest on BIS investments which were used to pay the dividends of shareholders, including the Bank of England, the Third Reich financed through the BIS the war that England was waging against it (LeBor, 2014: 94).[4]

Therefore, it was not Bretton Woods that laid the foundations for a new liberal order that would only finally take hold in the 1980s (Panitch and Gindin, 2009: 19). From the interwar period onwards, the conditions for private international cooperation were recreated, the role and importance of which were directly proportional to the degree of freedom of movement of capital. This is why, as a public institution offering an alternative source of financing to governments, the IMF was immediately condemned by the bankers as being inflationary and detrimental to private investment. Yet, the IMF had emerged from the Bretton Woods Agreement much weaker than Keynes and White had intended: it had been designed to make capital controls no longer compulsory but at most permissible by states wishing to control the flow of money across their borders (Burn, 2006: 4). In the eyes of the bankers, this possibility alone in the IMF's Articles of Agreement protected governments from the virtues of market discipline that would be imposed by the free movement of capital. It was indeed "highly doubtful that an institution run by governments could match the efficiency and rationality of a market-oriented system" (Helleiner, 1994: 40). But New York could no longer rely on London to organise the counter-offensive. With the fragility of the British accounts and the protectionism of the sterling zone, the Bank of England was momentarily won over to Keynes and White's projects (Helleiner, 1994: 45). However, the US foreign policy was in favour of a more open international financial system and, above all, of the liberalisation of foreign exchange in Western Europe. Yet, the European crisis, to which Wall Street contributed by welcoming European capital flight without limit (Helleiner, 1994: 6) and which intensified the risk of a communist Europe, gave way with the Marshall Plan to the largest public intervention that capitalism had ever known in peacetime. But, the Plan itself contributed to the weakening of the Bretton Woods institutions. For as the issuer of the universal currency, the US not only provided capital in place of the World Bank, but opened its markets to foreign exports and capital inflows, and provided short-term funds in case of a currency crisis (Cohen, 1977: 95). Thus, the Plan provided "more than four times the drawing rights of the European countries in the IMF and more than six times the maximum obligations of the United States under the IMF Articles of Agreement" (Ocampo, 2017: 88). It was not until 1958 and the return of external convertibility of European currencies that market discipline once again replaced public control (Eichengreen, 2008: 134). From then onwards, all the Bretton Woods dikes would give way one by one to the ever-increasing and ever-more-intense global capital flows.

As we have seen above, the turning point came in March 1961 with the agreement by the finance ministers of the 10 major economies (G10) on the General Agreements to Borrow, which provided for greater freedom of movement of short-term capital and more liquidity to the IMF (Seabrooke, 2001: 55). The IMF therefore allowed for compensatory financing to finance deficits caused by capital flows. This permission not only prevented the need for increased capital controls, but was intended to promote a more liberal global financial system (Helleiner, 1994: 96). In the same year, the OECD countries agreed on a "code of liberalization of capital movements" in order to progressively abolish restrictions on capital movements to the extent necessary for economic cooperation (Seabrooke, 2001: 56). In the meantime, the BIS, which had already been resurrected as the clearing bank for the European Payments Union, returned to the international game when the 1960 dollar crisis necessitated swap line agreements between central banks (Triffin, 1978: 7). The gold pool was created to prevent fluctuations in the price of gold on the private market (Seabrooke, 2001: 55–56): there was a shift from cooperation between public treasuries to more flexible and informal cooperation between central banks to react to speculative capital flows and to use large sums of money quickly for the defence of foreign exchange, etc. (Schenk, 2017: 75–76) Between 1962 and 1963 alone, the Fed had entered into swap agreements with 11 foreign central banks without any IMF involvement. But these agreements were made not to facilitate dollar credit to foreign central banks but to obtain foreign exchange for the defence of the dollar (McDowell, 2017: 42). The 1974 crisis confirmed this shift, with the creation of the Standing Committee on Banking Regulation and Supervisory Practices, better known as the Basel Committee. The Basel Concordat (1975), i.e. 13 years before the Basel I agreements (1988), replaced the Bretton Woods regulations with jurisdictional rules supervising the international banking markets to prevent financial crises (Helleiner, 1995: 332; Cassis, 2011: 124).

Before that, the Eurodollar market re-launched the privatisation of the international financial system in which even the central banks intervened as in the heyday of the BIS, i.e. as private actors (Schenk, 1998: 237). And once the Eurodollar banks were intermediating between the surplus countries and the developing borrowing countries, the IMF would serve as a simple agency for assessing the solvency of the borrowing countries:

> the Euro-dollar banks seem to have chosen the I.M.F. as their 'international auditors', so that they will feel more comfortable when lending to a country after the I.M.F. has vetted it and has made it accept an I.M.F. loan on conditions agreed with the I.M.F. The periodic reviews of the situation which the I.M.F. also imposes on its borrowers serve as guiding lights to the Euro-dollar market for its own behaviour towards the same borrowers.
>
> *(de Cecco, 1982: 24)*

It was not until the debt crisis of the developing countries in the 1980s that the IMF became the body that defended the interests of the international banks by making its aid conditional on structural adjustment in the indebted economies. However, it is not to be believed that the IMF has taken over the functions once performed by the Fed and the Treasury. On more than 50 occasions in the 1980s and 1990s, the Fed supplemented IMF loans through the Treasury's Exchange Stabilization Fund (McDowell, 2017: 65). But as early as 1976, and while the US had vigorously opposed petrodollar loans to developing countries being channelled through the IMF (Helleiner, 1995: 323), a Fed report suggested mobilising the IMF and World Bank to facilitate such structural adjustment in the South (Newstadt, 2009: 98). But in the meantime, the Eurodollar market would also replace the IMF as a regulator of global imbalances: it would serve as a balance-of-payments "adjustment chamber" for surplus and deficit countries: the former encouraged their commercial banks to deposit funds in the market to reduce their surpluses, while the latter borrowed from it to finance their deficits (Webb, 2019: 96–97). The joint launch of liberalisation measures in the US and Great Britain cannot be explained otherwise than by the competition between the two financial capitals in the Eurodollar business. In 1979, for example, the Thatcher government's liberalisation of exchange controls was a response to the New York Clearing House Association's aborted project to turn Wall Street into a monetary free trade zone (Burn, 2006: 147). If the intellectual project of neoliberalism had to wait until 1979 to find its open political translation in both London and Washington, it is because only then was it politically necessitated by the stateless market of the universal currency.

11.2 The new consensus on endogenous money in the age of ordomonetarism

Volcker's monetarism may have constrained banks on their reserve requirements, but we have seen that it did not limit the issuance of debt by banks and other financial institutions.

> As banking innovation accelerated in the 1960s and 1970s, it became clear that there were many types of money and that their natures changed as institutions evolved. It is not possible to understand money, banking and finance without taking into account banking evolution and innovation: in reality, money is an endogenously determined variable – supply is responsive to demand and is not mechanically controlled by the Federal Reserve.
>
> *(Minsky, 1986: 252–53)*

This was soon recognised by Volcker, who had abandoned targeting of monetary aggregates as early as 1982 (Singleton, 2011: 201–2). It was then that a consensus gradually developed between the monetary orthodoxy of the New Keynesians and the central bankers to make the short-term interest rate the exclusive instrument of monetary policy. The effectiveness of this instrument is based on the principle that, since prices and wages are rigid in the short term, a change in the nominal interest rate can lead to an increase or decrease in the real interest rate, i.e. the nominal rate adjusted for inflation. This consensus crystallised in the form of a rule laid down by John B. Taylor, according to which the central bank sets its key interest rate according to the difference between the desired inflation rate and the actual rate (inflation gap), which is itself determined by the difference between current output and potential output (Taylor, 1993; Woodford, 2001). Following this rule, the monetary aggregate, which does not appear in any of the equations combining the monetary policy variables, is considered as a simple "residual" based on the demand for money (Arestis and Sawyer, 2006: 848). This official recognition of endogenous sources of the quantity of money in circulation caused great embarrassment among post-Keynesians, whose endogenous money was the distinguishing criterion of their monetary heterodoxy. Post-Keynesians had to take refuge in their own realm of the dead, i.e. in the long run, to find lines of demarcation.[5] Where the post-Keynesians believe that it is possible to influence long-term real interest rates, employment and growth, the NMC remains convinced of the neutrality of monetary policy in the long term; where for the post-Keynesians demand continues to determine the level of activity over the long term, for the NMC supply factors alone determine potential output over the short term, when prices and wages become flexible again (Lavoie, 2006). The embarrassment is such that they sometimes criticise the NMC for adopting the very conceptions of some post-Keynesian currents: for example, for using the exogenous interest rate as a substitute for control of the money supply (Fontana and Passarella, 2018); or for adopting a horizontal money supply curve as an effect of the behaviour of the central bank and not, as post-Keynesian horizontalism would have it, of the behaviour of commercial banks (Sawyer, 2013).

For although money arises from the demand for credit, it is true that the transformation of credit into money or, what amounts to the same thing, the validation of the banks' money supply, does not take place in the same way for the NMC and the circuitist post-Keynesians. For the NMC, the interest rate is sufficient to conduct monetary policy because it is like the "a priori condition of possibility" of the money issue that the central bank does not control but that it constrains because of its position as external issuer of ultimate means of payment. For the post-Keynesian theory, the interest rate being only a distribution variable, it is the conversion of credit into wages, and therefore the conversion of these into securities of the enterprise (final finance) as well as into goods and services produced by the enterprise that validates the credit of banks. Between the two conceptions, the difference lies not between exogeneity and endogeneity – as some post-Keynesians insist on stressing (Lavoie, 2013b) – but between the a priori and the a posteriori validation of social labour by money. But this a posteriori validation proper to the circuit theory entirely ignores the fact that the product contains surplus value which can never be converted into monetary units spent by the employees. This fallacious simplification is not accidental but is due to the fact that in the framework of the circuit theory, the demand for money is structurally a demand for social production and consumption.[6] No doubt these differences remain formal for the post-Keynesians, according to whom the short-term interest rate has little impact on demand compared to that of wages and public spending (Dow, 2017: 1554) but also compared to the long-term interest rate. And Alan Blinder, close to the NMC, himself notes that no significant transaction is affected by the interest rate on which the central bank acts (1999: 70). But practice has shown both that the Fed's rate hike precipitated the financial crashes of 2007–8 through its effect on mortgage rates, and that the Fed's action on long-term rates was futile until the crisis broke.

Post-Keynesians neglect that the interest rate is not only a distributional variable, but is also, at the age of neoliberalism, a speculative variable (Neilson, 2019: 27).[7] Money does not only provide means of payment to wage earners but means of transaction to speculators (despite the principle of SFC models integrating financial variables with real variables).[8] Yet,

> the development of the money supply since 1990 presents a very contradictory picture. With the recovery from the recession at the beginning of the 1990s, there was once again an increase in money supply. Nonetheless, the effects were very different on the various forms of money supply. If money supply is viewed in relation to growth in price-adjusted GDP then M1 remains constant to the present-day at approximately 10 per cent of GDP. By contrast, since about 1997, M2 and M3 have exploded. Since 1980, the relationship of M2 to GDP has risen by 100 per cent and that of M3 by 145 per cent (and the years 1997–2003 accounted for half of this increase).
>
> *(Lehner, 2010: 98–99)*

The post-Keynesians see the low interest rate as the expression of a balance of power in favour of debtors without taking into account the fact that money conditions the purchase of securities and thus the constitution of claims on social production, in particular during the upward phase of the cycle, when the interest rate is still low. This is the condition of the paradox of tranquillity, according to which stability leads to instability through the use of leverage (Minsky, 1975: 127). Financial booms occur precisely in periods of low inflation, when the price of money remains low, when the credibility of monetary policy on price stability is such that it incites agents to widen imbalances (Borio and Lowe, 2002: 1). The post-Keynesians ignore this dimension of the interest rate all the more because its pre-crisis rise, which Minsky incorporates into his hypothesis of financial instability, can only be explained by the remnants of the loanable funds theory against which Keynes had fought (Lavoie, 2020). But Minsky only included this phenomenon of rise in relation to an excess of indebtedness, i.e. an excess of speculation in relation to bank indebtedness. He merely recognised the role of money and the interest rate in speculation – and the growth of the liquidity preference with the increase in indebtedness – or, in other words, the growth of the preference for the general equivalent that goes with the increase in promises to pay relative to the assets of banks (Minsky, 1964).

Post-Keynesians criticise the NMC for neglecting banks and especially financial markets (Fontana, 2011), but they do not link money to finance any more than the NMC cares about the destiny of money in financial circulation when the consumer price index remains stable. They call for asset prices and financial cycles to be taken into account in monetary policy choices but, faced with the rise of financial innovations and the instability inherent in the credit system, they themselves adopt the principle of interest rate stability to stabilise markets and anchor expectations (Carré and Le Héron, 2018). This is because they admit that the effects of the interest rate on other variables such as the exchange rate, investment and asset prices are uncertain (Arestis and Sawyer, 2006: 859), in the same way that they do not believe in the long-term effectiveness of prudential credit controls.

However, it is precisely because they only consider the effects of monetary policy on social production and consumption that the circuitist post-Keynesians share with the NMC not only an endogenous conception of money, but also the same implicit distinction between money and credit. For both, money is only that part of bank credit that enters the market of goods and services: for the NMC, only that part of bank issuance that affects the price level counts; for the post-Keynesians, credit is transformed into means of payment as soon as it is paid out to employees. When granted to financial institutions, credit functions as a simple cash flow for the purchase of assets (debt instruments, repos, money market funds, ABCP). In comparison with Keynes, therefore, the major change is that in times of prosperity money is no longer the reserve asset par excellence, but the basis for the creation of assets that are more or less liquid depending on the ease with which they can be converted at par, i.e. into itself (see Mehrling, 2012). This is first and foremost the financialisation of the banking system: the elimination of money in its function as a store of value in favour of "safe assets" backed by social wealth: tax revenues, real estate, etc. But unconventional policies such as quantitative easing have revealed to post-Keynesians that there is indeed a demand for money for its own sake. Post-Keynesians criticise monetary orthodoxy on the basis of the failures of these policies, as if this failure demonstrates the falsity of their supposedly exogenous conception of money: if firms do not borrow despite the abundant liquidity injected into the banking system, it is because money is not exogenous and bank loans are not dependent on the quantity of money offered by the central bank. But the fact is that there is nevertheless a demand for money by banks that is not further explained by endogenous money revolutionaries (Monvoisin and Rochon, 2018: 177–78. See also Rochon and Rossi, 2013).

For monetary heterodoxy, the merit of the endogenous approach was that it directly integrated money as a condition of production and trade, but also reversed the causality of the relationship between prices and money and thus justified the principle of accommodating monetary policy. But the implicit adoption of this approach by the NMC demonstrated that the problem lay elsewhere: not in the conditions of money issuance but in the forms of constraint exercised by money on social production. It is indeed through a constraint that money is integrated into the market order, not through its conditions of entry (helicopter or bank issue). Keynes had understood this when, for the convenience of his presentation, he made the hypothesis of exogenous money in the *General Theory*. Not only does the NMC recall, after Wicksell, that endogenous money was inherent to the credit money system, but it shows us that it does not integrate itself into that system any more than if we assume money thrown into circulation from a helicopter (Fiebiger and Lavoie, 2020).

This is because money has always been both endogenous and exogenous: endogenous because prices and the demand for credit determine the quantity of money necessary for the circulation of commodities; exogenous because the very nature of the capitalist market mode of production implies that commodities do not automatically convert into their appropriate form of social existence, i.e. into the quantity of money corresponding to the prices set by the borrowing firms:

> Price [...] expresses the value of a commodity (e.g., a ton of iron), by stating that a given quantity of the equivalent (e.g., an ounce of gold), is directly exchangeable for iron. But it by no means states the converse, that iron is directly exchangeable for gold. [...] To fix its price, it suffices to equate it to gold in imagination. But to enable it to render to its owner the service of a universal equivalent, it must be actually replaced by gold.
>
> *(Marx, 1867a: 112–13)*

The exogenous character of money does not come from the fact that the supply of money by the monetary authorities determines the price or quantity of money in circulation, but by the fact that the supply of money determines the transformation of credit demanded by enterprises into the ultimate means of settlement.

Notes

1 Slobodian suggests that the international neoliberal order should be described as "embedded", meaning that capital would be less isolated from states than framed by supra-state institutions such as the European Court of Justice or the WTO (Slobodian, 2018: 12–13). He justifies this expression by saying that it is not the state itself that would disappear from the neoliberal order, but the nation-state. Yet, Hayek was very sceptical about the desirability of creating an international government that would involve a multitude of authorities in charge of regulating the system. He preferred a genuine international law "which would limit the powers of national governments to harm each other" (Hayek, 2013: 482). This is because, unlike the state, this law would have no sovereignty, being devoid of its own will. If this right can be described as a conscious organ of capital, it is only insofar as its function consists in protecting itself from the attempts at control and regulation by the state, which, even as a bourgeois state, has the function of ensuring the compromises necessary to any society

composed of antagonistic social classes. This is why neoliberalism does not define an inverted re-embedding of the market (Slobodian, 2018: 19). Rather, it is the state itself that is embedded in the institutions of the global market. This is therefore neither an "embedding" of capital nor its isolation from the state, but its subtraction by the addition of international law.

2 Just as on inflation, Friedman's entire article on the Phillips curve is summarised in a 1945 speech by Hayek to the Economic Club of Detroit:

> I think there is a great educational task to be fulfilled. We must make the masses of people learn and understand the problem that is before us, make them capable of discriminating between methods which will achieve the end and methods which are empty promises, and particularly tell them that there may be desperate palliatives like inflationary measures which in the short run may keep employment high, but in the long run make the situation much more difficult than it was before.
>
> *(Quoted in Van Horn and Mirowski, 2009: 140)*

3 Just as Keynes had coped very well with the suspension of the gold standard. While he had become famous for *The Economic Consequences of the Peace* in which he denounced the fate of Germany inflicted by the victors of the war, three years later, after some ill-fated speculation bailed out by his father, Keynes staked his fortune on the deutsche mark, whose imminent collapse was a direct result of the terms of the Treaty of Versailles (Ahamed, 2009: 272). Keynes's personality had not escaped Montagu Norman who, delivering his assessment of the *Tract* to Strong, wrote: "For the moment Mr. Keynes seems to have rather outdone himself, a fact that perhaps comes from his trying to combine the position of financial mentor to this and other countries with that of a high-class speculator" (quoted in Ahamed, 2009: 278).

4 The complacent formalism with which the BIS had helped the Nazis to loot gold from the vaults of the Czechoslovak National Bank had turned into appalled moralism when the Soviets made the same demands regarding the occupied Baltic territories. This time McKittrick "just couldn't do it" (quoted in LeBor, 2014: 90).

5 In an article reviewing the Great Moderation, Perry and Cline present the explanation of low inflation by falling real wages and low import prices as properly post-Keynesian (2013). But as noted above, this is exactly the explanation given by Alan Greenspan, one of the three central bankers of the New Consensus.

6 If there are remnants of exogeneity in the NMC, it is therefore through the role it gives to interest rates as the price of the conversion of bank money into ultimate means of payment (banknotes, deposits, etc.).

7 For an in-depth analysis of the duality of monetary policy today, see Pierre Manigat (2022b).

8 As Minsky says, the bank differs from the firm in that while the firm adjusts quantities by keeping prices equal, it keeps quantities (of assets) equal by adjusting prices (Minsky, 1967: 276 n.).

PART 4
The politics of money

12

THE EUTHANASIA OF THE RENTIER AND THE SKELETON OF SOCIALISM

12.1 The dollar and the NEP

The history of the dollar that we have traced since the creation of the Fed was only intended to show how a national currency, once it imposes itself as a universal equivalent, acquires autonomy from its domestic base, and above all how the contradiction immanent to this universalisation, in relation to the national character of the Fed's monetary policy, expressed the deeper contradiction between the social and private functions of the dollar, between money as a form of general exchangeability and money as a general form of value. We have seen in particular how the crises inspired the Fed to take on missions akin to those of a world bank of issue and how the Fed's interest rate imposed itself as the universal rate conditioning the entire global financial cycle. But we have also seen how, even before the abolition of the gold standard, the role of universal reserve asset played by the Treasury bond had transformed the US fiscal system into the guarantor of the whole international financial system, in return for the exorbitant privileges offered to the country issuing the universal reserve of value. It is these functions that give the dollar a specificity unparalleled in the history of capitalism and that determine the criteria on which to evaluate the contenders for the universal currency competing with the dollar. But whatever the evolution of the international monetary system (replacement of the dollar by another key currency, or generalisation of Special Drawing Rights (Aglietta, Bai and Macaire, 2022; Guttmann, 2022)), the autonomy of the dollar as a purely fiat currency will have laid the foundations of a new global organisation of production and social exchange.

Through its various international functions, the Fed guarantees the dollar as a form of universal exchangeability, while the Treasury, through its bond issue, assumes the function of issuing quasi-money as a universal form of value: on the one hand, the dollar as a means of universal circulation and payment, and on

DOI: 10.4324/9780429261299-17

the other, the Treasury bond as a universal reserve of value. This is how the US monetary and financial system, at least since the Marshall Plan, has continued to loosen the market constraint imposed by money in the monetary economy of production. The dollarisation of the world, whose forced march and jolts we have described through the exchange rate crises, has not come without a relative decommodification of universal production, which finds in the crises both its manifestation (financial excess) and the conditions for its further progress (non-conventional policies). A detailed analysis of the crises from this point of view would indicate precisely the degree of relaxation of the commodity constraint achieved, while an analysis of the rescue measures would show, notably through the extension of the forms of money guaranteed by the payment system, the new conditions without which this commodity constraint continues to impose itself on social production.

In the aftermath of the unilateral US withdrawal from the Bretton Woods agreements in August 1971, Nixon described the measures taken to peel the dollar off gold and to fight inflation by freezing wages and prices as "the most comprehensive new economic policy to be undertaken by this nation in four decades". It has been questioned whether he was aware that he was using the same phrase that Lenin had used five decades earlier to describe the tactical return to market production in the aftermath of the civil war as a means of building the foundations of socialism (Solomon, 1982: 187).

In reality, Nixon was using this phrase to describe not his immediate measures, but the fate of world capitalism as a result of the measures he had taken the day before by suspending the convertibility of the dollar and letting it float on the foreign exchange market. This made the dollar the currency of the progressive decommodification of the capitalist world. And this decommodification is not contradictory to the growing commodification of social life; on the contrary, the more the market constraint on the products of social activity is relaxed, the more this relaxation allows products that are ever more distant from market production proper to enter the market sphere. This is what the Bolsheviks did with the currency inherited from the tsarist period, but first by returning to a certain market order after its brutal abolition in October 1917. And like everything else they did in economic matters, they went quickly.

In 1917, the convergence of the peasants' war against feudal oppression with the workers' movement determined the singular nature of the Russian revolution and conditioned its victory. In 1921, after four years of exhausting civil war, the convergence of the interests of a peasantry bled by requisitions and those of a proletariat decimated by the fighting forced the Bolshevik power to change its economic policy. For Lenin, the *smychka* (the workers–peasants bloc) was never a simple tactical watchword for a country divided between a peasant majority and a working class minority. Since Marx's epistolary exchanges with the Russian populists, it was a real possibility, and, since the 1905 revolution, a permanent challenge. The convergence of struggles was undoubtedly the condition of victory against capital; the convergence of interests became the condition of the victory of socialism (Dobb, 1948: 161). For the two fronts dividing the social struggle in Russia actually entailed two distinct revolutions demanding distinct practices. No doubt the distance from the prospects of revolution in Europe coupled with the ravages of civil war had precipitated the transition to the New Economic Policy (NEP) in 1921. However, these conditions, as well as the particular features of the development of capitalism in Russia, do not exhaust the issue of the turn to the NEP.

These circumstances only exacerbated a deeper tension which had been revealed by the debates and controversies of the first months of the seizure of power: between the workers and peasants' aspirations for autonomy and the demands for social organisation and control of the economic life of the new Soviet Republic. And this tension, in turn, posed a difficulty that had been agitating Lenin ever since *The State and Revolution*: how to mobilise the old apparatuses of control and regulation in the service of the new society without associating them with the despotic and repressive dimensions characterising the state apparatus under capitalism. And this problem was all the more acute in relation to the credit system, whose almost absolute power over society was precisely the hallmark of the highest stage of capitalism. In a text rightly entitled "Can the Bolsheviks retain state power?", written a few days before the insurrection and the seizure of power, Lenin wrote:

> The big banks *are* the 'state apparatus' which we *need* to bring about socialism, and which we *take ready-made* from capitalism; our task here is merely to lop off what *capitalistically mutilates* this excellent apparatus, to make it *even bigger*, even more democratic, even more comprehensive. Quantity will be transformed into quality. A single State Bank, the biggest of the big, with branches in every rural district, in every factory, will constitute as much as nine-tenths of the *socialist* apparatus. This will be country-wide *book-keeping*, country-wide *accounting* of the production and distribution of goods, this will be, so to speak, something in the nature of the *skeleton* of socialist society.
>
> *(Lenin, 1917: 106)*

12.2 What Soviet finance owes to wartime communism

No layer of Russian society made its aversion to the new power more apparent than the banking sector: rigged accounts, restrictions on withdrawals, artificial shortages of liquidity to pay salaries, refusal to grant loans. With the support of the big merchants and the owners of the factories now controlled by the workers, the banking personnel used the most devious expedients to boycott the Soviet power. In addition, the Central Bank rejected the loan applications of the new government, the Council of People's Commissars (*Sovnarkom*). The Union for the Regeneration, a clandestine association financed by private banks and parties of the former provisional governments, organised an undercover strike of civil servants. As the lesson of the Commune had been learned, which had not dared to attack the Bank of France and its reserves, emergency measures were taken as the situation demanded. On 14 December, soldiers stormed the main banks in Russia and a decree was issued making banking operations a state monopoly. As the managers and employees were reluctant to put themselves at the service of the new power, the reserves were confiscated and the vaults opened manu militari (Carr, 1969: 166). But it was ensured that the interests of small depositors would be protected. All the money was therefore deposited in personal current accounts in the State Bank and the gold coins or bars were confiscated (Baykov, 1970: 34). In a second decree, the private banks were merged with the State Bank, which consequently took over all assets and liabilities, as well as the existing staff. Subsequently, the State Bank absorbed the Chancellery of Credit and the Treasury Department. After all insurance companies were brought under state control, the insurance sector was finally declared a state monopoly in 1918.

But the re-appropriation of the banking system was hardly socialist in character, and above all was not enough to take control of the economic organisation of Russia. To these decrees was added one of Lenin's last struggles: the state monopoly on foreign trade, without which Russia would have suffered the stranglehold of foreign capital on grain reserves and the opposition of the entire peasantry to the trading conditions imposed on them by the Soviet authorities (Quigley, 1974: 33). The country's dependence on the world market would have hampered its industrialisation and condemned it to join the peripheral zone of countries supplying raw materials to the major capitalist powers. Generally speaking, the construction of socialism by means of the credit system was only possible on this condition (Goland, 1994: 1260), together with the nationalisation of the large industrial sectors, because without the latter, there would be no autonomous credit policy directed towards the development of the productive forces of large-scale industry. In fact, it was in state industry in 1923 that the first planning experiments were carried out with the so-called promfinplans (production and financial plans). With the decision to draw up a promfinplan for industry as a whole in 1925–26, the Vesenkha assumed the central steering role for the first time. The control of the economy would thus pass back into the hands of the central administrations of the Soviet state (Carr and Davies, 1969: 824).

So even before the NEP, non-financial measures were taken that would provide the credit system with a completely new basis for financing industry and the economic life of Soviet Russia. Thus the return of the Vesenkha to the forefront meant more than a return to the state centralisation of war communism. From now on, the Vesenkha would be backed up by a whole banking system, a national accounting system based on control figures from the Gosplan. It would build a closer cooperation between cities and the countryside and generate a dense and intense exchange system between agricultural and industrial products. In the meantime, it was necessary to reconstitute a banking and financial system dedicated not only to the development of the productive forces, but to the analysis and accounting control of the entire economy.

12.3 "Redeeming" the capitalist monster

Lenin was very amused that what was called the NEP was basically a return to capitalism. The measures he was forced to defend in the spring of 1921 were indeed the very ones he had fought so hard against throughout the civil war. Compared to wartime communism, which had practically abolished money, the banking system and private ownership of the major means of production, the NEP marked a clear step backwards in the construction of socialism (Carr, 1969: 286). But the situation at that time left little choice. Politically, the peasantry could not stand the policy of requisitioning agricultural products and its opposition to the regime was growing. As for the working class proletariat, the war had decimated it to the point where it represented only 2% of a population of 130 million and Lenin could be described as the leader of a vanguard of a class that no longer existed (Marie, 2011: 393). Industry was declining, not only because of the poor supply of agricultural products, but because it was deprived of people capable of organising work and directing production.

Yet, by the very fact that it was aimed at preparing the future leap forward of socialism, and by the very fact that it was based on an already large nationalised industrial sector, this retreat set Soviet society on a new course and anticipated what the capitalist nations would much later experience in their own way. And if the experience of the NEP can still inspire possible forms of transition in our own societies today, it is because of the way it subverted from within the monetary and financial system inherited from advanced capitalism to create a whole apparatus dedicated to the distribution, organisation and social control of production and exchange in society. The system inherited from the previous world had bequeathed to the Soviet authorities a set of specifically capitalist tools, means and institutions that they were able, through the great ruptures decreed in the first months of the seizure of power, to put at the service of specifically socialist ends.

12.4 The peasants and the harvest of money

For Lenin, the Russian revolution could only succeed on two conditions: if it was supported by a socialist revolution in the advanced countries, and if the proletariat in power got along with the peasantry. But for as long as the international revolution was delayed, Soviet Russia would remain at the mercy of the peasantry that formed the vast majority of the population. Under these conditions, the socialist transformation of social relations in the countryside was postponed. For the time being, the aim was to re-establish acceptable living conditions, to ensure the supply of food to the cities, to organise balanced exchanges between agriculture and industry, and to eliminate unemployment without delay (Carr, 1969: 288–89). In March 1921, the Executive Committee took two types of measures to consolidate the *smychka*. The system of requisitions of agricultural produce, imposed for war purposes, was replaced by a tax in kind; and partial freedom of trade was re-established for peasants, small traders and small manufacturers. Other measures were taken in this direction: concessions to foreign enterprises, privatisation of industrial enterprises and encouragement of party cadres to learn trade (Carr, 1969: 311). More generally, the principle of *khozrachet* was applied to all economic units, i.e. autonomous management, including profit-making (Carr, 1969: 315–16). At the same time, however, it was necessary to strengthen state capitalism, especially in order to revive industry, and to forge new links between the proletariat and the peasantry through cooperation, i.e. in fact through socialist (non-monetary) exchanges between the cities and the countryside (Dobb, 1948: 161–62).

The amount of the tax in kind was initially fixed in advance, which left the peasants with a quantity of products that was all the greater as their production was more considerable. The overall amount was to cover the needs of the army and the functioning of part of the state apparatus. Only the fraction of the peasants' production that was not consumed by them or absorbed by taxes or barter (exchange with state enterprises) could be sold freely on the local market (Carr, 1969: 342–43). But the 1921 harvest was disastrous and led Russia into an abominable famine. In addition, industrial production hardly progressed and the supply to the cities remained seriously deficient. So much so that in the autumn of 1921, Lenin supported a new conception of the NEP: abandonment of state capitalism in favour of a real, lasting and solid alliance with the peasantry, which meant a wider re-establishment of market and monetary relations between the city and the country (Arnold, 1937: 114). In addition, the government established new taxes, also payable in money, and in 1923 the agricultural tax, in turn, became monetary.

12.5 From sign to money

The monetary and financial system of the NEP was built on these renewed exchanges which, as soon as they expanded to a national scale, required monetary regulation. Before the NEP, the People's Commissariat for Finance (Narkomfin) had issued monetary units that were modestly called "Soviet signs": *sovznaks*. But the inflation caused by the over-issuance of sovznaks to finance the war had depreciated this quasi-currency. The first decision was to replace the old notes with new ones. These notes would be of a higher value and this time considered as real currency units (Arnold, 1937: 143–44).

But the major turning point in the Narkomfin's monetary policy was the decree of 12 October 1921 for the creation of a State Bank, which was to promote the development of industry, agriculture and trade through credit and other banking operations. Its statutes authorised it to grant short-term commercial credit and long-term investment credit, to the state of course, but above all to cooperative enterprises, agricultural producers and private enterprises in general (Arnold, 1937: 118). It took over all the credit operations of the banks and got preferential rights for the purchase and sale of gold and foreign trade transactions, even after the abolition of the system of compulsory transfer of gold and foreign currency to the state by private individuals. However, the Bank also had to adopt the khozrachet principle, which required it to cover its expenses with its revenues (Carr, 1969: 359–60) and this principle could conflict with its mission to contribute to price stability, as it gave it the right to buy and sell goods on its own account and to make profits on these transactions. Part of its profits was to be used to build up a capital reserve, and, in case of a loss, the difference was to be financed from the state budget, after confirmation of the annual report by the Narkomfin. In fact, the Bank was a constituent part of the Narkomfin and was allowed to establish district offices in the capitals of the republics, branches in provincial cities and local agencies. The only feature that distinguished it from a central bank was that, until 1922, it was not allowed to issue money, which was the exclusive privilege of the state (Arnold, 1937: 120–24).

From this top-down reform, the entire banking system was recreated (Hubbard, 1936: 11): Bank for Industry (Prombank) to provide short-term commercial credits and loans of up to three years to enterprises; Bank of Consumers' Cooperatives (Pokobank), which in 1923 became the All-Russian Bank of Cooperatives (Vsekobank); municipal banks to finance local industries and local government works; and mutual credit associations to cater for the needs of the small traders that flourished under the NEP (Arnold, 1937: 274 sq.)

Once this banking system was established, the State Bank was authorised by a decree of 11 October 1922 to issue a new monetary unit with a gold backing: the chervonetz rouble (literally pure gold), which was equivalent to 10 gold rubles. Its issue was strictly controlled, with 25% covered by precious metal reserves and 75% by short-term bonds and cash. The aim of the decree was to allow the Bank to increase its resources, to expand its commercial operations without recourse to Treasury money, and to regulate money circulation. The Bank was also allowed to use its right of issue to expand its lending to the Narkomfin, which was to be backed 50% by precious metals and 50% by government bonds (Arnold, 1937: 147–48). However, this currency did not have legal tender status, unlike the sovznak which was used for tax payment. In fact, until the summer of 1923, the chervonetz was not really used as a domestic medium of exchange, but as a store of value and an international currency, i.e. as a general form of value.

12.6 The scissors crisis and the financialisation of the NEP

In the history of the NEP, 1923 is the year of the scissors crisis. It was so-called following a presentation by Trotsky using a graph to illustrate the evolution of agricultural and industrial prices, initially favourable to the former, then continually moving away to the benefit of the latter. The scissors crisis was directly linked to the credit policy decided by the government and implemented by the State Bank. On the one hand, the trusts and unions of state enterprises benefited from large credits and could, by virtue of the khozrachet which encouraged enterprises to make profit their guiding principle, afford to speculate by withdrawing goods from the market in order to raise prices. On the other hand, private traders, to whom the Bank applied a restrictive credit policy, turned to private lenders who imposed very high interest charges on them, which again had the effect of driving up prices (Arnold, 1937: 201). More generally, the Treasury currency, the sovznak, issued in large quantities to finance the budget deficit, depreciated constantly against a relatively stable chervonetz (Carr, 1954: 9). Little by little, Gresham's law that bad money drives out good money was verified: chervonetz left the sphere of circulation to be hoarded from circulation while sovznak saw its velocity of circulation increase with inflation.

But in a strange twist, this crisis signalled the victory of finance over production in the hierarchy of priorities. This was because the crisis had initiated a muted and permanent struggle between the Narkomfin, which was committed to pursuing financial reform, and the Gosplan, whose views Trotsky shared, and for whom the development of heavy industry required large capital advances and planning (Carr, 1954: 9). For the Narkomfin, financial reform meant balancing the budget and therefore cutting state subsidies to industry. But above all, monetary stability required gold and foreign currency to build up the reserves of the Bank of Issue, which could only be obtained by exporting agricultural products. Encouraging grain exports meant encouraging the peasantry, especially the rich peasants of the kulaks. It was thought that this would kill two birds with one stone, since the policy of exporting grain would prove to be the most practical and effective way of achieving the dual objective of satisfying the peasantry and supplying the reserves necessary for monetary stabilisation.

However, the crisis forced the Gosplan to align itself with the Narkomfin policy, which suddenly and severely limited credit to industry. It was believed that the fall in the purchasing power of the chervonetz was due to a too-rapid expansion of credit. This tightening of the screws had immediate consequences, forcing consumer industries, which had benefited most from the credit policies at the expense of heavy industry, to lower their prices and liquidate their stocks on the market. It thus also had the effect of closing the gap between light and heavy industry. From then on, the question of credit to industry would be treated as a whole within the framework of industrial policy in general, without distinction as to which sectors should be favoured (Carr, 1954: 88–89). The anarchy of the first years of the NEP was thus brought to an end, but in a very particular way.

The victory of the Narkomfin over the Gosplan had an even more important result than the strengthening of the rich peasantry and the subordination of industrial development to monetary stability. From now on, monetary and financial policy would control the entire Soviet economy. In other words, the Soviet economy would be organised through money and credit. While the financial dimension of the NEP was initially the last of the government's concerns, from 1923 onwards, it became the only really active and forward-looking field of action of the authorities (Barnett, 2004: 69). Between 1921 and 1923, we moved from the dominant heights of heavy industry, as Lenin said, to the "new dominant heights" of money and credit.[1]

This was done first of all through prices. Thus, the Scissors Crisis Committee set up by the government decided to control not only wholesale prices, which was already the case, but also retail prices, especially for goods that were uniform in quality and available in large quantities (Carr, 1954: 112). And since in a market economy the control of some prices must inevitably extend to the control of all prices, price control meant controlling the whole economy and gradually placing planning at the heart of the organisation of production and trade. A good harvest in 1923, the resumption of grain exports, but also industrial concentration leading to better productivity and therefore lower industrial prices, completed the solution of the scissors crisis. The conditions were therefore ripe for the continuation and completion of a monetary reform that would sanction Soviet Russia's temporary rapprochement with capitalism.

12.7 From money to numbers

This reform, whose main goal was financial stability, required two conditions: monetary stability and fiscal balance. Monetary stability would be guaranteed by the creation of a new legal tender, pegged to gold, and by stopping the issue of sovznaks and buying them back by the Bank. As for fiscal balance, it would be applied by the Narkomfin, which examined the estimates submitted by the various departments on the basis of what were called control figures and aggregated these estimates with the budgets of the various republics to make a single Union budget, after approval by the Central Executive Committee (Carr, 1958: 500).[2]

But in 1925 the famous transition from "restoration" to "reconstruction" was the occasion of a decisive turn in the monetary and financial policy of the NEP. Since 1923, the economic recovery had been strong enough to approach the full capacity of the means of production left unused during the period of wartime communism (Linhart, 2017). The continuation of the industrialisation process therefore required the construction or acquisition of new means of production which, in turn, required a much higher rate of industrial accumulation than had prevailed during the "restoration". It was with this in mind that the Central Committee took the decision in early 1925 to remove the State Bank's control over fiscal policy. A USSR Budget Commission was created to implement a policy of budgetary expansion that was incompatible with the support of the ruble rate. The flow of credit to heavy industry naturally led to inflation, but the debate on what to do about it led to a solution that would change the course of the NEP. Instead of seeing this inflation as a classic price increase, it was seen primarily as a decrease in the external purchasing power of the chervonetz. In other words, the problem was no longer the internal purchasing power of the currency, but its external value. The chervonetz in foreign trade transactions had become negligible and there was no connection between the purchasing power of the currency and the gold exchange rate of the chervonetz; above all the state had a monopoly on foreign trade. The Treasury therefore stopped offering gold and foreign currency for chervonetz in March 1926, leaving their value to deteriorate on the black market, aptly named the "American market" (Carr, 1958: 487). The export of chervonetz was prohibited and any supply of Russian currency abroad was considered smuggling. Russia thus abandoned not only its parity with gold but all links with the international monetary system. The ruble became a purely domestic currency whose rate would be set by a government commission.

Prior to 1925, the monetary reform provided for the pegging of the new currency to gold and the Bank intervened in the market to maintain the official parity of the rouble against gold and foreign currencies. These interventions required gold and foreign exchange reserves which not only implied a policy of exports, especially of agricultural products, which as we have seen favoured the rich peasants at the expense of the middle-ranked and poor peasants, but also implied a decrease in industrial production, since industrial development was unable to provide export products quickly, which put the working class at a disadvantage (Bettelheim, 1977: 52–53). By freeing itself from the gold standard, the Soviet Union was freeing itself from these constraints; it was breaking the link that maintained its dependence on the world market and its status as an agriculturally oriented developing country. But to break with the capitalist world was also, in a sense, to break with the world proletariat that sustains it and to give up the idea of relying on an international revolution to build socialism. This is why abandoning the gold standard meant, consciously or not, abandoning the hypothesis of a European revolution (Carr, 1958: 489).

The reform provided a solid basis for the subsequent expansion of credit and the reconstruction phase. The number of credit institutions and their branches increased until 1927: they quadrupled in three years, and their branches tripled in the same period (Garvy, 1977: 28). At the same time, the Bank consolidated its status as the predominant credit institution and the bank of banks (loans and discounts doubled, with deposits four times larger than total deposits in other banking institutions in 1927) (Arnold, 1937: 269). The Bank gradually became the main institution for providing short-term credit, especially when, after 1925–26, it became clear that deposits at Prombank and Vneshtorgbank were beginning to decline, not because of the level of economic activity, but because of the start of the investment process in the national economy (Carr and Davies, 1969: 774). However, it had resources for its credit operations that the other credit institutions did not have: money issue and Treasury deposits, which from 1 October 1925 were transferred to the Bank (Arnold, 1937: 265).

12.8 State Bank versus Central Bank

The State Bank thus gradually moved away from the traditional monetary role of capitalist central banks to become an administrative control body for the credit operations of all other banking institutions. In mid-1927, a decree entitled "Principles of organization of the credit system" took a further step by granting the Bank the right to direct the activities of all credit institutions, which allowed it to place representatives on the boards and audit committees of all those where state capital predominated. In addition, the free reserves of banks were to be deposited in the State Bank, as well as the funds of the state budget, savings banks and insurance companies. It was also decided to strengthen the co-ordination activities of the Banking Committee by attaching it to the USSR People's Commissariat on Finance (Baykov, 1970: 101). In September 1928, the State Bank was given sole responsibility for collecting revenue and making payments on behalf of the state and local budgets (Hubbard, 1936: 14).

One way of appreciating the nature of the transformations that Soviet power brought about in the monetary and financial system inherited from capitalism is to compare the Bank's balance sheet in 1928, when production reached pre-war levels for the first time, with that of the Imperial Bank on the eve of the war. First, gold, which made up 60% of the Bank's assets at the time, now accounts for only about 8%. Second, while banknotes had previously been issued to acquire precious metals, they were now mainly used to provide credit to the nation. Since 1924, money in circulation had been increasing steadily, but the new issues were no longer intended to balance the state budget, which from that year onwards was in systematic surplus, but to expand credit for production (Carr and Davies, 1969: 774). In addition, the amount of Treasury deposits had decreased significantly, precisely because the Treasury money had been used to a large extent for the reconstruction of the national economy. But this numerical comparison expresses a more essential qualitative difference: most of the Tsarist Bank's clients had been private, whereas all of the Bank's clients were state agencies. In addition, speculative and investment activities in stocks and bonds were completely abolished, as were deposits created by companies in exchange for the sale of shares or loans in exchange for these securities. Deposits from shareholder dividends and loans against mortgages were also eliminated as a result of the abolition of private property. Finally, as a result of price controls and government regulation of the markets, large-scale speculative transactions in commodities were eliminated, and thus also the banking transactions that resulted from them (Arnold, 1937: 269–74).

12.9 NEP, Keynes and trust in money

On the one hand, the NEP broke with everything that characterised wartime communism: the concentration of economic authority and power; the centralisation of management, decisions and control; the promotion of large production units at the expense of smaller ones; production for direct use; and exchanges and payments in kind. But on the other hand, all the measures taken to reintroduce the market into economic relations led to the promotion of the quasi-exclusive economic authority and power of the Gosplan and the Gosbank,[3] as well as to the planning of all branches of the economy, and to the submission of the market to the control of prices mediated by a currency entirely freed from external constraints.

More generally, an overview of the successive stages of the NEP between 1921 and 1928 reveals a succession of measures that overlapped at unprecedented velocity all the stages of the development of capitalism to its most advanced form. The NEP begins with an agricultural policy, notably by means of taxation: this would be the phase of agrarian capitalism. It continues with a policy of internal and external trade aimed at the development of large-scale industry, which would correspond to the mercantilist phase, itself followed, with the reconstruction phase, by the period of industrial capitalism. Finally, it ends with a monetary and financial policy which subjects the whole social process of production and exchange to the credit system. This would be the moment of finance capital where Marx, and later Hilferding, Kautsky and Lenin himself, identified a form of proto-communism within capitalism.

This was because, precisely in the financial sphere, Russia entrusted monetary policy with tasks that Keynes, too concerned with preserving the market economy, was unwilling to consider. However, relations between Keynes and Soviet Russia did not start well. In 1918, Keynes was sent by the British Treasury to implement a monetary reform in northern Russia, which was then in the hands of the White Army supported by France and England. The measures he advocated were inspired by the strictest monetary orthodoxy: monetary stability, a fixed exchange rate and therefore a rigorous issuing policy (Ponsot, 2007: 381). With the collapse of the White Army, the reform was long in coming, but by 1923 Keynes had assessed and welcomed the Soviet dual currency system: the paper rouble, whose more or less controlled depreciation as a result of over-issue was akin to a tax on the population, and the chervonetz, used for large transactions and subject to the gold standard: "Russia provides an instructive example (at least for the moment) of a sound money for substantial transactions alongside small change for daily life, the progressive depreciation on which merely represents a quite supportable rate of turnover tax" (Keynes, 1923: 49). The crisis of 1929 and its consequences then led Keynes to design monetary instruments on a much larger scale (Toye, 1993: 251). Henceforth, monetary policy should serve to reduce the preference for liquidity, stimulate investment spending and increase the level of employment.

But from the 1924 reform onwards, the Soviet government reinvented the monetary system through a series of measures that Keynes could not have imagined in the context of private property.[4] With the nationalisation of major industries and the monopoly of foreign trade, the abandonment of the gold standard emancipated the currency far beyond what Keynes had predicted for the pound sterling in 1931. Even when liberated from gold, capitalist money remained chained on all sides: internally by its status as an appropriable and accumulable asset;[5] externally by the exchange rate system and the circulation of capital. The euthanasia of the rentier requires much more than an inflationary policy or a dissuasive tax. By controlling industry and trade, Soviet power pulled the plug on the breathing apparatus that would later revive it in the West. Without a state monopoly on foreign trade, the abandonment of the gold standard would have meant hastening the country's dependence on the world market and on the sale of its agricultural product. Without the nationalisation of large-scale industry, there could be no autonomous credit policy directed towards the development of the productive forces. It was in state industry that the first planning experiments were carried out in 1923 with the so-called promfinplans (production and financial plans). With the decision to draw up a promfinplan for industry as a whole in 1925–26, the Vesenkha, whose function was to control the nationalised industries, again assumed the central steering role. The control of the economy thus returned to the hands of the central administrations of the Soviet state, but this time backed by a whole banking system, national accounting based on control figures produced by the Gosplan, but also closer cooperation between cities and the countryside, and a dense and intense system of exchange between agricultural and industrial products.

On this basis, Soviet Russia experimented long before the "free world" with a monetary system whose stability depended essentially on the stability of the relationship between political power and the different classes of society. Not only is Russia the first European country that took part in the war to have succeeded in stabilising its currency, but it is also first in experimenting with a monetary system based entirely on political stability. Trust in money only means trust in the stability of capitalism as long as money does not emanate from collective institutions for the satisfaction of social needs.[6]

Notes

1 The expression is by Kamenev.

2 These control figures were in reality the numerical expressions of the very first annual plan of the national economy elaborated by the Gosplan, intended only to guide the various People's Commissariats but without any compulsory character (see Bettelheim, 1977: 71).

3 "Krijanovski, president of the Gosplan, asserts at the beginning of 1925 that 'credit and plan [are] brothers in a single system of socialisation'" (Bettelheim, 1977: 60).

4 "By 1926 the Soviet Government had increased nationalized production and extended socialized distribution to a degree that enabled it to resume its campaign of exterminating private enterprise. [...] By the beginning of the first Five-Year Plan in 1928 it was impossible for a private citizen to purchase any means of production [...] and very nearly impossible to obtain finished goods for resale. [...] Money had therefore lost the quality of capital; as far as the individual citizen was concerned, it was only a means of satisfying his personal day-to-day wants" (Hubbard, 1936: 5–6).

5 "But the most stable, and the least easily shifted, element in our contemporary economy has been hitherto, and may prove to be in future, the minimum rate of interest acceptable to the generality of wealth-owners" (Keynes, 1936: 309).

6 "The existence of the 'fiat' is by no means sufficient to guarantee the stability of money; for this stability not to be called into question, the 'general will' of those who hold money and commodities must be maintained" (Bettelheim, 1977: 55).

CONCLUSION

Digital currencies and post-capitalism

C.1 Digital currencies and social labour

Digital currencies and crypto-currencies, i.e. currencies issued and circulating on the basis of cryptographic systems of the blockchain type, have rekindled the debate between institutionalists and mainstream economists on the very nature of money and its role in a monetary economy of production: a public good used to settle debts between members of society versus a private good used for the immediate exchange of economic agents' resources. Thus, the former disqualify private digital currencies, both as a unit of account and as a medium of exchange, in the name of the public good character and social functions of money (Aglietta and Valla, 2021: 73–74). However, the orthodoxy praises their character as a private good and a potentially stable and secure object of value precisely because, unlike bank currencies, they do not arise from bank liabilities and a policy of endless credit to companies, households and, above all, states (Walker and Luu, 2016). For the former, the idea is to convert the cryptographic payment system into a centralised system controlled by a sovereign authority; for the latter, to abolish any central authority in the operation and preservation of that system. For the former, money is defined as a simple unit of account created and issued by the sovereign; for the latter, as a simple medium of exchange whose quantity is predefined in advance and whose value depends on the transactions decided by the exchangers: the dream of quantity theory (Bransbourg, 2015). Thus, the institutionalists demand the guarantee of a sovereign authority against the private deviation of the eminently social purpose of money, while the orthodox demand radical decentralisation against the monopolistic uses of sovereign currencies. Some want centralisation without capital, others capital without centralisation; both want money dedicated to its social functions exclusively, but the former artificially separate monetary sovereignty from the capitalist birth of

DOI: 10.4324/9780429261299-18

the centralised credit system, the latter separate the generalisation of monetary circulation from the capitalist conditions of this generalisation, i.e. the transformation of labour power into commodities. However, we have seen how institutionalism and quantity theory both rested on subjective bases which made the integration of money into the structure of exchange impossible. Even if they disagree on the birth of money – convention for some, direct exchange for others – these theories only measure the ultimate quality of money as a means of payment by the extent of its functions.

Since the functions of money are simply stated without being related to the genesis of money and the two modes of being that the development of this genesis gives rise to in the general equivalent, the debate on digital currencies is limited to examining to what extent and under what conditions these currencies could replace the fiat money of the current credit system. Thus, stablecoins, which are digital currencies anchored on one or more fiat units of account, at one stage seemed liable to replace existing monetary forms in their function as a medium of exchange, but not in their function as a store of value, which would continue to be fulfilled by the monetary forms of the anchor units of account (Brainard, 2019). Conversely, certain digital currencies, which, like gold and indeed even more so than it, are becoming scarcer in relation to the growth of transactions, could be thought to form a long-term store of value provided that the conditions for their reproduction and convertibility are assured (Baur and Dimpfl, 2021: 2681). But as a unit of account, only the currency in which social production is financed and represented determines the value of the units of account of digital currencies (Brunnermeier, James and Landau, 2021: 26).

We have seen that money derives its quality of ultimate means of payment from the fact that, as the objectivity of value, it represents in an objective form the private labour of social individuals: this character confers on it both its modes of being as a form of general exchangeability and as a general form of value. This double mode of being arises from the fact that money forms both the object by the exchange of which the products of labour are exchanged as commodities and the object representing the value of exchange, that is, the social character of the labour contained in the commodity. The contradiction between the social destination and the private uses of digital currencies is thus the contradiction of money itself as a general equivalent, which we have seen defines money both as a form of general exchangeability and as a general form of value. Now, this character of general equivalent, this quality of ultimate means of settlement, distinguishes money from other monetary forms precisely by the unity of these contradictory functions and derives this unity from its existence as an objectified form of labour in commodity society. That bitcoin and other crypto-currencies, after being launched as a currency of exchange, turn into stores of value or speculative assets is less proof of Gresham's law than evidence of the fact that these digital units do not mediate the exchange of labour in society. These currencies can sometimes constitute a reserve asset (Halaburda, Sarvary and Haeringer, 2022), and sometimes serve to exchange goods and services between producers and consumers, but on the basis of the capitalist mode of production, where the society's labour is financed by the advance of capital, only the means of settlement belonging to the payment system on which social capital is based have the character of money. As long as the income derived from the participation of agents in the general social activity is not financed in them, they remain dependent on the unit of account in which the income of society is denominated. It may be that each of the functions of money taken separately will give rise to a distinct monetary form (Brunnermeier, James and Landau, 2021). But the ultimate form will always be that which represents and objectifies society's labour. Hence the pivotal role of the US Treasury bill which, on a global scale, most surely represents universal labour.

Therefore, the question of whether digital currencies are real currencies or whether they can replace existing currencies amounts to asking whether they are intended to mediate the entirety of social activity. Only if they are part of the payment system and thus convertible at par with the monetary unit in which society's labour is financed could digital currencies or crypto-currencies be called proper means of payment. On the basis of the capitalist mode of production, in which money serves both as a means of social circulation and as privately appropriable social wealth, the centralisation of the payment system is as inevitable as the fragmentation of the means of payment themselves. With the autonomisation of the unit of account function fixed by law in relation to the value-measurement function arising from the exchange of goods, monetary theory is used to consider the currency in which the tax is paid as the ultimate means of payment and the object of the centralisation of the payment system. But it is from the character of a general equivalent, i.e. an objectified and separate form of value, that the unification of the means of payment results, and the centralisation of the payment system will remain necessary as long as social labour takes the form of a thing distinct from the activity and products of society's labour.

C.2 Central bank digital currencies or the digital Gosbank

However, don't central bank digital currency (CBDC) projects seek to overcome the contradiction of digital currencies by combining the centralisation of the payment system with the removal of the private store of value function that hard cash makes possible? It is known that there are two competing models for the creation of CBDCs: an account-based system, in which cash would disappear entirely from monetary transactions, and a token-based system, in which money would instead be represented exclusively by monetary units in the form of notes or coins circulating between agents (Fiedler, Gern and Stolzenburg, 2019: 17). So far, the respective virtues and vices of these models have been compared based on the issue of the authentication of transactions and users' identity: in the account-based system, you do not need to authenticate a transaction as long as the identity of the parties is known; in the token-based system, however, the identity of the parties is not necessary, but the amount of the transaction needs to be validated, just as when you are counting notes received in payment (Brunnemeier, James and Landau, 2021: 5). But the deeper issue at stake in these models is not the identification of agents or the validity of transactions, but the identity of money itself. First, the mere possibility that the central bank issues money through accounts open to all individuals or in the form of tokens circulating through a blockchain not only restores the centralisation inherent in the current payment system, but also removes the remnants of decentralisation that the system retains through its network of commercial banks (Bordo and Levin, 2017: 6). Under these conditions, credit policy would be conducted directly by the central bank itself, so that all credit money issuance in the covered currency area would be determined by a central authority whose choices would depend on considerations such as the balance between sectors, aggregate supply and demand, or the price level both generally and in each particular sector. In short, it would depend on considerations related to the level and structure of global production. But above all, a CBDC system based on a system of accounts would weaken the private function of the store of value by the impossibility of getting the money accumulated in the accounts out of the official payment system and would place the central bank "in a position of omnipotence" (Aglietta, Bai and Macaire, 2022: 211). This consequence would mainly result from the new possibilities of monetary policy that the CBDCs would make possible and which would bring the central bank closer to the Gosbank, and the Treasury closer to the Gosplan, under the conditions of a monetary production economy.

With a monopoly on digital currency accounts, the central bank could, in the event of a crisis or recession, charge negative interest rates on digital currency accounts instead of resorting to quantitative easing or causing inflation through money issuance (Prasad, 2021). It would force agents to make exclusively social use of money, as Gesell dreamed of with his "stamp money" (Rogoff, 2016: 163–67), abolishing money as a general form of value (Bordo and Levin, 2017: 13; Fiedler, Gern and Stolzenburg, 2019: 17). Conversely, it could directly increase the interest rate on these accounts in case of inflationary pressures, for example. Thus, the value of monetary assets would no longer be basically determined by market forces but directly by the steering of the central bank according to criteria subordinating the preservation of private wealth to the conditions for the reproduction of social wealth. This is because the control of the money value by the current account interest rate would lead to the replacement of a policy targeting inflation by price level targeting (Bordo and Levin, 2017: 16). So far, monetary policy has been limited to controlling the price level according to its growth rate, regardless of the initial price level. Direct price level targeting would in fact mean not only the control of supply and demand, which determine the evolution of prices, but, taking into account the evolution of the world market and the production conditions of the goods and services included in the targeted price index, the control of the production conditions of these goods and services themselves. This is what makes one of the specialists in digital currencies fear the confusion between monetary and fiscal policies that such a monetary instrument would entail (Prasad, 2021). The CBDC would fulfil both its social function as a pure medium of exchange and, as a unit of account, as a means of social control over production. But this confusion would already be taking place with the remuneration of accounts in CBDC. For what is it to attribute positive interest rates to accounts if not to immediately issue government bonds in digital form? (Aglietta, Bai and Macaire, 2022: 214). The difference between monetary and fiscal policies, as intended by MMT, would be abolished. But the merger of the central bank and the treasury in the absence of banking intermediaries would in fact imply a complete transformation of our mode of production. While the central bank would directly issue CBDC by directly controlling prices through the interest rate on the accounts of economic agents, the treasury would directly decide to which sectors and in what quantity to allocate these digital currencies whose monetary unit of account would merge with the unit of activity it represents. The central bank and the treasury would become the great planners of production in the digital age.

C.3 Capitalism and archaism

It is at the borders of digital technology that the creators of bitcoin have resurrected the most archaic forms of commodity money (Bransbourg, 2015). Distributed ledgers were designed to counter the principle of a currency based on the infinite credit of banks serving states, by artificially creating scarcity, subjecting transactions to cumbersome and costly validation procedures, and decentralising the control of operations (Yermack, 2015). This coexistence of archaism and innovation in crypto-currencies is born out of the project to return to the monetary forms of simple circulation whose issuance does not coincide with a liability of its creator: pure money of account whose value is entirely determined by supply and demand, i.e. by the amount of transactions (Walker and Luu, 2016: 9). Crypto-currencies trace monetary archaism back to the cryptographic background of distributed ledgers, whereas the financial revolution in England freed money from its archaic basis through the cyclical form of capital and the state tax system (Dickson, 2013: 11). In the first case, the revolution stems from the decentralised nature of the transaction system; in the second case, it arises from the increasing centralisation of the means of payment. In the first case, everything is based on the alternation of 0 and 1; in the second case, on the exponential growth that takes the value 1 in 0. Crypto-currencies are the currencies of finitude, divisible ad infinitum, in contrast to credit currencies whose infinite growth is fit for a world of unlimited expansion (Bataille and Favier, 2017). Bitcoin ushers in the era of infinite envelopment, of the infinitely small (the potentially infinite divisibility of the bitcoin), whereas credit money was projected into the infinitely large (the conquest of space).

While the credit system permanently frees the development of capitalism from the archaic basis of the value law, crypto-currencies attempt to restore this archaism on a revolutionary basis that dispenses with both private banks and states.

Moreover, it is this revolutionary basis that makes it possible to return to the root of monetary exchanges in simple circulation, in the same way that centralisation and the monopoly of issuance made it possible for the credit system to free itself from the archaic basis of the value law. This is because monetary policy, insofar as it forms a late product of the credit system and acts upon it, is also an action of balance between the before and after of capitalism, between ante-capitalism and post-capitalism. For it is the very nature of the credit system to be composed of financial products that push capitalism beyond itself, and at the same time of a monetary base that existed prior to the emergence of capitalism and now constantly constrains the capitalist present.

If the crises of modern capitalism are always first and foremost monetary or financial crises, this is because the credit system is always both ahead and behind the dynamics of capital. It never coincides with the capitalist present.

> The world would not yet have railways if it had had to wait until accumulation had enabled a few singular capitals to be able to take on the construction of a railway. Centralisation, on the other hand, has achieved this in no time at all by means of joint stock companies.
>
> *(Marx, 1887: 442)*

But at the same time as the credit system creates the conditions that accelerate the development of production and exchange beyond its present possibilities, it remains dependent on its monetary base inherited from commodity production, which pre-dates capitalism and makes it a heterogeneous system. The credit system is both post-capitalist through its sophisticated credit instruments and financial products and ante-capitalist through the money into which financial securities must be able to be converted at any time. In short, the credit system is never truly contemporary with capitalism; it is constantly torn between its tendency to override all the constraints of the capitalist present (through credit itself) and the need, which manifests itself brutally in times of crisis, to convert all these securities into hard cash. Even when adapted to the needs of capitalism, the financing system born of capitalist circulation remains a bastard financing system. "And its 'monetary base' appears as soon as it is in danger of being rendered useless, whether in domestic or international financial circuits" (de Brunhoff, 1979: 147). But insofar as this system is inherent to the capitalist mode of production, we must go further and generalise this combination of survivals and novelties to all dimensions of capitalism.

Marx often observed how the fact that different countries were at different levels of economic development led to the coexistence of archaic and modern bourgeoisies and state apparatuses. Thus, at the height of the Industrial Revolution, the German bourgeoisie was engaged in tasks of industrialising the country that the French and Germans had accomplished in the age of mercantilism. Similarly, France was developing a costly state apparatus because of the control of the Bank and the Stock Exchange over the country, while England had a cheap state adapted to the needs of industrial development (de Brunhoff, 1978: 119). For Marx, anachronism is involved in the tasks of the present, as when the French bourgeoisie, in order to accomplish its revolution, had to borrow from the Roman Empire the elements which made it the bearer of universal interests. However, as Suzanne de Brunhoff points out, "This was no mere ideological duplicity, but a necessity for the establishment of bourgeois hegemony" (de Brunhoff, 1978: 119), which informs us about the articulation of space and time in capitalist social formations.

For this combination of old and new is not unique to the financial system, but permeates, in varying degrees and forms, every stage of capitalism. Whatever the period considered, there is always a combination of relatively disparate elements, of different origins and ages, which makes it very difficult to identify and define stages of capitalism:

> the periods illustrated in terms of state monetary practices do not directly reflect those which traditionally allow us to define stages of capitalism, because of the division linked to the concept of general equivalent, and to the transformations of practices which correspond to the reproduction of this equivalent.
>
> *(de Brunhoff, 1973: 102)*

We cannot therefore apply the same mode of temporal division according to whether we are dealing with money and monetary practices or with labour and the composition of labour power.

The credit system institutes the conditions for a post-capitalist money circulation on the basis of a pre-capitalist money system, while the private digital currency system institutes the conditions for a pre-capitalist money circulation on the basis of a post-capitalist payment system. Hence the non-contemporaneity per se of crypto-currencies, which both rely on meta-national issuing systems and payment technologies and replicate archaic monetary forms of simple circulation. But it is precisely these asynchronous aspects that provide the conditions for post-capitalist uses of the credit system. For private digital money systems, by their very nature as anational, translate this contradiction directly to the global scale, providing both the technological conditions for the establishment of global currencies and, insofar as these currencies are anchored to the large units of account, the conditions for a wider and deeper dollarisation of peripheral social formations (Brunnermeier, James and Landau, 2021: 22). But even before these possible developments take place, the quantum computer is already threatening the encryption algorithm of crypto-currency transactions: a new quantum space-time after the relativistic space-time of the credit system.

But isn't this coexistence of the old and the new, of the pre-capitalist and the post-capitalist within capitalism itself, the expression of the very contradiction of money, always divided between its social function, which attracts to itself an ever-increasing quantity of the products of social activity, and its private function as a store of value, which withdraws it from circulation and paralyses the process of production and exchange in society? The abolition of monetary archaism would necessarily upset the nature of money itself, since it would mean abolishing the character of money as a general equivalent, that is, its character as an objective and separate representative of the exchange value of commodities, as a representative of social labour. A money reduced to its function as a means of exchange or circulation would mean the end of production based on the valorisation of value, i.e. production for money as "value for itself". The role of money would thus be as superfluous as it is in the general equilibrium models discussed above, where prices are set in money in the absence of any prior exchange of goods. Money would become what the neo-chartalists wrongly consider to define capitalist fiat money and which is at the origin of their simplistic voluntarism: a pure unit of account serving for the measurement and allocation of natural and social resources and for the organisation of human activity.

REFERENCES

Aftalion, Albert. 1927. *Monnaie, prix et change.* Paris: Sirey.

Aglietta, Michel. 2007. "Universalité et transformations de la monnaie: la nature des crises monétaires." In *Crises monétaires en Russie et en Allemagne au XXe siècle,* edited by Bruno Théret, 17–41. Vol. 2 of *La monnaie dévoilée par ses crises.* Paris: Éditions de l'École des Hautes Études en Sciences Sociales.

Aglietta, Michel. 2016. *La monnaie. Entre dettes et souveraineté.* Paris: Odile Jacob.

Aglietta, Michel, Guo Bai, and Camille Macaire. 2022. *La course à la suprématie monétaire mondiale. À l'épreuve de la rivalité sino-américaine.* Paris: Odile Jacob.

Aglietta, Michel, and Jean Cartelier. 1998. "Ordre monétaire des économies de marché." In *La monnaie souveraine,* edited by Michel Aglietta and André Orléan, 129–57. Paris: Odile Jacob.

Aglietta, Michel, and André Orléan. 1982. *La Violence de la monnaie.* Paris: Presses Universitaires de France.

Aglietta, Michel, and André Orléan. 1998. *La monnaie souveraine.* Paris: Odile Jacob.

Aglietta, Michel, and André Orléan. 2002. *La monnaie. Entre violence et confiance.* Paris: Odile Jacob.

Aglietta, Michel, and Sandra Rigot. 2009. *Crise et rénovation de la finance.* Paris: Odile Jacob.

Aglietta, Michel, and Natacha Valla. 2017. *Macroéconomie financière.* Paris: La Découverte.

Aglietta, Michel, and Natacha Valla. 2021. *Le futur de la monnaie.* Paris: Odile Jacob.

Ahamed, Liaquat. 2009. *Lords of Finance.* London: Windmill Books.

Akhtar, Michael Akbar. 1995. "Monetary Policy and Long-Term Interest Rates: A Survey of Empirical Literature." *Contemporary Economic Policy* 13: 110–30.

Akhtar, Mahmūd A., and Howard Howe. 1991. "The Political and Institutional Independence of U.S. Monetary Policy." *Research Paper 9110,* Federal Reserve Bank of New York.

Aldasoro, Iñaki, and Torsten Ehlers. 2018. "Global Liquidity: Changing Instrument and Currency Patterns." *BIS Quarterly Review* 2018: 17–27.

Allen, Roy E. 2016. "Financial globalization since the 1970s." In *Financial Crises and Recession in the Global Economy,* 4th ed., edited by Roy E. Allen, 1–35. Cheltenham: Edward Elgar Publishing.

Allingham, Michael. 2008. "Numeraire." In *The New Palgrave Dictionary of Economics*, edited by Steven N. Durlauf and Lawrence E. Blume, 9670–72. Palgrave Macmillan, London.

Aquanno, Scott. 2009. "US Power and the International Bond Market: Financial Flows and the Construction of Risk Value." In *American Empire and the Political Economy of Global Finance*, edited by Leo Panitch and Martijn Konings, 119–34. Basingstoke: Palgrave Macmillan.

Arestis, Philip, and Malcolm Sawyer. 2006. "The Nature and Role of Monetary Policy When Money Is Endogenous." *Cambridge Journal of Economics* 30 (6): 847–60.

Aristotle. 1996. *The Complete Works: The Revised Oxford Translation*. Princeton, NJ: Princeton University Press.

Arnold, Arthur Z. 1937. *Banks, Credit, and Money in Soviet Russia*. New York: Columbia University Press.

Arnon, Arie. 2011. *Monetary Theory and Policy from Hume and Smith to Wicksell*. Oxford: Oxford University Press.

Arthur, Christopher J. 2005. "Value and Money." In *Marx's Theory of Money*, edited by Fred Moseley, 111–23. London: Palgrave Macmillan.

Asimakopulos, A. 1991. *Keynes's General Theory and Accumulation*. Modern Cambridge Economics Series. Cambridge: Cambridge University Press.

Avdjiev, Stefan, Valentina Bruno, Catherine Koch, and Hyun Song Shin. 2019. "The Dollar Exchange Rate as a Global Risk Factor: Evidence from Investment." *IMF Economic Review* 67 (1): 151–73.

Avdjiev, Stefan, Wenxin Du, Cathérine Koch, and Hyun Song Shin. 2017. "The Dollar, Bank Leverage, and Deviations from Covered Interest Parity." *American Economic Review: Insights* 1 (2): 193–208.

Avdjiev, Stefan, Robert N. McCauley, and Hyun Song Shin. 2015. "Breaking Free of the Triple Coincidence in International Finance." *BIS Working Papers* 524.

Avrane, Patrick. 2015. *Petite psychanalyse de l'argent*. Paris: Presses Universitaires de France.

Baba, Naohiko, Robert N. McCauley, and Srichander Ramaswamy. 2009. "US Dollar Money Market Funds and Non-US Banks." *BIS Quarterly Review* 2009: 65–81.

Backhouse, Roger. 1999. *Keynes: Contemporary Responses to the General Theory*. South Bend, IN: St. Augustine Press.

Bailly, Jean-Luc, and Claude Gnos. 2003. "Définition et intégration de la monnaie: l'apport de la thèse de l'endogénéité." In *Théories monétaires post Keynésiennes*, edited by Pierre Piégay and Louis-Philippe Rochon, 243–58. Paris: Economica.

Barnett, Vincent. 2004. *The Revolutionary Russian Economy, 1890–1940*. London: Routledge.

Baronian, Laurent. 2013. *Marx and Living Labour*. London: Routledge.

Barredo-Zuriarrain, Juan. 2016. "The Inherent Instability of National Monetary Power in the 21st Century: The Triffin Dilemma Revisited." *Research in Political Economy* 30B: 25–52.

Bataille, Adlit Takal, and Jacques Favier. 2017. *Bitcoin, la monnaie acéphale*. Paris: CNRS Éditions.

Battilossi, Stefano. 2000. "Financial Innovation and the Golden Ages of International Banking: 1890–1931 and 1958–81." *Financial History Review* 7 (2): 141–75.

Battilossi, Stefano. 2020. "International Money Markets: Eurocurrencies." In *Handbook of the History of Money and Currency*, edited by Stefano Battilossi, Youssef Cassis, and Kazuhiko Yago, 269–314. Singapore: Springer Verlag.

Baur, Dirk G., and Thomas Dimpfl. 2021. "The Volatility of Bitcoin and Its Role as a Medium of Exchange and a Store of Value." *Empirical Economics* 61: 2663–83.

Baxter, Nevins D. 1968. "Marketability, Default Risk, and Yields on Money Market Instruments." *Journal of Financial and Quantitative Analysis* 3 (1): 75–85.

Baykov, Alexander. 1970. *The Development of the Soviet Economic System: An Essay on the Experience of Planning in the USSR*. Cambridge: Cambridge University Press.

Beckhart, Benjamin H. 1972. *Federal Reserve System*. Atlanta, GA: American Institute of Banking.

Bekerman, Gérard. 1997. *Les euro-dollars*. Paris: Presses Universitaires de France.

Bénassy-Quéré, Agnès, Sophie Béreau, and Valérie Mignon. 2009. "Taux de change d'équilibre: une question d'horizon." *Revue économique* 60 (3): 657–66.

Bensa, Alban, and Wiegratz, Michèle. 1992. "Genèse et nature de la monnaie. Extraits du chapitre 5 de Bernhard Laum, Argent sacré. Analyse historique de l'origine sacrée de l'argent." *Genèses* 8: 60–85.

Bernanke, Ben S. 1995. "The Macroeconomics of the Great Depression: A Comparative Approach." *Journal of Money, Credit and Banking* 27 (1): 1–28.

Bernanke, Ben S. 2015. "Federal Reserve Policy in an International Context." Mundell-Fleming Lecture Presented at the 16th Jacques Polak Annual Research Conference, International Monetary Fund, Washington, DC.

Bernanke, Ben S., and Kevin Carey. 1996. "Nominal Wage Stickiness and Aggregate Supply in the Great Depression." *The Quarterly Journal of Economics* 111 (3): 853–83.

Bernanke, Ben S., and Harold James. 1991. "The Gold Standard, Deflation, and Financial Crisis in the Great Depression: An International Comparison." In *Financial Markets and Financial Crises*, edited by R. Glenn Hubbard, 33–68. Chicago, IL: University of Chicago Press.

Bertaut, Carol C., Stephanie E. Curcuru, and Bastian von Beschwitz. 2021. "The International Role of the U.S. Dollar." FEDS Notes 2021-10-06-2, Board of Governors of the Federal Reserve System (U.S.).

Bertocco, Giancarlo. 2013. "On Keynes's Criticism of the Loanable Funds Theory." *Review of Political Economy* 25 (2): 309–26.

Bettelheim, Charles. 1977. *Les luttes de classes en URSS*, Vol. 2, Paris: Maspero/Seuil.

Bezhanidze, Tinatin. 2020. "Disruption in the Repo Market: A Sign of Systemic Issues." Senior Projects Spring 2020. 307. Accessed June 26, 2022. https://digitalcommons.bard.edu/senproj_s2020/307.

Bibow, Jörg. 1995. "Some Reflections on Keynes's 'Finance Motive' for the Demand for Money." *Cambridge Journal of Economics* 19: 647–66.

Bibow, Jörg. 1998. "On Keynesian Theories of Liquidity Preference." *The Manchester School* 66: 238–73.

Bibow, Jörg. 2000a. "The Loanable Funds Fallacy in Retrospect." *History of Political Economy* 32 (4): 789–832.

Bibow, Jörg. 2000b. "On Exogenous Money and Bank Behaviour: The Pandora's Box Kept Shut in Keynes' Theory of Liquidity Preference?" *The European Journal of the History of Economic Thought* 7 (4): 532–68.

Bibow, Jörg. 2007. "Liquidity Preference Theory." In *A Handbook of Alternative Monetary Economics*, edited by Philip Arestis and Malcolm Sawyer, 328–45. Cheltenham: Edward Elgar Publishing.

Blair, Andrew R. 1961. "The Dollar Shortage in Retrospect." *Review of Social Economy* 19 (2): 166–87.

Blaug, Mark. 1997. *Economic Theory in Retrospect*, 5th ed. Cambridge: Cambridge University Press.

Blinder, Alan S. 1999. *Central Banking in Theory and Practice*. Cambridge: MIT Press.

Bogoslovsky, Evgeny S. 1987. "On the Process of Appearance of Money in Ancient Egypt." *Altorientalische Forschungen* 14 (1–2): 227–36.
Bohannan, Paul. 1955. "Some Principles of Exchange and Investment among the Tiv." *American Anthropologist* 57: 60–70.
Bongenaar, Arminius Cornelius Valentinus Maria. 1999. "Money in the Neo-Babylonian Institutions." In *Trade and Finance in Ancient Mesopotamia*, edited by Jan Gerrit Dercksen, 159–74. Leiden: Nederlands Historisch-Archelogisch Instituut Istanbul.
Bordo, Michael D. 1993. "The Bretton Woods International Monetary System: A Historical Overview." In *A Retrospective on the Bretton Woods System: Lessons for International Monetary Reform*, National Bureau of Economic Research, Inc., 3–108. Chicago, IL: University of Chicago Press.
Bordo, Michael D. 2018. "The Imbalances of the Bretton Woods System 1965 to 1973: U.S. Inflation, The Elephant in the Room." NBER Working Paper No. 25409.
Bordo, Michael D., Michael Edelstein, and Hugh T. Rockoff. 1999. "Was Adherence to the Gold Standard a 'Good Housekeeping Seal of Approval' During the Interwar Period?" NBER Working Paper No. w7186.
Bordo, Michael, Barry Eichengreen, Daniela Klingebiel, Maria Soledad Martinez-Peria, and Andrew K. Rose. 2001. "Is the Crisis Problem Growing More Severe?" *Economic Policy* 16 (32): 53–82.
Bordo Michael, and Harold James. 2009. "Le dollar américain et son rôle dans l'ordre monétaire international." Revue d'économie financière, 94: 171–86.
Bordo, Michael D., Owen F. Humpage, and Anna J. Schwartz. 2014. "The Evolution of the Federal Reserve Swap Lines since 1962." NBER Working Paper No. 20755.
Bordo, Michael D., and John Landon-Lane. 2010. "Exits from Recessions: The U.S. Experience 1920–2007." NBER Working Paper No. w15731.
Bordo, Michael D., and Andrew T. Levin. 2017. "Central Bank Digital Currency and the Future of Monetary Policy." NBER Working Paper No. 23711.
Borio, Claudio and Philip Lowe. 2002. "Asset Prices, Financial and Monetary Stability: Exploring the Nexus." *BIS Working Papers* 114, Bank for International Settlements.
Borneman, Ernest. 1978. *Psychanalyse de l'argent*. Paris: Presses Universitaires de France.
Boyce, Robert W. D. 1987. *British Capitalism at the Crossroads 1919–1932*. Cambridge: Cambridge University Press.
Boyce, Robert. 2009. *The Great Interwar Crisis and the Collapse of Globalization*. Basingstoke: Palgrave.
de Boyer, Jérôme. 1982. "Demande effective et théorie monétaire." *Cahiers d'économie politique* 8: 51–64.
de Boyer des Roches, Jérôme. 1998. "Keynes et le risque de taux d'intérêt de la banque." *Cahiers d'économie politique* 30–31: 105–21.
Boyer, Robert, Mario Dehove, and Dominique Plihon, eds. 2004. "Les Crises financières." Rapport du Conseil d'analyse économique n° 50.
Boz, Emine, Gita Gopinath, and Mikkel Plagborg-Møller. 2017. "Global Trade and the Dollar." NBER Working Paper No. 23988.
Bradley, Xavier, Pierre Piégay, and Sergio Rossi. 2003. "Taux d'intérêt et 'propriétés fondamentales' de la monnaie." In *Théories monétaires post Keynésiennes*, edited by Pierre Piégay and Louis-Philippe Rochon, 226–242. Paris: Economica.
Brainard, Lael. 2019. "Digital Currencies, Stablecoins, and the Evolving Payments Landscape: A Speech at the Future of Money in the Digital Age, Sponsored by the Peterson Institute for International Economics and Princeton." Speech 1095, Board of Governors of the Federal Reserve System (U.S.).
Bransbourg, Gilles. 2015. "Fides in Instrumento Computatorio. The Rise of Digital Currencies." *American Numismatic Society* 1: 39–47.

Bridel, Pascal. 1987. *Cambridge Monetary Thought: Development of Saving-investment Analysis from Marshall to Keynes*. New York: St. Martin's Press.
Bridel, Pascal. 2002. "Patinkin, Walras and the 'Money-in-the-utility-function' Tradition." *European Journal of the History of Economic Thought* 9 (2): 268–92.
Bridel, Pascal. 2014. "Why Is There Money? Or Yet a New Attempt at Solving the Hahn Problem." *Oeconomia* 4 (4): 623–35.
Brown, William Adams Jr. 1940. *The International Gold Standard Re-Interpreted: 1914–1934*. New York: NBER Research Publications.
Broz, J. Lawrence. 1999. "Origins of the Federal Reserve System: International Incentives and the Domestic Free-Rider Problem." *International Organization* 53 (1): 39–70.
Broz, J. Lawrence. 2015. "The Politics of Rescuing the World's Financial System: The Federal Reserve as a Global Lender of Last Resort." *Korean Journal of International Studies* 13 (2): 323–51.
de Brunhoff, Suzanne. 1973. *La politique monétaire. Essai d'interprétation marxiste*. Paris: Presses Universitaires de France.
de Brunhoff, Suzanne. 1976. *Marx on Money*. Translated by Maurice Goldbloom. New York: Urizen Books.
de Brunhoff, Suzanne. 1978. *The State, Capital and Economic Policy*. Translated by Mike Sonenscher. London: Pluto Press.
de Brunhoff, Suzanne. 1979. *Le rapports d'argent*. Paris: Maspero; Grenoble: PUG.
de Brunhoff, Suzanne. 1986. *L'heure du marché*. Paris: Presses Universitaires de France.
de Brunhoff, Suzanne. 1998. "Money, Interest and Finance in Marx's Capital." In *Marxian Economics: A Reappraisal, Essays on Volume III of "Capital"*, edited by Riccardo Bellofiore, 176–88. London: Palgrave Macmillan.
Brunner, Karl, and Allan H. Meltzer. 1971. "The Uses of Money: Money in the Theory of an Exchange Economy." *The American Economic Review* 61 (5): 784–805.
Brunnermeier, Markus K., Harold James, and Jean-Pierre Landau. 2021. "The Digitalization of Money." BIS Working Papers No 941.
Bruno, Valentina, and Hyun Song Shin. 2015. "Cross-Border Banking and Global Liquidity." *Review of Economic Studies* 82 (2): 535–64.
Bruno, Valentina, and Hyun Song Shin. 2020. "Dollar and Exports." BIS Working Papers No 819.
Buchanan, Bonnie G. 2017. *Securitization and the Global Economy: History and Prospects for the Future*. New York: Palgrave Macmillan.
Bukharin, Nikolai I. (1919) 1970. *The Economic Theory of the Leisure Class*. New York: Augustus M. Kelley.
Burn, Gary. 2006. *The Re-Emergence of Global Finance*. London: Palgrave.
Calomiris, Charles, and David Wheelock. 1998. "Was the Great Depression a Watershed for American Monetary Policy?" In *The Defining Moment: The Great Depression and the American Economy in the Twentieth Century*, National Bureau of Economic Research, Inc., 23–65. Chicago, IL: University of Chicago Press.
Calvo, Guillermo A., and Morris Goldstein. 1996. "Crisis Prevention and Crisis Management after Mexico: What Role for the Official Sector?" In *Private Capital Flows to Emerging Markets after the Mexican Crisis*, edited by Guillermo A. Calvo, Morris Goldstein, and Eduard Hochreiter, 233–82.Washington, DC: Institute for International Economics.
Calvo, Guillermo A., Leonardo Leiderman, and Carmen M. Reinhart. 1996. "Inflows of Capital to Developing Countries in the 1990s." *Journal of Economic Perspectives* 10 (2): 123–39.
Calvo, Guillermo A., and Carmen M. Reinhart. 2002. "Fear of Floating." *The Quarterly Journal of Economics* 117 (2): 379–408.

Campbell, Martha. 2002. "The Credit System." In *The Culmination of Capital. Essays on Volume 3 of Marx's Capital*, edited by Martha Campbell and Geert Reuten, 212–27. London: Palgrave Macmillan.

Campbell, Martha. 2004. "The Objectivity of Value versus the Idea of Habitual Action." In *The Constitution of Capital. Essays on Volume 1 of Marx's Capital*, edited by Riccardo Bellofiore and Nicola Taylor, 63–87. London: Palgrave Macmillan.

Cardim de Carvalho, Fernando J. 1996. "Sorting Out the Issues: The Two Debates (1936/37; 1983–86) on Keynes' Finance Motive Revisited." *Revista brasileira de economia* 50 (3): 312–27.

Carr, Edward H. 1954. *The Interregnum, 1923–1924.* New York: Macmillan.

Carr, Edward H. 1958. *Socialism in One Country, 1924–1926.* New York: Macmillan.

Carr, Edward H.1969. *La révolution bolchévique (1917–1923).* Paris: Éditions de Minuit.

Carr, Edward H., and Robert W. Davies. 1969. *Foundations of a Planned Economy, 1926–1929.* New York: Macmillan.

Carré, Emmanuel, and Edwin Le Héron. 2018. "La politique monétaire post-keynésienne." In *L'économie post-keynésienne*, edited by Éric Berr, Virginie Monvoisin, and Jean-François Ponsot, 373–93. Paris: Seuil.

Carré, Emmanuel, and Laurent Le Maux. 2021. "*Dollar Swap Lines* et crédibilité: La réserve fédérale face à la globalisation financière." *Revue française d'histoire économique* 16 (2): 74–97.

Cartapanis, André. 2004. "Le déclenchement des crises de change: qu'avons-nous appris depuis dix ans?" *Économie internationale* 97 (1): 5–48.

Casas, Camila, Federico J. Díez, Gita Gopinath, Pierre-Olivier Gourinchas, and Mikkel Plagborg-Møller. 2016. "Dominant Currency Paradigm." NBER Working Paper No. w22943.

Cassel, Gustav. 1916. "The Present Situation of the Foreign Exchanges." *The Economic Journal* 26 (103): 319–23.

Cassel, Gustav. 1923. "The Restoration of the Gold Standard." *Economica* 9: 171–85.

Cassel, Gustav. 1932. "Monetary Reconstruction." *International Affairs (Royal Institute of International Affairs 1931–1939)* 11 (5): 658–77.

Cassidy, Mark. 1998. "The Development of John Fullarton's Monetary Theory." *The European Journal of the History of Economic Thought* 5 (3): 509–35.

Cassis, Youssef. 2011. *Crises and Opportunities: The Shaping of Modern Finance.* Oxford: Oxford University Press.

de Cecco, Marcello. 1975. *Money and Empire: The International Gold Standard, 1890–1914.* Totowa, NJ: Rowman and Littlefield.

de Cecco, Marcello. 1982. "Inflation and Structural Change in the Euro-Dollar Market." EUI Working Papers, Vol. 23. Florence: European University Institute.

Cencini, Alvaro. 1995. *Monetary Theory. National and International.* London and New York: Routledge.

Cencini, Alvaro. 2003. "Micro, macro et l'analyse du circuit." In *Théories monétaires post-Keynesiennes*, edited by Pierre Piégay and Louis-Philippe Rochon, 209–25. Paris: Economica.

Cencini, Alvaro. 2017. "Introduction: The Research Work and Scientific Legacy of Bernard Schmitt." In *Quantum Macroeconomics: The Legacy of Bernard Schmitt*, edited by Jean-Luc Bailly, Alvaro Cencini, and Sergio Rossi, 1–20. London: Routledge.

Cesaratto, Sergio. 2017. "Initial and Final Finance in the Monetary Circuit and the Theory of Effective Demand." *Metroeconomica* 68 (2): 228–58.

Chang, Roberto, and Andrés Velasco. 1998. "The Asian Liquidity Crisis." FRB Atlanta Working Paper No. 98-11.

Cheng, Jeffrey, and David Wessel. 2020. "What is the Repo Market? And Why Does It Matter?" *Brookings*. Last modified January 28, 2020. https://www.brookings.edu/blog/up-front/2020/01/28/what-is-the-repo-market-and-why-does-it-matter/.

Chesnais, François. 2011. *Les dettes illégitimes. Quand les banques font main basse sur les politiques publiques*. Paris: Raisons d'agir.

Chesnais, Francois. 2016. *Finance Capital Today Corporations and Banks in the Lasting Global Slump*. Leiden: Brill.

Chick, Victoria. 1983. *Macroeconomics after Keynes: A Reconsideration of the General Theory*. Cambridge, MA: MIT Press.

Chick, Victoria. (1986) 1992. "The Evolution of the Banking System and the Theory of Saving, Investment, and Interest." In *On Money, Method and Keynes: Selected Essays*, edited by Philip Arestis and Sheila C. Dow, 193–205. New York: St Martin's Press. Originally published in *Economies et sociétés*, Cahiers de l'IS-MEA (Paris), Serie Monnaie et Production, no. 3.

Chick, Victoria. 2000. "Money and Effective Demand." In *What Is Money?*, edited by John Smithin, 124–38. London: Routledge.

Chick, Victoria, and Sheila Dow. 2002. "Monetary Policy with Endogenous Money and Liquidity Preference: A Nondualistic Treatment." *Journal of Post Keynesian Economics* 24 (4): 587–607.

Chick, Victoria, and Sheila Dow. 2013. "Post-Keynesian Theories of Money and Credit: Conflicts and (Some) Resolutions." In *Theory and Origins*, edited by G. C. Harcourt and Peter Kriesler, 152–67. Vol. 1 of *The Oxford Handbook of Post-Keynesian Economics*. Oxford Handbooks in Economics. Oxford: Oxford University Press (Online).

Chick, Victoria, and Geoff Tily. 2014. "Whatever Happened to Keynes's Monetary Theory?" *Cambridge Journal of Economics* 38 (3): 681–99.

Clark, Peter B., and Ronald R. MacDonald. 1998. "Exchange Rates and Economic Fundamentals: A Methodological Comparison of BEERs and FEERs." IMF Working Paper No. 98/67.

Clastres, Pierre. 1980. *Recherches d'anthropologie politique*. Paris: Seuil.

Clower, R. 1967. "A Reconsideration of the Microfoundations of Monetary Theory." *Economic Inquiry* 6: 1–8.

Cohen, Benjamin J. 1977. *Organizing the World's Money*. New York: Basic Books.

Cohen, Benjamin J. 1998. *The Geography of Money*. Ithaca, NY: Cornell University Press.

Cohen, Benjamin J. 2008. *International Political Economy: An Intellectual History*. Princeton, NJ: Princeton University Press.

Cohen, Benjamin J. 2013. "Currency and State Power." In *Back to Basics: State Power in a Contemporary World*, edited by Martha Finnemore and Judith Goldstein, 159–76. Oxford: Oxford University Press.

Cömert, Hasan. 2012. "Decoupling between the Federal Funds Rate and Long-Term Interest Rates: Decreasing Effectiveness of Monetary Policy in the U.S." Working Paper wp295, Political Economy Research Institute, University of Massachusetts at Amherst.

Committee on the Global Financial System. 2020. "US Dollar Funding: An International Perspective." CGFS Papers No. 65 (BIS).

Coombs, Charles A. 1976. *The Arena of International Finance*. New York: Wiley.

Corsetti, Giancarlo, Paolo Pesenti, and Nouriel Roubini. 1999. "What Caused the Asian Currency and Financial Crisis?" *Japan and the World Economy* 11 (3): 305–73.

Crump, Thomas. 1981. *The Phenomenon of Money*. London: Routledge & Kegan Paul.

Darimon, Alfred. 1856. *La réforme des banques*. Paris: Guillaumin.

D'Arista, Jane. 2009. "The Evolving International Monetary System." *Cambridge Journal of Economics* 33 (4): 633–52.

Dalton, George. 1965. "Primitive Money." *American Anthropologist* 67 (1): 44–65.

Dardot, Pierre, and Christian Laval. 2014. *Commun essai sur la révolution au XXIe siècle*. Paris: La Découverte.

Dardot, Pierre, and Christian Laval. 2017. *The New Way of the World: On Neoliberal Society*. London: Verso.

Daumas, François. 1977. "Le problème de la monnaie dans l'Égypte antique avant Alexandre." *Mélanges de l'école française de Rome* 89 (2): 425–42.

Davidson, Paul. 1972. "Money and the Real World." *The Economic Journal* 82 (325): 101–15.

Davies, Glyn. 1994. *A History of Money from Ancient Times to the Present Day*. Cardiff: University of Wales Press.

Davis, Ann E. 2010. "Marx and the Mixed Economy: Money, Accumulation, and the Role of the State." *Science & Society* 74 (3): 409–28.

Deleidi, M. 2020. "Post-Keynesian Endogenous Money Theory: Horizontalists, Structuralists and the Paradox of Illiquidity." *Metroeconomica* 71: 156–75.

Deleuze, Gilles, and Félix Guattari. 1983. *Anti-Oedipus: Capitalism and Schizophrenia*. Minneapolis: University of Minnesota Press.

DeLong, James Bradford. 1990. "'Liquidation' Cycles: Old-Fashioned Real Business Cycle Theory and the Great Depression." NBER Working Paper No. w3546.

Denizet, Jean. 1971. "Chronique d'une décennie." In *Inflation, Dollar, Euro-Dollar*, edited by Henri Bourguinat, Jean Denizet and François Perroux, 25–103. Paris: Gallimard.

Denizet, Jean. 1977. *La grande inflation. Salaire, intérêt et change*. Paris: Presses Universitaires de France.

Denizet, Jean. 1985. *Le dollar. Histoire du système monétaire international depuis 1945*. Paris: Fayard.

Desai, Radhika. 2013. *Geopolitical Economy: After US Hegemony, Globalization and Empire*. London: Pluto Press.

Desmedt, Ludovic. 2008. "Généalogie d'une monnaie mondiale: aux origines du dollar." In: *L'argent des anthropologues, la monnaie des économistes*, edited by Eveline Baumann, Laurent Bazin, Pepita Ould-Ahmed, Pascale Phelinas, Monique Selim, and Richard Sobel, 269–89. Paris: L'Harmattan.

Diatkine, Sylvie. 1995. *Théories et politiques monétaires*. Paris: A. Colin.Bas du formulaire

Dickson, Peter George Muir. 2013. *The Financial Revolution in England: A Study in the Development of Public Credit, 1688–1756*. Aldershot: Gregg Revivals.

Dobb, Maurice. 1946. *The Studies in the Development of Capitalism*. London: Routledge and Sons.

Dobb, Maurice. 1948. *Soviet Economic Development since 1917*. London: Routledge & Kegan.

Dodd, Nigel. 2014. *The Social life of Money*. Princeton, NJ: Princeton University Press.

Dooley, Michael P., David Folkerts-Landau, and Peter M. Garber. 2003. "An Essay on the Revived Bretton Woods System." NBER Working Paper No. w9971.

Dooley, Michael P., David Folkerts-Landau, and Peter M. Garber. 2004. "The Revived Bretton Woods System." *International Journal of Finance and Economics* 9: 307–13.

Dornbusch, Rudiger. 1976. "Expectations and Exchange Rate Dynamics." *Journal of Political Economy* 84 (6): 1161–76.

Dornbusch, Rudiger. 2001. "A Primer on Emerging Market Crises." NBER Working Papers 8326.

Dornbusch, Rudiger, and Paul Krugman. 1976. "Flexible Exchange Rates in the Short Run." *Brookings Papers on Economic Activity* 7 (3): 537–84.

Dosoo, George, and Peter Gallant. 1992. *The Eurobond Market*. New York: Woodhead-Faulkner.

Dostaler, Gilles. 2009. *Keynes et ses combats (new revised and expanded edition)*. Paris: Albin Michel.

Dow, Sheila. 1997. "Endogenous Money." In *Overview, Extensions, Method and New Developments*, edited by Geoffrey Harcourt and Peter Riach, 43–55. Vol. 2 of *A Second Edition of The General Theory*. London: Routledge.

Dow, Sheila. 2017. "Central banking in the twenty-first century." *Cambridge Journal of Economics*, 41 (6): 1539–1557.

Driver, Rebecca L., and Peter F. Westaway. 2005. "Concepts of Equilibrium Exchange Rates." Bank of England Working Papers 248.

Drummond, Ian. 1987. *The Gold Standard and International Monetary System 1930–1939*. London: Macmillan.

Drunat, Jérôme, Gilles Dufrenot, and Laurent Mathieu. 1994. "Les théories explicatives du taux de change: de Cassel au début des années quatre-vingt." *Revue française d'économie* 9 (3): 53–111.

Duménil, Gérard, and Dominique Lévy. 2004. *Capital Resurgent: Roots of the Neoliberal Revolution*. Cambridge: Harvard University Press.

Duménil, Gérard, and Dominique Lévy. 2018. *Managerial Capitalism*, 1st ed. Chicago: University of Chicago Press.

Duncan, Richard. 2005. *The Dollar Crisis: Causes, Consequences, Cures*. Singapore: J. Wiley & Sons.

Eaton, Jonathan, Mark Gersovitz, and Joseph E. Stiglitz. 1986. "The pure theory of country risk," *European Economic Review*. 30 (3): 481–513.

Edwards, Sebastian. 2017. "Gold, the Brains Trust, and Roosevelt." *History of Political Economy* 49 (1): 1–30.

Eichengreen, Barry. 1990. *Elusive Stability: Essays in the History of International Finance, 1919–1939*. Cambridge: Cambridge University Press.

Eichengreen, Barry. 1992. *Golden Fetters: The Gold Standard and the Great Depression, 1919–1939*. New York: Oxford University Press.

Eichengreen, Barry. 1996. *Globalizing Capital: A History of the International Monetary System*. Princeton, NJ: Princeton University Press.

Eichengreen, Barry. 2000. "The EMS Crisis in Retrospect." NBER Working Paper No. w8035.

Eichengreen, Barry. 2004. "Viewpoint: Understanding the Great Depression." *The Canadian Journal of Economics/Revue Canadienne d'Economique* 37 (1): 1–27.

Eichengreen, Barry. 2007. *Global Imbalances and the Lessons of Bretton Woods*. Cambridge, MA: MIT Press.

Eichengreen Barry. 2008. *Globalizing capital: a history of the international monetary system*. Princeton, NJ: Princeton University Press.

Eichengreen, Barry, and Marc Flandreau. 1997. *The Gold Standard in Theory and History*. London: Routledge.

Eichengreen, Barry, and Marc Flandreau. 2009. "The Rise and Fall of the Dollar (Or When Did the Dollar Replace Sterling as the Leading Reserve Currency?)." *European Review of Economic History* 13 (3): 377–411.

Eichengreen, Barry, and Peter Temin. 2000. "The Gold Standard and the Great Depression." *Contemporary European History* 9 (2): 183–207.

Eichner, Alfred S. 1987. *The Macrodynamics of Advanced Market Economies*. Armonk, NY: M.E. Sharpe.

Einzig, Paul. 1962. *The History of Foreign Exchange*. London: Macmillan.

El-Gamal Mahmoud A. and Amy Myers Jaffe. 2010. *Oil, Dollars, Debt, and Crises: The Global Curse of Black Gold*. Cambridge: Cambridge University Press.

Ellis, Howard S. 1934. *German Monetary Theory, 1905–1933*. Vol. 44 of *Harvard Economic Studies*. Harvard: Harvard University Press.

Elson, Diane, ed. 2015. *Value: The Representation of Labour in Capitalism*. London: Verso Press.

Epstein, Gerald. 2019. *What's Wrong with Modern Money Theory? A Policy Critique*. London: Palgrave Macmillan.

Epstein, Gerald. 2020. "The Empirical and Institutional Limits of Modern Money Theory." *Review of Radical Political Economics* 52 (4): 77–80.

Epstein, Gerald, and Thomas Ferguson. 1984. "Monetary Policy, Loan Liquidation, and Industrial Conflict: The Federal Reserve and the Open Market Operations of 1932." *The Journal of Economic History* 44 (4): 957–83.

Erturk, Korkut A. 2007. "Speculation, Liquidity Preference and Monetary Circulation." In *Handbook of Alternative Monetary Economics*, edited by Philip Arestis and Malcolm Sawyer, 454–70. Cheltenham: Edward Elgar.

Farhi, Emmanuel, Pierre-Olivier Gourinchas, and Hélène Rey. 2011. *Reforming the International Monetary System*. London: Centre for Economic Policy Research.

Febrero, Eladio. 2008. "The Monetization of Profits in a Monetary Circuit Framework." *Review of Political Economy* 20 (1): 111–25.

Feinstein, Charles H., Peter Temin, and Gianni Toniolo. 2008. *The World Economy between the Wars*. New York: Oxford University Press.

Fellner, William. 1956. "Patinkin's Integration of Monetary and Value Theory." *The American Economic Review* 46 (5): 947–55.

Fetter, Frank Whitson. 1965. *Development of British Monetary Orthodoxy, 1797–1875*. Cambridge: Harvard University Press.

Fiebiger, Brett, and Marc Lavoie. 2020. "Helicopter Ben, Monetarism, the New Keynesian Credit View and Loanable Funds." *Journal of Economic Issues* 54 (1): 77–96.

Fiedler, Salomon, Klaus-Jurgen Gern, and Ulrich Stolzenburg. 2019. "The Impact of Digitalisation on the Monetary System." ECON Committee Monetary Dialogue Papers.

Fine, Ben. 1985–86. "Banking Capital and the Theory of Interest." *Science and Society* 49 (4): 387–413.

Fisher, Franklin M. 1983. *Disequilibrium Foundations of Equilibrium Economics*. Cambridge: Cambridge University Press.

Fisher, Irving. 1911. *The Purchasing Power of Money*. New York: The Macmillan Company.

Fisher, Irving. 1933. "The Debt-Deflation Theory of Great Depressions." *Econometrica* 1 (4): 337–57.

Flanders, M. June, and Elhanan Helpman. 1978. "On Exchange Rate Policies for a Small Country." *The Economic Journal* 88 (349): 44–58.

Fleming, Michael J. 2000. "Financial Implications of the Federal Debt Paydown." *Brooking Papers on Economic Activity* 2: 221–51.

Flood, Robert P., and Peter M. Garber. 1984. "Collapsing Exchange Rate Regimes: Some Linear Examples." *Journal of International Economics* 17 (1–2): 1–13.

Fontana, Giuseppe. 2011. "The Role of Money and Interest Rates in the Theory of Monetary Policy: An Attempt at Perspective." *History of Economic Ideas* 19 (3): 113–34.

Fontana, Guiseppe, and Marco Veronese Passarella. 2018. "The Role of Commercial Banks and Financial Intermediaries in the New Consensus Macroeconomics (NCM): A Preliminary and Critical Appraisal of Old and New Models." In *Alternative Approaches in Macroeconomics: Essays in Honour of John McCombie*, edited by Philip Arestis, 77–103. Cham, Switzerland: Palgrave Macmillan.

Forstater, Mathew. 2006. "Tax-Driven Money: Additional Evidence from the History of Economic Thought, Economic History and Economic Policy." In *Complexity, Endogenous Money and Macroeconomic Theory: Essays in Honour of Basil J. Moore*, edited by Mark Setterfield, 202–20. Northampton, MA: Edward Elgar Publishing.

Foucault, Michel. 1998. *The Will to Knowledge*. Vol. 1 of *The History of Sexuality*. London: Penguin Books.

Foucault, Michel. 2008. *The Birth of Biopolitics: Lectures at the Collège de France, 1978–79*. Basingstoke: Palgrave Macmillan.

Foucault, Michel. 2013. *Lectures on the Will to Know: Lectures at the Collège de France 1970–1971 and Oedipal Knowledge*. Basingstoke: Palgrave Macmillan.

Frankel, Jeffrey A. 1984. "Tests of Monetary and Portfolio Balance Models of Exchange Rate Determination." In *Exchange Rate Theory and Practice*, edited by John F. Bilson and Richard C. Marston, 239–60. Chicago, IL: University of Chicago Press.

Frankel, Jeffrey. 2012. "Internationalization of the RMB and Historical Precedents." *Journal of Economic Integration* 27 (3): 329–65.

Frankel, Jeffrey A., and Andrew K. Rose. 1995. "A Panel Project on Purchasing Power Parity: Mean Reversion within and between Countries." NBER Working Paper No. w5006.

Frankel, Jeffrey A., and Andrew K. Rose. 1996. "Currency Crashes in Emerging Markets: An Empirical Treatment." *Journal of International Economics* 41 (3–4): 351–66.

Frenkel, Jacob A. 1976. "A Monetary Approach to the Exchange Rate: Doctrinal Aspects and Empirical Evidence." *The Scandinavian Journal of Economics* 78 (2): 200–24.

Freud, Sigmund. (1909) 1953. "Notes upon a Case of Obsessional Neurosis." In *Two Case Histories: "Little Hans" and the "Rat Man"*, 151–249. Vol. 10 of *The Standard Edition of the Complete Psychological Works of Sigmund Freud*, edited by James Strachey. London: Vintage.

Freud, Sigmund. (1917) 1955. "On Transformations of Instinct as Exemplified in Anal Erotism." In *An Infantile Neurosis and Other Works (1917–1919)*, 125–34. Vol. 17 of *The Standard Edition of the Complete Psychological Works of Sigmund Freud*, edited by James Strachey. London: Vintage.

Friedman, Benjamin M. 1975. "Regulation Q and the Commercial Loan Market in the 1960s." *Journal of Money, Credit and Banking* 7 (3): 277–96.

Friedman, Milton. 1953. "The Case for Flexible Exchange Rates." In *Essays in Positive Economics*, 157–203. Chicago: University of Chicago Press.

Friedman, Milton. 1956. "The Quantity Theory of Money: A Restatement." In *Studies in the Quantity Theory of Money*, edited by Milton Friedman, 3–24. Chicago, IL: University of Chicago Press.

Friedman, Milton. 1959. "The Demand for Money: Some Theoretical and Empirical Results." *Journal of Political Economy* 67 (4): 327–51.

Friedman, Milton. 1961. "The Demand for Money." *Proceedings of the American Philosophical Society* 105 (3): 259–64.

Friedman, Milton. 1992. *Money Mischief: Episodes in Monetary History*. New York: Harcourt Brace Jovanovich.

Friedman, Milton, and Anna J. Schwartz. 1963. *A Monetary History of the United States, 1867–1960*. Princeton, NJ: Princeton University Press.

Fullarton, John. 1845. *On the Regulation of Currencies; Being an Examination of the Principles, on Which It Is Proposed to Restrict, within Certain Fixed Limits, the Future Issues on Credit of the Bank of England, and of the Other Banking Establishments throughout the Country*. London: J. Murray.

Furman, Jason, and Joseph E. Stiglitz. 1998. "Economic Crises: Evidence and Insights from East Asia." *Brookings Papers on Economic Activity* 1998 (2): 1–135.

Gabor, Daniela. 2016. "The (Impossible) Repo Trinity: The Political Economy of Repo Markets." *Review of International Political Economy* 23 (6): 967–1000.

Galbraith, John Kenneth. 1955. *The Great Crash, 1929*. Boston, MA: Houghton Mifflin.

Gallarotti, Giulio M. 1995. *The Anatomy of an International Monetary Regime: The Classical Gold Standard*. Oxford: Oxford University Press.

Garvy, George. 1977. "The Origins and Evolution of the Soviet Banking System: A Historical Perspective." In *Money, Financial Flows, and Credit in the Soviet Union*, edited by George Garvy, 13–35. Cambridge: NBER.

Gerardi, Kristopher S., Harvey S. Rosen, and Paul S. Willen. 2010. "The Impact of Deregulation and Financial Innovation on Consumers: The Case of the Mortgage Market." *The Journal of Finance* 65 (1): 333–60.

Germer, Claus. 2005. "The Commodity Nature of Money in Marx's Theory." In *Marx's Theory of Money: Modern Appraisals*, edited by Fred Moseley, 21–35. London: Palgrave Macmillan.

Ghosh, Atish R., and Mahvash S. Qureshi. 2017. "From Great Depression to Great Recession: An Overview." In *From Great Depression to Great Recession: The Elusive Quest for International Policy Cooperation*, International Monetary Fund, 1–33. Washington, DC: IMF.

Gibeault, Alain. 1989. "Symbolique de l'argent et psychanalyse." *Communications* 50 (1): 51–79.

Giddy, Ian, Gunter Dufey, and Sangkee Min. 1979. "Interest Rates in the U. S. and Eurodollar Markets." *Review of World Economics* 115 (1): 51–67.

Gill, Stephen, and David Law. 1993. "Global Hegemony and the Structural Power of Capital." In *Gramsci, Historical Materialism and International Relations*, edited by Stephen Gill, 1–18. Cambridge: Cambridge University Press.

Gilpin, Robert. 1987. *The Political Economy of International Relations*. Princeton, NJ: Princeton University Press.

Gnos, Claude. 2003. "Circuit Theory as an Explanation of the Complex Real World." In *Modern Theories of Money: The Nature and Role of Money in Capitalist Economies*, edited by Louis-Phillippe Rochon and Sergio Rossi, 322–38. Cheltenham: Edward Elgar Publishing.

Gnos, Claude. 2006. "Accounting Identities: More than Just Bookkeeping Conventions." In *Complexity, Endogenous Money and Macroeconomic Theory: Essays in Honour of Basil J. Moore*, edited by Mark Setterfield, 21–35. Northampton, MA: Edward Elgar Publishing.

Gnos, Claude. 2007. "French Circuit Theory." In *A Handbook of Alternative Monetary Economics*, edited by Philip Arestis and Malcolm Sawyer, 87–104. Cheltenham: Edward Elgar Publishing.

Godley, Wynne, and Marc Lavoie. 2007. *Monetary Economics: An Integrated Approach to Credit, Money, Income, Production, and Wealth*. Basingstoke: Palgrave Macmillan.

Goland, Yurii. 1994. "Currency Regulation in the NEP Period." *Europe-Asia Studies* 46 (8): 1251–96.

Goodfriend, Marvin. 1998. "Eurodollars." In *Instruments of the Money Market*, edited by T. Cook, 48–58. Richmond: Federal Reserve Bank of Richmond.

Gopinath, Gita. 2015. "The International Price System." NBER Working Paper No. 21646.

Gopinath, Gita and Jeremy C. Stein. 2018. "Banking, Trade, and the Making of a Dominant Currency." NBER Working Paper No. w24485.

Gorton, Gary. 2017. "The History and Economics of Safe Assets." *Annual Review of Economics* 9: 547–86.

Gourinchas, Pierre-Olivier, and Hélène Rey. 2007. "From World Banker to World Venture Capitalist: US External Adjustment and the Exorbitant Privilege." In *G7 Current Account Imbalances: Sustainability and Adjustment*, edited by Richard H. Clarida, 11–66 (National Bureau of Economic Research Conference Report). Chicago, IL: University of Chicago Press.

Gourinchas, Pierre-Olivier, Hélène Rey, and Maxime Sauzet. 2019. "The International Monetary and Financial System." NBER Working Paper No. w25782.

Goux, Jean-François. 1987. "La théorie monétaire de la 'finance' chez Keynes: une réinterprétation." *Revue d'économie Politique* 97, (5): 592–612.

Gowan, Peter. 1999. *The Global Gamble: Washington's Faustian Bid for World Dominance.* London: Verso.

Graeber, David. 2011. *Debt: The First 5,000 Years*. Brooklyn, NY: Melville House.

Gray, John. 1848. Lectures on the *Nature and Use of Money*: delivered before the members of the "Edinburgh Philosophical Institution" during the months of February and March. Edinburgh: London: Adam and Charles Black; Longman, Brown, Green and Longmans.

Grandmont, Jean-Michel, and Yves Younes. 1972. "On the Role of Money and the Existence of Monetary Equilibrium." *Review of Economic Studies* 39 (3): 355–72.

Grandpierre, Vérinique. 2010. *Histoire de la Mésopotamie*. Paris: Gallimard.

Graziani, Augusto. 1987. "Keynes's Finance Motive." *Économies et sociétés* 4: 23–42.

Graziani, Augusto. 2003. *The Monetary Theory of Production*. Cambridge: Cambridge University Press.

Green, Jeremy. 2016. Anglo-American Development, the Euromarkets, and the Deeper Origins of Neoliberal Deregulation. *Review of International Studies* 42 (3): 425–49.

Greenberg, Ronald David. 1983. "The Eurodollar Market: The Case for Disclosure." *California Law Review* 71 (5): 1492–515.

Greenspan, Alan. 1997. Remarks by Chairman Alan Greenspan at the *15th Anniversary Conference of the Center for Economic Policy Research* at Stanford University, Stanford, California. https://www.federalreserve.gov/boarddocs/speeches/19970905.htm.

Greenspan, Alan. 2008. *The Age of Turbulence: Adventures in a New World*. Waterville, ME: Thorndike Press.

Greider, William. 1987. *Secrets of the Temple: How the Federal Reserve Runs the Country.* New York: Simon & Schuster.

Grin, Gilles. 1999. "L'évolution du système monétaire international dans les années 1960: les positions des économistes Robert Triffin et Jacques Rueff." *Relations internationales* 100: 377–92.

Gumbau-Brisa, Fabia, and Catherine L. Mann. 2009. "Reviving Mortgage Securitization: Lessons from the Brady Plan and Duration Analysis." FRB of Boston Public Policy Discussion Paper No. 09-3.

Guttmann, Robert. 1994. *How credit-money shapes the economy: the United States in a global system*. Armonk , NY: M.E. Sharpe.

Guttmann, Robert. 2022. *Multi-Polar Capitalism: The End of the Dollar Standard*. London: Palgrave Macmillan.

Guzzini, Stefano. 1993. "Structural Power: The Limits of Neorealist Power Analysis." *International Organization* 47 (3): 443–78.

Hahn, Frank. 1965. "On Some Problems of Proving the Existence of an Equilibrium in a Monetary Economy." In *Theory of Interest Rates*, edited by James Tobin, F. H. Hahn, and F. P. R. Brechling. London: Macmillan.

Halaburda, Hanna, Miklos Sarvary, and Guillaume Haeringer. 2022. "Future Full of Possibilities." In *Beyond Bitcoin: The Economics of Digital Currencies and Blockchain Technologies,* edited by Hanna Halaburda, Miklos Sarvary, and Guillaume Haeringer, 197–99. Cham: Palgrave Macmillan.

Hamilton, James D. 1988. "Role of the International Gold Standard in Propagating the Great Depression." *Contemporary Economic Policy* 6: 67–89.

Hartmann, Philip. 2003. *Currency Competition and Foreign Exchange Markets.* Cambridge: Cambridge University Press.

Harvey, David. 2005. *A Brief History of Neoliberalism.* New York: Oxford University Press.

von Hayek, Friedrich A. 2010. *The Road to Serfdom.* London: Routledge.

von Hayek, Friedrich A. 2013. *Law, Legislation and Liberty: A New Statement of the Liberal Principles of Justice and Political Economy.* London: Routledge.

He, Dong, and Robert N. McCauley. 2012. "Eurodollar Banking and Currency Internationalisation." *BIS Quarterly Review* June 2012: 33–46.

Hein, Eckhard. 2006. "Money, Interest and Capital Accumulation in Karl Marx's Economics: A Monetary Interpretation and Some Similarities to Post-Keynesian Approaches." *The European Journal of the History of Economic Thought* 13 (1): 113–40.

Heinsohn, Gunnar, and Otto Steiger. 2000. "The Property Theory of Interest and Money." In *What is Money?,* edited by John Smithin, 67–100. London: Routledge.

Helfferich, Karl. 1927. *Money.* Translated by Louis Enfield. New York: Adelphi.

Helleiner, Eric. 1994. *The States and the Reemergence of Global Finance. From Bretton Woods to the 1990s.* Ithaca and London: Cornell University Press.

Helleiner, Eric. 1995. "Explaining the Globalization of Financial Markets: Bringing States Back In." *Review of International Political Economy* 2 (2): 315–41.

Helleiner, Eric. 2005. "Structural Power in International Monetary Relations." EUI RSCAS, 2005/10.

Helleiner, Eric. 2016. "Still an Extraordinary Power after All These Years: US and the Global Financial Crisis of 2008." In *Susan Strange and the Future of Global Political Economy: Power, Control and Transformation,* edited by Randall Germain, 93–108. London: Routledge.

Henry, John F. 2004. "The Social Origins of Money: The Case of Egypt." In *Credit and State Theories of Money: The Contributions of A. Mitchell Innes,* edited by L. Randall Wray, 70–98. Cheltenham: Edward Elgar Publishing.

Hicks, John. 1935. "A Suggestion for Simplifying the Theory of Money." *Economica* 2 (5): 1–19.

Hicks, John. 1937. "Mr. Keynes and the 'Classics'; A Suggested Interpretation." *Econometrica* 5 (2): 147–59.

Hicks, John. 1967. *Critical Essays on Monetary Theory.* Oxford: Oxford University Press.

Hicks, John. 1989. *A Market Theory of Money.* Oxford: Clarendon Press.

Hilferding, Rudolf. (1910) 1981. *Finance Capital.* London: Routledge & Kegan Paul.

Hitchcock, William I. 2010. "The Marshall Plan and the Creation of the West." In *The Cambridge History of the Cold War* edited by Melvyn P. Leffler and Odd Arne Westad, 154–74. New York and London: Cambridge University Press.

Hobbes, Thomas. (1651) 1998. *Leviathan.* Oxford: Oxford University.

Hobson, John M., and Leonard Seabrooke. 2009. "Everyday International Political Economy." In *Routledge Handbook of International Political Economy (IPE),* edited by Mark Blyth, 290–306. London: Routledge.

Howells, Peter. 2007. "The Endogeneity of Money: Empirical Evidence." In *A Handbook of Alternative Monetary Economics,* edited by Philip Arestis and Malcolm Sawyer, 134–78. Cheltenham: Edward Elgar Publishing.

Hubbard, Leonard E. 1936. *Soviet Money and Finance*. London: Macmillan.

Hudson, Michaël. 2003. *Super Imperialism: The Origin and Fundamentals of U.S. Dominance. London*: Pluto Press.

Humphrey, Thomas M. 1978. "The Monetary Approach to Exchange Rates: Its Historical Evolution and Role in Policy Debates." *Economic Review, Federal Reserve Bank of Richmond* 64 (July): 2–9.

Hyman, Louis. 2010. "American Debt, Global Capital: The Policy Origins of Securitization." In *The Shock of the Global. The 1970s in Perspective*, edited by Niall Ferguson, Erez Manela, and Daniel J. Sargent, 128–42. London: Belknap Press.

Ilzetzki, Ethan, Carmen M. Reinhart, and Kenneth S. Rogoff. 2017. "Exchange Arrangements Entering the 21st Century: Which Anchor Will Hold?" NBER Working Paper No. 23134.

Ingham, Geoffrey. 2000. "Babylonian Madness: On the Historical and Sociological Origins of Money." In *What Is Money?*, edited by John Smithin, 16–41. London/New York: Routledge.

Ingham, Geoffrey. 2002. "New Monetary Spaces?" In *The Future of Money*, OECD, 139–64. Paris: OECD.

Ingham, Geoffrey. 2004a. *The Nature of Money*. Malden, MA: Polity Press.

Ingham, Geoffrey. 2004b. "The Emergence of Capitalist Credit Money." In *Credit and State Theories of Money: The Contributions of A. Mitchell Innes*, edited by L. Randall Wray, 173–222. Cheltenham: Edward Elgar Publishing.

Ito, Hiro, and Robert N. McCauley. 2018. "A Key Currency View of Global Imbalances." BIS Working Papers No. 762.

Ivanova, Maria N. 2013. "The Dollar as World Money." *Science & Society* 77 (1): 44–71.

James, Harold. 1996. *International Monetary Cooperation since Bretton Woods*. Washington, DC: International Monetary Fund.

James, Harold. 2017. "Learning Lessons from Previous Crises: The Capital Account and the Current Account." In *From Great Depression to Great Recession*, edited by Atish R. Ghosh and Mahvash S. Qureshi, 37–55. Washington, DC: International Monetary Fund.

Jeanne, Olivier. 2000. *Currency Crises: A Perspective on Recent Theoretical Developments*. Special Papers in International Economics No. 20, International Finance Section, Princeton University.

Jeanne, Olivier. 2003. "Comprendre les crises financières internationals." *Revue d'Économie Financière* 70 (1): 23–31.

Jespersen, Jesper. 2009. "Bridging the Gap between Monetary Circuit Theory and Post-Keynesian Monetary Theory." In *The Political Economy of Monetary Circuits*, edited by Jean-François Ponsot and Sergio Rossi, 21–35. London: Palgrave Macmillan.

Jevons, William Stanley. (1871) 1965. *Theory of Political Economy*, 5th ed. New York: August M. Kelley.

Jiang, Zhengyang, Arvind Krishnamurthy, and Hanno Lustig. 2020. "Dollar Safety and the Global Financial Cycle." NBER Working Paper No. 27682.

Johnson, Harry G. 1951. "Some Cambridge Controversies in Monetary Theory." *Review of Economic Studies* 19 (2): 90–104.

Johnson, Harry G. 1969. "The Case for Flexible Exchange Rates, 1969." *Federal Reserve Bank of St. Louis Review* 51 (June): 12–24.

Joly, Hervé, Céline Prigent, and Nicolas Sobczak. 1996. "Le taux de change réel d'équilibre: une introduction." *Économie & prévision* 123 (2): 1–21.

Junne, Gerd. 1973. "Euromoney, Multinational Corporations, and the Nation State." *Instant Research on Peace and Violence* 3 (2): 74–83.

Jursa, Michael. 2010. *Aspects of the Economic History of Babylonia in the First Millennium BC*. Münster: Ugarit-Verlag.

Kadochnikov, Denis V. 2013. "Gustav Cassel's Purchasing Power Parity Doctrine in the Context of His Views on International Economic Policy Coordination." *The European Journal of the History of Economic Thought* 20 (6): 1101–21.

Kahn, Richard F. 1954. "Some Notes on Liquidity Preference." *The Manchester School* 22: 229–57.

Kahn, Richard F. 1958. "Memorandum of evidence submitted to the Radcliffe Committee (May 27)." In *Selected Essays on Employment and Growth*, 124–152, Cambridge: Cambridge University Press.

Kaldor, Nicholas. 1960. "Keynes' Theory of the Own Rates of Interest." In *Essays on Economic Stability and Growth. Collected Economic Essays by Nicholas Kaldor*, 59–74. London: Duckworth.

Kamin, Steven B., Shawna L. Samuel, and John W. Schindler. 2001. "The Contribution of Domestic and External Factors to Emerging Market Devaluation Crises: An Early Warning Systems Approach." International Finance Discussion Papers 711, Board of Governors of the Federal Reserve System (U.S.).

Keohane, Robert O. 1984. *After Hegemony: Cooperation and Discord in the World Political Economy*. Princeton, NJ: Princeton University Press.

Keohane, Robert O. 2000. "Foreword." In *Strange Power: Shaping the Parameters of International Relations and International Political Economy*, edited by Thomas C. Lawton, James N. Rosenau and Amy C. Verdun, ix–xv. Aldershot, UK: Ashgate.

Keynes, John Maynard. (1923) 2013. *A Tract on Monetary Reform*. Vol. 4 of *The Collected Writings of John Maynard Keynes*. Cambridge: Cambridge University Press for the Royal Economic Society.

Keynes, John Maynard. 1930. *The Pure Theory of Money*. Vol. 1 of *A Treatise on Money*. Vol. 5 of *The Collected Writings of John Maynard Keynes*. London: Macmillan.

Keynes, John Maynard. (1936) 1993. *The General Theory of Employment, Interest and Money*. Vol. 7 of *The Collected Writings of John Maynard Keynes*, edited by Elizabeth Johnson and Donald Moggridge. London: Macmillan for the Royal Economic Society.

Keynes, John Maynard. 1937a. "Alternative Theories of the Rate of Interest." *Economic Journal* 47 (June): 241–52.

Keynes, John Maynard. 1937b. "The Ex-ante Theory of the Rate of Interest." *Economic Journal* 47 (December): 663–69.

Keynes, John Maynard. 1938. "Mr Keynes and Finance. Comment." *Economic Journal* 48 (190): 318–22.

Keynes, John Maynard. (1942) 1980. "Proposals for an International Clearing Union." In *Activities 1940–1944: Shaping the Post-War World: The Clearing Union*, edited by Donald Moggridge, 168–96. Vol. 25 of *The Collected Writings of John Maynard Keynes*. London: Macmillan.

Keynes, John Maynard. 1973a. *The General Theory and After. Part 1: Preparation*. Vol. 13 of *The Collected Writings of John Maynard Keynes*, edited by Donald Moggridge. London: Macmillan for the Royal Economic Society.

Keynes, John Maynard. 1973b. *The General Theory and After. Part 2: Defence and Development*. Vol. 14 of *The Collected Writings of John Maynard Keynes*, edited by Donald Moggridge. London: Macmillan for the Royal Economic Society.

Kindleberger, Charles P. 1973. *The World in Depression, 1929–1939*. Berkeley: University of California Press.

Kindleberger, Charles P. 1984. *A Financial History of Western Europe*. London: Allen & Unwin.

Kirchner, Stephen. 2019. "The 'Reserve Currency' Myth: The US Dollar's Current and Future Role in the World Economy." United States Studies Centre at the University of Sydney. Accessed June 26, 2022. https://assets.realclear.com/files/2019/11/1485_dollar.pdf.

Kirshner, Jonathan. 2014. "Same as It Ever Was? Continuity and Change in the International Monetary System." *Review of International Political Economy* 21 (5): 1007–16.

Kiyotaki, Nobuhiro, and Randall Wright. 1989. "On Money as a Medium of Exchange." *Journal of Political Economy* 97 (4): 927–54.

Klopstock, Fred H. 1968. *The Euro-Dollar Market: Some Unresolved Issues*. Essays in International Finance, No. 65. Princeton, NJ: International Finance Section, Princeton University.

Klossowski, Pierre. 2017. *Living Currency: Followed by Sade and Fourier*. London and New York: Bloomsbury Academic.

Knapp, George Friedrich. 1924. *The State Theory of Money*. London: Macmillan and Company.

Kojima, Kiyoshi. 1951. "Ricardo's Theory of International Balance of Payments Equilibrium." *The Annals of the Hitotsubashi Academy* 2 (1): 76–92.

Konings, Martijn. 2009. "American Finance and Empire in Historical Perspective." In *American Empire and the Political Economy of Global Finance: International Political Economy*, edited by Leo Panitch and Martijn Konings, 48–68. Basingstoke: Palgrave Macmillan.

Konings, Martijn. 2011. *The Development of American Finance*. Cambridge: Cambridge University Press.

Krasner, Stephen D. 1983. *International Regimes*. Ithaca, NY: Cornell University Press.

Kregel, Jan. 2019. "MMT: The Wrong Answer to the Wrong Question." *Real-World Economics Review* 89 (1): 85–96.

Krippner, Greta R. 2011. *Capitalizing on Crisis: The Political Origins of the Rise of Finance*. Cambridge, MA: Harvard University Press.

Krishnamurthy, Arvind, and Annette Vissing-Jorgensen. 2012. "The Aggregate Demand for Treasury Debt." *Journal of Political Economy* 120 (2): 233–67.

Krugman, Paul. 1979. "A Model of Balance-of-Payments Crises." *Journal of Money, Credit and Banking* 11 (3): 311–25.

Krugman, Paul. 1991. "Increasing Returns and Economic Geography." *Journal of Political Economy* 99 (3): 483–99.

Krugman, Paul. 1995. "Dutch Tulips and Emerging." Markets. *Foreign Affairs*. 74 *(4)*: 28–44.

Krugman, Paul. 1996. "Are Currency Crises Self-Fulfilling?" *NBER Macroeconomics Annual* 11: 345–407.

Krugman, Paul. 1998. "What Happened to Asia?" Mimeo, MIT. Accessed June 26, 2022. http://web.mit.edu/krugman/www/DISINTER.html.

Krugman, Paul. 2000. "Crises: The Price of Globalization?" In *Global Economic Integration: Opportunities and Challenges: A Symposium*, 75–106. Kansas City, MO: Federal Reserve Bank of Kansas City. New York: Books for Business.

Krugman, Paul. 2001a. "Analytical Afterthoughts on the Asian Crisis." In *Economic Theory, Dynamics and Markets: Essays in Honor of Ryuzo Sato*, edited by Takashi Negishi, Rama V. Ramachandran, and Kazuo Mino, 243–55. Vol. 5 of *Research Monographs in Japan–U.S. Business and Economics*. New York: Springer.

Krugman, Paul. 2001b. "Could've Been Worse." *New York Times*, December 28, 2001. https://www.nytimes.com/2001/12/28/opinion/could-ve-been-worse.html.

Krugman, Paul. 2002. "Dubya's Double Dip?" *New York Times*, August 2, 2002. https://www.nytimes.com/2002/08/02/opinion/dubya-s-double-dip.html.

Laidler, David E. W. 1991. *The Golden Age of the Quantity Theory*. Princeton, NJ: Princeton University Press.

Laidler, David, and Rowe, Nicholas, 1980. "Georg Simmel's Philosophy of Money: A Review Article for Economists." *Journal of Economic Literature* 18 (1): 97–105.

Lapavitsas, Costas. 2017. *Marxist Monetary Theory*. Leiden: Brill.

Lavoie, Marc. 1987. "Monnaie et production: une synthèse de la théorie du circuit." *Economie et sociétés, monnaie et production* 9: 65–101.

Lavoie, Marc. 1996. "Horizontalism, Structuralism, Liquidity Preference and the Principle of Increasing Risk." *Scottish Journal of Political Economy* 43: 275–300.

Lavoie, Marc. 2006. "A Post-Keynesian Amendment to the New Consensus on Monetary Policy." *Metroeconomica* 57 (2): 165–92.

Lavoie, Marc. 2013a. "Post-Keynesian Monetary Economics, Godley-Like." In *The Oxford Handbook of Post-Keynesian Economics, Volume 1: Theory and Origins*, edited by G. C. Harcourt and Peter Kriesler, 203–17. New York: Oxford University Press.

Lavoie, Marc. 2013b. "The Monetary and Fiscal Nexus of Neo-Chartalism: A Friendly Critique." *Journal of Economic Issues* 47 (1): 1–32.

Lavoie, Marc. 2014. *Post-Keynesian Economics: New Foundations*. Cheltenham: Edward Elgar Publishing.

Lavoie, Marc. 2019. "Modern Monetary Theory and Post-Keynesian Economics." *Real-World Economics Review* 89 (1): 97–108.

Le Maux, Laurent. 2012. "The Banking School and the Law of Reflux in General." *History of Political Economy* 44 (4): 595–618.

Le Rider, Georges. 2001. *La naissance de la monnaie: pratiques monétaires de l'Orient ancien*. Paris: Presses Universitaires de France.

LeBor, Adam. 2014. *Tower of Basel: The Shadowy History of the Secret Bank that Runs the World*. New York: PublicAffairs.

Lehner, Markus. 2010. "Marx, Money and Modern Finance Capital." In *Marx, Money and the Modern World. Finance Capital and Imperialism Today*, Fifth International, 53–128.

Lenin, Vladimir Ilitch. (1917) 1972. "Can the Bolsheviks Retain State Power?" In *September 1917–February 1918*, 87–136. Volume 26 in *Collected Works*. Moscow: Progress Publishers.

Lévi-Strauss, Claude. 1969. *The Elementary Structures of Kinship*. Boston: Beacon Press. Levy Economics Institute.

Lichtenstein. Cynthia C. 1995. "The Mexican Crisis: Who Should Be a Country's Lender of Last Resort?" *Fordham International Law Journal* 18 (5): 1769–77.

Linhart, Robert 2017. "Pour une théorie concrète de la transition: Pratique politique des blochéviks au pouvoir." Accessed June 27, 2022. http://revueperiode.net/pour-une-theorie-concrete-de-la-transition-pratique-politique-des-bolcheviks-au-pouvoir/.

Logan, Francis D., William J. Mahoney, David R. Slade, and Harry E. White. 1986. "The Securitization of U.S. Bank Activities in the Eurodollar Market." *North Carolina Journal of International International Law* 11 (3): 539–82.

Lordon, Frédéric, and André Orléan. 2006. "Genèse de l'état et genèse de la monnaie: le modèle de la potentia multitudinis." RR Working Paper n° 2006-1. Série MF.

Lutz, Friedrich A. 1938. "The Outcome of the Saving-Investment Discussion." *The Quarterly Journal of Economics* 52 (4): 588–614.

Maes, Ivo. 2013. "On the Origins of the Triffin Dilemma." *The European Journal of the History of Economic Thought* 20 (6): 1122–50.

Manning, Joseph G. 2013. "Money, Ancient near East and Pharaonic Egypt." In *The Encyclopedia of Ancient History*, edited by Roger S. Bagnall, Kai Brodersen, Craige B. Champion, Andrew Erskine and Sabine R. Huebner, 4574–76. Malden, MA: Wiley-Blackwell.

Marcuse, Herbert. 1955. *Eros and Civilization: A Philosophical Inquiry into Freud*. Boston: Beacon Press.

Marcuzzo, Maria Christina. 2001. "Sraffa and Cambridge Economics, 1928–1931." In *Piero Sraffa's Political Economy: A Centenary Estimate*, edited by Terenzio Cozzi and Roberto Marchionatti, 81–99. London: Routledge.

Marie, Henry Gérard. 2009. "La lente et irrésistible ascension du dollar des États-Unis au statut de monnaie internationale (1914–1958)." In: *Revue d'économie financière* 94: 21–54.

Marie, Jean-Jacques. 2011. *Lénine: La révolution permanente*. Paris: Payot.

Markham, Jerry W. 2002. *From J. P. Morgan to the Institutional Investor (1900–1970)*. Vol. 2 of *A Financial History of the United States*. Armonk, NY, and London: M.E. Sharpe.

Markham, Jerry W. 2002b. *A Financial History of the United States*, Volume 3. Armonk, NY, and London: M.E. Sharpe.

Marshall, Alfred. 1923. *Money, Credit and Commerce*. London: Macmillan & Co.

Marshall, Alfred. 1996. *Official Papers of Alfred Marshall: A Supplement*, edited by Peter Groenewegen. Cambridge: Cambridge University Press.

Marty, Éric. 2011. *Pourquoi le XXe siècle a-t-il pris Sade au sérieux?* Paris: Seuil.Bas du formulaire.

Marx, Karl. (1844) 1975. *Marx and Engels: 1843–1844*. Vol. 3 of *Collected Works*. London: Lawrence & Wishart.

Marx, Karl. (1852) 1979. *The Eighteenth Brumaire of Louis Bonaparte*. Vol. 11 of *Collected Works*. London: Lawrence and Wishart.

Marx, Karl. (1859) 1987. *A Contribution to the Critique of Political Economy*. Vol. 29 of *Collected Works*. London: International Publishers.

Marx, Karl. (1861–63) 1989. *Economic manuscripts of 1861–1863*. Vol. 32 of *Collected Works*. London: Lawrence & Wishart.

Marx, Karl. (1867a) 1996. *Capital, Volume 1*. Vol. 35 of *Collected Works*. London: International Publishers.

Marx, Karl. (1867b) 1962. *Das Kapital*. Volume 23 of *Werke*. Berlin: Dietz.

Marx, Karl. 1887. *Capital. A Critique of Political Economy*, Volume I. Moscow: Progress Publishers.

Marx, Karl. (1857–58) 1986. *Outlines of the Critique of Political Economy I (Grundrisse)* Vol. 28 of *Collected Works*. London: Lawrence & Wishart.

Marx, Karl. (1894) 1998. *Capital, Vol. III*. Vol. 37 of *Collected Works*. London: Lawrence & Wishart.

Mason, David L. 2004. *From Buildings and Loans to Bail-Outs: A History of the American Savings and Loan Industry, 1831–1995*. Cambridge: Cambridge University Press.

Masson, Paul R. 1999. "Multiple Equilibria, Contagion, and the Emerging Market Crises." IMF Working Paper No. 99/164.

Matthews, Peter Hans. 1996. "The Modern Foundations of Marx's Monetary Economics." *The European Journal of the History of Economic Thought* 3 (1): 61–83.

Mauss, Marcel, 1990. *The Gift: The Form and Reason for Exchange in Archaic Societies*. Translated by W. D. Halls. London: Routledge.

McCauley, Robert N. 2019. "Safe Assets: Made, Not Just Born." BIS Working Papers No 769.

McCauley, Robert N., and Catherine R. Schenk. 2020. "Central Bank Swaps Then and Now: Swaps and Dollar Liquidity in the 1960s." BIS Working Paper No. 851.

McDowell, Daniel. 2017. *Brother, Can You Spare a Billion? The United States, the IMF, and the International Lender of Last Resort.* New York: Oxford University Press.
McKinnon, Ronald. 1982. "Currency Substitution and Instability in the World Dollar Standard." *American Economic Review* 72 (3): 320–33.
McKinnon, Ronald. 2001. "The International Dollar Standard and the Sustainability of the U.S. Current Account Deficit." *Brookings Papers on Economic Activity* 2001 (1): 227–39.
McKinnon, Ronald. 2010. "Rehabilitating the Unloved Dollar Standard." *Asian-Pacific Economic Literature* 24 (2): 1–18.
McKinnon, Ronald. 2013. *The Unloved Dollar Standard from Bretton Woods to the Rise of China.* New York: Oxford University Press.
Mehra, Yash P. 1996. "Monetary Policy and Long-Term Interest Rates." *FRB Richmond Economic Quarterly* 82 (3): 27–49.
Mehrling, Perry. 2002. "Economists and the Fed: Beginnings." *Journal of Economic Perspectives* 16 (4): 207–18.
Mehrling, Perry. 2012. "The Inherent Hierarchy of Money." In *Social Fairness and Economics: Economic Essays in the Spirit of Duncan Foley*, edited by Lance Taylor, Armon Rezai, and Thomas Michl, 394–404. Abingdon: Routledge.
Mehrling, Perry. 2015. "Elasticity and Discipline in the Global Swap Network." *International Journal of Political Economy* 44 (4): 311–24.
Mehrling, Perry, Zoltan Pozsar, James Sweeney, and Daniel H. Neilson. 2013. "Bagehot Was a Shadow Banker: Shadow Banking, Central Banking, and the Future of Global Finance." In *Shadow Banking Within and Across Borders*, edited by Stijn Claessens, Douglas D. Evanoff, and George G. Kaufman. Singapore: World Scientific Publishing Company.
Meltzer, Allan H. 1988. *Keynes's Monetary Theory: A Different Interpretation.* Cambridge, MA: Cambridge University Press.
Meltzer, Allan H. 2002. *A History of the Federal Reserve, Volume 1: 1913–1951.* Chicago: University of Chicago Press.
Mendez, Julien, and Christian Tutin. 2010. "De la crise bancaire à la régulation: l'expérience américaine de 1907." *L'Économie politique* 48: 42–63.
Menger, Carl. (1871) 1981. *Principles of Economics.* Translated by J. Dingwall and B. F. Hoselitz, with an introduction by Friedrich A. Hayek. New York: New York University Press.
Menger, Carl. 1892. "On the Origin of Money." Translated by C.A. Foley. *Economic Journal* 2 (6): 239–55.
Messori, Marcello. 1997. "The Theory of Value without Commodity Money?" *International Journal of Political Economy* 27 (2): 51–96.
Michalet, Charles-Albert. 2002. *Qu'est-ce que la mondialisation?* Paris: La Découverte.
Michie, Ranald C. 2006. *The Global Securities Market: A History.* Oxford: Oxford University Press.
Miles, Marc A. 1978. "Currency Substitution, Flexible Exchange Rates, and Monetary Independence." *The American Economic Review* 68 (3): 428–36.
Minsky, Hyman. 1964. "Financial Crisis, Financial Systems, and the Performance of the Economy." In *Private Capital Markets*, Commission on Money and Credit Research Study, 173–380. Englewood Cliffs: Prentice Hall.
Minsky, Hyman. 1967. "Money, Other Financial Variables and Aggregate Demand in the Short Run." In *Monetary Process and Policy: A Symposium*, edited by G. Horwich, 265–94. Homewood, IL: Irwin.
Minsky, Hyman. 1975. *John Maynard Keynes.* New York: McGraw-Hill.

Minsky, Hyman. 1986. *Stabilizing an Unstable Economy*. New Haven, CT: Yale University Press.

Mishra, Deepak, Poonam Gupta, and Ratna Sahay. 2003. "Output Response to Currency Crises." IMF Working Papers 2003/230.

Mitchell, William F. 1998. "The Buffer Stock Employment Model and the Path to Full Employment." *Journal of Economic Issues* 32 (2): 547–55.

Monvoisin, Virginie, and Louis-Philippe Rochon. 2018. "La monnaie endogène et la question du financement de l'économie." In *L'économie postkeynésienne en théorie et en pratique* edited by Éric Berr, Virginie Monvoisin, and Jean-François Ponsot, 165–81. Paris: Le Seuil.

Moore, Basil J. 1988. *Horizontalists and Verticalists: The Macroeconomics of Credit and Money*. Cambridge: Cambridge University Press.

Moore, Basil J. 2001. "Some Reflections on Endogenous Money." In *Credit, Interest Rates and the Open Economy: Essays on Horizontalism*, edited by Louis-Philippe Rochon and Matias Vernengo, 11–30. Cheltenham and Northampton, MA: Edward Elgar Publishing.

Moore, Basil J. 2003. "L'endogénéité de l'offre de monnaie: fixe-t-on le prix ou la quantité des réserves?" In *Théories monétaires post keynésiennes*, edited by Pierre Piégay and Louis-Philippe Rochon, 41–51. Paris: Economica.

Moran, Michael. 1991. *The Politics of the Financial Services Revolution: The USA, UK, and Japan*. Basingstoke: Macmillan.

Moreno Garcià, Juan Carlos. 2014. "Penser l'économie pharaonique." *Annales. Histoire, Sciences Sociales* 69 (1): 7–38.

Mosler, Warren. 1997. "Full Employment and Price Stability." *Journal of Post Keynesian Economics* 20 (2): 167–82.

Mouré, Kenneth. 2006. "La politique monétaire et la tyrannie de l'or pendant les années trente." In *L'économie française dans la compétition internationale au XXe siècle,* edited by Maurice Lévy-Leboyer, 169–96. Paris: Institut de la gestion publique et du développement économique.

Mullin, John. 2020. "The Repo Market is Changing (And What Is a Repo, Anyway?)" *Econ Focus* (1): 14–17.

Murau, Steffen. 2018. "Offshore Dollar Creation and the Emergence of the Post-2008 International Monetary System." IASS Discussion Paper.

Murau, Steffen, Joe Rini, and Armin Haas. 2020. "The Evolution of the Offshore US-Dollar System: Past, Present and Four Possible Futures." *Journal of Institutional Economics* 16 (6): 767–83.

Musacchio, Aldo. 2012. "Mexico's Financial Crisis of 1994–1995." Harvard Business School Working Paper No. 12–101.

Myers, Margaret G. 1931. *The New York Money Market*. New York: Columbia University Press.

Narsey, Wadan. 2016. *British Imperialism and the Making of Colonial Currency Systems*. Basingstoke: Palgrave Macmillan.

Neilson, Daniel. 2019. *Minsky*. Cambridge: Polity Press.

Nell, Edward J. 1986. "On Monetary Circulation and the Rate of Exploitation." *Thames Papers in Political Economy*, Summer: 1–36.

Nell, Edward J. 2002. "On Realizing Profits in Money." *Review of Radical Political Economy* 14 (4): 519–30.

Nelson, Anitra. 2005. "Marx's Objections to Credit Theories of Money." In *Marx's Theory of Money: Modern Appraisals*, edited by Fred Moseley, 65–77. London: Palgrave Macmillan.

Newstadt, Eric. 2009. "Neoliberalism and the Federal Reserve." In *American Empire and the Political Economy of Global Finance*, edited by Leo Panitch and Martijn Konings, 90–118. Basingstoke: Palgrave Macmillan.

Niehans, Jürg. 1987. "Classical Monetary Theory, New and Old." *Journal of Money, Credit and Banking* 19 (4): 409–24.

Niveau, Maurice, and Yves Crozet. 2010. *Histoire des faits économiques contemporains*. Paris: Presses Universitaires de France.

Norel, Philippe. 1995. "La financiarisation du change." Les études du CERI, n°9.

Norrlof, Carla, 2014. "Dollar Hegemony: A Power Analysis." *Review of International Political Economy* 21 (5): 1042–70.

Norrlof, Carla, Paul Poast, Benjamin J. Cohen, Sabreena Croteau, Aashna Khanna, Daniel McDowell, Hongying Wang, and W. Kindred Winecoff. 2020. "Global Monetary Order and the Liberal Order Debate." *International Studies Perspectives* 21 (2): 109–53.

Nurkse, Ragnar. 1944. *L'expérience monétaire internationale: enseignements de la période d'entre les deux guerres*. Geneva: Société des nations.

Obstfeld, Maurice. 2011. "International Liquidity: The Fiscal Dimension." NBER Working Paper No. 17379.

Obstfeld, Maurice, and Alan M. Taylor. 2017. "International Monetary Relations: Taking Finance Seriously." *The Journal of Economic Perspectives* 31 (3): 3–28.

Ocampo, Jose Antonio. 2017. *Resetting the International Monetary (Non) System*. A study prepared by the United Nations University World Institute for Development Economics Research (UNU-WIDER). Oxford: Oxford University Press.

O'Malley, Chris. 2015. *Bonds without borders: A history of the Eurobond market*. Chichester: Wiley.

Orléan, André. 2018. "De quelques débats à propos de la production marchande chez Marx." In *Penser la monnaie et la finance avec Marx*, edited by Riccardo Bellofiore, Cédric Durand, Daniel Cohen, and André Orléan, 45–74. Rennes: Presses universitaires de Rennes.

Ostroy, Joseph M. 1987. "Money and General Equilibrium Theory." In *The New Palgrave: A Dictionary of Economics*, 1st ed., edited by John Eatwell, Murray Milgate and Peter Newman. London: Palgrave Macmillan.

Padoa-Schioppa, Tommaso. 2010. "The Ghost of Bancor: The Economic Crisis and the Global Monetary Disorder." Working Papers 1294, Robert Triffin International.

Palan, Ronen. 1998. "Trying to Have Your Cake and Eating It: How and Why the State System Has Created Offshore." *International Studies Quarterly* 42 (4): 625–43.

Palley, Thomas. 2008. "Endogenous Money: Implications for the Money Supply Process, Interest Rates, and Macroeconomics." Working Paper wp178, Political Economy Research Institute, University of Massachusetts at Amherst.

Palley, Thomas. 2013. "Horizontalists, Verticalists, and Structuralists: The Theory of Endogenous Money Reassessed." *Review of Keynesian Economics* 1 (4): 406–24.

Palley, Thomas. 2019. "What's Wrong with Modern Money Theory (MMT): A Critical Primer." Forum for Macroeconomics and Macroeconomic Policies. FMM Working Paper 2019–44.

Panitch, Leo, and Sam Glidin. 2012. *The Making of Global Capitalism: The Political Economy of American Empire*. London: Verso.

Panitch, Leo, and Martijn Konings, eds. 2009. *American Empire and the Political Economy of Global Finance: International Political Economy*. Basingstoke: Palgrave Macmillan.

Parguez, Alain. 1981. "Keynes et la révolution." *Cahiers d'économie politique* 6: 171–87.

Parguez, Alain. 1999. "The Expected Failure of the European Economic and Monetary Union: A False Money against the Real Economy." *Eastern Economic Journal* 25 (1): 63–76.

Parguez, Alain. 2003. "Monnaie et capitalisme: la théorie générale du circuit." In *Théories monétaires post keynésiennes*, edited by Pierre Piégay and Louis-Philippe Rochon, 129–42. Paris: Economica.

Parguez, Alain, and Mario Seccareccia. 2000. "The Credit Theory of Money: The Monetary Circuit Approach." In *What Is Money?*, edited by John Smithin, 101–23. London: Routledge.

Parry, Jonathan, and Maurice Bloch, eds. 1989. *Money and the Morality of Exchange*. Cambridge: Cambridge University Press.

Patinkin, Don. 1965. *Money, Interest, and Prices; An Integration of Monetary and Value Theory*. New York: Harper & Row.

Patinkin, Don. 1989. "Real Balances." In *Money*, edited by John Eatwell, Murray Milgate, and Peter Newman, 303–9. New York: W. W. Norton & Company.

Paulani, Leda Maria. 2014. "Money in Contemporary Capitalism and the Autonomisation of Capitalist Forms in Marx's Theory." *Cambridge Journal of Economics* 38 (4): 779–95.

Perry, Nathan, and Nathaniel Cline. 2013. "Wages, Exchange Rates, and the Great Inflation Moderation: A Post-Keynesian View." *Levy Economics Institute Working Paper Series* 759: 1–28.

Pesenti, Paolo, and Cedric Tille. 2000. "The Economics of Currency Crises and Contagion: An Introduction." *Economic Policy Review* 6 (3): 3–16.

Pierre Manigat, Matari. 2022a. "Usura." In *Diccionario de injusticias*, edited by Carlos Pereda, 764–70. Mexico: XXI Century Edition.

Pierre Manigat, Matari. 2022b. *El Leviathan domesticado. Las relaciones entre el Estado y el capital financiero*. Mexico: IIS UNAM.

Pilkington, Philip Clarke. 2014. "Endogenous Money and the Natural Rate of Interest: The Reemergence of Liquidity Preference and Animal Spirits in the Post-Keynesian Theory of Capital Markets." Levy Economics Institute Working Papers Series. Accessed June 26, 2022. http://dx.doi.org/10.2139/ssrn.2509361.

Plehwe, Dieter. 2017. "Neoliberal Think Tanks and the Crisis." In *Liberalism and the Welfare State*, edited by Roger E. Backhouse, Bradley W. Bateman, and Tamotsu Nishizawa, 190–211. Oxford: Oxford University Press.

Plihon, Dominique. 2017. *Les taux de change*. Paris: La Découverte.

Polanyi, Karl. 2001. *The Great Transformation: The Political and Economic Origins of Our Times*. Boston, MA: Beacon Press.

Polanyi, Karl, Conrad M. Arensberg, and Harry W. Pearson. 1957. *Trade and Market in the Early Empires: Economies in History and Theory*. Glencoe, IL: Free Press.

Pollin, Robert. 1991. "Two Theories of Money Supply Endogeneity: Some Empirical Evidence." *Journal of Post Keynesian Economics* 13 (3): 366–96.

Ponsot, Jean-François. 2007. "Ordre monétaire et intervention militaire britannique dans la guerre civile russe: Le *currency board* d'Arkhangelsk." In *Crises monétaires d'hier et d'aujourd'hui*, edited by Bruno Théret, 375–99. Vol. 1 of *La monnaie dévoilée par ses crises*. Paris: Éditions de l'École des Hautes Études en Sciences Sociales.

Poulon, Frédéric. 2016. *La pensée monétaire*. Malakoff: Dunod.

Powell, Marvin A. 1996. "Money in Mesopotamia." *Journal of the Economic and Social History of the Orient* 39 (3): 224–42.

Pozsar, Zoltan. 2014. "Shadow Banking: The Money View." Office of Financial Research, US Department of the Treasury Working Papers 14-04.

Pozsar, Zoltan. 2015. "A Macro View of Shadow Banking: Levered Betas and Wholesale Funding in the Context of Secular Stagnation." *Macroeconomics: Monetary & Fiscal Policies eJournal*. Accessed June 25, 2022. http://dx.doi.org/10.2139/ssrn.2558945.

Prasad, Eswar S. 2014. *The Dollar Trap: How the US Dollar Tightened Its Grip on Global Finance*. Gurgaon: Penguin.

Prasad, Eswar S. 2021. *The Future of Money*. Cambridge, MA: Belknap Press.

Proudhon, Pierre-Joseph. 1849. *Voix du Peuple du 3 décembre*. Vol. 29 in *Œuvres complètes*. Paris/Brussels: Lacroix-Verboeckhoven.

Pulak, C. 2000. "The Balance Weights from the Late Bronze Age Shipwreck at Uluburun." In *Metals Make the World Go Round*, edited by Christopher F. E. Pare, 247–66. Oxford: Oxbow.

Quigley, John B. 1974. *The Soviet Foreign Trade Monopoly*. Columbus: Ohio State University Press.

Rachline, François. 1982. "La nature de la monnaie." *Revue économique* 33 (3): 446–75.

Rafferty, Devin T. 2009. "Horizontalists, Structuralists, and the Latest Global Financial Crisis: What Can Be Learned." Proceedings of 4th Bi-Annual Cross Border Post Keynesian Conference. Buffalo, NY.

Rainelli, Michel. 1986. "Loi du prix unique et théorie de la parité des pouvoirs d'achat: un retour à G. Cassel, A. Aftalion et J. Viner." *Revue d'économie Politique* 96 (1): 25–38.

Ranieri, Lewis S. 1996. "The Origins of Securitization, Sources of Its Growth, and Its Future Potential." In *A Primer on Securitization*, edited by Leon Kendall and Michael Fishman, 31–43. Cambridge, MA: MIT Press.

Realfonzo, Riccardo. 2007. "The Italian Circuitist Approach." In *A Handbook of Alternative Monetary Economics*, edited by Philip Arestis and Malcolm Sawyer, 105–20. Cheltenham: Edward Elgar Publishing.

Renger, Johannes. 1995. "Institutional, Communal, and Individual Ownership or Possession of Arable Land in Ancient Mesopotamia from the End of the Fourth to the End of the First Millennium B.C." *Chicago-Kent Law Review* 71(1): 269–319.

Renger, Johannes. 2011. "The Role and the Place of Money and Credit in the Economy of Ancient Mesopotamia." In *New approaches to monetary theory*, edited by Heiner Ganssmann, 14–36. New York: Routledge.

Reuten, Geert. 2005. "Money as Constituent of Value." In *Marx's Theory of Money: Modern Appraisals*, edited by Fred Moseley, 78–92. London: Palgrave Macmillan.

Rey, Hélène. 2015. "Dilemma not Trilemma: The Global Financial Cycle and Monetary Policy Independence." CEPR Discussion Papers 10591.

Ricardo, David. (1821) 2004. *On the Principles of Political Economy and Taxation*. Vol. 1 of *The Works and Correspondence of David Ricardo*, edited by P. Sraffa. Indianapolis: Liberty Fund.

Rist, Charles. 1940. *History of Monetary and Credit Theory: From John Law to the Present Day*, 1st ed. London: Routledge.

Robinson, Joan. 1951. "The Rate of Interest." *Econometrica* 19, no. 2 (April): 92–111.

Robinson, Joan. 1956. *The Accumulation of Capital*. London: Macmillan.

Rochon, Louis-Philippe. 1997. "Keynes's Finance Motive: A Re-assessment. Credit, Liquidity Preference and the Rate of Interest." *Review of Political Economy* 9 (3): 277–93.

Rochon, Louis-Philippe. 2001. "Horizontalism: Setting the Record Straight." In *Credit, Interest Rates and the Open Economy: Essays on Horizontalism*, edited by Louis-Philippe Rochon and Matias Vernengo, 31–65. Cheltenham: Edward Elgar Publishing.

Rochon, Louis-Phillippe. 2005. "The Existence of Monetary Profits within the Monetary Circuit." In *The Monetary Theory of Production*, edited by Guiseppe Fontana and Riccardo Realfonzo, 125–38. London: Palgrave Macmillan.

Rochon, Louis-Phillippe. 2009. "The Existence of Profits within the Monetary Circuit: Some Unanswered Questions Revisited." In The Political Economy of Monetary Circuits, edited by Jean-François Ponsot and Sergio Rossi, 46–76. London: Palgrave Macmillan.

Rochon, Louis-Philippe, and Sergio Rossi. 2013. "Endogenous Money: The Evolutionary versus Revolutionary Views." *Review of Keynesian Economics* 1 no. 2 (Summer): 210–29.

Rochon, Louis-Philippe, and Mario Seccareccia, eds. 2003. *Dollarization: Lessons from Europe for the Americas*. London: Routledge.

Rogoff, Kenneth Saul. 2016. *The Curse of Cash*. Princeton, NJ: Princeton University Press.

Roley, V. Vance, and Gordon H. Sellon. 1995. "Monetary Policy Actions and Long-Term Interest Rates." *Economic Review* 80 (4): 73–89.

de Roover, Raymond. 1953. *L'évolution de la lettre de change XIVe–XVIIIe siècles*. Paris: Armand Colin.

Rossi, Sergio. 2005. "Central Banking in a Monetary Theory of Production: The Economics of Payment Finality from a Circular-Flow Perspective." In *The Monetary Theory of Production*, edited by Guiseppe Fontana and Riccardo Realfonzo, 139–51. London: Palgrave Macmillan.

Rossi, Sergio. 2007. "The Theory of Money Emissions." In *A Handbook of Alternative Monetary Economics*, edited by Philip Arestis and Malcolm Sawyer, 121–38. Cheltenham: Edward Elgar Publishing.

Rothbard, Murray N. 1998. "The Gold- Exchange Standard in the Interwar Years." In *Money and the Nation State: The Financial Revolution, Government and the World Monetary System*, edited by Kevin Dowd and Richard H. Timberlake, Jr., 105–65. New Brunswick, NJ: Transactions Publishers.

Rubin, Isaak Il'ich. (1926–28) 2017. "Essays on Marx's Theory of Money." In *Responses to Marx's Capital: From Rudolf Hilferding to Isaak Illich Rubin*, edited by Richard B. Day and Daniel Gaido, 629–727. Leiden: Brill.

Ruggie, John Gerard. 1982. "International Regimes, Transactions, and Change: Embedded Liberalism in the Postwar Economic Order." *International Organization* 36 (2): 379–415.

Sahlins, Marshall. 2017. *Stone Age Economics*. London: Routledge.

Sarai, David. 2009. "US Structural Power and the Internationalization of the US Treasury." In *American Empire and the Political Economy of Global Finance*, edited by Leo Panitch and Martijn Konings, 71–89. Basingstoke: Palgrave Macmillan.

Sardoni, Claudio. 1998. "Marx's Theory of Money and Interest: A Reconsideration in the Light of Robertson and Keynes." In *Method, Value and Money,* edited by Anthony Brewer, 271–85. Vol. 1 of *Marxian Economics: A Reappraisal. Essays on Volume III of Capital*. Durham, NC: Duke University Press.

Sardoni, Claudio. 2017. "Circuitist and Keynesian Approaches to Money: A Reconciliation?" *Metroeconomics*, 68: 205–227.

Sartre, Jean-Paul. (1960) 2004. *Critique of Dialectical Reason*. London: Verso.

Sawyer, Malcolm. 2013. "Endogenous Money, Circuits and Financialization." *Review of Keynesian Economics* 1 no. 2 (Summer): 230–41.

Schaps, David M. 1997. "The Monetisation of the Marketplace in Athens." In *Economie antique: Prix et formation des prix dans les économies antiques*, edited by Jean Andreau, Pierre Briant, and Raymond Descat, 91–104. Vol. 3 of *Entretiens d' Archéologie et d'Histoire*. Toulouse: Saint-Bertrand-de-Comminges.

Schenk, Catherine R. 1998. "The Origins of the Eurodollar Market in London: 1955–1963." *Explorations in Economic History* 35: 221–38.

Schenk, Catherine. 2017. "Coordination failures during and after Bretton Woods." In *From Great Depression to Great Recession*, edited by Atish R. Ghosh and Mahvash S. Qureshi, 69–89. Washington, DC: International Monetary Fund.

Schenk, Catherine. 2018. "The Sterling Area 1945–1972." In *Handbook of the History of Money and Currency*, edited by Stefano Battilossi, Youssef Cassis, and Catherine Schenk, 1-20. Singapore: Springer.

Schinasi, Garry J., Charles F. Kramer, and R. T. Smith. 2001. "Financial Implications of the Shrinking Supply of U.S. Treasury Securities." International Monetary Fund Working Paper N°01.

Schmelzer, Matthias. 2020. "What Comes After Bretton Woods? Neoliberals Debate and Fight for a Future Monetary Order." In *Nine Lives of Neoliberalism*, edited by Dieter Plehwe, Quinn Slobodian, and Philip Mirowski, 197–218. London: Verso Books.

Schmitt, Bernard. 1975. *Monnaie, Salaires, Profits*. Albeuve: Castella.

Schmitt, Bernard. 1982. "Time as Quantum." In *Advances in Economic Theory*, edited by Mauro Baranzini, 115–25. Oxford and New York: Basil Blackwell and St. Martin's Press.

Schmitt, Bernard. 1984. *Inflation, Chômage et malformations du capital*. Albeuve: Castella, and Paris: Economica.

Schmitt, Bernard. 2003. "Circuit économique et pensée néoclassique." In *Théories monétaires post Keynésiennes*, edited by Pierre Piégay and Louis-Philippe Rochon, 198–205. Paris: Economica.

Schmitt, Bernard. 2012a. "Money, Effective Demand, and Profits." In *Modern Monetary Macroeconomics*, edited by Claude Gnos and Sergio Rossi, 71–99. Cheltenham: Edward Elgar Publishing.

Schmitt, Bernard. 2012b. "Relative Prices are Undermined by a Mathematical Error." In *Modern Monetary Macroeconomics*, edited by Claude Gnos and Sergio Rossi, 19–38. Cheltenham: Edward Elgar Publishing.

Schularick, Moritz, and Alan M. Taylor. 2012. "Credit Booms Gone Bust: Monetary Policy, Leverage Cycles, and Financial Crises, 1870–2008." *American Economic Review* 102 (2): 1029–61.

Schulz-Forberg, Hagen. 2020. "Embedded Early Neoliberalism: Transnational Origins of the Agenda of Liberalism Reconsidered." In *Nine Lives of Neoliberalism*, edited by Dieter Plehwe, Quinn Slobodian, and Philip Mirowski, 169–96. London: Verso Books.

Schulzinger, Robert D. 2010. "Détente in the Nixon–Ford years, 1969–1976." In *Crises and Détente*, edited by Melvyn P. Leffler and Odd Arne Westad, 273–94. Vol. 2 of *The Cambridge History of the Cold War*. New York and London: Cambridge University Press.

Schumpeter, Joseph Alois. (1954) 2009. *History of Economic Analysis*. Abingdon: Routledge.

Scott-Quinn, Brian. 1975. *The New Euromarkets: A Theoretical and Practical Study of International Financing in the Eurobond, Eurocurrency, and Related Financial Markets*. New York: Wiley.

Seabrooke, Leonard. 2001. *US Power in International Finance: The Victory of Dividends*. New York: Palgrave.

Seaford, Richard. 2004. *Money and the Early Greek Mind: Homer, Philosophy, Tragedy*. Cambridge: Cambridge University Press.

Seccareccia, Mario. 1996. "Post Keynesian Fundism and Monetary Circulation." In *Money in Motion*, edited by Ghislain Deleplace and Edward J. Nell, 400–16. London: Palgrave Macmillan.

Seccareccia, Mario. 2003. "Pricing, Investment and the Financing of Production within the Framework of the Monetary Circuit: Some Preliminary Evidence." In

Modern Theories of Money: The Nature and Role of Money in Capitalist Economies, edited by Louis-Phillippe Rochon and Sergio Rossi, 173–97. Cheltenham: Edward Elgar Publishing.

Semenova, Alla, and L. Randall Wray. 2015. "The Rise of Money and Class Society: The Contributions of John F. Henry." Working Paper N° 832, Levy Economics Institute.

Senior, Nassau William. 1840. *Three Lectures on the Value of Money, Delivered before the University of Oxford in 1829.* London: B. Fellowes.

Serrano, Franklin, 2003. "From 'Static' Gold to the Floating Dollar." *Contributions to Political Economy* 22: 87–102.

Servet, Jean-Michel. 1993. "L'institution monétaire de la société selon Karl Polanyi." *Revue économique* 44 (6): 1127–50.

Servet, Jean-Michel, Bruno Théret, and Zeynep Yildirim. 2008. "Universalité du fait monétaire et pluralité des monnaies." In *L'argent des anthropologues, la monnaie des économistes,* edited by Eveline Baumann, Laurent Bazin, Pepita Ould-Ahmed, Pascale Phelinas, Monique Selim et Richard Sobel, 167–207. Paris: L'Harmattan.

Sgard, Jérôme. 2002. *L'économie de la panique: Faire face aux crises financières.* Paris: La Découverte.

Shafir, Eldar, Peter Diamond, and Amos Tversky. 1997. "Money Illusion." *The Quarterly Journal of Economics* 112 (2): 341–74.

Shin, H. 2012. "Global Banking Glut and Loan Risk Premium." *IMF Economic Review* 60: 155–92.

Simmel, Georg. (1900) 2011. *The Philosophy of Money.* London: Routledge.

Singleton, John. 2011. *Central Banking in the Twentieth Century.* Cambridge: Cambridge University Press.

Sissoko, Carolyn. 2019. "Repurchase Agreements and the (De)construction of Financial Markets." *Economy and Society* 48 (3): 315–41.

Skaggs, Neil T. 1991. "John Fullarton's Law of Reflux and Central Bank Policy." *History of Political Economy* 23 (3): 457–80.

Skaggs, Neil T. 2016. "Banking and Currency Schools." In *Schools of Thought in Economics,* edited by Gilbert Faccarello and Heinz D. Kurz, 180–87. Vol. 2 of *Handbook on the History of Economic Analysis.* Cheltenham: Edward Elgar Publishing.

Skidelsky, Robert. 2018. *Money and Government.* Newhaven, CT: Yale University Press, 2018.

Slobodian, Quinn. 2018. *Globalists. The End of Empire and the Birth of Neoliberalism.* Cambridge, MA: Harvard University Press.

Smith, Matthew. 2003. "On Central Banking 'Rules': Tooke's Critique of the Bank Charter Act of 1844." *Journal of the History of Economic Thought* 25: 39–61.

Smithin, John. 2000. "What is Money? Introduction." In *What Is Money?,* edited by John N. Smithin, 1–15. London and New York: Routledge.

Smithin, John. 2007. "The Theory of Interest Rates." In *A Handbook of Alternative Monetary Economics,* edited by Philip Arestis and Malcolm Sawyer, 273–90. Cheltenham: Edward Elgar Publishing.

Snippe, Jan. 1985. "Finance, Saving and Investment in Keynes's Economics." *Cambridge Journal of Economics* 9 (3): 257–69.

Solomon, Robert. 1982. *The International Monetary System, 1945–1981.* New York: Harper & Row.

Solomon, Robert. 1999. *Money on the Move: The Revolution in International Finance since 1980.* Princeton, NJ: Princeton University Press.

Starr, Ross M. 1972. "The Structure of Exchange in Barter and Monetary Economies." *The Quarterly Journal of Economics* 86 (2): 290–302.

Steil, Benn. 2013. *The Battle of Bretton Woods: John Maynard Keynes, Harry Dexter White, and the Making of a New World Order.* Princeton, NJ: Princeton University Press.

Steil, Benn. 2021. *The Marshall Plan: Dawn of the Cold War.* Oxford: Oxford University Press.

Stiglitz, Joseph E. 2002a. *Globalization and Its Discontents.* London: Allen Lane/Penguin Books.

Stiglitz, Joseph E. 2002b. "The Lessons of Argentina for Development in Latin America." In *Argentina in Collapse? The Americas Debate,* edited by Michael Cohen and Margarita Gutman, 151–70. New York: The New School.

Stiglitz, Joseph E. 2002c. "Argentina, Shortchanged: Why the Nation That Followed the Rules Fell to Pieces." *Washington Post,* May 12, 2002.

Stiglitz, Joseph E. 2003. *The Roaring Nineties: A New History of the World's Most Prosperous Decade.* New York: W. W. Norton & Co.

Stigum, Marcia L., Anthony Crescenzi, and Marcia L. Stigum. 2007. *Stigum's Money Market.* New York: McGraw-Hill.

Strange, Susan. 1989. *States and Markets.* London: Pinter.

Sumner, Scott. 1992. "The Gold Standard, Monetary Policy, and the Banking School: Currency School Debate." *Eastern Economic Journal* 18 (3): 345–58.

Sylla, Richard. 2002. "United States Banks and Europe: Strategy and Attitudes." In *European Banks and the American Challenge: Cooperation and Competition in International Banking under Bretton Woods,* edited by Stefano Battilossi and Youssef Cassis, 53–73. Oxford: Oxford University Press.

Sylla, Richard. 2012. "U.S. Government Debt Has Always Been Different!" In *Is US Government Debt Different?,* edited by Franklin Allen, Anna Gelpern, Charles Mooney, and David Skeel, 1–12. Philadelphia, PA: FIC Press.

Taylor, Alan M., and Taylor, Mark P. 2004. "The Purchasing Power Parity Debate." *Journal of Economic Perspectives* 18 (4): 135–58.

Taylor, John B. 1993. "Discretion versus Policy Rules in Practice." *Carnegie-Rochester Conference Series on Public Policy* 39: 195–214.

Taylor, John B. 1995. "Changes in American Economic Policy in the 1980s: Watershed or Pendulum Swing?" *Journal of Economic Literature* 33 (2): 777–84.

Taylor, Mark P. 1995. "The Economics of Exchange Rates." *Journal of Economic Literature* 33 (1): 13–47.

Taylor, Mark P. 2006. "Real Exchange Rates and Purchasing Power Parity: Mean-Reversion in Economic Thought." *Applied Financial Economics* 16 (1–2): 1–17.

Tcherneva, Pavlina R. 2007. "Chartalism and the Tax-Driven Approach to Money." In *A Handbook of Alternative Monetary Economics,* edited by Philip Arestis and Malcolm Sawyer, 69–86. Cheltenham: Edward Elgar.

Tcherneva, Pavlina R. 2016. "Money, Power, and Monetary Regimes." Levy Economics Institute Working Paper No. 861.

Tcherneva, Pavlina R. 2018. "Money and Monetary Regimes." In *The Routledge Handbook of Heterodox Economics,* edited by Tae-Hee Jo, Lynne Chester, and Carlo D'Ippoliti, 237–50. Abingdon and New York: Routledge.

Temin, Peter. 1989. *Lessons from the Great Depression.* The Lionel Robbins Lectures for 1989. Cambridge: MIT Press.

Testart, Alain. 2001. *Aux origines de la monnaie.* Paris: Éditions Errance.

Théret, Bruno. 2007. "La monnaie au prisme de ses crises d'hier et d'aujourd'hui." In *Crises monétaires d'hier et d'aujourd'hui,* edited by Bruno Théret, 17–74. Vol. 1 of *La monnaie dévoilée par ses crises.* Paris: Éditions de l'École des Hautes Études en Sciences Sociales.

Théret, Bruno. 2008. "Les trois états de la monnaie. Approche interdisciplinaire du fait monétaire." *Revue économique* 59 (4): 813–41.

Thorn, Richard S. 1971. *Théorie monétaire.* Translated by Françoise Duboeuf. Paris: Dunod.

Thornton, Daniel L. 2012. "Greenspan's Conundrum and the Fed's Ability to Affect Long-Term Yields." Working Paper 2012-036, Federal Reserve Bank of St. Louis.

Tily, Geoff. 2007. *Keynes's General Theory, the Rate of Interest and "Keynesian" Economics Keynes Betrayed.* London: Palgrave Macmillan.

Tooke, Thomas. 1840. *A History of Prices and of the State of the Circulation 3: 1838–1839.* London: Longmans.

Tooke, Thomas. 1844. *An Inquiry into the Currency Principle.* London: Longman, Brown, Green and Longmans.

Tooke, Thomas. 1848. *A History of Prices and of the State of the Circulation 4: 1839–1847.* London: Longmans.

Toye, John. 1993. "Keynes, Russia and the State in Developing Countries." In *Keynes and the Role of the State,* edited by Derek Crabtree and A. P. Thirlwell, 239–65. London: Macmillan.

Triffin, Robert. 1960. *Gold and the Dollar Crisis.* New Haven, CT: Yale University Press.

Triffin, Robert. 1964. *The Evolution of the International Monetary System: Historical Reappraisal and Future Perspectives.* Princeton, NJ: Princeton University Press.

Triffin, Robert. 1968. *Our International Monetary System: Yesterday, Today, and Tomorrow.* New York: Random House.

Triffin, Robert. 1978. "Gold and the Dollar Crisis." Essays in International Finance 132, Princeton University.

Tsiang, Sho-Chieh. 1956. "Liquidity Preference and Loanable Funds Theories, Multiplier and Velocity Analysis: A Synthesis." *American Economic Review* 46: 539–64.

Tutin, Christian. 2009. *Les grands textes de la pensée monétaire.* Paris: Flammarion.

Tymoigne, Eric. 2014. "Modern Money Theory, and Interrelations between the Treasury and Central Bank: The Case of the United States." *Journal of Economic Issues* 48 (3): 641–62.

Vallée, Olivier. 2016. "Le FMI et la dette. De la discipline aux arrangements." *Savoir/Agir* 35 (1): 53–62.

van Horn, Rob, and Philip Mirowski. 2009. "The Rise of the Chicago School of Economics and the Birth of Neoliberalism." In *The Road from Mont Pèlerin,* edited by Philip Mirowski and Dieter Plehwe, 139–78. Cambridge, MA: Harvard University Press.

Veenhof, Klaas R. 1972. *Aspects of Old Assyrian Trade and its Terminology.* Leiden: Brill.

Veenhof, Klaas R. 1999. "Silver and Credit in Old Assyrian Trade." In *Trade and Finance in Ancient Mesopotamia,* edited by Jan Gerrit Dercksen, 55–83. Leiden: Nederlands Historisch-Archelogisch Instituut Istanbul.

Walker, Martin C. W., and Jose Luu. 2016. "Blockchain and the Nature of Money." *Banque et Stratégie,* N°350. Accessed June 28, 2022. http://www.revue-banque.fr/management-fonctions-supports/article/blockchain-and-nature-money.

Wallace, Neil. 1983. "A Legal Restrictions Theory of the Demand for 'Money' and the Role of Monetary Policy." *Federal Reserve Bank of Minneapolis Quarterly Review* 7(1): 1–7.

Walras, Léon. 1900. *Éléments d'économie politique pure ou théorie de la richesse sociale,* 4th ed. Lausanne: F. Rouge.

Walras, Léon. 1926. *Elements of Pure Economics: On the Theory of Social Wealth.* Translated by William Jaffé (1965). London: J. Allen and Unwin.

Walras, Léon. 1988. *Eléments d'économie politique pure: ou théorie de la richesse sociale.* Paris: Economica.

Wansleben, Leon. 2020. "Formal institution building in financialized capitalism: the case of repo markets." *Theory and Society* 49: 187–213.

Webb, Michael C. 2019. *The Political Economy of Policy Coordination: International Adjustment since 1945*. Ithaca, NY: Cornell University Press.

Weber, Max. 1950. *General Economic History*. Glencoe, IL: Free Press.

Weeks, John. 2012. "The Theory and Empirical Credibility of Commodity Money." *Science & Society* 76 (1): 66–94.

Weill, Raymond. 1925. "L'unité de valeur Shat et le Papyrus de Boulaq n° 11." *Revue de l'Egypte ancienne* 1: 45–87.

Wicksell, Knut. (1898) 1965. *Interest and Prices: A Study of the Causes Regulating the Value of Money*. Translated by R. F. Kahn. New York: A.M. Kelley.

Wicksell, Knut. 1978. *Money*. Vol. 2 in *Lectures on Political Economy*. Fairfield, NJ: Auguste M. Kelley.

Wigmore, Barrie A. 1997. *Securities Markets in the 1980s: The New Regime, 1979–1984*. Oxford: Oxford University Press.

Williams, Michael. 2000. "Why Marx Neither Has Nor Needs a Commodity Theory of Money." *Review of Political Economy* 12 (4): 435–51.

Williamson, John. 1985. *The Exchange Rate System*. Washington, DC: Institute for International Economics.

Williamson, John. 1986. "Target Zones and the Management of the Dollar." *Brookings Papers on Economic Activity* 1986 (1): 165–74.

Williamson, John. 1990. "What Washington Means by Policy Reform." In *Latin American Adjustment: How Much Has Happened?*, edited by John Williamson, 7–20. Washington, DC: Institute for International Economics.

Wojnilower, Albert M. 1980. "The Central Role of Credit Crunches in Recent Financial History." *Brookings Papers on Economic Activity* 11 (2): 277–340.

Wolfson, Martin H. 1986. *Financial Crises: Understanding the Postwar U.S. Experience*. Armonk, NY: Sharpe.

Woodford, Michael. 2001. "The Taylor Rule and Optimal Monetary Policy." *American Economic Review* 91 (2): 232–37.

Wray, L. Randall. 1990. *Money and Credit in Capitalist Economies*. Cheltenham: Edward Elgar.

Wray, L. Randall. 1992. "Alternative Approaches to Money and Interest Rates." *Journal of Economic Issues* 26 (4): 1145–78.

Wray, L. Randall. 2000. "Modern Money." In *What Is Money?*, edited by John Smithin, 42–66. London: Routledge.

Wray, L. Randall. 2003. "Functional Finance and US Government Budget Surpluses." In *Reinventing Functional Finance: Transformational Growth and Full Employment*, edited by Edward J. Nell and Mathew Forstater, 141–59. Northampton, MA: Edward Elgar.

Wray, L. Randall. 2004. "Conclusion: The Credit Money and State Money Approaches." In *Credit and State Theories of Money: The Contributions of A. Mitchell Innes*, edited by L. Randall Wray, 223–62. Northampton, MA: Edward Elgar.

Wray, L. Randall. 2006. "When are Interest Rates Exogenous?" In *Complexity, Endogenous Money and Macroeconomic Theory: Essays in Honour of Basil J. Moore*, edited by Mark Setterfield, 271–89. Northampton, MA: Edward Elgar.

Wray, L. Randall. 2007. "Endogenous Money: Structuralist and Horizontalist." Levy Economics Institute Working Paper No. 512.

Wray, L. Randall. 2010. "Alternative Approaches to Money." *Theoretical Inquiries in Law* 11 (1): 29–49.

Wray, L. Randall. 2011. "Money in Finance." Levy Economics Institute Working Paper No. 656.

Wray, L. Randall. 2014a. "Central Bank Independence: Myth and Misunderstanding." Levy Economics Institute Working Paper No. 791.

Wray, L. Randall. 2014b. "From the State Theory of Money to Modern Money Theory: An Alternative to Economic Orthodoxy." Levy Economics Institute Working Paper No. 792.

Yang, Jian, Jaeun Shin, and Moosa Khan. 2007. "Causal Linkages between US and Eurodollar Interest Rates: Further Evidence." *Applied Economics* 39 (2): 135–44.

Yermack, David. 2015. "Is Bitcoin a Real Currency? An Economic Appraisal." In *Handbook of Digital Currency Bitcoin, Innovation, Financial Instruments, and Big Data*, edited by David Lee Kuo Chuen, 31–43. Amsterdam: Elsevier. Haut du formulaire.

INDEX

Note: Page numbers followed by "n" denote endnotes.